L. H. Bailey

The Survival Of The Unlike 1896

L. H. Bailey

The Survival Of The Unlike 1896

ISBN/EAN: 9783741197338

Manufactured in Europe, USA, Canada, Australia, Japa

Cover: Foto ©Andreas Hilbeck / pixelio.de

Manufactured and distributed by brebook publishing software (www.brebook.com)

L. H. Bailey

The Survival Of The Unlike 1896

THE SURVIVAL OF THE UNLIKE

A COLLECTION OF EVOLUTION ESSAYS SUGGESTED BY THE STUDY OF DOMESTIC PLANTS

BY

L. H. BAILEY

The study of domestic productions will rise immensely in value.
—*Darwin, Origin of Species.*
Botanists have generally neglected cultivated varieties as beneath their notice
—*Darwin, Animals and Plants under Domestication.*

New York
THE MACMILLAN COMPANY
LONDON: MACMILLAN & CO., Ltd.
1896

COPYRIGHT, 1896
BY L. H. BAILEY

Mount Pleasant Printery
J. Horace McFarland Company
Harrisburg, Pa.

PREFACE.

For several years it has been my habit, when called upon to address horticultural societies, to choose some topic intimately associated with the evolution of domestic plants. My motives have been several. I have chiefly desired to attempt to answer many of the common questions which puzzle horticulturists by appealing to the evidences of evolution, for I am convinced that many of these questions can be answered in no other way. I have also desired to spread a knowledge of the evolution speculations and of the methods of research which they suggest, amongst those who deal with plants and animals, and who lead a rural life. Again, I have wished to make a record of a great class of most common and significant facts vitally related to the study of organic evolution, but which are almost wholly overlooked by students and philosophers. In making these essays, I have constantly had in mind the collation and publication of them, and I have, therefore, endeavored to discuss the leading problems associated with the variation and evolution of cultivated plants, in order that the final collection should be somewhat consecutive.

The results of this intermittent labor I now give

to those for whom it was from time to time conceived, —for horticulturists first, for evolutionists next. The essays are of unequal merit, and there are necessarily repetitions in them; but I conceive that they are the more valuable for having been written at different times and for different occasions, for they thereby present the subjects in more diverse aspects. The audiences to whom the greater number of the essays have been addressed have been composed of persons who observe widely of facts, but who are unused to making broad inductions from them. It is only in the first two essays that I have ventured to state any general convictions respecting the bolder problems of organic evolution, but I count these of much less merit than the statements of many plain and simple facts of observation and experiment which are made in the humbler essays. If the author has been fortunate enough to make any contribution to positive science in these pages, it is probably that associated with the vexed question of bud-variation, which is chiefly presented in the third essay; but even this is novel only in its treatment. The underlying motive of the collection is the emphasis which is placed upon unlikenesses, and of their survival because they are unlike. The author also denies the common assumption that organic matter was originally endowed with the power of reproducing all its corporeal attributes, or that, in the constitution of things, like produces like. He conceives, as explained on pages 20 to 24, that heredity is an acquired force, and that, normally or originally, unlike produces unlike.

It may be well to state what are the chief lines of proof of evolution as they appeal to the author. *A priori* reasons for belief in the hypothesis are the two facts, that there must be struggle for existence from the mere mathematics of propagation, and that there have been mighty changes in the physical character of the earth. These facts argue that organisms must either have changed or perished. To me, the chief demonstrative reason for belief in evolution is the fact that plants and animals can be and are modified profoundly by the care of man. In fact, I should be convinced that the organic creation is an evolution if I had no other proof than this. But the proofs are abundant:

1. Those afforded by paleontology.

2. Those of embryology.

3. Those of comparative anatomy and structure.

4. Resemblances of types, which allow the objects to be classified. If species were specially created, there would have been no relationships.

5. The successive increase in complexity and differentiation, or divergence, in this classification, or the growth of the "tree of life."

6. The fact of adaptation to environment.

7. The vagaries of distribution. (See Essay XV.)

8. The fact of variation, and the frequency of intergradient forms.

9. The observed behavior of animals and plants under the hand of man.

The reader who desires more explicit information upon the means of producing new varieties may consult "Plant-Breeding," in which some of the more obvious speculations which are concerned with the breeding of plants are set forth in some detail. Historical narratives of our indigenous cultivated fruits will be found in "The Evolution of our Native Fruits."

L. H. BAILEY.

CORNELL UNIVERSITY,
ITHACA, N. Y., September 1, 1896.

Note to the Second Issue.

In this issue, a few minor alterations have been made, and a fuller statement is given to the concluding paragraph of the first Essay. The author takes this occasion to say — what, it would seem, is perfectly obvious — that in his denial of design, he uses the word design in its biological significance, and that he has no reference to the larger question of purposiveness in the creation. He refers to the notion of immediate or proximate interference in shaping the forms of life. The larger question of purposive design is one which can be neither denied nor affirmed from biological evidence; but the author would argue that the entire evolution scheme is a nobler conception of purposive creation than any mere interjection of special forces into a discontinuous, and, therefore, in a meaningless, creation.

November 17, 1896.

CONTENTS.

PART I.

ESSAYS TOUCHING THE GENERAL FACT AND PHILOSOPHY OF EVOLUTION.

                                                                         Page

I. The Survival of the Unlike 13
II. Neo-Lamarckism and Neo-Darwinism 55
III. The Plant Individual in the Light of Evolution. The Philosophy of Bud-Variation, and its Bearing upon Weismannism. 81
IV. Experimental Evolution amongst Plants 107
V. Van Mons and Knight, and the Production of Varieties 138
VI. Some Bearings of the Evolution-Teaching upon Plant-Cultivation 162
VII. Why have our Enemies Increased? 180
VIII. Coxey's Army and the Russian Thistle. A Sketch of the Philosophy of Weediness 193
IX. Recent Progress in American Horticulture 202

PART II.

ESSAYS EXPOUNDING THE FACT AND CAUSES OF VARIATION.

A. The Fact.   Page

    X. On the Supposed Correlations of Quality in Fruits 219
    XI. The Natural History of Synonyms 237
    XII. Reflective Impressions of the Nursery Business . . 245
    XIII. The Relation of Seed-Bearing to Cultivation . . . 251

B. The Causes.

    XIV. Variation after Birth 256
    XV. A Pomological Alliance. Sketch of the Relationships between American and Eastern Asian Fruits 267
    XVI. Horticultural Geography 278

CONTENTS.

		Page
XVII.	Some Emphatic Problems of Climate and Plants. Comprising "Speculative Notes upon Phenology (the Physiological Constant, and the Climatal Modification of Phenological Phenomena);" and "Some Interrelations of Climatology and Horticulture"................	288
XVIII.	Are American Fruits Best Adapted to American Conditions?................	311
XIX.	Acclimatization: Does it Occur?........	320
XX.	On the Longevity of Apple Trees........	334
XXI.	Sex in Fruits..................	347
XXII.	Are Novelties Worth their Cost?........	356
XXIII.	Why Do Promising Varieties Fail?.......	364
XXIV.	Reflections upon the Longevity of Varieties. Comprising "Do Varieties Run Out?" "Are the Varieties of Orchard Fruits Running Out?" "Studies in the Longevity of the Varieties of Tomatoes"................	376

PART III.

ESSAYS TRACING THE EVOLUTION OF PARTICULAR TYPES OF PLANTS.

		Page
XXV.	Whence Came the Cultivated Strawberry?.....	400
XXVI.	The Battle of the Plums.............	418
XXVII.	The Evolution of American Grapes........	431
XXVIII.	The Progress of the Carnation. Comprising "Types and Tendencies in the Carnation;" "John Thorpe's Ideal Carnation;" and "Border Carnations.".............	438
XXIX.	Evolution of the Petunia...........	465
XXX.	The Amelioration of the Garden Tomato. Comprising "The Origin of the Tomato from a Morphological Standpoint;" "History of the Trophy Tomato;" "The Probable Course of Evolution of the Tomato;" and "Direction of Contemporaneous Improvement of the Tomato."...............	473
Glossary.................		491
Index...................		499

PART I

I.

THE SURVIVAL OF THE UNLIKE.[1]

We all agree that there has been and is evolution; but we probably all disagree as to the exact agencies and forces which have been and are responsible for it. The subject of the agencies and vehicles of evolution has been gone over repeatedly and carefully for the animal creation, but there is comparatively little similar research and speculation for the plant creation. This deficiency upon the plant side is my excuse for calling your attention, in a popular way, to a few suggestions respecting the continuing creation of the vegetable world, and to a somewhat discursive consideration of a number of illustrations of the methods of advance of plant types.

I.

Nature of the Divergence of the Plant and the Animal.

It is self-evident that the development of life upon our planet has taken place along two divergent lines. These lines evidently originated at a common point. The common life-plasma was probably at first more ani-

---

[1] Originally an address before the Philosophical Club of Cornell University, April 20, 1890. Revised and presented, in part, before the American Philosophical Society, Philadelphia, May 1, 1890, and printed in the proceedings of the Society. vol. xxxv. pp. 88 to 110.

mal-like than plant-like. The stage in which this life-plasma first began to assume plant-like functions is closely and possibly exactly preserved to us in that great class of organisms which are known as mycetozoa when studied by zoölogists and as myxomycetes when studied by botanists. At one stage of their existence, these organisms are amœba-like, that is, animal-like, but at another stage they are sporiferous or plant-like. The initial divergencies in organisms were no doubt concerned chiefly in the methods of appropriating food, the animal-like organisms apprehending their food at a more or less definite point, and the plant-like organisms absorbing food throughout the greater or even the entire part of their periphery. It is not my purpose to trace the particular steps or methods of these divergencies, but to call your attention to what I believe to be a characteristic distinction between the two lines of development, and one which I do not remember to have seen stated in the exact form in which it lies in my mind.

Both lines probably started out with a more or less well marked circular arrangement of the parts or organs. This was consequent upon the peripheral arrangement of the new cells in the development of the multicellular organism from the unicellular one. A long line of animal life developed in obedience to this peripheral or rotate type of organization, ending in the echinoderms and some of the mollusks. This type long ago reached its zenith. No line of descent can be traced from it, according to Cope. The progressive and regnant type of animal life appeared in the vermes or true worms, forms which are characterized by a two-sided or bilateral, and therefore more or less longitudinal, structure. The animal-like organisms were strongly developed in the power of locomotion, and it is easy to see that the rotate or centrifugal construction would place the organism at a comparative disadvantage, because its seat of sensation is farthest removed from the external stimuli. But the worm-like organisms "being longitudinal and bilateral," writes Cope, "one extremity becomes differentiated by first contact with the environment." In other words, the animal type has shown a cephalic, or head-forming, evolution in consequence of the bilateralism of structure. The individual has become concentrated. Out of this worm-form type, therefore, all the higher ranges of zoötypic evolution have sprung, and one is almost tempted to read a literal truth into David's lamentation that "I am a worm, and no man."

If, now, we turn to plants, we find the rotate or peripheral arrangement of parts emphasized in all the higher ranges of forms. The most marked bilateralism in the plant world is amongst the bacteria, desmids, and the like, in which locomotion is markedly developed; and these are also amongst the lowest plant-types. But plants soon become attached to the earth, or, as Cope terms them, they are "earth-parasites." They therefore found it to their advantage to reach out in every direction from their support in the search for food. Whilst the centrifugal arrangement has strongly tended to disappear in the animal creation, it has tended with equal strength to persist and to augment itself in the plant creation. Its marked development amongst plants began with the acquirement of terrestrial life, and with the consequent evolution of the asexual or sporophytic type of vegetation. Normally, the higher type of plant bears its parts more or less equally upon all sides, and the limit to growth is still determined by the immediate environment of the given individual or of its recent ancestors. Its evolution has been acephalic, diffuse, or headless, and the individual plant or tree has no proper concentration of parts. For the most part, it is filled with unspecialized plasma, which, when removed from the parent individual (as in cuttings and grafts), is able to reproduce another like individual. The arrangements of leaves, branches, the parts of the flower, and even of seeds in the fruit, are thus rotate or circular, and in the highest type of plants the annual lateral increments of growth are disposed in like fashion; and it is significant to observe that in the compositæ, which is considered to be the latest and highest general type of plant-form, the rotate or centrifugal arrangement is most emphatically developed. The circular arrangement of parts is the typical one for higher plants, and any departure from this form is a specialization, and demands explanation.

The point I wish to urge, therefore, is the nature of the obvious or external divergence of plant-like and animal-like lines of ascent. The significance of the bilateral structure of animal-types is well understood, but this significance has been drawn, so far as I know, from a comparison of bilateral or dimeric animals with rotate or polymeric animals. I want to put a larger meaning into it, by making bilateralism the symbol of the onward march of animal evolution, and circumlateralism (if I may invent the term), the symbol of plant evolution. The suggestion, however, applies simply to the general arrangement of the parts or organs of the plant body, and has no relation to structural characteristics and relationships. It is a suggestion of analogues, not of homologues. We may, therefore, contrast these two great lines of ascent which, with so many vicissitudes, have come up through the ages, as Dipleurogenesis and Centrogenesis.

The two divergent directions of the lines or phyla of evolution have often been the subject of comment, but one of the sharpest contrasts between the two was made in 1884 by Cope, when he proposed that the vegetable kingdom has undergone a degenerate or retrogressive evolution. "The plants in general," he then wrote, "in the persons of their protist ancestors, soon left a free-swimming life and became sessile. Their lives thus became parasitic, more automatic, and in one sense degenerate." The evolution of the plant creation is, therefore, held to be a phenomenon of catagenesis or decadence. This, of course, is merely a method of stating a comparison with the evolution of the animal line or phylum, and is, therefore, of the greatest service. For myself, however, I dislike the terms retrogressive, catagenetic, and the like, as applied to the plant creation, because they imply intrinsic or actual degeneracy. True retrogressive or degenerate evolution is the result of loss of attributes. Cope holds that the chief proof of degeneracy in the plant world is the loss of a free-swimming habit; but it is possible that the first life-plasma was stationary: at any rate, we do not know that it was motile. Degeneracy is unequivocally seen in certain restricted groups where the loss of character can be traced directly to adaptive changes, as in the loss of limbs in the serpents. Retarded evolution expresses the development of the plant world better than the above terms, but even this is erroneous, because plant types exhibit quite as complete an adaptation to an enormous variety of conditions as animals do, and there has been rapid progress towards specialization of structure. As a matter of fact, the vegetable world does not exhibit, as a whole, any backward step, any loss of character once gained, nor any stationary or retarded periods; but its progress has been widely unlike that of the animal world, and it has not reached the heights which that line of ascent has attained. The plant phylum cannot be said to be catagenetic, but it is sui generis; or, in other words, it is centrogenetic, as distinguished from dipleurogenetic.

The hearer should be reminded, at this point, of the curious alternation of generations which has come about in the plant world. One generation performs sexual functions, and the product of the sexual union is an asexual generation, and this, in turn, gives rise to another sexual generation like the first. In the low sex-plants, as in some of the algæ, the sexual generation—or the gametophyte, as it is called—generally comprises the entire plant body, and the asexual generation—or sporophyte—develops as a part of the fructifying structure of the gametophyte, and is recognizable as a separate structure only by students of special training. In the true mosses, the gametophyte is still the conspicuous part of the plant structure. It comprises all that part of the moss which the casual observer recognizes as "the plant." The sporophytic generation is still attached to the persistent gametophyte, and it is the capsule, with its stem and appendages. In the ferns, however, the gametophytic stage is of short duration. It is the inconspicuous prothallus, which follows germination of the spore. Therefrom originates "the fern," all of which is sporophytic, and the gametophyte perishes. With the evolution of the flowering plants, the gametophyte becomes still more rudimentary, whilst the sporophyte is developed into the plant, tree or shrub, as we see it.

The gametophytic generation is associated with the act of fertilization, the male prothallus or gametophyte developing from the pollen grain and soon perishing, and the female prothallus or gametophyte developing in the ovule, and either soon perishing, or persisting, at least in the conifer-like plants, in the form of the albumen of the seed. The great development of the sporophyte in later time is, no doubt, a consequence of the necessity of assuming a terrestial life; and with this development has come the perfection of centro-genetic form.

II.

The Origin of Differences.

The causes which have contributed to the origin of the differences which we see in the organic creation have been and still are the subjects of the most violent controversy. Those persons who conceive these differences to have come into existence full-formed, as they exist at the present time, are those who believe in the dogma of special creations, and they usually add to the doctrine a belief in design in nature. This doctrine of special creation receives its strongest support when persons contrast individual objects in nature. Certainly nothing can seem more unlike in very fundamental character than an insect and an elephant, a star fish and a potato, a man and an oak tree. The moment one comes to study the genealogies of these objects or groups, however, he comes upon the astonishing fact that the ancestors are more and more alike the farther back they are traced. In other words, there are great series of convergent histories. Every naturalist, therefore, is compelled to admit that differences in nature have somehow been augmented in the long processes of time. It is unnecessary, therefore, that he seek the causes of present differences until he shall have determined the causes of the smallest or original indifferences. It is thus seen that there are two great and co-ordinate problems in the study of evolution,—the causes of initial differences, and the means by which differences are augmented. These two problems are no doubt very often expressions of the same force or power, for the augmentation of a difference comes about by the origination of new degrees of difference; that is, by new differences. It is very probable that the original genesis of the difference is often due to the operation of the very same physiological processes which gradually enlarge the difference into a gulf of wide separation.

In approaching this question of the origin of unlikenesses, the inquirer must first divest himself of the effects of all previous teaching and thinking. We have reason to assume that all beings came from one original life-plasma, and we must assume that this plasma had the power of perpetuating its physiological identity. Most persons still further assume that this plasma must have been endowed with the property of reproducing all its characters of form and habit exactly, but such assumption is wholly gratuitous and is born of the age-long habit of thinking that like produces like. We really have no right to assume either that this plasma was or was not constituted with the power of exact reproduction of all its attributes, unless the behavior of its ascendents forces us to the one or the other conclusion. Inasmuch as no two individual organisms ever are or ever have been exactly alike, so far as we can determine, it seems to me to be the logical necessity to assume that like never did and never can produce like. The closer we are able to approach to plasmodial and unspecialized forms of life in our studies of organisms, the more are we impressed with the weakness of the hereditary power. Every tyro in the study of protoplasm knows that the amœba has no form. The shapes which it assumes are individual, and do not pass to the descendants. To my mind, therefore, it is a more violent assumption to suppose that this first unspecialized plasma should exactly reproduce all its minor features than to suppose that it had no distinct hereditary power, and therefore, by the very nature of its constitution, could not exactly reproduce itself. The burden of proof has been thrown upon those who attempt to explain the initial origin of differences, but it should really be thrown upon those who assume that life-matter was originally so constructed as to rigidly recast itself into one mould in each succeeding generation. I see less reason for dogmatically assuming that like produces like than I do for supposing that unlike produces unlike.

I advanced this proposition a year ago in my "Plant-Breeding"* (pages 9 and 10), and I am now glad to find, since writing the above paragraph, that H. S. Williams has reached similar conclusions in his new "Geological Biology." He regards mutability as the fundamental law of organisms, and speaks of the prevalent notion that organisms must necessarily reproduce

---

*As an example of the common and unreserved acceptance of the notion that like produces like, I may cite the opinion of A. S., in a review of Plant-Breeding in the Bulletin of the Torrey Botanical Club (April, 1890). He dogmatically asserts that the statement that inherent plasticity of organisms may allow of variation without an immediate inciting cause, is "certainly unscientific." It is only fair to ask that he explain why it is.

themselves exactly as "one of the chief inconsistencies in the prevalent conception of the nature of organisms." "While the doctrine of mutability of species has generally taken the place of immutability," he writes, "the proposition that like produces like in organic generation is still generally, and I suppose almost universally, accepted. It therefore becomes necessary to suppose that variation is exceptional, and that some reason for the accumulation of variation is necessary to account for the great divergencies seen in different species. * * * * The search has been for some cause of the variation; it is more probable that mutability is the normal law of organic action, and that permanency is the acquired law." I do not suppose that Professor Williams makes definite variation an inherent or necessary quality of organic matter, but that he conceives this matter to have had no original hereditary power, and that its form and other attributes in succeeding generations have been moulded into the environment, and that the burden of proof is thrown upon those who assume that life-matter was endowed with the property that like necessarily produces like. At all events, this last is my own conception of the modification of the lines of ascent.

This conception of the unstable constitution of the original forms of life is by no means novel, but it appears to have been held most freely by those thinkers who are not themselves professed biologists. One of the best statements of it which I know is that of E. P. Powell in his powerful book, "Our Heredity from God." "But Nature never fails to remind us," he says, "that heredity is only a slowly established tendency, and that permutation is the original tendency in nature; for, if you succeed in breaking up an established order or species, you will find the most persistent effort necessary to prevent unlimited variation. * * * The difficulty is not so much to secure a new variety or a new species as it is to establish and confirm it."

In other words, I look upon heredity as an acquired character, the same as form or color or sensation is, and not as an original endowment of matter. The hereditary power did not originate until, for some reason, it was necessary for a given character to reproduce itself, and the longer any form or character was perpetuated, the stronger became the hereditary power.

It is now pertinent to enquire what determined the particular differences which we know to have persisted. The mere statement that some forms became sessile or attached to the earth, and that others became or remained motile, is an assumption that these differences were direct adaptations to environment. Every little change in environment incited a corresponding change in the plastic organization; and the greater and more various the changes in the physical attributes of the earth with the lapse of time, the greater became the modifications in organisms. I believe, therefore, that the greater part of present differences in organisms are the result, directly and indirectly, of external stimuli, until we come into those higher ranges of being in which sensation and volition have developed, and in which the effects of use and disuse and of psychological states have become increasingly more important as factors of ascent. The whole moot question, then, as to whether variations are definite or multifarious, is aside from the issue. They are as definite as the changes in the environment are, which determine and control their existence. More differences arise than can persist, but this does not prove that those which are lost are any the less due to the impinging stimuli. Those who write of definite variation usually construe the result or outcome of some particular evolution into a measure of the variation which is conceived to have taken place in the group. Most or all of the present characters of any group are definite because they are the survivals in a process of elimination; but there may have been, at various times, the most diverse and diffuse variations in the very group which is now marked by definite attributes. As the lines of ascent developed, and generation followed generation in countless number, the organization was more and more impressed with the features of ancestral characters, and these ancestral characters are the more persistent as they have been more constant in the past. But these characters, which appear as hereditary or atavistic variations in succeeding generations, were no doubt first, at least in the plant creation, the offspring, for the most part, of the environment reacting upon the organism. As life has ascended in the time-scale and has become increasingly complex, so the operation of any incident force must ever produce more diverse and unpredictable results. What I mean to say is that, in plants, some of the variations seem to me to be the resultants of a long line of previous incident impressions, or to have no immediate inciting cause. Such variation is to all appearances fortuitous. It is, therefore, evident that the study of the effects of impinging environments at the present day may not directly elucidate the changes which similar conditions may have produced in the beginning.

Whilst the steadily ascending line of the plant creation was fitting itself into the changing moods of the external world, it was, at the same time, developing an internal power. Plants were constantly growing larger and stronger or more specialized. The accumulation of vital energy is an acquired character, the same as peculiarities of form or structure are. It is the accumulated result of every circumstance which has contributed to the well-being and virility of the organism. The gardener knows that he can cause the plant to store up energy in the seed, so that the resulting crop will be the larger. Growth is itself but the expression or result of this energy which has been picked up by the way through countless ages. Now, mere growth is variation. It results in differences. Plants cannot grow without being unlike. The more luxuriant the growth, the more marked the variation. Most plants have acquired or inherited more growth-force than they are able to use, because they are held down to certain limitations by the conditions in which they are necessarily placed by the struggle for existence. I am convinced that many of the members of plants are simply outgrowths resulting from this growth-pressure, or, as Bower significantly suggests ("A Theory of the Strobilus in Archegoniate Plants," Annals of Botany, viii. 358, 359), they are the result of an "eruptive process." The pushing out of shoots from any part of the plant body, upon occasion, the normal production of adventitious plantlets upon the stems and leaves of some begonias (especially *Begonia phyllomaniaca*), bryophyllum, some ferns, and many other plants, are all expressions of the growth-force which is a more or less constant internal power. This growth-force may give rise to more definite variations than impinging stimuli do; but the growth-force runs in definite directions because it, in its turn, is the survival in a general process of elimination. Many of the characters of plants which—for lack of better explanation—we are in the habit of calling adaptive, are no doubt simply the result of eruption of tissue. Very likely some of the compounding of leaves, the pushing out of some kinds of prickles, the duplication of floral organs, and the like, are examples of this kind of variation. We know that the characters of the external bark or cortex upon old tree trunks are the result of the internal pressure in stretching and splitting it. This simply shows how growth-force may originate characters of taxonomic significance when it is expressed as mere mechanical power acting upon tissue of given anatomical structure. This power of growth is competent, I think, to originate many and important variations in plants. I suppose my conception of it to be essentially the same as that of the bathmism of Cope, and the "theory of the organic growth" of Eimer. Darwin seems to have come near to the same law when he supposed that excess of food supply is the chief cause of variation, for he thereby recognizes the correlation of growth and variability; but in his conception, the growth is the result of a direct and immediate external stimulus, and not an internal acquired force.

We have now considered two general types of forces or agencies which start off variations in plants,—purely external stimuli, and the internal acquired energy of growth. There is still a third general factor, crossing, or, as Eimer writes it, "sexual mixing." The reason for the very existence of sex, as we now understand it, is to originate differences by means of the union of two parents into one offspring. (See Essay II.) This sexual mixing cannot be considered to be an original cause of unlikeness, however, since sex itself was at first a variation induced by environment or other agencies, and its present perfection, in higher organisms, is the result of the process of continuous survival in a conflict of differences.

The recent rise of Lamarckian views seems to have been largely the result of an attempt to discover the *vera causa* of variations. Darwin's hypothesis of natural selection assumes variability without inquiring into its cause, and writers have therefore said that Darwin did not attempt to account for the cause of variations. Nothing can be farther from his views. Yet some of our most recent American writings upon organic evolution repeat these statements. Cope, in his always admirable "Primary Factors of Organic Evolution," writes that "Darwin only discussed variation after it came into being." Yet Darwin's very first chapter in his "Origin of Species" contains a discussion of the "Causes of variability," and the same subject is gone over in detail in "Variation of Animals and Plants under Domestication." Darwin repeatedly refers the cause or origin of variation to "changed conditions of life," which is essentially the position maintained by the Lamarckians, and he as strenuously combats those who hold that definite variation is an innate attribute of life. "But we must, I think, conclude * * *," writes Darwin in the latter book, "that organic beings, when subjected during several generations to any change whatever in their conditions, tend to vary." He discussed at length the particular agencies which he considered to be most potent in inducing variability, and enumerated, amongst other factors, the kind and amount of food, climate, and crossing. "Changes of any kind in the condition of life," he repeats, "even extremely slight changes, often suffice to cause variability. Excess of nutriment is perhaps the most efficient single exciting cause." (See Essay XIV.) Cope, in his discussion of the "Causes of variation," starts out with the proposition "to cite examples of the direct modifying effect of external influences on the characters of individual animals and plants;" and he closes with this paragraph: "I trust that I have adduced evidence to show that the stimuli of chemical and physical forces, and also molar motion or use and its absence, are abundantly sufficient to produce variations of all kinds in organic beings. The variations may be in color, proportions, or details of structure, according to the conditions which are present." This is, in great part, the thesis to which Darwin extended the proofs of a most laborious collection of data from gardeners and stock-breeders and from feral nature. It has been the great misfortune of the interpretation of Darwin's writings that his hypothesis of natural selection has so completely overtopped everything else in the reader's mind that other important matters have been overlooked.

Whilst the one central truth in the plant creation is the fact that differences arise as the result of variations in environment, there are, nevertheless, many exceptions to it. There are various types of differences, which are merely incidental or secondary to the main stem of adaptive ascent. Some of these are such as arise from the cessation of the constructive agencies, and others are mere correlatives or accompaniments of type differences. As an example of the former, we may cite the behavior of the potato. By high cultivation and careful breeding, the plant has been developed to produce enormous crops of very large tubers, so heavy a crop that the plant has been obliged to spare some of its energy from the production of pollen and berries for the purpose of maintaining the subterranean product. It is evident that this high state of amelioration can be maintained only by means of high cultivation. The moment there is a letdown in the factors which have bred and maintained the plant, there is a tendency towards a breaking up and disappearance of the high-bred type. This is an illustration of the phenomenon of panmixia, as outlined by Weismann, except that the force which has ceased to act is human selection rather than natural selection. "This suspension of the preserving influence of natural selection," Weismann writes, "may be termed Panmixia." In his opinion, "the greater number of those variations which are usually attributed to the direct influence of external conditions of life are to be attributed to panmixia. For example, the great variability of most domesticated animals and plants essentially depends upon this principle." In other words, certain differences are preserved through the agency of natural selection, and certain differences are lost; if the organism is removed from this restraining and directing agency, all variations have the chance of asserting themselves. "All individuals can reproduce themselves," Weismann explains, "and thus stamp their characters upon the species, and not only those which are in all respects, or in respect to some single organ, the fittest." I am convinced that this term expresses a very important truth, and one which, as Wiesmann says, is particularly apparent in domestic animals and plants; but panmixia does not express an original force. If new differences arise in consequence of the cessation of the directive agency of natural selection, it is because they were impressed upon the organization by some unaccountable agency; or, if there is simply a falling away from accumulated characters, the residuary or secondary features which appear are probably the compound and often deteriorated result of various previous incident forces. In short, panmixia is a name for a class of phenomena, and it cannot be considered as itself an original cause of variation. It is, to my mind, largely the unrestrained expression or unfolding of the growth-force consequent upon the removal of the pressure under which the plant has lived.

III.

The Survival of the Unlike.

The one note of the modern evolution speculations which has resounded to the remotest corner of civilization and which is the chief exponent of current speculation respecting the origin and destiny of the organic world, is Spencer's phrase, "the survival of the fittest." This epigram is an epitome of Darwin's law of natural selection, or "the preservation, during the battle for life, of varieties which possess any advantage in structure, constitution or instinct." In most writings, these two phrases—"natural selection" and "the survival of the fittest"—are used synonymously; but in their etymology they really stand to each other in the relation of process and result. The operation of natural selection results in the survival of the fittest. One must not be too exact, however, in the literal application of such summary expressions as these. Their particular mission is to afford a convenient and abbreviated formula for the designation of important principles, for use in common writing and speech, and not to express a literal truth. Darwin was himself well aware of the danger of the literal interpretation of the epigram "natural selection." "The term 'natural selection,'" he writes, "is in some respects a bad one, as it seems to imply conscious choice; but this will be disregarded after a little familiarity." This technical use of the term "natural selection" is now generally accepted unconsciously; and yet there have been recent revolts against it, upon the score that it does not itself express a literal principle or truth. If we accept the term in the sense in which it was propounded by its author, we are equally bound to accept "survival of the fittest" as a synonymous expression, because its author so designed it. "By natural selection or survival of the fittest," writes Spencer, "—by the preservation in successive generations of those whose moving equilibria happen to be least at variance with the requirements, there is eventually produced a changed equilibrium completely in harmony with the requirements."

It should be said that there is no reason other than usage why the phrase "survival of the fittest" should not apply to the result of Lamarckian or functional evolution as well as of Darwinian or selective evolution. It simply expresses a fact without designating the cause or the process. Cope has written a book upon the "Origin of the Fittest," in which the argument is Lamarckian. The phrase implies a conflict, and the loss of certain contestants and the salvation of certain others. It asserts that the contestants or characters which survive are the fittest, but it does not explain whether they are fit because endowed with greater strength, greater prolificness, completer harmony with surroundings, or other attributes. I should like to suggest, therefore, that the chief merit of the survivors is unlikeness, and to call your attention for a few minutes to the significance of the phrase— which I have used in my teaching during the last year— the survival of the unlike.

This phrase—the survival of the unlike—expresses no new truth, but I hope that it may present the old truth of vicarious or non-designed evolution in a new light. It defines the fittest to be the unlike. You will recall that in this paper I have dwelt upon the origin and progress of differences rather than of definite or positive characters. I am so fully convinced that, in the plant creation, a new character is useful to the species because it is unlike its kin, that the study of differences between individuals has come to be, for me, the one absorbing and controlling thought in the contemplation of the progress of life. These differences arise as a result of every impinging force,—soil, weather, climate, food, training, conflict with fellows, the strain and stress of wind and wave, and insect visitors,—as a complex resultant of many antecedent external forces, the effects of crossing, and also as the result of the accumulated force of mere growth; they are indefinite, non-designed, an expression of all the various influences to which the passive vegetable organism is or has been exposed; those differences which are most unlike their fellows or their parents find the places of least conflict, and persist because they thrive best, and thereby impress themselves best upon their offspring. Thereby there is a constant tendency for new and divergent lines to strike off, and these lines, as they become accented, develop into what we, for convenience sake, have called species. There are, therefore, as many species as there are unlike conditions in physical and environmental nature, and in proportion as the conditions are unlike and local are the species well defined. But to Nature, perfect adaptation is the end; she knows nothing, *per se*, as species or as fixed types. Species were created by John Ray, not by the Lord; they were named by Linnæus, not by Adam.

I must now hasten to anticipate an objection to my phrase which may arise in your minds. I have said that when characters are unlike existing characters, they stand a chance of persisting; but I do not desire to say that they are useful in proportion as they are unlike their kin. I want to express my conviction that mere sports are rarely useful. Sports are no doubt the result of very unusual or complex stimuli or of unwonted refrangibility of the energy of growth, and not having been induced by conditions which act uniformly over a course of time, they are likely to be transient. I fully accept Cope's remark that there is "no ground for believing that sports have any considerable influence on the course of evolution. * * * The method of evolution has apparently been one of successional increment and decrement of parts along definite lines." Amongst domestic animals and plants the selection and breeding of sports, or very unusual and marked variations, has been a leading cause of their strange and diverse evolution. In fact, it is in this particular thing that the work of the breeder and the gardener is most unlike the work of nature. But in feral conditions, the sport may be likened to an attribute out of place; and I imagine that its chief effect upon the phylogeny of a race—if any effect it have—is in giving rise in its turn to a brood of less erratic unlikenesses. This question of sports has its psychological significance, for if the way becomes dark the wanderer invokes the aid of this *ignis fatuus* to cut short his difficulties. Sir William Thomson suggests that the basis of life may have come to earth upon a meteor, and Brinton proposes that man is a sport from some of the lower creation. It is certainly a strange conception which ascribes a self-centered and self-sufficient power to the tree of life, and then, at the very critical points, adopts a wholly extraneous force, and one which is plainly but a survival of the old cataclysmic doctrines; and it is the stranger, too, because such type of explanation is not suggested by observation or experiment, but simply by an insuperable barrier of our present ignorance of natural processes. If evolution is true at all, there is reason to suppose that it extends from beginning to finish of creation, and the stopping of the process at obscure intervals can be only a temporary satisfaction to one who is not yet fully committed to the eternal truth of ascent. The tree of life has no doubt grown steadily and gradually, and the same forces, variously modified by the changing physical conditions of the earth, have run on with slow but mighty energy until the present time. Any radical change in the plan would have defeated it, and any mere accidental circumstance is too trivial to be considered as a modifying influence of the great onward movement of creation, particularly when it assumes to account for the appearing of the very capstone of the whole mighty structure.

Bear with me if I recite a few specific examples of the survival of the unlike, or of the importance, to organic types, of gradually widening differences. Illustrations might be drawn from every field of the organic creation, but I choose a few from plants because these are the most neglected, and because I am most familiar with them. These are given to illustrate how important external stimuli are in originating variation, and how it is that some of these variations persist.

Let me begin by saying that a good gardener loves his plants. Now, a good gardener is one who grows good plants, and good plants are very unlike poor plants. They are unlike because the gardener's love for them has made them so. The plants were all alike in November; in January, the good gardener's plants are strong and clean, with large, dense leaves, a thick stem, and an abundance of perfect flowers; the poor gardener's plants are small and mean, with curled leaves, a thin, hard stem, and a few imperfect flowers. You will not believe now that the two lots were all from the same seed-pod three months ago. The good gardener likes to save his own seeds or to make his own cuttings; and next year his plants will be still more unlike his neighbor's. The neighbor tries this seed and that, reads this bulletin and that, but all avails nothing, simply because he does not grow good plants. He does not care for them tenderly, as a fond mother cares for a child. The good gardener knows that the temperature of the water and the air, the currents in the atmosphere, the texture of the soil, and all the little amenities and comforts which plants so much enjoy, are just the factors which make his plants successful; and a good crop of anything, whether wheat or beans or apples, is simply a variation.

And do these unlikenesses survive? Yes, verily! The greater part of the amelioration of cultivated plants has come about in just this way,—by gradual modifications in the conditions in which they are grown, by means of which unlikenesses arise, and then by the selection of seeds from the most coveted plants. Even at the present day, there is comparatively little plant-breeding. The cultivated flora has come up with man, and if it has departed immensely from its wild prototypes, so has man. The greater part of all this has been unconscious and unintended on man's part, but it is none the less real.

As an illustration of how large the factors of undesigned choice and selection are in the amelioration of the domestic flora, let me ask your attention to the battle of the seed-bags. In the year 1890 the census records show, for the first time, the numbers of acres in the United States devoted to the growing of seeds. I give the acreage of three representative crops, and these figures I have multiplied by the average seed-yields per acre, in order to arrive at an approximate estimate of the entire crop produced, and the number of acres which the crop would plant. I have used low averages of yields in order to be on the safe side, and I have likewise used liberal averages of the quantity of seed required to plant an acre when making up the last column:

	Acres in seed-crops.	Average yields per acre.	Approximate crop of seeds.	Would plant
Cabbage	1,208	200 lbs.	253,600 lbs.	1,014,400 acres.
Cucumber	10,219	120 "	1,220,280 "	613,140 "
Tomato	4,356	80 "	308,480 "	1,473,020 "

The last column in this table has particular interest, because it shows the enormous acreage which these seeds, if all planted, would cover. We are now curious to know if such areas really are planted to these species, and if they are not, it will be pertinent to inquire what becomes of the seeds. Unfortunately, we have no statistics of the entire acreages of these various truck-garden crops, but the same census gives the statistics of

BATTLE OF THE SEED-BAGS.

the commercial market-gardens of the country. Inquiry of seed-merchants has convinced me that about one-fourth of all the seeds sold in any year go to market-gardeners. I have therefore multiplied the census figures of market gardens by four for the purpose of arriving at an estimate of the total acreage of the given crops in the United States; and I have introduced the last column from the previous table for purposes of comparison:

	Acreage of market-gardens.	Probable total acreage.	There are seeds enough to plant	Difference.
Cabbage	77,094	308,376	1,014,400 acres.	706,024 acres.
Cucumber	4,721	18,884	613,140 "	594,256 "
Tomato	22,802	91,208	1,473,920 "	1,382,712 "

It will thus be seen that there are enough cabbage seeds raised in this country each year—if the census year is a fair sample—to plant nearly three-quarters of a million acres more than actually are planted; about the same surplus of cucumber seeds; and a surplus of tomato seeds sufficient to plant over one and a quarter million acres. It is possible, of course, that the figures of actual acreage of these crops are too low; but such error, if it occur, must be much overbalanced by the large quantities of home-grown and imported seeds which are used every year. These startling figures would not apply so well to many other crops which are detailed in the census bulletin. For instance, the peas raised in this country would plant only about 46,000 acres, whilst there are over 100,000 acres actually grown; but this discrepancy is probably accounted for by the fact that the larger part of the seed peas are grown in Canada, and therefore do not figure in our census. There is a somewhat similar discrepancy in the watermelon, but in this crop the seeds are very largely home-saved by the heavy planters in the south and west. I do not give these figures for their value as statistics, but simply for the purpose of graphically expressing the fact that many more seeds are raised by cultivators each average year than are ever grown into plants, and that struggle for existence does not necessarily cease when plants are taken under the care of man.

What, now, becomes of this enormous surplus of seed? Let us take a rough survey of the entire seed crop of any year. In the first place, a certain percentage of the seeds are laid aside by the seedsman as a surety against failure in the year to come. Much of this old stock never finds its way into the market, and is finally discarded. We will estimate this element of waste as 20 per cent. Of the 80 per cent. which is actually sold, perhaps another 10 per cent. is never planted, leaving about 70 per cent. which finds its way into the ground. These two items of loss are pure waste, and have no effect upon the resulting crop. Now, of the seeds which are planted, no more than 75 per cent. can be expected to germinate. That is, there is certainly an average loss of 25 per cent. in nearly all seeds—and much more in some—due to inherent weakness, and 75 per cent. represents the survival in a conflict of strength. We have now accounted for about half of the total seed product of any year. The remaining half produces plants; but here the most important part of the conflict begins. In the crops mentioned above, much less than half of the seeds which are grown ever appear in the form of a crop. We must remember, moreover, that in making the estimate of the number of acres which these seeds would plant, I have used the usual estimates of the quantity of seeds required to plant an acre. Now, these estimates of seedsmen and planters are always very liberal. Every

DISRUPTION OF SPECIFIC TYPES.

farmer sows from five to twenty times more seed than he needs. Some years ago, I sowed seeds according to the recommendation of one of our best seedsmen, and I found that peas would be obliged to stand four-fifths of an inch apart, beets about twenty to the foot, and other vegetables in like confusion. I suppose that of all the seeds which actually come up, not more than one in ten or a dozen, in garden vegetables, ever give mature plants. What becomes of the remainder? They are thinned out for the good of those which are left.

This simple process of thinning out vegetables has had a most powerful effect upon the evolution of our domestic flora. It is a process of undesigned selection. This selection proceeds upon the differences in the seedlings. The weak individuals are disposed of, and those which are strongest and most unlike the general run are preserved. It is a clear case of the survival of the unlike. The laborer who weeds and thins your lettuce bed unconsciously blocks out his ideas in the plants which he leaves. But all this is a struggle of Jew against Jew, not Jew against Philistine. It is a conflict within the species, not of species against species. It, therefore, tends to destroy the solidarity of the specific type, and helps to introduce much of that promiscuous unlikeness which is the distinguishing characteristic of domestic plants.

Let us now transfer this emphatic example to wild nature. There we shall find the same prodigal production of seeds. In the place of the gardener undesignedly moulding the lines of divergence, we find the inexorable physical circumstances into which the plastic organisms must grow, if they grow at all. These circumstances are very often the direct causes of the unlikenesses of plants, for plants which start like when they germinate may be very unlike when they die. Given time and constantly but slowly changing conditions, and the vegetable creation is fashioned into the unlikenesses which we now behold. With this conception, let us read again Francis Parkman's picturesque description of the forests of Maine in his "Half-Century of Conflict:" "For untold ages Maine had been one unbroken forest, and it was so still. Only along the rocky seaboard or on the lower waters of one or two great rivers a few rough settlements had gnawed slight indentations into this wilderness of woods, and a little farther inland some dismal clearing around a blockhouse or stockade let in the sunlight to a soil that had lain in shadow time out of mind. This waste of savage vegetation survives, in some part, to this day, with the same prodigality of vital force, the same struggle for existence and mutual havoc that mark all organized beings, from men to mushrooms. Young seedlings in millions spring every summer from the black mold, rich with the decay of those that had preceded them, crowding, choking, and killing each other, perishing by their very abundance; all but a scattered few, stronger than the rest, or more fortunate in position, which survive by blighting those about them. They in turn, as they grow, interlock their boughs, and repeat in a season or two the same process of mutual suffocation. The forest is full of lean saplings dead or dying with vainly stretching towards the light. Not one infant tree in a thousand lives to maturity; yet these survivors form an innumerable host, pressed together in struggling confusion, squeezed out of symmetry and robbed of normal development, as men are said to be in the level sameness of democratic society. Seen from above, their mingled tops spread in a sea of verdure basking in light; seen from below, all is shadow, through which spots of timid sunshine steal down among legions of dark, mossy trunks, toadstools and rank ferns, protruding roots, matted bushes, and rotting carcasses of fallen trees. A generation ago one might find here and there the rugged trunk of some great pine lifting its verdant spire above the indistinguished myriads of the forest. The woods of Maine had their aristocracy; but the axe of the woodman has laid them low, and these lords of the wilderness are seen no more.''

In such bold and generalized examples as this, the student is able to discern only the general fact of progressive divergency and general adaptation to conditions, without being able to discover the particular directive forces which have been at the bottom of the evolution. It is only when one considers a specific example that he can arrive at any just conclusions respecting initial causes of modification. Of adaptive modifications, two general classes have been responsible for the ascent of the vegetable kingdom; one a mere moulding or shaping into the passive physical environments, the other the direct result of stress or strain imposed upon the organism by wind and water, and by the necessities of a radical change of habit from aquatic to terrestrial life, and later on by the stimuli of insects upon the flowers. One of the very best examples of the mere passive ascent is afforded by the evolution of the root as a feeding organ; and a like example of development as a result of strain is afforded by the evolution of the stem and vascular or fibrous system. Our present flora, like our present fauna, is an evolution from aquatic life. The first

Perhaps the best illustration which I can bring you of the origin of the unlike by means of environmental conditions, and the survival of some of this unlikeness in the battle for life, is the development of the winter quiescence of plants. What means all this bursting verdure of the liquid April days? Why this annually returning miracle of the sudden expansion of the leaf and flower from the lifeless twigs? Were plants always so? Were they designed to pass so much of their existence in this quiescent and passive condition? No! The first plants had no well-defined cycles, and they were born to live, not to die. There were probably no alternations of seasons or even of days, in the primordial world. The account in Genesis places the creation of plants in the third cosmogonic day, and the setting of "lights in the firmament of heaven" to "be for signs, and for seasons, and for days, and years," in the fourth day. As late as the Carboniferous time, according to Dana, the globe "was nowhere colder than the modern temperate zone, or below a mean temperature of 60° F." The earth had become wonderfully diverse by the close of the Cretaceous time, and the cycads and their kin retreated from the poles. Plants grew the year round; and as physical conditions became diverse and the conflict of existence increased, the older and the weaker died. So a limit to duration,—that is, death,—became impressed upon the individuals of the creation; for death, as seen by the evolutionist, is not an original property of life-matter, but is an acquired character, a result of the survival of the fittest. The earth was, perhaps, ages old, even after life began, before it saw a natural death; but without death all things must finally have come to a standstill. When it became possible to sweep away the old types, opportunity was left for new ones; and so the ascent must continue so long as physical conditions which are not absolutely prohibitive of life shall become unlike.

Species have acquired different degrees of longevity, the same as they have acquired different sizes and shapes and habits,—by adaptation to their conditions of life. Annual plants comprise about half of the vegetable kingdom, and these are probably all specializations of comparatively late time. Probably the greater part of them were originally adaptations to shortening periods of growth,—that is, to seasonal changes. The gardener, by forceful cultivation and by transferring plants towards the poles, is able to make annuals of perennials. Now, a true annual is a plant which normally ripens its seeds and dies before the coming of frost. Many of our garden plants are annuals only because they are killed by frost. They naturally have a longer season than our climate will admit, and some of them are true perennials in their native homes. These plants are, with us, plurannuals, and amongst them are the tomato, red pepper, egg-plant, potato, castor bean, cotton, lima bean, and many others. But there are some varieties of potatoes and other plants which have now developed into true annuals, normally completing their entire growth before the approach of frost. It is all the result of adaptation to climate, and essentially the same phenomenon is the development of the annual and biennial flora of the earth from the perennial. An interesting example of the effect of climate upon the seasonal duration of plants is the indeterminate or prolonged growth of plants in England as compared with the same plants in America. The cooler summer and very gradual approach of winter in England develop a late and indefinite maturity of the season's growth. When English plants are grown in America, they usually grow until killed by fall frosts; but after a few generations of plants, they acquire the quick and decisive habit of ripening which is so characteristic of our vegetation. I once made an extended test of onions from English and American seeds (Bull. 31, Mich. Agric. College), and was astonished to find that nearly all of the English varieties continued to grow until frost and failed to "bottom," whilst our domestic varieties ripened up in advance of freezing weather. This was true even of the Yellow Danvers and Red Wethersfield, varieties of American origin and which could not have been grown very many years in England. Every horticulturist of much experience must have noticed similar unmistakable influences of climate upon the duration of plants.

A most interesting type of examples of quick influence of climate upon plants—not only upon their duration but upon habit and structural characters—is that associated with the growing of "stock seed" by seedsmen. Because of uncertainties of weather in the eastern states, it is now the practice to grow seeds of onion, lima bean and other plants in California or other warm regions; but the plants so readily acquire the habit of long-continuing growth as to be thereafter grown with difficulty in the northeastern states. It is, therefore, necessary that the seedsman shall raise his stock seed each year in his own geographical region, and this seed is each year sent to California for the growing of the commercial seed crop. In other words, the seed of California-grown onions is sold only for the purpose of growing onion bulbs for market, and is not planted for the raising of a successive crop of seed. This results in growing only a single generation of the crop in the warm country. Onion seed from stock which has been grown in California for several years is considered to produce onions which do not "bottom," much as I found to be the case with the English onion seed.

But some plants, in Geologic time, could not thus shorten up their life-history to adjust themselves to the oncoming of the seasons. They ceased their labors with the approach of the cold or the dry, tucked up their tender tissues in buds, and resigned themselves to the elements. If a man could have stood amongst those giant mosses and fern forests of the reeking Carboniferous time, and could have known of the refrigeration which the earth was to undergo, he would have exclaimed that all living things must utterly perish. Consider the effects of a frost in May. See its widespread devastation. Yet, six months hence the very same trees which are now so blackened will defy any degree of cold. And then, to make good the loss of time, these plants start into activity relatively much earlier in spring than the same species do in frostless climates. This very day, when frosts are not yet passed, our own New York hillsides are greener with surface vegetation than the lands of the Gulf states are, which have been frostless for two months and more. The frogs and turtles, the insects, the bears and foxes, all adjust themselves to a climate which seems to be absolutely prohibitive of life, and some animals may freeze during their hibernation, and yet these April days see them again in heyday of life and spirits! What a wonderful transformation is all this! This enforced period of quiescence is so impressed upon the organization that the habit becomes hereditary in plants, and the gardener says that his begonias and geraniums and callas must have a "rest," or they will not thrive. But in time he can so far break this habit in most plants as to force them into activity for the entire year. These budding days of April, therefore, are the songs of release from the bondage of winter which has come on as the earth has grown aged and cold.

I must bring still one more illustration of the survival of the unlike, out of the abundance of examples which might be cited. It is the fact that, as a rule, new types are variable and old types are inflexible. The student of fossil plants will recall the fact that the liriodendrons, ginkgos, sequoias, sassafrasses and other types came into existence with many species, and are now going out of existence with one or two species. Williams has considered this feature, for extinct animal forms, at some length in his new "Geological Biology." "Many species," he writes, "which by their abundance and good preservation in fossil state give us sufficient evidence in the case, exhibit greater plasticity in their characters at the early stage than in later stages of their history. A minute tracing of lines of succession of species shows greater plasticity at the beginning of the series than later, and this is expressed, in the systematic description and tabulation of the facts, by an increase in the number of the species." "When species are studied historically, the law appears evident that the characters of specific value * * * present a greater degree of range of variability at an early stage in the life-period of the genus than in the later stages of that period." So marked is this incoming of new types in many cases that some students have supposed that actual special creation of species has occurred at these epochs.

It should be said that there is apt to be a fallacy in observation in these instances, because the records which are, to our vision, simultaneous in the rocks may have extended over ages of time; but it is nevertheless true that some important groups seem to have come in somewhat quickly with many or several species, and to have passed out with exceeding slowness.

To my mind, all this is but the normal result of the divergence of character, or the survival of the unlike. A new type finds places of least conflict, it spreads rapidly and widely, and thereby varies immensely. It is a generalized type, and therefore adapts itself at once to many and changing conditions. A virile plant is introduced into a country in which the same or similar plants are unknown, and immediately it finds its opportunity and becomes a weed, by which we mean that it spreads and thrives everywhere. Darwin and Gray long ago elucidated this fact. The trilobites, spirifers, conifers, ginkgos, were weed-types of their time, the same as the composites are to-day. They were stronger than their contemporaries, the same as our own weeds are stronger than the cultivated plants with which they grow. After a time, the new types outran their opportunity, the remorseless struggle for existence tightened in upon them, the intermediate unlikenesses had been blotted out, and finally only one or two types remained, struggling on through the ages, but doomed to perish with the continuing changes of the earth. They became specialized and inelastic; and the highly specialized is necessarily doomed to extinction. Such remnants of a vanquished host remain to us in the equisetums and tree-ferns, in our single liriodendron, the single ginkgo and sassafras, and the depleted ranks of the conifers.

My attention was first called to this line of thought by contemplating upon the fact that cultivated plants differ widely in variability, and I was struck by the fact that many of our most inextricably variable groups—as the cucurbits, maize, citrus, and the great tribes of composites—are still unknown in a fossil state, presumably because of their recent origin. Many other variable genera, to be sure, are well represented in fossil species, as roses (although these are as late as the Eocene), pyrus, prunus, and musa; but absolute age is not so significant as the comparative age of the type, for types which originated very far back may be yet in the comparative youth of their development. The summary conclusions of a discussion of this subject were presented to the American Association for the Advancement of Science two years ago.* A modification of these points, as I now understand them, would run something as follows:

1. There is a wide difference in variability in cultivated plants. Some species vary enormously, and others but little.

2. This variability is not correlated with age of cultivation, degree of cultivation, nor geographical distribution.

3. Variability of cultivated plants must be largely influenced and directed, therefore, by some antecedent causes.

4. The chief antecedent factor in directing this variability is probably the age of the type. New types, in Geologic time, are polymorphous; old types are mono-

---

* See Proc. A. A. A. S. 1894, 255; Botanical Gazette, xix. 381.

morphous, and finally tend towards extinction. The most flexible types of cultivated plants are such as have probably not yet passed their zenith, as the cucurbits, composites, begonias, and the like. The varieties of cereals, which are old types, are so much alike that expert knowledge is needed to distinguish them.

5. New types are more variable and flexible because less perfectly moulded into and adjusted to the circumstances of life than the old types are. They have not yet reached the limits of their dissemination and variation. They are generalized forms.

The reader will please observe that I have here regarded the origin and survival of the unlike in the plant creation in the sense of a plastic material which is acted upon by every external stimulus, and which must necessarily vary from the very force of its acquired power of growth; and the unlikenesses are preserved because they are unlike. I have no sympathy with the too prevalent idea that all the attributes of plants are direct adaptations, or that they are developed as mere protections from environment and associates. There is a type of popular writings which attempts to evolve many of the forms of plants as a mere protection from assumed enemies. Perhaps the plant features which have been most abused in this manner are the spines, prickles, and the like, and the presence of acrid or poisonous qualities. As a sample of this type of writing, I will make an extract from Massee's "Plant World:"

"Amongst the most prominent and general modes of protection of vegetative parts against the attacks of living enemies may be mentioned *prickles*, as in roses and brambles, which may either be straight, and thus prevent the nibblings of animals, or in more advanced species, curved, thus enabling the weak stem to climb and carry its leaves out of harm's way. *Spines*, that are sharp-pointed abortive branches, serving the same purpose as prickles, as in the common sloe or blackthorn (*Prunus spinosa*). *Rigid hairs* on leaves and stem, as in the borage (*Borago officinalis*), and comfrey (*Symphytum officinale*). *Stinging hairs*, as in the common nettles (*Urtica dioica*, and *U. urens*); in these cases the stinging hairs are mixed on the leaves and stem with ordinary rigid hairs, of which they are higher developments, distinguished by the lower or basal swollen portion of the hair containing an irritating liquid that is ejected when the tip of the hair is broken off. *Bitter taste*, often accompanied by a strong scent, as in wormwood (*Artemisia vulgaris*), chamomile (*Anthemis nobilis*), and the leaves and fruit of the walnut (*Juglans regia*). *Poisonous alkaloids*, as in the species of *Strychnos*, which contain two very poisonous alkaloids, strychnine and brucine, in the root and the seeds; decoctions of species of strychnos are used by the Javanese and the natives of South America to poison their arrows. Some of the species, as *Strychnos nux-vomica*, are valuable medicines, depending on the strychnine they contain, which acts as a powerful excitant of the spinal cord and nerves; thus the most effective protective arrangements evolved by plants can be turned to account, and consequently lead to the destruction of the individuals they were designed to protect. Our common arum (*Arum maculatum*), popularly known as 'Lords and Ladies,' has an intensely acrid substance present in the leaves, which effectually protects it from the attacks of mammals and caterpillars, but not from the attacks of parasitic fungi, which appear to be indifferent to all protective contrivances exhibited by plants, nearly every plant supporting one or more of these minute pests, the effects of which will be realized by mentioning the potato disease, 'rust' and 'smut' in the various cereals, and the hop disease, all due to parasitic fungi."

Now, this is merely a gratuitous and *ad captandum* species of argument—one which is suited to please the fancy, and to satisfy those persons who are still determined to read the element of proximate design into organic nature. It does not account for the facts. These particular attributes of plants are specialized features, and it is always unsafe to generalize upon specializations. Each and every one of such specialized features must be investigated for itself. Probably the greater number of spinous processes will be found to be the *residua* following the contraction of the plant body; others are no doubt mere correlatives of the evolution of other attributes, and some may be the eruptions of the growth-force; and the acrid and poisonous properties are quite as likely to be wholly secondary and useless features. The attempt to find a definite immediate use and office for every attribute in the creation is unphilosophical. There are many attributes of organisms which are not only useless but positively dangerous to the possessor, and they can be understood only as one studies them in connection with the long and eventful history of the line of ascent.

The thought which I want to leave with you, therefore, is that unlikenesses are the greatest facts in the organic creation. These unlikenesses in plants are (1) the expressions of the ever-changing environmental conditions in which plants grow, and of the incidental stimuli to which they are exposed; (2) the result of the force of mere growth; (3) the outcome of sexual mixing. Some of them may still be the expression of the normal or original plasticity of organic matter, although it is probable that most of this normal mutability has been suppressed in the long process of elimination. These variations survive because they are unlike, and thereby enter fields of least competition. The possibility of the entire tragic evolution lay in the plasticity of the original life-plasma. The plastic creation has grown into its own needs day by day and age by age, and it is now just what it has been obliged to be. It could have been nothing else.

II.

NEO-LAMARCKISM AND NEO-DARWINISM.[1]

It is difficult to accept the hypothesis of organic evolution in the abstract. In the first place, there must be some reason for the operation of a law of transformation or development; and this is found in the ever-changing physical or external conditions of existence, which are more or less opposed to established organisms. And it may also be said that the very fact of the increase of organisms through multiplication must impose new conditions of competition upon every succeeding generation. Again, it is necessary to conceive of some means or machinery by which the process of evolution is carried forward. It was long known that all species vary, that is, that no two individuals in nature are exactly alike; yet there was lacking any hypothesis to show either why these varieties appear or how it is that some become permanent and some do not. The first scientific explanation of the process of evolution was that made in 1809 by the now famous Lamarck. He saw two factors which, he thought, were concerned in the transformation of species—the habitat and the habit. The habitat is the condition in which the organism lives, the environment. This environment, subject to change with every new individual, calls for new habits to adapt the organism to the new needs—inducing greater exercise of some

---

[1] Extract from an address before the Philosophical Club of Cornell University. Printed in American Naturalist, xxviii. 661 (August, 1894).

powers or organs and less exercise of others. This greater or less use gradually strengthens or enfeebles the organ concerned, and the modifications thus acquired are preserved "through heredity to the new individuals that are produced by them, provided the changes are common to the two sexes, or to those that have produced these new individuals." There are three things to be considered in this hypothesis: 1. Changes in environment or the conditions of life react upon organisms in the direction of their needs or functions. 2. Organs or powers thus affected are modified to satisfy the new demands. 3. The modifications acquired by the individual are hereditary. This, then, is Lamarckism—that the controlling factor or process in evolution is functional, and that acquired characters are readily transmissible. It is important that I still repeat Lamarck's belief in the transmission of a character obtained by any individual during its own lifetime, for this is the starting point of the definition of an "acquired character," concerning the hereditability of which the scientific world is now rent. "All that nature has caused individuals to acquire or lose through the influence of the circumstances to which their race has been for a long time exposed," says Lamarck, "it preserves," etc. And again: "Every change acquired in an organ by an habitual exercise sufficient to have brought it about is preserved thereafter through heredity," etc. We shall presently observe how far this definition of an acquired character has been maintained by recent philosophers.

Just fifty years after the publication of Lamarck's theory, Darwin proposed a hypothesis which has had a greater influence upon the habit of scientific thought than any enunciation since the promulgation of inductive philosophy. Darwin, like Lamarck, saw that all forms of life vary; and like him, too, he perceived that there must be a fierce struggle for place or existence amongst the individuals of the rapidly succeeding generations. This variation and struggle are particularly apparent in cultivated plants; and Darwin saw that the gardener selects the best, and thereby "improves" the breed. "Can it, then, be thought improbable," says Darwin, "seeing that variations useful to man have undoubtedly occurred, that other variations useful in some way to each being in the great and complex battle of life, should occur in the course of many successive generations? If such do occur, can we doubt (remembering that many more individuals are born than can possibly survive) that individuals having any advantage, however slight, over others, would have the best chance of surviving and procreating their kind?" "This preservation of favorable individual differences and variations, and the destruction of those which are injurious, I have called Natural Selection, or the Survival of the Fittest." This, then, is Darwinism—that the controlling factor or process in evolution is selective, the survival, in the struggle for existence, of those individuals which are best fitted to survive. But while this is the naked core of Darwinism, there are various correlative or incidental hypotheses attached to it. Darwin, for instance, accepted in some degrees the views of Lamarck as to the importance of functional characters; he considered that sexual selection, or the choice exercised in securing mates, is often an important factor in modifying species; he thought that variation is induced by the modifications of environment, or the "changed conditions of life;" and he was a firm believer in the hereditability of acquired characters. It is around these two great hypotheses—the functional or Lamarckian on the one hand, and the selective or Darwinian upon the other—in various forms and modifications, that the discussions of the philosophy of organic nature are at present revolving.

Before leaving the subject of Darwinism, I wish to touch upon Darwin's view of the cause of variation and his belief in the transmission of acquired characters. We shall presently see that the rehabilitation of the theories of Lamarck, under the name of Neo-Lamarckism, is undertaken, very largely, for the purpose of assigning the origin of variations to external causes, or to the environment, in opposition to those who consider the source of variation to be essentially innate, or at least internal. But Darwin also believed that variation is induced by the environment, and the chief factor in this environment, so far as its reaction upon the organism is concerned, is probably excess of food supply, although climate and other impinging circumstances are potent causes of modification. He marshaled arguments to support "the view that variations of all kinds and degrees are directly or indirectly caused by the conditions of life to which each being, and more especially its ancestors, have been exposed," and that "each separate variation has its own proper exciting cause." I do not understand how it has come about that various writers declare that Darwin did not believe explicitly in the external cause of variation, and that they feel obliged to go back to Lamarck in order to find a hypothesis for the occasion. It is true that Darwin believed that the nature or direction or particular kind of variation in a given case is determined very largely by the constitution of the organism, but that variation itself, that is, variability, proceeds largely from external causes; and the characters arising in the lifetime of an individual may become hereditary. (See page 27.) I must hasten to explain, however, that Darwin clearly recognized the importance of the union of sexes, or crossing, as a cause of variation.

While Darwin believed that the effects of variability arise "generally from changed conditions acting during successive generations," he nevertheless believed that the first increment of change—that arising in the first individual of a given series—might be directly carried over to the first offspring. That is, he believed in the hereditability of acquired or new external characters, a fact which is emphasized by his conviction that certain mutilations, and even the effects of use and disuse, may be transmitted. Yet, whilst Darwin accepted the doctrine, he believed it much less thoroughly than Lamarck did, and it is but an incidental part of his philosophy, while it is an essential tenet of Lamarckism.

Thus far, the hereditability of all important characters had not been disputed. In other words, heredity as a general law or force in the organic world had been assumed. But with the refinement of the discussions it became necessary to conceive of some definite means through which the transmission of particular characters or features should operate; and it was soon found, also, that no philosophy of evolution can expect to explain the phenomena of organic life unless it is connected and coordinated with some hypothesis of the method of heredity. While, therefore, a hypothesis of heredity need not necessarily be associated with the abstract theory of evolution, all such hypotheses which are now before the scientific world have for their particular object the explanation of the assumed progressive tendency of the forms of life.

It is incomprehensible that the minute fertilized ovum or egg-cell should reconstruct the essential characters of the two individuals from which it proceeds, unless it has in some way derived distinct impressions from every part and organ of the parental bodies which it is to reproduce. It would seem as if it must of itself be an epitome or condensation of its parents, with the power of unfolding its impressions or attributes during the whole life-course of the organism to which it gives rise. Several hypotheses have been announced to account for the phenomena of heredity, of which one of the most important is still Darwin's theory of pangenesis. Darwin supposed, provisionally, that besides the ordinary multiplication of the cell, each cell may "throw off minute granules which are dispersed throughout the whole system; that these, when supplied with proper nutriment, multiply by self-division, and are ultimately developed into units like those from which they were originally derived." These granules, or gemmules, have a natural affinity for each other, and they collect themselves "from all parts of the system" to form the sexual materials or elements. These sexual elements, therefore, which unite to form the new individual, are an epitomized compound of the parents. The value of this hypothesis, it seems to me, lies not so much in the particular constitution and behavior of these gemmules, as in the fact that it attempts to account for the known phenomena of life by supposing each corporeal element to be represented in the sexual elements. The hypothesis has never gained wide support, because of the supposed physical improbability of the gemmules and of their concentration in sexual system; yet it should be said that a simpler one which can account for the facts has not yet been advanced, unless it be the bathmic hypothesis of Cope (or similar formulations of the conception of the growth-force), which supposes that each body-cell transmits "a mode of motion" to the germ-cell.

For the present purpose, we need consider but one other hypothesis of heredity—that advanced in 1883 by Weismann, which has given rise to the philosophy now called Neo-Darwinism. Weismann's point of view is interesting and unique. He places himself at the threshold of organic life, and contemplates what takes place in the reproduction of one-celled organisms. These organisms multiply largely by simple division, or fission. When the organism reaches a certain size, it becomes constricted near its middle, and finally parts into two cells or organisms. It is evident that one organism is twin of the other, neither is older, neither is parent, but each has partaken of the common stock of protoplasm. The protoplasm again multiplies itself in the two organisms, and at length it is again divided; and so, to the end of time, the remotest individual of the series may be said to contain a portion of the original protoplasm; in other words, the protoplasm is continuous. And inasmuch as protoplasm is the seat or physical basis of life, it may be said that the one-celled organism is immortal, or is not confronted by natural death.

In time, however, there came a division of labor—cells living together in colonies, and certain cells performing one function and certain other cells other functions. This was, perhaps, the beginning of the many-celled organism, in which certain cells developed the specific function of reproduction, or eventually became elements of sex. As organisms became more complex in their structure, there came to be great differences between this reproductive or germ portion and the surrounding or body portion; and Weismann assumes that these two elements are different and distinct from each other in kind, and, inasmuch as the one-celled organisms propagated their exact kind by simple division, that therefore the reproductive elements of the many-celled or complex body must continue to perpetuate their kind or enjoy immortality, while all the surrounding or body cells die and are reproduced only through the reconstructive power of the sexual elements. There are, then, according to this hypothesis, two elements or plasms in every organized being, the germ-plasm and the soma-plasm or body-plasm; and every organism which procreates thereby preserves its germ-plasm to future generations, while death destroys the remainder. A vital point in this hypothesis is the method by which the soma-plasm, or the organs and body of the organism, can be so impressed upon the germ that they shall become hereditary. At first it would seem as if some assumption like that of Darwin's might be useful here—that this germ-plasm is impressed by particles thrown off from all the surrounding or soma-cells; but this Weismann considers to be too unwieldy, and he ascribes the transfer of these characters through the medium of the germ-plasm to "variations in its molecular constitution." In other words, there can be no heredity of a character which originates at the periphery of the individual, because there is no means of transferring its likeness to the germ. All modification of the offspring is predetermined in the germ-plasm; and if the new organism becomes modified through contact with external agencies, such modification is lost with the death of the individual. "Characters only acquired by the operation of external circumstances acting during the life of the individual cannot be transmitted." "All the characters exhibited by the offspring are due to primary changes in the germ." It is admitted that the continued effect of impinging environment may, now and then, finally reach the germ-plasm, but not in the first generation in which such extraneous influence may be exercised. In other words, acquired characters cannot be hereditary.

It would seem as if this hypothesis precludes the possibility of evolution or the continued modification of species, inasmuch as it does not accept the modifications arising directly from external sources. But Weismann supposes that variation originates—or at least all variation which is of permanent use to the species—from a union of the sexes, inasmuch as the unlike germ-plasms of two individuals unite; and from the variations thus induced are derived the materials upon which natural selection works in the struggle for existence. "I am entirely convinced," Weismann writes, "that the higher development of the organic world was only rendered possible by the introduction of sexual reproduction." "Sexual reproduction has arisen by and for natural selection, as the only means by which the individual variations can be united and combined in every possible proportion."

It will be seen that Weismann is a Darwinian—a believer in natural selection as the one controlling process of evolution; but, unlike Darwin, he refers variation to sex, and declares that any new or acquired character originating in the body of the organism cannot be transmitted. The exact means or machinery through which he supposes heredity to act is rather more an embryological matter than a philosophical one. We are particularly concerned in its results, which are the distinguishing marks of Neo-Darwinism—that variation is of sexual or internal origin, and that acquired characters are not hereditary.

In opposition to this body of belief, which has been upheld, particularly in England, with much aggressiveness, is Neo-Lamarckism, which is a compound of both Lamarckism and Darwinism, and which has an especially strong following in North America. The particular canons of this philosophy are the belief that external causes, or the environment, are directly responsible for much variation, and that acquired characters are often hereditary. Other features of it, held in varying degrees by different persons, are the belief in the transforming effects of use and disuse, and in natural selection.

The one great schism between the Neo-Darwinians and the Neo-Lamarckians is the controversy over the hereditability of acquired characters, and just at present this question has come so strongly to the fore that other differences in the two hypotheses have been obscured. It is worthy of remark that Darwinism and Neo-Lamarckism see first the facts or phenomena and then try to explain then; while Neo-Darwinism or Weismannism assumes first a hypothesis and then tries to prove it. I think that any one will be struck with this difference of attitude, if he read Darwin's chapter upon pangenesis, and then read Weismann's essay upon heredity. The Neo-Darwinians are loud in demand of facts or proofs that acquired characters are hereditary, and they attempt to throw the burden of proof upon their opponents; while, at the same time, they give no proofs of their own position, and confound their adversaries with verbal subtleties. The burden of proof, however, lies clearly upon the Neo-Darwinians, inasmuch as they have assumed to deny phenomena which were theretofore considered to be established.

A voluminous issue of polemics has arisen during the last five or six years between the Neo-Darwinians and the Neo-Lamarckians; but whatever may have been its effects upon the older philosophy, it is clear, to my mind, that some of the attacks upon Neo-Darwinism are un-answerable in any rational manner, and it is certain that they have forced Weismann into a change of position with reference to some of his definitions. Certain phases of this discussion appeal with particular force, of course, to some minds, while they exert little influence upon others. My own objections to Neo-Darwinism—and I admit that my bias is strong against it—seem to be somewhat different from those most commonly urged in opposition to it; and the three which chiefly influence me I shall present very briefly.

1. I cannot see that the non-transmissibility of acquired characters is a necessary assumption to Weismann's fundamental arguments. I have already explained his reasoning from the reproduction of the one-celled organism. I cannot attempt any opinion of the probable facts upon which the hypothesis is founded. It may be said, in passing, that one of the prominent objections to the fundamental basis of the theory is the difficulty of deriving the mortal soma-plasm from the immortal germ-plasm, a question to which, however, Weismann has made a somewhat full reply.

When organisms became complex, it was necessary to assume either that the soma-plasm does or does not directly influence the germ-plasm. Weismann discarded the various hypotheses which suppose that there is a vital and necessary connection between the body units and reproductive units, and then to avoid the difficulties which the hereditability of acquired characters would entail, he supposed that such characters are not hereditary. His subsequent labors have been largely employed in trying to show that they are not. This supposition was made for the purpose of simplifying the hypothesis by removing the cumbrous gemmules of Darwin and the similar bodies or movements of other philosophers, and, therefore, by localizing the seat of the germ-plasm. But he immediately encounters difficulties quite as great as those which he avoids. In cases where there are alternate generations of asexual and sexual organisms, he must suppose that the germ-plasm is united with the soma-plasm, and is probably, therefore, distributed throughout the body. "There may be, in fact, cases," Weismann writes, "in which such separation [of the germ-plasm from the soma-plasm] does not take place until after the animal is completely formed, and others, as I believe that I have shown, in which it first arises one or two generations later, viz., in the buds produced by the parent." And he has been compelled to admit that in the case of begonias, which are propagated by leaves, the germ-plasm is probably distributed throughout the foliage; and he must make a similar admission for all plants, for they can all be propagated and modified through asexual or vegetative parts.* (Compare Essay III.) This is ad-

---

* Throughout these essays, I have used the terms "asexual" and "sexless"

mitting, then, that there is no localized germ-plasm in the vegetable kingdom, and, in many instances, in the animal kingdom; and if the germ-plasm is distributed to the very periphery of the organism, why may it not be directly affected by environment, the same as the soma-plasm is? Or why is the hypothesis any the less objectionable than Darwin's pangenesis, which supposes that every organic unit can communicate with the germ?

Weismann also supposes, as I have said, that the means by which the germ-plasm is able to reconstruct the soma-plasm in the offspring is through some mod-

---

to designate plants which arise from buds (as bud-sports, cutting-made plants, grafts, and the like) in distinction to those which arise from the direct result of sexual union, that is, from seeds. "Male," "female," and like terms, are occasionally used to designate paternal and maternal parents. This ascription of sex-relations to the plant itself is held by some botanists to be erroneous, but I consider it to be a perfectly proper use of the terms, and one which is often necessary to perspicuous treatment of the subject. My own convictions upon this subject are set forth in the following note, which appeared in "Science" June 5, 1896. (Professor Charles R. Barnes made a rejoinder to this position in "Science" for June 26, 1896):

ON THE UNTECHNICAL TERMINOLOGY OF THE SEX-RELATION IN PLANTS.

The modern conception of the sex-relation and the alternation of generations in plants has so changed our point of view respecting the morphologies of various members that an entirely new terminology has recently come into use to express the new-found homologies. At the same time, there is an attempt to restrict or to specialize the use of such age-long words as male and female, sex and the like, when applying them to plants. This part of the new terminology which touches common language is not above criticism, and I wish briefly to advert to it.

It should be said, in the first place, that the original conceptions of sexuality in plants, from Camerarius down to the middle of this century, were borrowed and adapted very largely from analogy with the animal kingdom. The stamens were considered to be male organs of sex and the pistils to be female organs, the idea of the necessity of a conformed sex-member being evidently borrowed from a knowledge of animal morphology. At the present time, however, our conception of the sex-relation of the higher plants is borrowed from a study of the flowerless plants, which, with every reason, are believed to represent a more primitive stage of evolution than the flowering plants. The true significance of the sex-process in plants was first clearly conceived by Hofmeister in 1849, when he propounded the hypothesis that certain great groups of plants undergo an alternation

ification in its "molecular constitution," an assumption which was by no means novel when Weismann announced it. "The exact manner in which we imagine the subsequent differentiation of the colony to be potentially present in the reproductive cell," he writes, "becomes a matter of comparatively small importance. It may consist in a different molecular arrangement, or in some change of chemical constitution, or it may be due to both these causes combined." In whatever manner the germ-plasm receives its somatic influences, there must be a direct connection between the two, and it is quite as easy to assume the existence of gemmules as any less tangible influence. I am not arguing in favor

---

of generations, a sex-bearing generation being followed by a sexless generation. In certain plants, as the ferns, the sex-generation soon disappears and the sexless generation leads a wholly independent life; this sex-generation is the prothallus of the fern, and the sexless generation is the foliaceous fern-plant. But in certain other plants, as the mosses, the sexless generation remains attached to or incorporated with the sex-generation. Many of these flowerless plants produce a prothallus from the spore, and upon this prothallus are two minute unlike organs, one female in function, because it develops the succeeding generation, and the other male in function, because it produces the cells which fertilize the female cells. Recent morphological studies have shown that in the flowering plants the asexual generation is enormously developed, and is "the plant," whilst the sex-generation is reduced to the minimum and is represented by a female organ developed within the ovule and a male organ developed in the pollen-grain. The prothallus within the ovule encloses the germ of the asexual generation in its fertilized sexual cell, and this germ becomes the embryo of the seed; and the prothallus is absorbed, or else it remains as the albumen—or endosperm or perisperm—of the seed.

This very brief and imperfect outline is sufficient to bring the point which I have in mind before the reader, namely, how far can we use the terms "male" and "female," and what must be the common language of the sex-relation in plants? Some morphologists now object to calling a stamen a male organ, or a pistil a female organ; and they base their reform upon the undisputed morphological fact that the male sex-phase of the plant is comprised within the short span and function of the generative cell developing from the pollen grain, and that the female phase is associated only with the development of the prothallus in the ovule. It should be pointed out, however, that the discovery of these morphological facts does not in the least shift the old-time attribute of maleness as applied to the stamen or of femaleness as applied to the pistil; for whether the pollen grain is sperm, as older naturalists supposed, or whether it is a spore

of pangenesis, but only stating what seems to me to be a valid objection to the fundamental constitution of the Weismannian hypothesis—that it is quite as easy to assume, from the argument, one interpretation of the process or means of heredity as another. And if there is any vital connection whatever between the soma-plasm and the germ-plasm—as the hypothesis itself must admit—then why cannot the soma-plasm directly influence the germ-plasm?

Again, I wish to point out that modification and evolution of vegetable species may and does proceed wholly without the interposition of sex—that is, by propagations through cuttings or layers of various parts. This proves either one of two things—that the

---

and gives rise to a secondary generation which discharges the office of sperm, it is still all contained in the stamen; and the stamen is, in the broad sense of common language, a sexual member, because its entire office is the discharge of the paternal relation. It is as much a member or organ of sex as the root is an organ of nutrition. The meaning of the sex-process has not been materially changed by the recent studies. "Male" and "female" never did and never can be made to express strict morphological homologies. An organ of an animal or a plant is male if it exercises the functions of paternity and not of maternity. The stamen is such an organ. Its entire office is that of maleness. The attempt to restrict the terms male and female to the ultimate sexual process seems to me to be unwarranted and hypercritical. It is interesting to observe that the morphologists fall into the very pit which they have digged, when they talk of male and female prothalli. Surely the prothallus is no more sexual than a stamen or a leaf. The egg-cell and the male cell are the sexual organs, unless we choose to carry the purism to the physiological units; and since these organs soon disappear, as such, it follows that we cannot apply the terms "male," "female," "sex," and the like, to plants, save in the very brief period during which impregnation is taking place. This practically means that we must eliminate any reference to sexuality in all untechnical speech about plants, and the result would contribute to anything but clearness.

The common language of sex has always dealt in analogies. There are perfectly good and sufficient technical terms to designate the homologies and the ultimate physiological processes. If the hypercriticism of the plant morphologists were to be accepted for the animal creation, pandemonium would come of it. One could not speak of the members of generation as sex organs, nor of any animal as male or female. I insist that it is perfectly proper to speak of a staminate willow as male, because its ultimate function is paternity; if I cannot speak of it as a male plant, then I cannot call a bull a male animal.

germ-plasm is not necessary to the species, or else that it is not localized but distributed throughout the entire body of the individual, as I have shown above; and either horn of this dilemma is fatal, it seems to me, to Weismannism. If the germ-plasm is not necessary to this reproduction, then we must discard the hypothesis of the continuity of the germ-plasm; if the germ-plasm is distributed throughout the plant, then we are obliged to admit that it is not localized in germ-cells beyond the reach of direct external influences.

This asexual or vegetative propagation of plants has been brought to Weismann's attention by Strasburger, who cited the instance of the leaf-propagation of begonia, and said that plants thus asexually multiplied afterwards produce flowers and seeds, or develop germ-plasm. Weismann meets the objection by supposing that it is possible for "all somatic nuclei to contain a minute fraction of unchanged germ-plasm," but he considers the begonia, apparently, to be an exception to most other plants, inasmuch as he declares that "no one has ever grown a tree from the leaf of the lime or oak, or a flowering plant from the leaf of the tulip or convolvulus." Henslow meets this latter statement by saying that this has not been accomplished simply because "it has never been worth while to do it. If, however, a premium were offered for tulips or oak trees raised from leaf-cuttings, plenty would soon be forthcoming." What Weismann wishes to show is that the begonia is an exception to other plants in allowing of propagation from leaf-cuttings, although he should have known that hundreds of plants can be multiplied in this way, and that—what amounts to the same thing—all plants can be propagated by asexual parts, as stems or roots. Various writers have objected to the continuity of the germ-plasm because of this power of a plant to reconstruct itself from purely vegetative parts. Eimer, who is Weismann's chief German opponent, speaks of this power of reconstruction in both animals and plants, following division, as follows: "The new complete individual produced by this method has the same characters as the animal or plant produced at another time from a germ-cell—a proof that the substance possessing the property of heredity is not confined to the germ-plasm, and that it cannot be something altogether different from other parts of the organism."

But there is another aspect to this asexual multiplication of plants which I do not remember to have seen stated in this connection. It has been said that the asexually multiplied plants may afterwards produce flowers and resume the normal method of reproduction and variation. I now wish to add, what I have already said, that plants may be continuously multiplied asexually and yet the offspring may vary, and the variations may be transmitted from generation to generation, quite as perfectly as if seed-production intervened. This has been true with certain plants through a long period of time, as with the banana, and every intelligent gardener knows that plants propagated by cuttings often "sport" or vary. Here are cases, then, in which variation does not originate from sexual union, unless Weismann is willing to concede that the result of previous sexual union has remained latent through any number of generations and has been carried to all parts of the plant by a generally diffused germ-plasm; and if this is admitted, then I must again insist that this germ-plasm must be just as amenable to external influences as the soma-plasm with which it is indissolubly associated. I have repeated this argument in order to introduce the subject of "bud-variations," or those "sports" which now and then appear upon certain limbs or parts of plants, and which are nearly always readily propagated by cuttings. These variations cannot be attributed to sex, in the ordinary and legitimate application of the Weismannian hypothesis. Whilst these "sports" are well known to horticulturists, they are generally considered to be rare, but nothing can be farther from the truth. As a matter of fact, every branch of a tree is different from every other branch, and when the difference is sufficient to attract attention, or to have commercial value, it is propagated and called a "sport." This leads me to recall the old discussion of the phytomer, or the hypothesis that every node and internode of a tree—and, we might add, the roots—is in reality a distinct individual, inasmuch as it possesses the power of leading an independent existence when severed from the plant, and of reproducing its kind. (See Essay III. for a fuller discussion of this question.) However this may be as a matter of speculation, it is certainly true as regards the phenomenon, and shows conclusively that if the germ-plasm exists at all, it exists throughout the entire structure of the plant.

This conclusion—that the germ-plasm resides throughout the soma—is also unavoidable from another consideration: the fact that plants are asexual organisms at all times previous to flowering, and that the germ-plasm must be preserved, in the meantime, along with the soma-plasm. In his essay upon the "Continuity of the Germ-Plasm," Weismann cites the observation of Sachs that "in the true mosses almost any cell of the roots, leaves, and shoot-axes * * * may grow out under favorable conditions, become rooted, form new shoots, and give rise to an independent living plant." Weismann meets this statement as follows: "Since such plants produce germ-cells at a later period, we have here a case which requires the assumption that all or nearly all cells must contain germ-plasm." I do not understand the significence of the phrase "such plants." The mosses are no exceptions, for all higher plants develop their germ-cells "at a later period." All plants are perfectly sexless or somatic for a longer or shorter period after germination,—that is, until they bloom. This somatic stage extends over several years in many trees. In all higher plants, therefore, the germ-plasm must be developed from the soma-plasm; and since any part of the plant may, upon occasion, develop sexual organs and germ-plasm, it follows that the germ-plasm cannot be localized in any part of maiden plant-body. Every plant possesses the same power of making new individuals from "roots, leaves and shoot-axes" which Sachs ascribes to the mosses. If, therefore, Weismann admits the association of germ-plasm with the soma-plasm in "all or nearly all cells" of moss, he thereby admits it for all plants. It is pertinent to call attention, also, to the fact that recent morphological studies have demonstrated that all plants—except certain low or specialized forms—undergo an alternation of generations (see Essay I. and the foot-note on page 66), one generation being sexual or gametophytic in office and the other sexless or sporophytic. The sporophytic generation is "the plant" in ferns and the flowering-plants, the gametophytic generation perishing as soon as the sporophyte has been developed to the point of supporting itself. Another sexual or gametophytic generation does not arise, in the flowering-plants, until the plant arrives at the stage of seed-production. Wheredoes the germ-plasm reside in the sporophyte? All these facts and conclusions are inconsistent with Weismannism as taught at present, and these alone would lead me to discard the hypothesis for plants, however well it may apply to the animal kingdom.

Henslow has made a different argument to show that the germ-plasm of plants may be directly exposed to external influence (Origin of Floral Structures). The germ-plasm is assumably located in the sex-elements in the flower, and the egg-cell of the embryo-sac and the sperm-cell of the pollen grain are close to the surface, and are directly impressed by the interference of bees and other external stimuli. Henslow endeavors to show "that the infinite variety of adaptations to insects discoverable in flowers may have resulted through the direct action of the insects themselves, coupled with the responsive power of protoplasm." And these characters must be in part acquired during the lifetime of a given individual.

2. It seems to me, also, that the presumption, upon general philosophical grounds, is against the doctrine that immediate external influences are without permanent effect. If we admit—as all philosophers now do—that species are mutable, and that the forms of life have been shaped with reference to their adaptations to environment, then we are justified in assuming that every change in that environment must awaken some vital response in the species. If this response does not follow, then environment is without influence upon the organism; or if it follows and is then not transmitted, it is lost

just the same, and environment is impotent. And it does not matter if we assume, with the Neo-Darwinians, that this effect does not become hereditary until the germ is affected—that is, until two or more generations have lived under the impinging environment—it must nevertheless follow that the change must have had a definite beginning in the lifetime of an individual; for it is impossible to conceive that a change has its origin in two generations. In other words, the beginning is singular; two generations is plural. And whether the modification is directly visible in the body of the organism, or is an intangible force impressed upon the germ, it is nevertheless of an environmental character, and was at first acquired. If this is not true—that the changed conditions of life exert a direct effect upon the phylogeny of the species—then no variation is possible save that which comes from the recompounding of the original or ancestral sex-elements; and it would still be a question how these sex-elements acquired their initial divergence.

The Neo-Darwinians would undoubtedly meet this argument by saying that their hypothesis fully admits the importance of these external influences, the only reservation being that they shall have affected the germ. It is true that this is a common means of escape; but it cannot be gainsaid that the denial of the influence of the external or environmental forces is really the fundamental difference between them and the Darwinians or Neo-Lamarckians, as the following quotation from Weismann will show: "Our object is to decide whether changes in the soma (the body, as opposed to the germ-cells) which have been produced by the direct action of external influences, including use and disuse, can be transmitted; whether they can influence the germ-cells in such a manner that the latter will cause the spontaneous appearance of corresponding changes in the next generation. This is the question which demands an answer; and, as has been shown above, such an answer would decide whether the Lamarckian principles of transformation must be retained or abandoned."

If, then, to repeat, organisms are adapted to their environment, it must be equally true that this environment directly affects its inhabitants; and, considering the intense struggle for existence under which all organisms live, it is highly probable that any advantageous variation can be seized upon at once. I cannot conceive that nature allows herself to lose every possibility of obtaining the result of any effort.

3. My third conviction against Neo-Darwinism arises from the fact that its advocates are constantly explaining away the arguments of their opponents by verbal mystifications and ingenious definitions. This charge is so frequently made, and the fact is so well known, that it seems almost useless to refer to it here; and yet there are some phases of it upon which I cannot forbear to touch.

Weismann declares that he uses the term "acquired character" in its original sense. This term, or at least the idea, was first employed, as we have seen, by Lamarck, who used it or an equivalent phrase to designate "every change acquired in an organ by a habitual exercise sufficient to have brought it about." In fact, the basis of Lamarck's philosophy is the assumption of the hereditability of characters arising directly from use or disuse; and his idea of an acquired character is, therefore, one which appears in the lifetime of the individual from some externally inciting cause. Darwin's notion, while less clearly defined, was essentially the same, and he collected a mass of evidence to show that such characters are transmissible; and he even went further than Lamarck, and attempted to show that mutilations may be hereditary. Weismann's early definition of acquired characters is plain enough. Such characters, that is, the somatogenic, "not only include the effects of mutilation, but the changes which follow from increased or diminished performance of function, and those which are directly due to nutrition and any of the other external influences which act upon the body." Standing fairly and squarely upon this definition, it is easy enough to disprove it—that is, to show that some characters thus acquired are hereditary. But the moment proofs are advanced, the definition is contracted, and the Neo-Darwinians declare that the given character was potentially present in the germ and was not primarily superinduced by the external conditions—a position which, while it allows of no proof, can neither be overthrown. A cow lost her left horn by suppuration, and two of her calves had rudimentary left horns; but Weismann immediately says, "The loss of a cow's horn may have arisen from a congenital malformation." Certainly! And it may not; and the presumption is that it did not. A soldier loses his left eye by inflammation, and two of his sons have defective left eyes. Now, "the soldier," says Weismann, "did not lose his left eye because it was injured, but because it was predisposed to become diseased from the beginning, and readily became inflamed after a slight injury!" This gratuitous manner of explaining away the recorded instances of the supposed transmission of mutilations, and the like, is common with the Neo-Darwinians, but it must always create the impression, it seems to me, of being labored and far-fetched; and inasmuch as it is incapable of proof, and is of no occasion beyond the mere point of upholding an assumed hypothesis, it is scarcely worthy serious attention. It would be far better for the Neo-Darwinians if they would flatly refuse to accept the statements concerning the transmission of mutilations, rather than to attempt any mere captious explanation of them; for it is yet very doubtful if the recorded instances of such transmissions will stand careful investigation.

But perhaps the most remarkable example of this species of Neo-Darwinian logic is produced by Weismann when he is hard pressed by Hoffman, who supposed that he had proved the hereditability of certain acquired characters in poppies. Weismann says: "Since the characters of which Hoffman speaks are hereditary, the term cannot be rightly applied to them,"* thus showing that his fundamental conception of an acquired character is one which cannot be transmitted! He then proceeds to elaborate this definition as follows: "I have never doubted about the transmission of changes which depend upon an alteration in the germ-plasm of the reproductive cells, for I have always asserted that these changes, and these alone, must be transmitted." Then he proceeds to say that it is necessary to have "two terms which distinguish sharply between the two chief groups of characters—the primary characters, which first appear in the body itself, and the secondary ones, which owe their appearance to variations in the germ, however such variations may have arisen. We have hitherto been accustomed to call the former 'acquired characters,' but

---

*Essays upon Heredity, I. 422 (note).

we might also call them 'somatogenic,' because they follow from the reaction of the soma under external influences; while all other characters might be contrasted as 'blastogenic,' because they include all those characters in the body which have arisen from changes in the germ. * * * We maintain that the 'somatogenic' characters cannot be transmitted, or rather, that those who assert that they can be transmitted must furnish the requisite proofs." That is: Changes in the soma-plasm are not transmitted; acquired characters are changes in the soma-plasm; therefore, acquired characters cannot be transmitted! Or, to use Weismann's shorter phrase, "Since the characters * * * are hereditary, the term ['acquired'] cannot be rightly applied to them!" Surely, Neo-Darwinism is impregnable!

Weismannism has unquestionably done much to elucidate some of the most intricate questions of biology, and it has weeded the old hypotheses of much that was ill-considered and false. It has challenged beliefs which have been too easily accepted. Its value to the science of heredity upon its biological side is admitted, and its explanation of the meaning of sex is one of the best of all contributions to the philosophy of organic nature. It has suffered, perhaps, from too ardent champions, and its great weakness lies in its stubborn refusal to accept an important class of phenomena associated with acquired characters, a sufficient explanation of which, it seems to me, could be assumed without great violence to the hypothesis.

Most Neo-Lamarckians accept much of Weismann's teachings. But, while there are comparatively few who believe that mutilations are directly transmissible, there is a general and strong conviction that many truly acquired characters are hereditary, and there seems to be demonstrable evidence of it; and while sex variation is fully accepted, it logically follows, if acquired characters are hereditary, that much variation is due directly to external causes. Perhaps the habit of thought of most Darwinians and Neo-Lamarckians is something as follows:

All forms of life are mutable. Variation affords the material or starting-points from which progress is derived. Variation is due to sexual union, changed conditions of life, the energy of growth, panmixia or the cessation of natural selection, and to direct use and disuse, although use and disuse are minor factors amongst plants. There is an intense struggle for existence. All forms or variations useful to the species tend to live, and the harmful ones tend to be destroyed through the operation of the simple agent of natural selection. These newly appearing forms tend to become permanent, sometimes immediately; but the longer the transforming environments are present, the greater is the probability, on the whole, that the resulting modifications will persist.

III.

THE PLANT INDIVIDUAL IN THE LIGHT OF EVOLUTION.[1]

THE PHILOSOPHY OF BUD-VARIATION, AND ITS BEARING UPON WEISMANNISM.

I.

WHILST the animal and vegetable kingdoms originate at a common point and are not clearly distinguishable in a number of the lower groups of organic beings, they nevertheless diverge rapidly, and finally become very unlike. I believe that we shall find that this divergence into two co-ordinate branches of organic nature is brought about by the operation of at least two fundamentally distinct laws. There is a most unfortunate tendency, at the present time, to attempt to account for all phenomena of evolution upon some single hypothesis which the observer may think to be operative in the particular group of animals or plants which he may be studying. For myself, I cannot believe that all forms of life are the results of any one law. It is probable that all recent explanations of evolution contain more or less truth, and that one of them may have been the cause of certain developments, whilst others have been equally fundamentally important in other groups of

[1] Address before the Biological Society of Washington, January 12, 1895. Printed in Science, new series, 1. 281 (March 15, 1895).

organisms. If I were a zoölogist, and particularly an entomologist, I should hold strongly to the views of Lamarck; but, being a horticulturist, I must accept largely, for the objects which come within the range of my vision, the principles of Darwin. In other words, I believe that both Lamarckism and Darwinism are true; and, in this connection, it is significant to observe that Lamarck propounded his theory from studies of animals, whilst Darwin was first led to his theory from observations of plants. I am willing to admit, also, at least for the sake of argument, that Weismannism, or the Neo-Darwinian philosophy, may be true for some organisms, but it seems to be wholly untenable for plants.

There is one feature of this difference between the animal and the plant to which I wish to call your attention on this occasion. It is the meaning of individuality in the two. I must say, at the outset, that when I speak of a plant or an animal I refer to those higher forms which the layman knows by these names, for it is not my purpose to discuss the original causes of divergence so much as those phenomena of individuality which are most apparent to the general observer. The animal may be said to have complete autonomy. It has a more or less definite span of life. It grows old and dies without having been impaired by decay, and the period of death may have no immediate relation to environment. It has a definite number of parts, and each part or organ is differentiated and performs one function, and this function serves the whole animal and not the organ itself. If any part is removed, the animal is maimed and the part cannot be supplied, and the severed portion has no power to reproduce either itself or the animal from which it came. The only means by which the animal can multiply is by a union of sexes. The plant, on the contrary, has no perfect or simple autonomy. It has no definite or pre-determined proximate span of life, except in those instances when it is annual or biennial, and here duration is an evident adaptation to environment. (See page 13.) The plant frequently dies as the result of decay. It has not a definite number of parts or members and each part of the plant may perform a function for itself, and the part may be useful to the remainder of the plant or it may not. One part is like what all other parts are or may be. If one portion is removed the plant may not be injured; in fact, the plant may be distinctly benefited. And the severed portion may not only have the power of reproducing itself, but it may even reproduce an organism like that from which it came. In other words, plants multiply both with and without sex. Potentially, every node and internode of the plant is an individual, for it possesses the power, when removed and properly cared for, of expanding into what we call a plant, and of perfecting flowers and seeds and of multiplying its kind.

Many of the lower animals possess the same phenomena of recrescence or multiple individuality that plants do, and Eimer has insisted that the animal is not "a complete, distinctly-defined unity." His position is certainly well taken, but the argument in this paper, as I have already stated, is drawn from a comparison of higher animals with higher plants. If the two kingdoms are similar in their lower strata, they are dissimilar in their upper strata, and this divergence of individuality in the two phyla represents an actual truth.

Those of you who are botanists now recall the contention of Gaudichaud concerning the plant unit or phyton. He proposed that the leaf, with its connecting tissues, is the vegetable individual, and that the plant is a colony of these individuals. Gaudichaud offered this theory as an explanation of the morphology and physiology of plants, and the hypothesis really has no place in the present discussion; but, inasmuch as I have borrowed the word which he proposed for the plant unit, it is no more than fair that I should explain his use of it; and this explanation may serve, incidentally, to illustrate some of the problems of individuality to which I shall recur. Gaudichaud, while recognizing that a cell which develops into a bud is itself an individual, nevertheless considered that the leaf, with its dependent tissues, represents the simple vegetable unit. Each of these units has an aërial or ascending part and a radicular part. The ascending part has three kinds of tissues or merithals—the stem merithal, the petiolar merithal and the limbic merithal. Now, each phyton fixes itself upon the trunk, or upon an inferior phyton, in the same manner as a plant fixes itself in the soil, and, sending its vascular threads downwards between the bark and the wood, is enabled to support itself upon the plant colony; and, at the same time, the extension of these threads produces the thickening of the stem, and the superposition of phytons increases the height of the plant. This mechanical theory of the morphology of plants was not original with Gaudichaud, but he greatly enlarged it and gave it most of its historic value, and, what is more to our purpose, he used the word phyton, which, in lieu of a better one, I shall use as a convenient expression for that asexual portion of any plant which is capable of reproducing itself. Gaudichaud's fanciful hypothesis was not completely overthrown until the exact studies

INDIVIDUALITY OF THE PHYTON.

of Von Mohl upon the vegetable cell established a rational basis of morphology and physiology.

What I wish now to show is that the evolution of the vegetable kingdom cannot be properly understood until we come to feel that the phyton, or each portion of the plant which, when removed, has the capability of reproducing itself and its parent, is in reality a potential autonomy. In doing this, I shall not forget that the plant also has an individuality as a whole; but as this feature is quite aside from my argument, and is the conception of the plant which is everywhere accepted, I must necessarily confine my remarks to the individual life of the phyton. The mere fact that the phyton may reproduce itself is not the most important point to consider, but, rather, that each part of the plant may respond in a different manner or degree to the effects of environment and heredity. Before proceeding to this matter, I should say that there is no doubt about the capability of every plant to be propagated asexually. It is true that all plants have not been so propagated, but there is every reason to suppose that the gardener can acquire the requisite skill to grow oaks and hickories from cuttings were it worth his while to do so. (See, also, page 70.) At present there are cheaper modes of multiplying these plants. But certain pines and spruces, which do not seed under cultivation, are propagated by cuttings, and the tissue of these trees is as little adapted to such use as that of any plants with which I am acquainted. The fact that plants are not grown from cuttings does not prove that they cannot be so propagated, for we know that the essential structure of all of them is very similar, and that each node and internode—or each phyton—does or may produce branches and flowers and seeds when it is borne upon its parent plant. And I should remind you that those plants which are not readily multiplied by cuttings are generally propagated by grafting, which, for illustration, amounts to the same thing, for we only substitute the stock of another plant for the soil. Plants of the most various kinds are readily multiplied by graftage. Even tuberous herbaceous stems, which are not commonly associated with the art of the grafter, unite with ease. One of the latest investigators in this field is a Frenchman, Daniel, and his conclusions upon the physiology of grafted plants show that the physiological modifications in these plants are largely such as arise from physical causes, showing that the parts still preserve their essential autonomy.

Now, if every plant varies in the number of parts, or phytons, of which it is composed, it follows that this number must be determined by agencies which act immediately upon the given plant itself. We all know that the number of these parts is determined very largely by environment. A dozen plants springing from the same capsule may vary immensely in the numbers of their branches, leaves and flowers, and this variation is generally obviously correlated with amount of food, amount of space which the plant is allowed to occupy, and other physical conditions which affect its welfare. But we not only find that no two plants have the same number of parts, but that no two branches in the same plant are alike. One part grows longer, one more erect, one has greener leaves, one bears more fruit. So, too, there may be different forms of flowers on the same plant, a subject to which Darwin has devoted an entire volume. We know, also, that this variation amongst the sisterhood or colony of branches is determined by very much the same conditions which determine variation in independent plants growing in soil. I believe that the primary and most important determinant of this variation is the variation in food supply, the same which Darwin believed to be the most potent factor in the origination of variations in general. That branch or phyton which receives the most food, because of its position or other incidental circumstance, is the one which grows the largest, has the heaviest and greenest leaves, and, in the end, is the most fruitful. I use the word food to designate not only the supply of nutriment which is derived from the soil, but also that obtained from the air and which is most quickly and thoroughly elaborated in the presence of the brightest sunlight. Thus the uppermost branches of the tree, whilst farthest from the root, are generally the strongest, because they are more freely exposed to light and air and their course is least impeded. Many branches in the interior of tree-tops are undoubtedly parasites upon the plant colony, taking from it more than they return.

If the number of the plant-members is determined by circumstances peculiar to that plant, and if there is variation amongst these members in any plant, then it follows that there must be struggle for existence between them. And this struggle differs from the conflict between independent plants in the complex battle for life only in the circumstance that it is more intense or severe, from the fact that the combatants are more closely associated. There are weak branches and strong branches, and the survival of the fittest is nature's method of pruning. The strong terminal branch, shooting upwards toward air and sunlight, makes the bole of the tree, whilst the less fortunate or side branches perish and fall. The leaf surface of any tree or large plant is always pushing outwards towards the periphery, which is only another way of saying that the interior branches die. I often find fruit-growers who refuse to prune their trees because they believe it to be unnatural, while at the same time their tree tops are full of dead limbs, every one a monument to the stupidity of the owner!

Now, the effect of this struggle for existence allows of mathematical measurement. Each bud should produce a branch or a cluster of fruit. A seedling peach tree may be two feet high the first year, producing thirty leaves, and in every axil a bud. Each of these buds should produce a branch, which should again produce thirty buds. The third year, therefore, whilst the tree is only six or eight feet high, it should have nine hundred branches, and in the fourth year twenty-seven thousand! Yet a peach tree twenty years old may not have more than one thousand branches! That is, many millions of possible branches have been suppressed or have died. I once made an actual observation of such a battle and counted the dead and wounded. A black cherry tree came up near my door. The first year it made a straight shoot nineteen inches high, which produced twenty-seven buds. It also sent out a branch eight inches long which bore twelve buds. The little tree had, therefore, enlisted thirty-nine soldiers for the coming conflict. The second year twenty of these buds did not grow. Nineteen of them made an effort, and these produced three hundred and seventy buds. In two years it made an effort, therefore, at four hundred and nine branches, but at the close of the second year there were only twenty-seven branches upon the tree.

At the close of the third year the little tree should have produced about thirty-five hundred buds or branch-germs. It was next observed in July of its fourth year, when it stood just eight feet high; instead of having between three and four thousand branches, it bore a total of two hundred and ninety-seven, and most of them were only weak spurs from one to three inches long. It was plain that not more than twenty, at the outside, of even this small number could long persist. The main stem or trunk bore forty-three branches, of which only eleven had much life in them, and even some of this number showed signs of weakness. In other words, in my little cherry tree, standing alone and having things all its own way, only one bud out of every hundred and seventy-five succeeded in making even a fair start towards a permanent branch. And this struggle must have proceeded with greater severity as the top became more complex, had I not put an end to its travail with the axe!

II.

I am now ready to say that I believe bud-variation to be one of the most significant and important phenomena of vegetable life, and that it is due to the same causes, operating in essentially the same way, which underlie all variation in the plant world. As some of you may not be familiar with the technical use of the term, I will explain that a bud-variety is an unusual or striking form or branch appearing upon a plant; or, as Darwin put it, bud variation is a term used to "include all those sudden changes in structure or appearance which occasionally occur in full-grown plants in their flower-buds or leaf-buds." A classical example is the origination of the nectarine from a branch of a peach-tree; and one often hears of Russet apples upon a branch of a Greening apple tree, of weeping, variegated or cut-leaved shoots on otherwise normal trees, or of potatoes that "mix in the hill." Now, this matter of bud-variation has been a most puzzling one to all writers upon evolution who have touched upon it. It long seemed to me to be inexplicable, but I hope that you will now agree with me in saying that it is no more unintelligible than seminal variation of plants, for I have already shown that there is abundant asexual or vegetative variation (of which bud-variation is itself the proof), and that this variation takes place as readily when the phyton is growing upon a plant as when it is growing in the soil. The chief trouble in the consideration of this subject has been that persons have observed and recorded only the most marked or striking variations, or those which appear somewhat suddenly (although suddenness of appearance usually means that the observer had not noticed it before), and that they had, therefore, thought bud-variation to be rare and exceptional. The truth is, as I have said, that every branch or phyton is a bud-variety, differing in greater or lesser degree from all other phytons on the same plant.

These differences, even when marked, may arise in every part of the parent plant, as on stems aërial and subterranean, from bulbs and tubers, or even from the adventitious buds of roots; and the characters of these varieties are as various as those originating from seeds. The nurseryman knows that branches differ amongst themselves, for he instructs his budders to cut buds only from the topmost shoots of the nursery rows, in order that he may grow straight, vigorous trees; and every farmer's boy knows that the reddest and earliest apples grow on the uppermost branches, and his father always tells him that he should never select cions from the center or lower part of a tree. Every skillful horticulturist will tell you that the character of the orchard is determined very largely by the judgment of the propagator in selecting cions. To select out the extreme forms of these variations and to attempt to explain bud-variation by them is exactly like selecting the extreme types of seminal variations, and, by ignoring the lesser ones and the intermediates, to attempt to build thereon a theory of the variation of plants. If you ask me why it is that the nectarine was produced upon the branch of a peach tree, I will ask you why it is that nectarines have also been produced from peach seeds. The answer to one answers the other. It is true that bud-variations, if we use that term, as we logically must, to denote all variations between phytons, are commonly less marked than seed variations, but this is only because the conditions of origin and environment of the phyton are less varied than those of the seedling. The phytons originate from one parent, not from two; and they all grow in very like conditions. But I am convinced that, when we consider the plant individual in the light of evolution, the bugbear of bud-variation vanishes.

A good proof that bud-variation and seed-variation are one in kind is afforded by the fact that selection can be practiced for the improvement of forms originating by either means. Darwin was surprised, as he says, to "hear from Mr. Salter that he brings the principle of selection to bear on variegated plants propagated by buds, and has thus greatly improved and fixed several varieties. He informs me that at first a branch often produces variegated leaves on one side alone, and that the leaves are marked only with an irregular edging, or with a few lines of white and yellow. To improve and fix such varieties, he finds it necessary to encourage the buds at the bases of the most distinctly marked leaves, and to propagate from them alone. By following, with perseverance, this plan during three or four successive seasons a distinct and fixed variety can generally be secured.'' This practice, or similar ones, is not only well known to gardeners, but we have seen that nature selects in the same manner, through the operation of the same struggle for subsistence which Darwin so forcibly applied to all other forms of modification. Once given the three fundamental principles in the phylogeny of the phyton, the variation amongst themselves, the struggle for existence, the capability of perpetuating themselves—an indisputable trinity—and there can no longer be any doubt as to the fundamental likeness of the bud-variety and the seed-variety.

Yet I must bring another proof of this likeness to your mind. It is well known that the seedlings of plants become more variable as the species is cultivated; and it is also true that bud-varieties are more frequent and more marked in cultivated plants. Note, for example, the tendency of cultivated plants to bear variegated or cut-leaved or weeping shoots, and the fact that the colors and doubleness of flowers often vary greatly upon the same plant. Many of our best known roses, carnations, chrysanthemums, violets and other garden plants originated as bud-sports. This fact is so well known that critical gardeners are always on the alert for such variations. In any house of two hundred roses, all grown from cuttings, the grower will expect to find more than one departure from the type, either in color or freedom of bloom or in habit of plant. Every gardener will recall the "sporting" tendencies of Perle des Jardins rose, and the fact that several commercial varieties have sprung from it by bud-variation. As early as 1865 Carrière gave a descriptive list of one hundred and fifty-four named bud-varieties, and remarked at length upon their frequency amongst cultivated plants. (See Plant-Breeding.) This fact of greater bud-variability under cultivation was fully recognized by Darwin, and he regarded this as one of the strongest proofs that such variation, like seed variation, is "the direct result of the conditions of life to which the plant has been exposed."

In order to extend the proofs of the essential ontogenetic likeness of bud and seminal variations, I will call to your remembrance the fact that the characters of the two phytons may be united quite as completely by means of asexual or graft hybridism as by sexual hybridism. I do not need to pursue this subject, except to say that we now believe that graft-hybrids are rare and exceptional chiefly because the subject has received little experimental attention. Certainly the list given by Focke, and the anatomical researches of Macfarlane, show that such hybrids may be expected in a wide variety of subjects and with some frequency. It is now stated positively by Daniel, as the result of direct experiment, that the seeds of cions of certain cultivated herbs which are grafted upon a wild plant give offspring which show a marked return to the wild type. I should also add that the breaking up of seminal hybrids into the characters of either parent may take place, as Darwin has shown, through either seed or bud-variation. You are all no doubt aware that hybrids generally tend to revert to the types from which they sprung, and this sometimes occurs even in hybrid offspring which is propagated exclusively by buds or cuttings.

Still another proof of the similarity of bud-varieties and seed-varieties is the fact that the seeds of bud-varieties are quite as likely to reproduce the variety as the seeds of seed-varieties are to reproduce their parents. Darwin and others have recorded this seminal transmission of bud-sports. "Notwithstanding the sudden production of bud-varieties," Darwin writes, "the characters thus acquired are sometimes capable of transmission by seminal reproduction. Mr. Rivers has found that moss-roses [which are bud-varieties] generally reproduce themselves by seed; and the mossy character has been transferred by crossing from one species to another." This general fact, that bud-sports may reproduce many of their essential acquired characters by seeds, is so well grounded in the minds of gardeners that the most critical of them make no distinction, in this respect, between varieties of bud and seed origin when selecting parents for making crosses.

If we can prove the similarity of bud and seed variations by showing that both bear the same relation to transmission of characters by means of seedage, we can demonstrate it equally well by the converse proposition —that both bear the same relation to the perpetuation of their features by cuttage. Some seed-varieties will not "come true" by cuttings, and there are also some bud-sports which will not, as every gardener of experience knows. I will cite a single case of "sporting" in bud offspring. One winter a chance tomato plant came up in one of my greenhouses. I let it grow, and it bore fruit quite unlike any other variety which I ever saw. There was no other tomato plant in the house. I propagated it both by seeds and cuttings. I had two generations of cuttings. Those taken directly from the parent plant "came true," or very nearly so; then a lot of cuttings from these cutting-grown plants was taken, making the second asexual generation from the original seedling. While most of the seeds "came true," few of these second cuttings did, and, moreover, they "sported" into several very unlike forms — so much unlike that I had both red and yellow fruits from them. In respect to transmission of characters, then, bud and seed-varieties are alike, because either class may or may not transmit its marks either by seeds or buds.

Finally, let me say, in proof of the further similarity of bud and seed-variations, that each class follows the incidental laws of external resemblance which pertain to the other class. For instance, there are analogous variations in each, giving rise to the same kinds of variegation, the same anomalies of cut and colored foliage, of weeping branches, party-colored fruits and the like; and the number of similar variations may be as great for any ameliorated plant in the one class as in the other. The most expert observer is not able to distinguish between bud-varieties and seed-varieties; the only way of distinguishing the two is by means of the records of their origins, and because such records of any varieties are few we have come to overlook the frequency of bud-variation, and to associate all progressive variability in the vegetable kingdom with seeds or the results of sexual union.

Whilst it is not my purpose to discuss the original sources or causes of bud-variations, I cannot forbear to touch upon one very remarkable fact concerning reversions. It is a common notion that all bud-varieties are atavistic, but this position is untenable if one accepts the hypothesis, which I have here outlined, of the ontogenetic individuality of the phyton, and if he holds, at the same time, to the transforming influence of environment. It is also held by some that bud-varieties are the effects of previous crossing, but this is controverted by Darwin in the statement that characters which do not pertain to any known living or extinct species sometimes appear in bud-varieties; and the observations which I am about to recite also indicate the improbability of such influence in a large class of cases. The instances to which I call your attention are, I think, true reversions to ancestral types. Those of you who have observed the young non-blooming shoots of tulip-tree, sassafras and some other trees will have noticed that the leaves upon them often assume unusual shapes. Thus the leaves of sassafras often vary from the typical oval form to three-lobed and mitten-shaped upon the strong shoots. There are the most various forms on many tulip-trees, the leaves ranging from almost circular and merely emarginate to long-ovate and variously lobed; all of them have been most admirably illustrated and discussed recently by Holm in the preceedings of the National Museum. Holm considers the various forms of these liriodendron leaves to be so many proofs of the invalidity of the fossil species which very closely resemble them. This may be true, for there are probably no specific names of organisms founded upon so fragmentary and scant material as those applied to fossil plants; and yet I cannot help feeling that some of these contemporaneous variations are reversions to very old types. I was first led to this opinion by a study of the sports in ginkgo leaves, and in finding them suggestive of Mesozoic types. "This variation in leaf characters," I wrote at the time,* "recalls the geologic history of the ginkgo, for it appears to be true that leaves upon the young and vigorous shoots of trees are more like their ancestors than are the leaves upon old plants or less vigorous shoots, as if there is some such genealogical record in leaves as there is in the development of embryos in animals." Subsequent observation has strengthened my belief in the atavistic origin of many of these abnormal forms, and this explanation of them is exactly in line with the characters of reversions in animals and in cultivated plants. It would, of course, be futile to attempt any discussion of the merits of the specific types proposed by palæobotanists, but in those cases, like the ginkgo, where the geologic types are fairly well marked, constant and frequent, and where the similar contemporaneous variations are rare, there is apparently good reason for regarding contemporaneous forms as fitful recollections of an ancient state; and this supposition finds additional support in the ginkgo, because the species is becoming extinct, a fact which also applies to the tulip-tree, which is now much restricted in its distribution. I am further reinforced in this view by Ward's excellent study of the evolution of the plane-tree, for, in this instance, it seems to be well determined that the geologic type has fairly well marked specific characters, and the auricular or peltate base upon

---

* American Garden, xii. 262 (1891).

7 SUR.

contemporaneous leaves, which records the connection between the two, is sufficiently rare to escape comment. Various writers have remarked upon the similarities of these occasional leaves to geologic types, but, so far as I recall, they regard them as remnants or vestiges of the ancient types rather than as reversions to them. There is this important difference between a remnant and a reversion. A remnant or rudiment is more or less uniformly present under normal conditions, and it should give evidence of being slowly on the decline; whilst a reversion is a reappearance of wholly lost characters under unusual or local conditions. Now, my chief reasons for considering these sports to be reversions is the fact that they occur upon the sterile and verdurous shoots, the very shoots which are most likely to vary and to revert, because they receive the greatest amount of food supply, as Darwin has shown to be the case with independent plants. I am thus able, therefore, to make still another analogy between phytons and plants, and to illustrate again the essential sameness of bud-variations and seed-variations.

III.

I now wish to recall your attention more specifically to the subject of asexual or purely vegetative variation. I have shown that no two branches are alike any more than any two plants are. I have also cited the frequent occurrence of differences so marked that they are called bud-varieties or sports. Carrière enumerated over one hundred and fifty of them of commercial importance in France, and, as nearly as I can estimate, there are no fewer than three hundred named horticultural varieties grown at the present moment in this country which had a like origin. It is also known that there are a number of species in which seeds are practically unknown, and yet which run into many varieties, as the pineapple, banana and bread-fruit; and note, if you will, the great variations in weeping willows, a tree which never fruits in this country. In our gardens there are three or four varieties of the common seedless "top" onion, and I have been able, by treatment, to vary the root of the horse-radish, a plant which rarely, if ever, produces viable seeds in this climate; and there are variable seedless plants in our greenhouses. I might also cite the fact that very many fungi are sexless, so far as we know, and yet they have varied into innumerable species. You will be interested in a concrete case of the apple. The Newtown Pippin, which originated upon Long Island, New York, has been widely disseminated by graftage. In Virginia it has varied into a form known as the Albemarle Pippin, and a New York apple exporter tells me that it is a poorer shipper than the northern Newtown and is not so long-keeping. In the extreme northwestern states the Newtown, while it has not been rechristened there, is markedly unlike the eastern fruit, being much longer and bearing distinct ridges about the apex. Finally, in New South Wales, the ridges are more marked and other characters appear, and the variety is there known as the Five-crowned Pippin. This is not an isolated case. Most northeastern varieties of apples tend to take on this elongated form in the Pacific Northwest, to become heavy-grained and coarse-striped in the Mississippi Valley and the Plains, and to take other characteristic forms in the higher lands of the South Atlantic states. This asexual variation is sometimes very rapid. An illustration came directly under my own observation (and upon which I have once reported) in the case of the Chilian strawberry. (Essay XXV.) Within two years this plant, growing in my garden, varied or departed from its wild type so widely as to be indistinguishable from the common garden strawberry, which has been regarded by many botanists to be specifically distinct from the Chilian berry. This remarkable departure, which has enabled me, as I believe, to reconstruct the evolution of the garden strawberry, was one in which no seedling plants were concerned. If all the common garden strawberries owe their origin to a like source—as I cannot doubt—then we have here a most instructive case of sexless evolution, but one in which the subsequent generations reproduce these characters of sexless origin by means of seeds.

This asexual modification is not confined to domesticated plants. Any plant which is widely distributed by man by means of cuttings or other vegetative parts may be expected to vary in the same manner, as much experiment shows; and if they behave in this way when disseminated by man, they must undergo similar modification when similarly disseminated by nature herself. I need only cite a few instances of habitual asexual or seedless distribution of wild plants to recall to your attention the fact that such means of distribution is common in nature, and that in some cases the dispersion over wide areas is quite as rapid as by means of seeds; and some plants, as various potamogetons, ceratophyllums and other aquatics are more productive of detachable winter buds and other separable vegetable organs than they are of seeds. The brittle willows drop their twigs when injured by storms of ice or wind, or by animals, and many of these cuttings take root in the moist soil, and they may be carried far down streams or distributed along lake shores; the may-apple and a host of rhizomatous plants march onward from the original starting-point; the bryophyllum easily drops its thick leaves, each one of which may establish a new colony of plants; the leaves of the lake-cress (*Nasturtium lacustre*) float down the streams and develop a new plant while they travel; the house-leeks surround themselves with colonies of offshoots, the black raspberry travels by looping stolons, and the strawberry by long runners; the tiger-lily scatters its bulb-like buds, and all bulbiferous plants spread quite as easily by their fleshy parts as by seeds. Now, all these vegetative parts, when established as independent plants, produce flowers and good seeds, and these seeds often perpetuate the very characters which have originated in the asexual generations, as we have seen in the case of many bud-varieties; and it should also be remarked that these phytons usually transmit almost perfectly the characters acquired by the plant from which they sprung. Or, to put the whole matter in a convenient phrase, there may be, and is, a progressive evolution of plants without the aid of sexual union.

Now, where is Weismann's germ-plasm? One of the properties of this material—if an assumption can receive such designation—is its localization in the reproductive organs or parts. But the phyton has no reproductive parts; or, if it has them, they are developed after the phyton has lived a perfectly sexless life, and possibly after generations of such life, in which it and its progeny may either have remained comparatively stable or may have varied widely, as the circumstances may have determined. If the sex-elements of any flower, therefore, contain germ-plasm, they must have derived it out of the asexual or vegetative or soma-plasm. And I will ask where the germ-plasm is in ferns. These plants are fertilized in the prothallic stage, the plant enjoys only one brief sexual state, and then the sex-organs die and wholly disappear. The fern, as the layman knows the plant, is wholly asexual, and the spores are as sexless as buds; yet these spores germinate and give rise to another brief prothallic or sexual stage, and if there is any germ-plasm at all in these fleeting sexual organs, it must have come from the sexless spores. (See pages 66 to 74.) It is interesting to note, in this connection, that this bud-variation is as frequent in ferns as in other plants. Or, if the Weismannians can locate the germ-plasm in all these instances, pray tell us where it is in the myriads of sexless fungi! There is no such thing as continuous localization of germ-plasm in plants!

Weismann himself admits that the germ-plasm must be distributed in "minute fraction" in all "somatic nuclei" of the begonia leaf, because that leaf is capable of giving rise to new plants by means of cuttings, and all the plants may produce good flowers, which, if they are sexual at all, are so only by virtue of containing some of this elusive germ-plasm. There is no other way for these plants to get their germ-plasm, except from the somatic leaf from which they came. It would seem that this admission undermines the whole theory of the localization of the germ-plasm in plants, for one exception in the hypothesis must argue that there are others. But not so! There are no insurmountable difficulties before the Weismannians. It is the begonia which is the exception, for it is abnormal for plants to propagate by any such means! The answer which has been made to this statement is that very many plants are propagated asexually by horticulturists, and that all plants can probably be so propagated if there were any occasion for the effort. This answer is true; but the philosophical answer is that every phyton is an autonomy, and that the mere accident of its growing on the plant, in the soil, or in a bottle of water, is wholly aside from the point, for wherever it grows it lives at first a sexless life, it has an individuality, competes with its fellows, varies to suit its needs, and is capable, finally, of developing sex.

Another fundamental tenet of Weismannism is the continuity of the germ-plasm, the passing down from generation to generation of a part or direct offspring of the original germ-plasm. Now, if it has any continuity in plants, this ancestral germ-plasm must be inextricably diffused in the soma-plasm, as I have said, for every part or phyton of these plants, even to the roots and parts of the leaves, is able to produce sexual parts or germ-plasm. Every plant, too, is wholly sexless or somatic in the early part of its existence (see page 73), and whatever germ-plasm it may have when it begins to develop germ-cells must come either from the soma-plasm itself or from latent germ-plasm, which is intimately associated with the soma-plasm. And if this germ-plasm is inextinguishably associated with every cell of the plant body, why may it not receive and transmit all incident impressions upon the plant? Why should acquired characters impress themselves upon the soma-plasm and not upon the germ-plasm, when this latter element is contained in the very nuclei, as Weismann admits, of somatic cells? If the theory of the continuity of the germ-plasm is true for plants, then acquired characters *must* be transmitted!* The only escape from this position is an arbitrary assumption that one plasm is impressionable and that the other is not; and, now that we can no longer relegate the germ-plasm to imaginary deep-seated germ-cells, such an assumption is too bold, I think, to be suggested.

The entire Weismannian hypothesis is built upon the assumption that all permanent or progressive variation is the result of sexual union; but I have shown that there is much progressive variation in the vegetable kingdom which is purely asexual or vegetative, and, for all we know, this type of modification may proceed indefinitely. There is no doubt of the facts; and the only answer to them which I can conceive the Weismannian to make is that these progressive variations arise because of the latent influence of ancestral sexual unions. In reply to this, I should ask for proofs. Hosts of fungi have no sex. I am not convinced but that there may be strains or types of some species of filamentous algæ and other plants in which there has never been sexual union, even from the beginning. And I should bring in rebuttal, also, the result of direct observation and experiment to show that given hereditable asexual variations are often the direct result of climate, soil or other impinging conditions. As a matter of fact, we know that acquired characters may be hereditary in plants; if the facts do not agree with the hypothesis, so much the worse for the hypothesis. Unfortunately, the hypothesis is too

---

* Essentially this position is expressed in Cope's theory of Diplogenesis, which insists that "the effects of use and disuse" [and, I suppose, of other stimuli] "are two-fold; viz., the effect on the soma, and the effect on the germ-plasma." The character which appears in the soma "must be potentially acquired by the germ-plasma as well as actually by the soma." See Cope, "Primary Factors of Organic Evolution," 1896, pp. 441 to 444.

apt to be capable of endless contractions and modifications to meet individual cases. I sometimes think that we are substituting for the philosophy of observation a philosophy of definitions.

I have now attempted to show:

1. That the plant is not a simple autonomy in the sense in which the animal is.

2. That its parts are virtually independent in respect to (*a*) propagation (equally either when detached or still persisting upon the parent plant), (*b*) struggle for existence amongst themselves, (*c*) variation, (*d*) transmission of their characters by means of either seeds or buds.

3. That there is no essential difference between bud-varieties and seed-varieties, apart from the mere fact of their unlike derivation; and the causes of variation in the one case are the same as those in the other.

4. That all these parts or phytons are at first sexless, but finally may or may not develop sex.

5. That much of the evolution of the vegetable kingdom is accomplished by wholly sexless means.

There is, then, a fundamental unlikeness in the ultimate evolution of animals and plants. A plant, as we ordinarily know it, is a colony of potential individuals, and each individual save the very first is derived from an asexual parent, yet each one may, and usually does, develop sex. Each individual is capable also of receiving a distinct or peculiar influence of the environment and struggle for existence, and is capable, therefore, of independent permanent modification. It is not possible, therefore, that there is any localization or continuity of a germ-plasm in the sense in which these conceptions are applied to animals; nor is it possible for the plant, as a whole, to make a simple functional adaptation to environment. If there is a continuity of germ-plasm in plants, this element must of necessity be intimately associated with every particle of the plant body, even to its very periphery, and it must directly receive external impressions; and this concept of Weismann—the continuity of the germ-plasm—becomes one of the readiest means of explaining the transmission of acquired characters. All these conclusions prove the unwisdom of endeavoring to account for the evolution of all the forms of life upon any single hypothesis; and they illustrate with great emphasis the complexity of even the fundamental forces in the progression of organic nature.

IV.

EXPERIMENTAL EVOLUTION AMONGST PLANTS.[1]

DE VARIGNY has written a most suggestive book upon experimental evolution, in which he contends for the establishment of an institution where experiments can be definitely undertaken for the purpose of transforming a species into a new species. "In experimental transformism," he writes, "lies the only test which we can apply to the evolutionary theory. We must use all the methods we are acquainted with, and also those, yet unknown, which cannot fail to disclose themselves when we begin a thorough investigation of the matter, and do our utmost to bring about the transmutation of any species. We do not specially desire to transform any

---

[1] Read before the Massachusetts Horticultural Society, Boston, February 23, 1895. Printed in the Society's Transactions for 1895, pp. 88 to 100. Abstract in American Naturalist, April, 1895, p. 318.

The minutes of the Society make the following record:

Before entering upon the proper subject of the hour, the speaker made some introductory remarks concerning the present state of belief in the theory of evolution. A brief abstract of these remarks is here given:

Every thoughtful person at the present day is an evolutionist, although he may not know it. Everyone now considers every movement, either of human society or of natural forces, in connection with its origin and gradual growth or development. A person may be an evolutionist without subscribing to any particular doctrine of the origin of species or to any specific dogma either of religion or science. Evolution in the abstract means merely a gradual unfolding or growth. In the organic world, the term is used to designate the belief in the origin of one form or one species from another. Its use does not necessarily imply that one believes in the origin of all things from one species or from many. It simply means that a person sees growth, development and progression in nature.

There are two chief reasons for the belief in the evolution of animals and plants: First, the fact of struggle for existence; second, the fact that there are constantly recurring physical changes. The struggle for existence is the necessary result of the multiplication of species, and the physical changes necessitate

one species into another known at present; we wish to transform it into a new species. * * * Experimental transformism is what we need now, and therein lies the only method we can use.''

The Species-Dogma.

This experiment is a most commendable object, and I hope that the attempt will be made to create a new species before our very eyes. This is what most people demand as a proof of evolution, and they are sometimes impatient that it has not been done; and it would seem, upon the face of it, that nothing more could be desired. When I reflect, however, upon the fact that this very thing has occurred time and again with the horticulturist, and then consider that botanists and philosophers persist in refusing to see it, I am constrained to offer some suggestions upon De Varigny's excellent ambition. If I show a botanist a horticultural type of recent or even contemporaneous origin which I consider to be specifically distinct from its ancestors, he

---

a constant modification of the species, in order that they may fit themselves into the environment.

There are several lines of proof of evolution: First, the record of the rocks, or palæontology; second, the fact that animals and plants are widely variable,—so much so that no two individuals in the world are exactly alike; third, we can see adaptive changes taking place, particularly among plants which are widely disseminated by man, or which are brought under domestication; fourth, the presence of missing links or breaks in the chain of life, which shows that those forms which are weakest or least adapted to live have dropped out, and have left the others to strengthen themselves; and, fifth, the fact that there is a perfect adaptation of all organisms to their environments or conditions of life.

The doctrine of evolution is old, although it was not until the opening of the present century that it began to take on specific and technical form. It was taught more or less vaguely by the Greeks, and, later, by the Arabs. Perhaps it may be said that two chief epochs in the history of the unfolding of the doctrine are those represented by Copernicus and Darwin. Copernicus disproved the old geocentric doctrine, or the notion that the earth is the center of the universe; Darwin disproved the homocentric doctrine, or the notion that man is the central object of nature. We now conceive of the universe as a whole, undergoing a general progressive or onward movement, in which all its parts are intimately concerned.

at once exclaims that it is not a species, but a horticultural variety. If I ask him why, he replies, "Because it is an artificial production!" If I show him that the type is just as distinct from the species from which it sprung as that species is from its related species, and that it reproduces its kind with just as much certainty, he still replies that, because it is a horticultural production, it cannot be a species. In what, then, does an accidental horticultural origin differ from any other origin? Simply in the fact that one takes place under the eye of man and the other occurs somewhere else! It is impossible at the present day to make a definition of a species which shall exclude many horticultural types, unless an arbitrary exception is made of them. The old definitions assumed that species are special creative acts, and the method of origin is therefore stated or implied in all of them. The definition itself, therefore, was essentially a statement of the impossibility of evolution. We have now revised our definitions so as to exclude the matter of origin, and thereby to allow free course to evolution studies; and yet here is a great class of natural objects which are practically eliminated from our consideration because, unhappily, we know whence they came! Or, to state the case differently, these types cannot be accepted as proofs of the transformation of species because we know certainly that they are the result of transformation!

Now, just this state of things would be sure to occur if De Varigny were to transform one species into another. People would say that the new form is not really a species, because it is the result of cultivation, domestication, and definite breeding by man. He could never hope to secure more remarkable transformations than have occurred a thousand times in the garden; and his scheme—so far as it applies to plants—is essentially that followed by all good gardeners. Or, if the prejudices of scientists respecting the so-called artificial production of species could be overcome, he could just as well draw his proofs of evolution from what has already been done with cultivated plants and domesticated animals as from similar results which might arise in the future from his independent efforts. I am not arguing against the scheme to create a species before our eyes, but I am simply stating what has been and is the insurmountable difficulty in just this line of endeavor,—the inability of the experimenter to satisfy the scientific world that he has really produced a species; for it is a singular thing that whilst all biologists now agree in defining a species upon its tangible and present characters, they nevertheless act, for the most part, upon the old notion that a species must have its origin somewhere beyond the domain of exact history.

This notion that a species, to be a species, must have originated in nature's garden and not in man's, has been left over to us from the last generation—it is the inheritance of an acquired character. John Ray, towards the close of the seventeenth century, appears to have been the first to use the word species in its technical, natural-history sense, and the matter of origin was an important factor in his conception of what a species is. Linnæus's phrase is familiar: "We reckon as many species as there were forms created in the beginning." Darwin elaborated the new conception—that a species is simply a congregation of individuals which are more like each other than they are like any other congregation, and with a freedom from prejudice which is rarely attained even by his most devoted adherents, he declared that "one new variety raised by man will be a more important and interesting subject for study than one more species added to the infinitude of already recorded species." The old naturalists threw the origin of the species back beyond known causes; Darwin endeavored to discover the "Origin of Species," and it is significant that he set out without giving any definition of what a species is. I have said this much for the purpose of showing that it is important, when we demand that a new species be created as a proof of evolution, that we are ourselves open to conviction that the thing can be done.

I have said that no modern naturalist would define a species in such terms that some horticultural types could be excluded, even if he desired that they should be omitted. Haeckel's excellent definition admits many of them. In his view, the word species "serves as the common designation of all individual animals or plants, which are equal in all essential matters of form, and are only distinguished by quite subordinate characters." It is impossible, however, actually to determine whether one has a species in hand by applying a definition. One must show that his new type—if it is a plant—has botanical characters as well marked as similar accepted species have, and these characters must show, as a whole, a general tendency towards permanency when the plant is normally propagated by seeds. He must measure his type by the rule of accepted botanical practice. If the same plant were found wild, so that all prejudice were removed, would the botanist unhesitatingly describe it as a new species? If yes, then we would say that a new species had been created under the hand of man; and this rule I wish now to apply to a very few familiar plants. In doing so, I do not wish to be understood as saying that I consider it advisable to describe these plants as species under the existing methods of botanical description and nomenclature, for, merely as a matter of convenience and perspicuity, I do not; but I wish to show that they really are, in every essential character, just as much species as very many other universally accepted species are.

The Forms of Tomatoes.

The evolution of forms which any botanist would at

A. Spray of old-time tomato.

once designate as species, were he ignorant of their origin, is well illustrated in the tomato. Dunal, the

IV.]   OLD-TIME AND NEW-TIME TOMATOES.   113

accepted authority upon the genus Lycopersicum, admits ten unqualified species into his account in De Candolle's Prodromus. Two of these, *L. pyriforme* and *L. cerasiforme*, are generally regarded as mere

B. Spray of new-time tomato.

forms of the common garden species, *L. esculentum*, both because they are very like the common tomato in botanical characters, and because we know, as a matter of history and experiment, that all three of these reputed species are modifications of one type. Omitting these two species, then, there remain eight to which we

8 SUR.

cannot attach any such suspicion as a knowledge of their origin. These are what botanists call good species. These species agree in having a weak and spreading habit of growth, much like the common tomato. The features by which they differ

C. Spray of the large-leaved tomato.

amongst themselves, that is, the specific characters, are founded chiefly upon the manner of divisions of the leaves, the shape of the leaflets, the character of the flower cluster and the relative hairiness or smoothness of the parts. If one applies these same tests in the same degree to the two modern offshoots of the tomato—the Upright and the Mikado types—he will find that these offshoots differ as much or even more from each other and from their own

D. Leaf of the large-leaved tomato.

common parent as any one of the wild species differs from any other species; and everyone knows that these characters come true from seed. The Upright type differs from all other tomatoes in its stiff and self-sustaining habit of growth, a character which belongs

E. Spray of Upright tomato.

to Solanum rather than to Lycopersicum; and this habit is so marked that persons unfamiliar with the variety usually think the plants potatoes rather than tomatoes, when the fruit is not seen. The entire foliage of the plant is so distinct that the most casual botanist could draw botanical characters from it to separate the plant specifically from any other species of Lycopersicum

F. Old-time and new-time forms of tomato fruit.

which is yet described. The leaflets are reduced in number, and are greatly modified in shape. Even the inflorescence shares in the transformation, for the flowers, instead of being six or more, as they are in its known ancestors, are reduced to two or three. If De Varigny were to experiment for centuries, he could scarcely expect to produce any "new species" which should have better characters than this singular race of tomatoes, the origin of which is so well known that we have the record of the year in which it originated, and the very

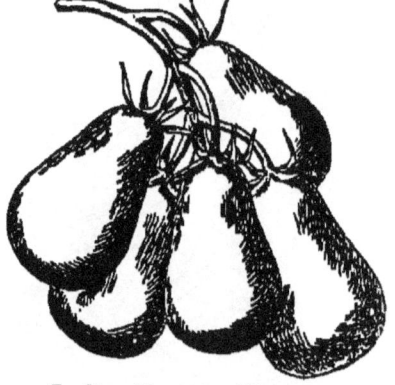

G. Pear-like type of tomato.

man who sowed the seed from which it sprung. This curious race came in suddenly, without any premonition, so far as we know, of its appearing, and the same thing has probably not originated a second time.

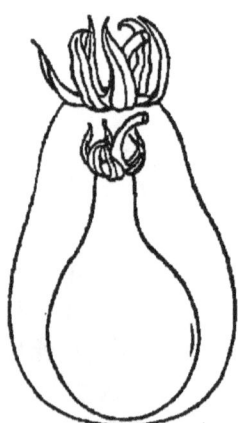

H. Augmentation of size in the pear-form tomato.

The other type to which I referred, the large-leaved or Mikado race (variety *grandifolium*), gave evidence of its coming. This type has a remarkable divergence from the species in the most fundamental botanical characters of its leaves. The leaflets are much fewer than in the common tomatoes, very large, the lower side strongly decurrent on the stem, the margins entire, and the blades plane or flat,—characters which are as far removed from *Lycopersicum esculentum*, from which it came, as the characters of the latter are from other recognized species. In young plants, the leaves are even entire, a character which is supposed to be foreign to the genus! The tendency towards this large leaved type was noticed many years ago in the old Keyes Prolific tomato, but appeared to have first attracted much attention in Nisbit Victoria, a variety which came from seed of Hathaway Excelsior, which has foliage very small, curled, and much divided. In very recent years, it has appeared again in a most emphatic form in the Mikado or Turner Hybrid, and in the Potato-Leaf. We have a good indication of how distinct these two races of tomatoes are from the fact

1. Lycopersicum pyriforme, from Dunal.

that we have a real species—that is, one which has no genealogy—in cultivation besides *Lycopersicum esculentum*, and it is not regarded by horticulturists as worthy such explicit description or separation from the common type of tomatoes as either the Upright or the Mikado type is. In fact, gardeners do not look

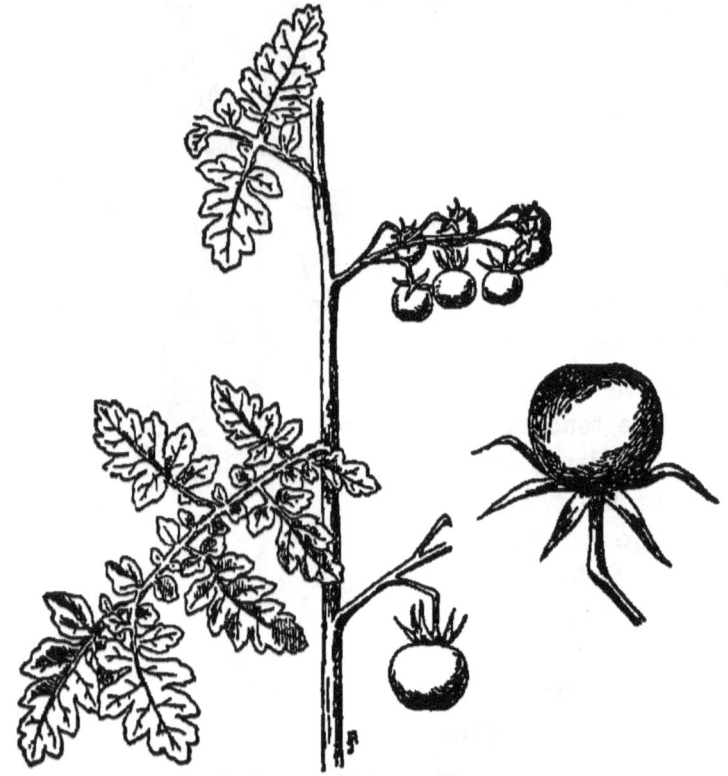

J. Lycopersicum cerasiforme.

upon it as a distinct species at all, although it is universally received by botanists, and Vilmorin even places it in the genus Solanum. This is the Currant tomato, or *L. pimpinellifolium*.

But the most remarkable feature of the evolution of

the tomato, to my mind, is one which appears to have escaped scientific comment. It is the fact that, in America at least, the whole body of garden forms is rapidly progressing, or departing from the original type. This original type, or something very like it, was the only tomato at the opening of the century, and it was essentially that which the older men of the present generation

K. Spray of Currant tomato (Lycopersicum pimpinellifolium).

knew in their boyhood. The plant was comparatively small, with an erect or upright tendency of the young shoots, with foliage light in color and small, and either thin or much curled, the leaflets tending somewhat to rounded forms; the flowers two-ranked in long and sometimes forking clusters, the fruit, in the simplest forms, strictly two-celled, and in the most developed forms flat on the top and bottom and corrugated or ridged on the sides. This angular tomato was apparently the only one known a century ago, aside from the little cherry and pear tomatoes. Martyn's Edition of Miller's Dictionary, in 1807, describes the fruit of the common tomato as follows: "The fruit in this is very large [in comparison with the cherry tomato and others], compressed both at top and bottom, and deeply furrowed all over the sides, red or yellow." Now all this is changed, and there is only an occasional variety, or the persistent cherry tomato, which recalls the old type. At present, the tomato plant is large and widely spreading, with scarcely an indication of the spire-like growths of the young shoots which character-

L. Currant tomato in Herb. Kew.

ized the old forms, with foliage very dark green and large, and the leaflets thick and flat and tending to pointed and jagged forms, the flowers reduced to irregular clusters of two to four, the fruit very many-celled, and, under the influence of recent selection, regularly rounded on top and apple-shaped. For nearly a century, the tomato has been steadily moving forward into this new type, with all its botanical characters profoundly modified; and it holds this form as uniformly when propagated from seeds as any wild species could be expected to do. If, as Haeckel declares, a species is a succession of organisms which exhibit the same form under the same environments, then even the common type of tomatoes might contend for specific distinction from its ancestors of a century ago. At all events, we have here as profound, onward, definite transformation as De Varigny could hope to secure in the same length of time; and if such productions as these of which I have spoken are not to be accepted as species, why should we accept those which we assume would arise under the care of an evolution

M. Currant tomato. The upper spray from a specimen in Herb. Kew. The lower one from a colored drawing of *L. racemiforme* in Botanisk Tidsskrift by Lange.

experiment station? Here we have absolutely new and unique types, and they are as distinct from each other and from their parents, in accepted botanical characters,

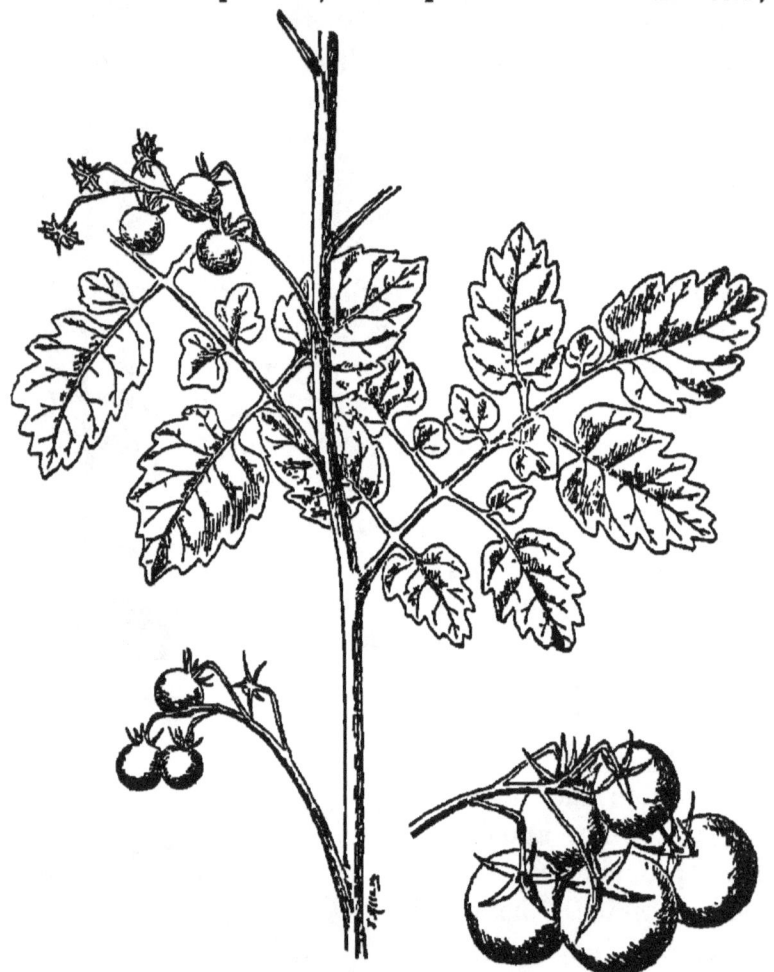

N. Lycopersicum Humboldtii. Tropical America.

as "good species" in the same genus are from each other, and they perpetuate these characters as unequivocally as those various species do. Moreover, we

THE TOMATO SPECIES.

know definitely what their origins were, and they, therefore, answer all the purposes of experimental evolution. The evolution of the tomato is so interesting and it is typical of so many garden plants, that it

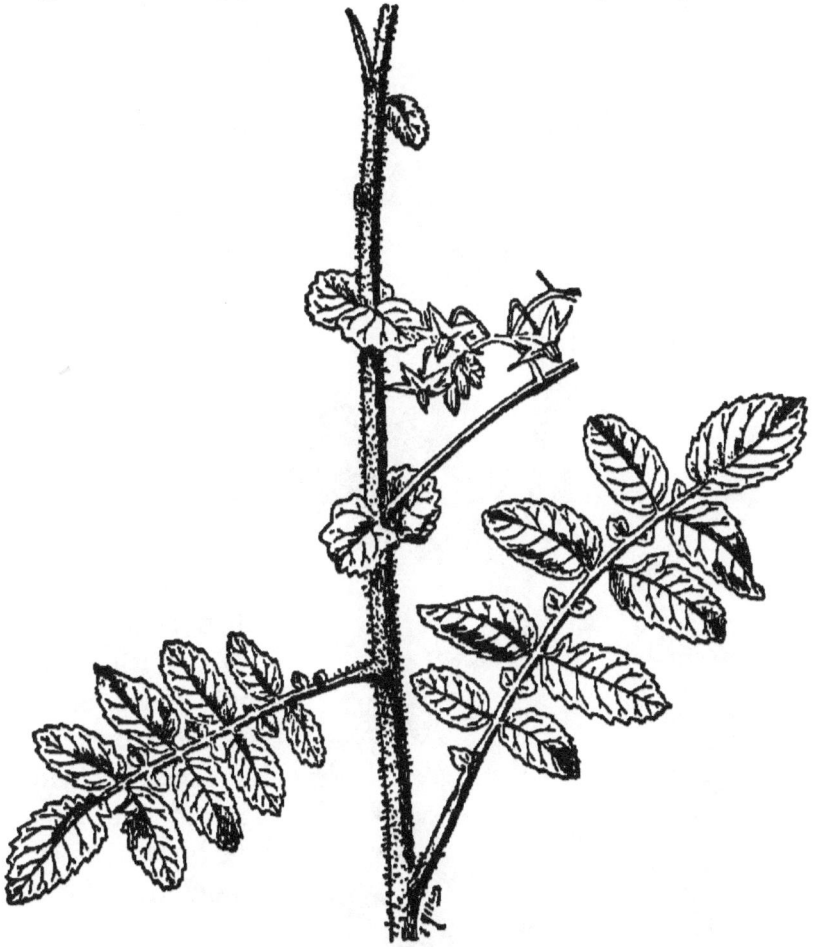

O. Lycopersicum agrimoniæfolium. Peru.

will profit us to give it even closer attention. The pictures will help us. Fig. A represents the foliage and fruit of the tomato of a generation and more ago, to which I have already alluded. The curled leaves and the cornered, flattened fruit are conspicuous. The plane or flat-leaved type of tomato, which is the usual form in cultivation to-day, is shown in B. The curious, large-leaved or grandifolium type which has sprung from this plane-leaved form—with its few and large and nearly entire leaflets, and the absence of the rudimentary leaflets on the rachis—is well shown in C, and a single leaf at D. With these should be contrasted the remarkable foliage and habit of the Upright tomato, at E. The old-time form of fruit is shown in the inner diagram in F, and the new-form or apple like type is

P. Lycopersicum Peruvianum. Peru.

IV.]   THE TOMATO SPECIES.   125

shown in the outer diagram. Some of the older forms which are still preserved to us, are seen in G and H. These are the pear-tomatoes, once known as a species under the name *Lycopersicum pyriforme*. Various offshoots of this type have given large-fruited tomatoes (as in the Criterion), but the type has been much less productive of improved forms than the cherry tomato has. It is in the rotate-formed or spherical-fruit types that the greater development has been possible because of the greater facility which they possess for the intercalation of interior carpels. (See the discussion of

Q. *Lycopersicum puberulum.* Chile.

this point, with illustrations, in Essay XXX.). When this pear-form type becomes markedly augmented in size, the distinctly clavate form tends to disappear, as if the fruit were making the attempt to throw itself into a spherical form. This is shown in the outer diagram in H, which represents the King Humbert tomato. I have already said that both the pear and cherry tomatoes were formerly described as species—*Lycopersicum pyriforme* and *L. cerasiforme* respectively. A picture of the pear tomato, drawn from a figure in Dunal's monograph, is shown in I. In J is shown a picture of an authentic specimen of the cherry tomato. All these various pictures, therefore—from A to J—represent forms of the common tomato species, *Lycopersicum esculentum*.

The reader will now be interested to compare with these pictures of various forms of *L. esculentum*, those of other accepted species of Lycopersicum. For this purpose, I have had Mr. John Allen make drawings of specimens in the Kew Herbarium, and these drawings are here laid before the reader. I expect that all the specimens from which these drawings are made are properly determined (many of them are truly authentic), but I do not vouch for them, and I do not submit the pictures for the purpose of making a contribution to the knowledge of the species of Lycopersicum, but I introduce them to show that the differences between the various accepted species do not strike one as being so marked or so valid as the differences between the various groups of *Lycopersicum esculentum* itself. I first show a spray of the Currant tomato, K, drawn from specimens of my own growing, a species to which I have already adverted on pages 117, 118. L and M are evidently the same thing, although they are labelled *L. racemiforme* of Lange at Kew.* *Lycopersicum Humboldtii*, N, closely resembles our garden tomato, and I should not be surprised if it proves to be only a racial offshoot of it. Dunal's *L. agrimoniæfolium* is shown at O, Miller's *L. Peruvianum* at P, and Phillippi's *L. puberulum* at Q. This last I know only from the drawing which Mr. Allen sends me. The last two species, P, Q, are most unlike the garden tomato types of any of the lot, yet they are not so widely removed from them in foliage as the Grandifolium and Upright sub-types are.

Other Garden Species.

Similar observations respecting the evolution of forms of specific importance could be made for most species of plants which have been widely cultivated for a considerable length of time. The case is singularly well illustrated in Indian corn. Maize has been very uniformly accepted as a single species by botanists. This arises mostly from the fact that corn is nowhere known truly wild, and has, therefore, attracted little attention from systematic botanists. There are some authors, however, who have made species of some of the marked cultivated types, either upon the hypothesis that these forms must have been derived from distinct wild

---

*According to "Index Kewensis," *Lycopersicum racemiforme* of Lange should be *L. racemigerum*, Lange. The Currant tomato of American gardens is to all appearances the same, and this was first referred to a botanical species—*L. pimpinellifolium*—in my Bulletin 19, Michigan Agricultural College, 1886. It is not there recorded, however, that this determination was made for me by Asa Gray. Vilmorin's "Plantes Potagères" calls the species *Solanum racemiflorum* of Dunal. The species seems to have been first described by Linnæus as *Solanum pimpinellifolium*, and Philip Miller took up the specific name and attached it to *Lycopersicum*. Dunal, however, upon the evidence of a specimen in Banks'

types, or that, independently of origin, they merit specific recognition. The chief author who takes the latter view is Sturtevant, who, whilst accepting the common origin of all types of maize, nevertheless prefers to recognize seven "agricultural species," as follows: *Zea tunicata*, "a primitive form," from which the other six are derived; *Zea everta*, pop corns; *Z. indurata*, flint corns; *Z. indentata*, dent corns; *Z. amylacea*, soft corns; *Z. saccharata*, sweet corns; *Z. amylea-saccharata*, the starchy-sweet corns. Whilst these species are not accepted by the regular botanists, there can be no doubt that some of them would be regarded as distinct species if they should turn up in an evidently wild state; and a proof of this statement is found in Watson's *Zea canina*, which was founded upon wild corn collected in southern Mexico. Now, Mr. Watson was one of our most conservative American botanists, and any new species which he should describe could be depended upon to have good botanical characters; yet this new *Zea canina* is so like our rice pop corns that Sturtevant unhesitatingly refers it to his *Zea everta*, thus showing that it is not more unlike ordinary corn than some types of pop corn are! Moreover, this corn is found to lose quickly the very botanical characters upon which the species is founded, when it is brought into

---

Herbarium, refers Miller's *Lycopersicum pimpinellifolium* to *L. Humboldtii* (see DC. Prodr. xiii. i. p. 25). Martyn's edition of Miller, 1807, however, refers it back to *Solanum*, and writes of it as follows: "Habit and structure of *S. Lycopersicum*. Fruit like that of its variety B [Cherry tomato]. But it differs altogether from *S. Lycopersicum* in having the stem smooth, without any hairs scattered over that or the peduncles, the leaves smooth entire cordate, not at all gashed or toothed as in that. However it agrees upon the whole in structure, it may perhaps come from that. The structure of the peduncles is the same as in *tuberosum*, *Lycopersicum* and *peruvianum*, with the pedicles also jointed, and the raceme naked, as in the two former, not leafy as in the last."

cultivation.* Even in its wild state it is scarcely more distinct from the common races of maize than the "husk corn" is, or the curious striped-leaved corn of Japan—and the latter would certainly be considered worthy of specific recognition by botanists were it not for the fact that historical evidence shows that maize was introduced into Japan directly or indirectly from the New World, and that, therefore, its origin is more or less enshrouded in knowledge! All this is but another illustration of how tenaciously botanists still hold to the Linnæan idea of species whilst they profess the Darwinian idea.

A similar evolution of types which are as distinct and permanent as accepted species in the same genus are, is well illustrated in the various beans. The common garden or kidney bean was made into two species by Linnæus, the pole beans (*Phaseolus vulgaris*) and the bush beans (*P. nanus*). Since it has been demonstrated by experience and experiment that these groups are interchangeable forms of one type, botanists have discarded Linnæus's designations of them, and now call the garden bean a single species; yet it should be said that a more explicit and satisfactory instance of the evolution of specific forms right under our own observation could not be demanded. The two groups are species until we discover that they have sprung from one type within historic times, whereupon we then regard them not as species but as anomalies of cultivation. Von Martens, however, discards origin as a mark of specific likeness or difference, and now proposes to erect seven species upon the obvious racial differences in the garden beans. But the most interesting feature of this bean botany is the

---
*For an account of this corn under cultivation, see Bulletin 49, Cornell Experiment Station.

9 SUR.

complete neglect, on the part of botanists, of the singular dwarf Limas, which have appeared in very recent years. Remember, now, that Linnæus regarded the common pole beans and the common bush beans as two distinct species, because one is a running or twining plant and the other is a dwarf erect plant. The Lima bean is a twining plant; but within the last few years three well-marked types of true bush beans have sprung independently from the old types of Lima. If these differences were worth specific recognition in the common garden beans, why are not the same differences worth at least a passing comment in the Lima bean? Yet, because these types have originated before our eyes, botanists consider them not worth notice, although, at the same moment, they are hoping for the time when they shall see the origination of a new species of plant! But this curious bean evolution has not stopped here. The old Scarlet Runner and White Dutch Runner of our gardens (*Phaseolus multiflorus*) have well marked botanical characters in the leaves, inflorescence, pods, beans, and particularly in the roots, which are fleshy and perennial, and in the very tall twining habit. Yet, at the moment when dwarf forms had sprung off the Lima stock—in the same way as the common bush beans undoubtedly had sprung off the stock of the common pole bean before Linnæus's time—a bush bean sprung off the stock of the old White Dutch Runner, and this is known in commerce as Barteldes Bush Lima. But this singular bean has other characters than the very dwarf complete bush habit to distinguish it from its parent, for it differs in a smaller inflorescence, in foliage, and particularly in a remarkable tendency towards a fibrous annual root.* Here is a new form which surely ought to satisfy any person who demands the direct origination of a new species as a proof of evolution.

There are other curiosities amongst the beans. Gardeners know two well-marked types or races of the Lima bean, the Sieva type and the Large Lima type. There are good and valid botanical distinctions between the two, which were amply recognized by Linnæus, who, supposing that one came from Bengal and the other from Africa, made species of them. The smaller, or what we now know as the Sieva type, he called *Phaseolus lunatus;* the other he called *P. inamœnus.* The term Lima bean, which all agree in associating with our *Phaseolus lunatus,* should properly be applied, therefore, to the Sieva type. For a century these species of Linnæus were generally considered to be good,—that is, distinct and valid. It is now pretty well established that both these beans came from Brazil. Only one of them is known in a truly wild state, and the suspicion is so strong, therefore, that the other sprung off from it under cultivation, that the two types are now united as one species. Still a third well-marked type, differing in shape and texture of leaflets, and characters of pods and seeds, has now originated from the Large Lima type; this is the Potato Lima type. It should also be said that Macfadyen, in his flora of Jamaica, made four new species out of the Lima type of beans. Here, then, are three groups of beans, each as distinct from the others and from its ancestors as accepted species of Phaseolus are from each other, yet, because of their origin under domestication, they are debarred specific distinction. Now, a most curious thing about these dwarf Lima beans, which have appeared so

---

*For an account of these beans, see Cornell Bulletin 87.

suddenly in the past few years, is that they have come from each of these three types,—Henderson from the Sieva type, Thorburn and Dreer from the Potato Lima type, and Burpee from the Large Lima type,— thus showing that each of these types or races is developing along independent but parallel lines; and these lines are also identical with the method of evolution which was early assumed by the common garden bean and with the departure which has just now appeared in the old White Dutch Runner.

The Soy bean, now coming into popular cultivation in the south, affords a most striking example of the evolution of a new species, and one, moreover, which is accepted by careful botanists. This plant is unknown wild, and there is every reason to consider it to be a modified form of the wild *Glycine Soja* of China and Japan; but its botanical characters are so unlike those of its ancestral household that Maximowicz,—a most conservative botanist,—describes it outright as a new species, *Glycine hispida*.

The Lesson of the Garden-Experiments.

I have now brought to your attention a few familiar plants for the purpose of showing that what are to all intents and purposes good species have originated in recent years; and that, whilst botanists demand that the origination of species within historic times shall constitute the only indisputable proof of organic evolution, they nevertheless refuse to accept as species those forms which have thus originated, and which answer every demand of their definitions and practice.

The proofs of the evolution of species, drawn from

the accepted practice of the best botanists themselves, could be indefinitely extended. We need only recall the botanical confusion in which most cultivated plants now lie, to find abundant proof of the evolution of hundreds of types so distinct that the best botanists have considered them to be species; but other botanists, basing their estimate of species upon origins, have reduced them or re-included them into the form or type first described. Consider the number of species which have been made in the genus Citrus, comprising the various oranges, lemons, limes and the like. Recall the roses. The Moss rose and others would be regarded as distinct species by any botanist if they were found wild, and if they held their characters as tenaciously as they do under cultivation. In fact, the Moss rose was long regarded as a good species, and it was only when its origin began to be understood that this opinion was given up. The earlier botanists, who were less critical about origins than the present botanists are, made species largely upon apparent features of plants, although their fundamental conception of a species was one which was created, as we find it, in the beginning. Yet, strangely enough, we at the present day, who profess to regard species as nothing more than loose and conventional aggregations of similar individuals, and which we conceive to have sprung from a common ancestor at some more or less late epoch in the world's history, make our species upon premises which we deny, by giving greater weight to obscurity of origin than we do to similarity of individuals!

The fact is that the practice of systematic or descriptive botany is at variance with the teachings of evolution. Every naturalist now knows that nature does not set out to make species. She makes a multitude of forms which we, merely for purposes of convenience in classifying our knowledge of them, combine into more or less marked aggregations, to which we have given the name species. Very often we find in nature an aggregation of successive individuals which is so well marked and set off from its associated groups that we consider nature to have made an out and out distinct species; but a closer acquaintance with such species shows that, in many cases, the intermediate or outlying forms have been lost, and that the type which we now know is the remainder in a continuous problem of subtraction. In other cases, a form appears to have arisen without intermediate forms, as a distinct offshoot from an older type. This is well illustrated in many remarkably distinct garden forms, which originated all at once with characters new to the species or even to the genus. I have mentioned such a case in the Upright tomato. Even the sudden appearance of these strange forms is proof that species may originate at any time, and that it can be no part of our fundamental conception of a species that it shall have originated in some remote epoch. Species-making forever enforces the idea of the distinctness and immutability of organic forms, but study of organisms themselves forever enforces an opposite conception.*

The intermediate and variable forms are perplexities

---

*If this position is well taken, it follows that the naturalist should not describe new species with the idea of adding another item or organism to the inventory of nature, but for the purpose of classifying and clarifying our knowledge of the kind and extent of variation which the given group presents. A new species, therefore, is made simply for convenience's sake. In very variable groups, it is perfectly justifiable to make species when it is known that occasional forms are intermediates, if thereby we are enabled to understand the relationships of the various forms more clearly. This is particularly true in narrow groups which have many forms of varying taxonomic importance. An illustration may be taken from the genus Carex. The *echinata* group contains four more or less coördinate main types, the *echinata* proper of the Old World, and three types in the United

to one who attempts to describe species as so many entities which have distinct and personal attributes. So the garden has always been the bugbear of the botanist. Even our lamented Asa Gray declared that the modern garden roses are "too much mixed by crossing and changed by variation to be subjects of botanical study." He meant to say that the roses are too much modified to allow of species-making. The despair of systematic botanists is the proof of evolution!

I repeat that mere species-making, in the old or con-

States. It has been the fashion to throw these all together into a composite species, calling it *Carex echinata*. In this arrangement, the sub-groups or sub-forms do not stand out clearly, and it is impossible to contrast them forcibly. Moreover, the characters which separate the most marked sub-forms are of as great or even greater classifactory importance than characters which are used to separate *Carex echinata* itself from its fellow species. The old arrangement might be graphically presented as follows:

Carex echinata.
  Group B.
    Sub-group a.
    Sub-group b.
    Sub-group c.
  Group C.
  Group D.
    Sub-group a.

This classification, from a taxonomic standpoint, is untrue, for, as Carex species go, groups B, C, D are coördinate with *C. echinata*, and not subordinate to it. The mere fact that there are now and then intermediate forms between these various groups should not deprive us of the privilege of expressing the taxonomic facts. In nearly every instance, specimens can be clearly referred to one or the other of the groups by one who is familiar with them; but so long as the various groups are represented to be of minor and variable importance—as the above arrangement does represent them to be, to a botanist's mind—so long will they remain to be comparatively little distinguished and understood. Consequently, I have erected (Bull. Torr. Bot. Club. xx. 422) the four groups into coördinate species, as follows:

  A. *Carex echinata.* Old World.
  B. *Carex sterilis.* New World.
    a. variety excelsior.
    b. var. cephalantha.
    c. var. angustata.
  C. *Carex Atlantica.*
  D. *Carex interior.*
    a. var. capillacea.

ventional sense, is an incubus to the study of nature. One who now describes a species should feel that he is simply describing a variable and plastic group of individuals for mere convenience's sake. He should not attempt to draw the boundary lines hard and fast, nor should he be annoyed if he is obliged to modify his description every year. This loose group may contain some forms which seem to be aberrant to the idea which he has in mind; and it would seem as if he should be ready to call them new or distinct species whenever, from whatever cause, they become so much modified that it is convenient, for purposes of identification and description, to separate them from the general type. Just as soon as botanists come to feel that all so-called species of plants are transitory and artificial groups maintained for convenience in the study of nature, they will not ask whether they are modified outside the garden or inside it, but will consider groups of equal distinctness and permanence to be of equal value in the classification of knowledge, wholly aside from the mere place of their origin. At the present time, the garden fence is the only distinction between many accepted species and many disregarded ones. The cultivation of man differs from the methods of nature only in degree, not in kind; and if man secures results sooner than nature does it is only another and indubitable proof of the evolution of organic forms. It is certainly a wholly unscientific attitude to demand that forms originating by one of nature's methods are species, while similar forms originating by another method are beneath notice.

If species are not original entities in nature, then it is useless to quarrel over the origination of them by means of experiment. All we want to know, as a proof

THE WORK OF THE HORTICULTURIST.

of evolution, is whether plants and animals can be profoundly modified by different conditions, and if these modifications tend to persist. Every man before me knows, as a matter of common observation and practice, that this is true of plants. He knows that varieties with the most marked features are passing before him like a panorama. He knows that nearly every plant which has been long cultivated, has become so profoundly and irrevocably modified that people are disputing as to what wild species it came from. Consider that we cannot certainly identify the original species of the apple, peach, plum, cherry, orange, lemon, wine grape, sweet potato, Indian corn, melon, bean, pumpkin, wheat, chrysanthemum, and nearly or quite a hundred other common cultivated plants. It is immaterial whether they are called species or varieties. They are new forms. Some of them are so distinct that they have been made the types of genera. Here is the experiment to prove that evolution is true, worked out upon a scale and with a definiteness of detail which the boldest experimenter could not hope to attain, were he to live a thousand years. The horticulturist is one of the very few men whose distinct business and profession is evolution. He, of all other men, has the experimental proof that species come and go.

V.

VAN MONS AND KNIGHT, AND THE PRODUCTION OF VARIETIES.[1]

EVERY species of plant which man has cultivated for any considerable length of time has numerous forms or varieties. This simple and undisputable statement represents one of the most significant facts in nature. There are two diverse types of inquiries which may grow out of a contemplation of this fact. One type attempts to collect information concerning the various forms, for the direct and immediate use of the cultivator. It endeavors to ascertain the best varieties for certain purposes or for given conditions. This is a matter of practical agriculture. The other type of inquiry asks why and how these various forms came to be. It seeks for fundamental truths, that is, for laws or principles; and inasmuch as principles are eternal, so far as we know, it follows that the enunciation of a law is prophecy of progress and destiny.

The type of mind which inquires into the reasons for the existence of these forms is essentially a modern one. It may almost be said to be recent. The inquiry into the nature of garden or domestic varieties of plants and animals is simply a special application of the desire to know the genesis and destiny of that congeries of objects

---

[1] Address before the Pennsylvania Horticultural Society, Philadelphia, March 17, 1896. Printed under the title, "New Varieties of Plants," in American Gardening for May 16, 23, 30, June 6 and 20, 1896.

knew that plants mix by crossing. He had also learned that the character of the entire plant is more important, when choosing seed-parents, than that of the particular fruit from which the seed is taken. "The common method of saving seed corn, by taking the ears from the crib or heap, is attended with two disadvantages, one is, the taking the largest ears, which have generally grown but one on a stalk. This lessens the production; the other is, taking ears which have ripened at different times, which causes the production to do the same." A year or two ago I wrote: "The practice of selecting large ears from a bin of corn, or large melons from the grocer's wagon, is much less efficient in producing large products the following season than the practice of going into the fields and selecting the most uniformly large-fruited parents would be." This remark was drawn from general experience and observation. I had not then read Cooper. I now find that my advice is a hundred years behind time! This is not the only instance in which I seem to have copied Cooper. I have said several times that the seeds of the southern watermelons are almost worthless for the north because they give late fruits, but that the variety may eventually be fitted to our conditions by a constant selection of seeds from the earliest plants. "A striking instance of plants being naturalized," writes Cooper, "happened by Colonel Matlack sending some water melon seed from Georgia, which, he informed me by letter, were of superior quality. Knowing that seed from vegetables which had grown in more southern climates, required a longer summer than what grow here, I gave them the most favourable situation, and used glasses to bring them forward, yet very few ripened to perfection;

author of nature, has so constructed that wonderful machine, if I may be allowed the expression, as to incline every kind of soil and climate to naturalize all kinds of vegetables, that it will produce at any rate, the better to suit them, if the agriculturists will do their part in selecting the most proper seed." For over fifty years he had maintained the "long, warty squash" on the farm "without changing," and he adds that they "are now far preferable to what they were at first." He had also maintained early peas and asparagus in vigorous and pure condition for over half a century. It is significant that both of these, also, had been "improved." He made similarly successful experiments in keeping and improving strains of the potato, for even at that time the complaint was "very general," as he writes, "that potatoes of every kind degenerate." Indian corn was equally plastic in his hands. "For many years past," he says, in closing, "I have renewed the whole seed of my winter grain, from a single plant which I have observed to be more productive, and of better quality than the rest; a practice which I am satisfied, has been of great use."

It will thus be seen that Cooper clearly apprehended the value of repeated selection for the amelioration of plants; and finding it so potent, he made the natural error of discouraging the change of seed. For himself, however, he was wholly correct in refusing a change of seed, because his own seed was better than that which he would be likely to secure by exchange; but we now know that while selection is the greater factor, change of seed is also important because it incites variation.* Cooper

---

*For a somewhat full discussion of the philosophy of the benefits resulting from change of seed, the reader is referred to my handbook upon "Plant-Breeding."

plants; important caution to secure permanent good quality of plants." The editors say that the paper "has already been published in the United States and in Europe; and has deservedly excited very general attention." It is further explained that "the writer is entitled to every degree of respect, both for his practical knowledge, and integrity of relation. His experience and opinions differ widely from those generally received. The results produced, require the care and attention which few will give. The merit of Mr. Cooper is therefore the greater." Cooper was also a pomologist of note, and was the originator, amongst other things, of the Cooper plum, a seedling of the Orleans, which William Coxe said, in 1817, "is the largest plum I have seen."

Cooper said that he was "greatly embarrassed at the opinion very generally entertained by farmers and gardeners, that changing seeds, roots and plants, to distant places, or different soils or climates, is beneficial to agriculture; such opinion not agreeing with my observations or practice." He deplored the general acceptance of this notion, because "it turns the attention of the husbandman from what appears to me one great object, viz. that of selecting seeds and roots for planting or sowing, from such vegetables as come to the greatest perfection, in the soil which he cultivates." Cooper's experiments were a credit to his time, and they have probably not yet been excelled in this country for simplicity and usefulness. "What induced me to make experiments on the subject," he writes, "was, my observing that all kinds of vegetables were continually varying in their growth, quality, production, and time of maturity. This led me to believe that the great

gle lesson is worth all the arduous labor of his long and useful life. This lesson has now been accepted as one of the canons of horticultural teaching, and it has been strengthened by the experience of every experimenter and every careful cultivator,—that the one and the only infallible means of producing better plants is through good care, and judicious and persistent selection.

Joseph Cooper.

Although Van Mons is the leading early apostle of selection for the amelioration of plants, there were other experimenters who had early demonstrated its value. One of these early explorers in the field of plant-breeding was Joseph Cooper, of Gloucester county, New Jersey, who, at the close of last century, had made most suggestive experiments in the improvement of plants, and who apprehended the value of selection more clearly than any other person of his time with whose work I am acquainted. Unfortunately, Joseph Cooper appears to be almost unknown and therefore I have the greater pleasure in introducing him to his posterity; although he had been discovered by the patient search of Darwin, who cites his work to show that selection may accomplish much when it "has been silently carried on in places where it would not have been expected." Darwin, however, did not know the particular paper and experiments of Cooper's to which I am about to refer. This paper is a short letter which was written in 1799, and published in the first volume of the "Memoirs of the Philadelphia Society for Promoting Agriculture." The title given it in the Memoirs is: "Change of seed not necessary to prevent degeneracy; naturalization of

untrue. It is indisputable that he obtained many very excellent new varieties of pears, and that in some of his series the generations came into bearing earlier and earlier, until, in the fifth generation of certain pears, he was able to secure fruit at three years from the seed. This result was thought to be indubitable proof of his proposition that the first fruits from the newest varieties, —that is, from seedlings,—give the quickest and best results. In the first place, it should be said that the failures were much more numerous than the successes. We are told that he had as many as eighty thousand seedlings growing at one time, but the number of good new varieties which he obtained, whilst aggregating perhaps three or four hundred, was much less than one per cent of the total number of efforts. In the second place, Van Mons' methods of cultivation were such as to hasten precocious fruiting. He conceived the idea—which, unfortunately, is prevalent at the present day—that progress in amelioration of fruits is correlated with an enfeebled or refined condition of the tree. His seedlings were planted close together, and they were kept closely headed-in, in order to lessen their exuberant natural vigor. The seeds were also selected from unripe fruits, a process which is now known to result in more or less enfeeblement of the offspring, and consequently in precocity. In the third place, it must be observed that this increasing precocity and amelioration in the succeeding generations are also due to simple selection, and not to any inherent tendency towards perfection in the first fruits of seedlings. Probably no experimenter in plants has ever given the world more excellent proofs of the value of judicious and repeated selection than Van Mons has; and this sin-

perhaps all, variation is the result of the conditions or circumstances in which the organism is placed. Van Mons plainly propounds that the causes of variation are change of soil, of climate, or of temperature; but he assumed, in common with most thinkers of his time, that species are essentially distinct and immutable. Therefore, he could not look upon variation as anything more than an incidental feature in nature, and whatever the causes of this variation may be, they are significant only as they explain how the cultivator may manipulate his plants, not as throwing any light upon the evolution of the vegetable forms which cover the earth. It is reasonable to suppose that the origination of new kinds of plants in the garden is but a local or specialized expression of the means of orgination of all forms of plants, whether in the garden, field, swamps or woods. I am constantly reminded that horticulturists do not apprehend the fundamental principles of the origination of new varieties simply because they refuse to look at the problem broadly, in the light of evolution, and persist in asking for some short-cut or so-called practical method which they can apply in the garden without testing its probably fitness by comparing it with the means which are operative in the uplifting of the vegetable world. Horticulture has always suffered by being cut off from the studies of scientific men, so that it has grown too much into a mere art, which is not conceived to rest upon the very same fundamental laws, so far as plant-breeding is concerned, as have been and are the slow but mighty forces which have been operating throughout the ages.

You are now wanting to ask how it was that Van Mons obtained such useful results if his system were

which he accomplished, seem to place Van Mons in the very front rank of those bolder men who, by the aid of science and philosophy, have contributed to the permanent advancement of the cultivation of plants. Yet one will find that this fame rests more upon a regard for the man and the varieties which he produced, than upon an acceptance of his system. Van Mons was unfortunate in having a theory to prove by means of experiment, rather than in attempting to construct a theory as the result of experiment. He assumed, as most persons do at the present day, that there is some mysterious or hidden means which, if discovered, will enable the operator to produce forthwith and with certainty such plants as he desires. This appears to have been the almost universal type of mind in pre-Darwinian times. Even Loiseleur-Deslongchamps, whilst refusing to accept Van Mons' system, yet writes in 1842 that "we are still ignorant of a positive means by which we can proceed with certainty to produce new fruits of the best quality; it is a mystery of which nature guards the secret." We are now convinced that this attitude of mind is erroneous, and that it is rarely productive of useful results in investigation.

One might think, from the bare statement of his principles, that Van Mons had really anticipated some of the characteristic generalizations of Darwin. One of the most important and inextricable problems now before philosophical naturalists is the source or cause of variations or differences between individuals of any species. There are some thinkers who refer all useful or permanent tendencies towards variation to innate or predisposed inclinations; and there are others, like the Lamarckians and Darwinians, who believe that much, or

the American public by Robert Manning, who received and distributed his new varieties, and who described these novelties in Hovey's "Magazine of Horticulture," and in his own excellent "Book of Fruits," which was published at Salem in 1838. Van Mons' system was first clearly enunciated in this country by the brilliant Andrew Jackson Downing, in the first edition of his "Fruits and Fruit Trees," in 1845; and this outline of the theory has remained unchanged through the many editions and revisions of this work. American horticulturists now know Van Mons only from this historic record in Downing. In England, Van Mons' influence seems to have been comparatively small, owing largely, no doubt, to the overshadowing effect of the contemporaneous work of Thomas Andrew Knight, to whom we shall presently recur. Upon the continent, however, his authority was unbounded. Loiseleur-Deslongchamps, himself a great horticultural authority and yet one who did not subscribe to Van Mons' theories, writes of him: "We have no fear in saying that Van Mons himself accomplished more than had been accomplished since horticulture began; for there had been no labor, so far as I know, that resembles or even approaches it. Pomology owes him the greatest obligations. In fact, it is from his time that we have seen good fruits of all sorts, and principally of pears, multiplied in a most extraordinary manner; and that whatever reproaches one may make against his system (and I do not fear myself to raise objections to it), it is justice to him, which I am glad to grant, to say that there has never been a man who made known such a large number of new and good fruits as Van Mons did." The praise which was everywhere bestowed upon him, and the prodigious labors

name and disseminate such good kinds as might have originated, and there were no books or periodicals, or other public prints, into which accounts of them would be likely to find their way.

Van Mons set out with most commendable vigor to prove his theory, and he continued the work for about half a century. He conceived that the best results were to be obtained by taking the first seeds from wild or spontaneous plants, for the transfer to the new conditions would itself tend to awaken a variation, and the starting point would be a new type or variety. From the first fruits to ripen on any of the seedlings, he saved the seeds and sowed again; and this practice was continued generation after generation with unabated zeal. His experiments were begun in 1785. Thirty-eight years thereafter—in 1823—he had eighty thousand seedling trees in his "Nursery of Fidelity," at Louvain, and he had then begun to distribute cions in many countries. These were sent to America, also, chiefly to the elder Robert Manning, of Massachusetts. These cions were sent out freely under numbers, and were never sold. He gave his attention almost wholly to pears. In 1823, he issued his first catalogue, which contains ten hundred and fifty pears, three-fourths of them bearing names. Of this number, Van Mons himself appears to have originated four hundred and five varieties, two hundred of which were named. Amongst Van Mons' pears are the Diel, Louvain, Frederic of Wurtemburg, Bosc, Colmar, Manning's Elizabeth, and many others which are little known in this country.

The theories and work of Van Mons probably exerted the widest and most profound interest and influence of any horticulturist up to his time. He was introduced to

dislike to handle them, and so on. If we could trace out every case of the disappearance of varieties, we should no doubt find a special and separate reason for each one. On the other hand, we should find various varieties, like the Green Gage plum, the Ribston Pippin apple, Bergamot pear, and others, which have persisted for centuries in undiminished excellence; and everyone must recognize the fact that in the past a variety of apple has rarely gained much prominence until the first or second generation of trees has passed away. It is significant that many of our best fruits are also the oldest, as, for instance, the Baldwin, Greening, Roxbury Russet and King apples, and the Bartlett pear.

There are various other contributory reasons for the founding of this hypothesis of the different behavior of seeds from new and old varieties. It was conceived that new varieties, and particularly young trees of new varieties, are not yet fixed in their characters and are in a state of variation or amelioration. One of the best proofs of this, to Van Mons' mind, seemed to be the experiences of the colonists in America. At first, no famous or notable varieties of fruits appeared. This was conceived to be because the seeds had been taken from old varieties in the mother country; but after a time, through the successive generations of trees coming from these first sowings, there began to appear many excellent varieties of fruits. I am afraid that if this argument could be tested by historical facts, it would be found to rest upon a very slender foundation. The fact that pomologists know of the existence of few meritorious varieties in the early days does not prove that such varieties did not exist; for the fruit plantations were few and scattered, there was little incentive to

10 SUR.

that, on the contrary, the seeds of new varieties give wide variations, which are usually in the direction of improvement. It seems that this particular doctrine—to which we shall now restrict the name "Van Mons' theory,"—was not originally deduced from observation, but was a precognition. "The system of Van Mons upon the means of producing the best fruits for the table is not founded upon experience or practice," writes Loiseleur-Deslongchamps; "it is a preconceived idea of the earlier years of the author, which he has endeavored by every means to verify and develop, and which he made the fond child of his imagination." Yet there was some apparent basis for the generalization. Many of the old varieties of fruits seemed to be failing, whilst the new varieties were strong, healthful and productive. There seems at times to be a tendency for old varieties to deteriorate towards some assumed primitive or inferior type. In fact, we hear everywhere at the present day that varieties wear out with age, and we are cited to the disappearance of once cherished forms for proof of the statement. But we are learning to analyze these instances of wearing out, and we seem to find, in every instance, that there is some specific reason for the disappearance of given varieties, and that their loss is not the result of the operation of a general law. We now know that the Bordeaux mixture is a specific for the so-called running out of the Virgalieu pear, Catawba grape, and other fungus-infested fruits; that change in fashions and demands has stranded varieties of intrinsic merits; that certain varieties have failed because they have been taken into regions to which they were not adapted; that others have passed out because they are difficult to propagate or are wayward growers, so that the nurserymen

2. The causes of variation are a change in soil, climate or temperature.

3. Whenever a natural species of tree produces one or many varieties, these varieties continue to vary always, if they multiply by means of seeds, without ever being able to return to the primitive form.

4. The source of all variation, which is transmissible by sowing, resides in the seeds.

5. The older a variety of fruit or other tree, the less the seedlings vary and the more they tend to return towards the primitive form, without being able ever to reach that state; the younger or newer the variety, the more the seedlings vary, or, as we might say, the better the variations are for the use of man.

Another epitomist expresses Van Mons' theory as follows:

"In sowing the first seeds of a new variety of fruit tree, one obtains trees necessarily variable,—for they cannot escape this condition,—but they are less disposed to return to a wild state than those coming from seeds of an old variety; and as that which tends towards the wild state has less chance of being perfect, as measured by our tastes, than that which remains in the open field of variation [or tends to vary still further], it is, therefore, in the sowing of the first seeds of the most recent varieties of fruit trees that we must hope to find the most perfect varieties for our tastes."

The student will observe that there is little in these statements to challenge controversy, save only the last or fifth law,—that seeds from old varieties tend to give small differences in the seedlings, and that these differences are usually in the direction of inferiority, being reversions toward the primitive type of the species; and

gave up his pharmaceutical interests that he might devote himself wholly to science. He received the degree of Doctor of Medicine from the faculty of Paris in 1800, and he was one of the savants of the Institute of France from its formation. He came into correspondence with Lavoisier, Berthollet, Chaptal, Fourcroy, Volta, and other celebrities of the time. In 1817 Van Mons became professor of physics and chemistry in the University of Louvain, where he remained until the last. He was an expert linguist, a profuse correspondent and a facile writer. He published important works upon chemistry and electricity, many of which exerted wide influence.

This is the man who first propounded a complete system or theory of the philosophy of the origination of varieties of cultivated plants. His system was applied particularly to fruit trees, to which he devoted most of his attention, but it was conceived that the principles which he enunciated are of general application in the vegetable kingdom. This system was expounded in various papers, chiefly in his admirable "Arbres Fruitiers," which was published in 1835 and 1836, in two volumes, but he had conceived the fundamental idea of the propositions as early as his twentieth year, and the system had early become current amongst naturalists. The various characteristic features of the system were brought together and codified by the illustrious Poiteau shortly following Van Mons' death. They are as follows:

1. A natural species of tree does not vary through its seedlings, in the place in which it is born; so long as it remains in its natal place, it reproduces only plants which resemble itself, or, at most, only sub-varieties.

refinement and expansion of the old magic which smote the rock or swung the enchanted wand to disclose to some oracle the secret of the mysteries of nature. It needed the modern analytical mind to grasp the meaning of the forces of nature, to see that there was nothing supernatural, and to pick the kernel of truth from the husk of sophistry. It was in the latter half of this present century that such a mind grasped the entire sweep of organic nature and attempted to discover its meaning in order that the most common man, as well as the oracle, might apprehend the truth and apply it to his own life. This, as I think of it, is the transcendant merit of Darwin. His theories and conclusions may perish, but his life marks an epoch in the habit of thought. All the old notions and traditions, the panorama of nature, the rise of civilization, the destiny of beings and events,—all these are but links or factors in a grand spectacle whose beginning and end are one and whose concerns are every man's.

Van Mons.

With this introduction, you can understand the setting in which the theories of Van Mons and Knight appeared, and we may be able to construct a perspective in which to contemplate them. Jean Baptiste Van Mons was born in Brussels in 1765, and he died in Louvain in 1842. At the age of twenty he became a pharmacist, but at that time the brilliant experiments of Lavoisier and his contemporaries turned the attention of the young student to pure chemistry. With the French occupation of Belgium, he became professor of physics and chemistry in the department of the Dyle, and he

but finding them to be as excellent in quality as described, I saved seed from those first ripe; and by continuing that practice four or five years, they became as early water melons as I ever had."

With this digression, made for the purpose of introducing a worthy and unappreciated compatriot, and to still further illustrate the early development of the ideas associated with the amelioration of plants, we shall now return to the main course of our narrative.

Knight.

Whilst Van Mons was experimenting in Belgium, another bold and prophetic spirit was pursuing similar studies in England. This was Thomas Andrew Knight, who, in the variety, accuracy, significance and candor of his experiments, stands to the present day without a rival amongst horticulturists. Knight was born in 1759, and died in 1838. He completed his academic studies at Oxford, and soon removed into the country where, as he had intended, he spent the remainder of his days. He established himself at Elton, near the paternal home of Downton. He seems to have been brought into agricultural studies chiefly through the efforts of Sir Joseph Banks, who recommended him to the Board of Agriculture as a fit person to answer correspondents' inquiries. He soon became deeply interested in matters relating to the physiology and amelioration of plants, and entered upon investigations which have now come to be considered amongst the classics of botany. These experiments were concerned with the reasons for the upward growth of stems and the downward growth of roots, the motions of the fluids in plants, the physiology of the wood and bark, the motions of tendrils, and the like. In purely horticultural lines, he took hold of the common perplexities of the time and endeavored to solve them. He made studies touching the best methods of cultivating many plants, and he was amongst the first to make really scientific experiments with the growing of plants under glass. He gave particular attention to physiology and methods of grafting, and appears to have been the first to perfect the method of root-grafting which is now in common use. The activity and variety of his interests during the first third of the century attracted the widest attention, and placed him at the very front of English-speaking horticulturists.

But Knight did his greatest work in the direction of ecological studies, through which he desired to discover the best means of improving plants. He took up the vexed questions of the running out of varieties, and he made great efforts to produce new ones. It will thus be seen that the greatest problems which presented themselves to Knight were exactly those which appealed to Van Mons. But the two men were unlike in temper. Van Mons, as we have seen, projected a general theory and then set out to prove it. Knight, on the contrary, began an inquisitive study of nature, and never arrived at a general theory of the amelioration of plants. It is true that he had hypotheses for some of the minor problems which he undertook, but this is essential to any efficient study. An hypothesis is the line to which the axman works. But these hypotheses of Knight's were never of the dogmatic kind, which apply themselves with unvarying assurance to large classes of facts. One of these hypotheses is worth mentioning here, because it is so closely like that held by Van Mons. He was convinced that all varieties of fruit trees "become subject within no very distant period to the debilities and diseases of old age," and that each variety has a "most productive and eligible" epoch, and that this epoch occurs whilst the variety is still young; or, as Knight expresses it, "the most prolific period is that which immediately succeeds the age of puberty." That is, varieties are strongest and most productive early in their existence, and thence tend to gradually fail. He also maintained that the cions of any seedling tree cannot be "made to produce blossoms or fruit till the original tree has attained its age of puberty," and that the longevity and behavior of any variety are intimately connected with the behavior of the original seedling from which the variety had its birth. These ideas were suggested by experiment and observation, for he tells us that he was first convinced "that each variety possessed its greatest value in its middle age," but certain experiments led him to change his views. This dogmatic hypothesis of the duration of varieties was widely repeated, but it appears, fortunately, never to have exerted great influence, and it is so insignificent in comparison with Knight's greater work that we need not dwell further upon it.

Van Mons was the first horticulturist to boldly exemplify and demonstrate the value of the great principle of repeated selection in the origination of varieties. Knight was the first to show the value of crossing for the same purpose. Kœlreuter, at the middle of the last century, had made many suggestive experiments in the crossing of plants, but his studies were concerned with the immediate means and effects of the operation. Sprengel, at the close of the century, had observed some of the wonderful adaptations of flowers to insects, but he did not perceive the meaning of these adaptations to the progress of the vegetable world. Knight was the first to directly undertake the improvement of plants by means of crossing. "New varieties of every species of fruit will generally be better obtained," he writes in 1806, "by introducing the farina of one variety of fruit into the blossom of another, than by propagating any from a single kind." He made experiments in crossing which, for extent, variety and importance, would do great credit to any experimenter of the present day, even after we have obtained much definite knowledge of the results of cross-breeding. The varieties of fruits which he raised, largely by means of crossing, were many and important. Amongst those which American horticulturists know are Elton and Black Eagle cherries, Ickworth Impératrice plum and Downton nectarine. He originated many varieties of potatoes, and several of peas, cabbages, pears, strawberries and apples.

The transcendent merit of Knight's studies and experiments lies, however, in the fact that he made them contributions to our knowledge of the general forces and processes of nature, rather than to restrict them to a special application to horticulture. He was one of the pioneers of that inductive type of experiment which reached such a high level in the work of Darwin, and which has come to be a passion in our recent life. In other words, he was a philosopher. In the closing year of the last century, he hinted at the fact that nature employs intrabreeding for the purpose of improving plants and animals; he demonstrated the value of crossing as a means of producing new forms; and he propounded the idea, which is now very generally accepted, that the leading cause of variation, at least in plants, is an excess or modification of food supply.

Retrospect.

Such, then, are the leading features of the attitude of two great horticultural philosophers to the history of the ideas respecting the breeding of plants. The work of these men derives its chief value when it is interpreted by means of the work of Darwin and his successors. We now understand the fundamental nature of cultivated varieties, and we are able to specify many of the reasons why they come and go. The key to the entire subject lies in two propositions, which may be stated as follows:

First. Variation, or the truth that no two living things are alike, is the most important fact in organic nature. This variation is important because we know that it is the starting-point for the making of greater differences.

Second. Variation may be augmented by constantly propagating from the individuals possessing the most pronounced characteristics.

These two facts represent the sum total of the forces with which man has worked from the beginning for the improving of plants and animals. Even barbarians practice selection in the growing of their plants. Any being possessed of the faculty of choice and capable of planting seeds must habitually and necessarily choose from those plants which suit him best. The most ignorant workman in our fields does the same. This unconscious choice of parents, operating slowly during a very long period of time, had so profoundly modified plants and animals that when the descriptive naturalists appeared last century, they were unable to determine the origin of many of these domestic forms. Even at the present day, with all our study of nature and our inquisitive searching into the uttermost parts of the earth, there are more than a hundred domestic species of which we do not positively know the aboriginal forms. The overwhelming majority of ameliorated forms of plants have appeared in just this way,—as the result of half-conscious or even unconscious and unrecorded efforts. The definite breeding of domestic animals began about the middle of last century with Robert Bakewell, and the breeding of plants may be said to have begun with Van Mons and Knight. Even at the present day, the phenomenal amelioration of the chrysanthemum, rose, potato, and other plants has been, for the most part, undirected. They have developed rapidly because variation has been so rapid and so marked.

You now ask me why variation has been so marked of recent years. The question is readily answered: It is because the conditions under which plants have been grown are so varied. Better cultivation, greater attention to training and feeding, the growing of plants in many and unlike regions and soils and local conditions, the prodigal exchange of seeds and plants between dealers and buyers, crossing,—all these are the agents which tend to make plants more and more various and unlike. Selection of these variations, by means of which they have been intensified and augmented, has also been more universal and more thorough. The greater the number of persons who grow plants, the more diverse are the ideals of selection; and the more variable plants are, the more plastic they are in the hands of the breeder. These new forms have no limit of duration. They do not wear out. But as often as they are grown in new conditions and by different persons, they again vary and are again the subjects of selection. So there is a constant shifting of forms, but the longevity of any form depends, not upon any predestined limitations, but upon the accident of the conditions under which it is grown and bred. The same forces which have brought domestic plants and animals to their present condition, and which are largely responsible for the general uplift of the vegetable kingdom from the beginning, are the ones which, variously modified and refined, must carry the domestic flora and fauna on to the end. What, then, is the mystery of plant-breeding? Only this: Good care, varying circumstances, judicious selection for what you want!

VI.

SOME OF THE BEARINGS OF THE EVOLUTION-TEACHING UPON PLANT-CULTIVATION.[1]

THIS century will be known in history as an epoch in which the race came to a turning-point in its habit of contemplating the origin and destiny of itself and of the material universe. Various dominant philosophies had taught, with more or less steadfastness, that man is in kind wholly and eternally distinct from organic nature, that nature, therefore, possesses only an incidental or extrinsic interest to the race, and that the origin of organic forms is beyond the domain, or at least outside the concern, of the human intellect. With little knowledge of the external world and little incentive to inquire into it, men were content to ascribe the origin of a given object to a summary creation which was without distinct occasion or purpose. The result of this habit of thought was to depreciate the importance of remote events and to detach the present generation, so far as its organic constitution is concerned, from preceding generations, and even, also, from the effects of its environments. Phenomena were not studied with reference to their antecedents. Man, standing apart from nature, devoted his speculative philosophy to himself, and

---

[1] Address before the State Board of Agriculture, Trenton, N. J., Jan. 16, 1895. Printed in Twenty-second Annual Report of the State Board of Agriculture, 177–188.

thereby arrived at those metaphysical absurdities which are now amongst the curiosities of history. There had appeared at various times, however, revolts against this general body of opinion, and upon more than one occasion men had come to believe more or less dimly in some kind of a progressive movement in which both nature and man were in some way concerned. This belief was even known to the Greeks. The doctrine of the special or particular creation of the forms of life had been held with fierce tenacity in later times, and had become embodied in the forms of religious thought. Yet, at the opening of our century, there had accumulated a considerable body of belief in the spontaneous or natural origin of forms of life, and consequently in the present rejuvenescence or progressive tendency in nature. This movement has matured in our own time, and it has come to be known as evolution. I have said this much by way of introduction for the purpose of emphasizing two facts,—that this habit of thought, which is now well-nigh universal, is itself a gradual evolution from the centuries, and that to hold this belief does not necessarily imply assent to any particular dogma either of religion or science.

I have said that there was belief in evolution at the opening of the century. It was mostly confined to naturalists, especially to those under French influence. Amongst those who most clearly perceived it were gardeners or garden-authors, who, observing the wonderful transformations of plants under cultivation, were led to consider that whole groups of plants must have had a common origin. Thus Duchesne, in 1766, concluded that all the species of strawberries must have sprung from the ever-bearing strawberry of Europe. Gallesio, in 1811, presented an elaborate chart of the development of the orange tribe, "made according to the principles of the new theory of the reproduction of plants;" and at this time Thomas Andrew Knight had made some of his boldest statements, in reality anticipating some of the generalizations of Darwin. I am particular to call attention to this line of facts, because I am convinced that, neither in presenting the history of evolution nor in elucidating contemporaneous discussions, have most modern philosophical writers given adequate attention to horticultural literature and practice. The very fact that garden-plants are so modified and mixed that nearly every botanist avoids the systematic study of them, is proof enough that they afford the very materials in which to study the transformation of species.

This great movement or body of thought, originating in contemplation of natural or organic science, has now extended itself to every field of human thought and industry; and every teacher or investigator, even though he opposes the doctrine of the evolution of organic forms, now approaches his subject from the standpoint of its origin and its relation to all cognate questions. The present conditions of nature and, as well, of human institutions, are seen to have been the product of a gradual growth or evolution, and it is apparent that they must continue to change and develop for all time. The conception of the uniformity of the unfolding of this great law of growth in everything of which we have cognizance, has established a new philosophy, of which the core is monism, or the essential oneness of all things. The discussion of evolution, therefore, should no longer be confined to naturalists, for inasmuch as it concerns every enlightened person, its various theories and applications should be tested, in a candid spirit, by persons in every walk of life. Every enlightened person is in some degree an evolutionist, and every occupation is to some extent affected by the philosophy.

It is not my purpose at this time to enter into any discussion of the theories of evolution, but rather to specify some of the bolder directions in which they are capable of explaining or modifying the practices of the farmer, more particularly of the horticulturist. Leaving aside the specific inter-relations of evolution and horticulture, and ignoring the technicalities, let us take a broad sweep of the subject, and endeavor to discover those chief fundamental elements upon which the inquiring mind can permanently rest. I shall need to say something at the outset, however, of the shape in which these theories have formulated themselves in the minds of naturalists. That there is an evolution or progression of forms, one giving rise to another, is an assumption no longer doubted by biologists, and I shall, therefore, present no arguments in support of the general hypothesis. In the words of Haeckel, "The whole literature of modern biology, the whole of our present zoölogy and botany, morphology and physiology, anthropology and psychology, are pervaded and fertilized by the theory of descent." The difficulties in the hypothesis all turn upon the means or agencies which may be conceived to have brought about this evolution. For our purpose we may divide the philosophers of organic evolution into two classes,—those who believe that the environment, or conditions in which animals and plants live, directly modify the organisms from generation to generation; and those who conceive that immediate effects of environment have no permanent effect upon the species, but that all modifications are brought about through a union of the sexes. Amongst the leading philosophers who hold to the direct permanent transforming effect of environment are Lamarck and Darwin, but these writers differ as to the exact method by which this environment operates upon the animal or plant. Lamarck supposes that the environment or circumstances in which the organism lives,—as climates, food-supply, struggle for existence, care exercised by man, and the like,—cause the organism to acquire new habits or functions to adapt itself to these circumstances. The organism needs to use one part more and another part less in the constant changes in the physical conditions in which it lives, and the effects of this change or modification of function become hereditary. It is evident that this adaptation of the organism to the environment is largely an active one on the part of the organism, and that the Lamarckian theory is better adapted to an application to animals than to plants.

Darwin, on the other hand, supposed that the environments or "changed conditions of life" are themselves the causes of variations or modifications in the organism, and that those forms which are best adapted to these environments tend to live and to perpetuate their kind, and those which are least adapted to the environments tend to disappear. This is the well-known hypothesis of natural selection or survival of the fittest. It is evident that this survival of the fittest is largely a passive one upon the part of the organism, and that the Darwinian theory is better adapted to an application to plants than to animals.

It will be seen from the above outline that both Lamarckism and Darwinism teach that those characters or modifications which are acquired from the direct or indirect effects of environment in the lifetime of the individual may become hereditary.

In recent years, however, it has been strenuously denied that any such incidental or adaptive characters can be hereditary, and that all new forms come as a result of sexual union. This is the hypothesis of Weismann; but, inasmuch as Weismann's conception supposes that evolution takes place as a result of natural selection or survival of the fittest amongst the forms so originating, his theory is generally known as Neo-Darwinism, or the new Darwinism. The fundamental concepts of Weismann are too recondite for presentation here, but I have already said enough, I think, to bring the general trend of the three leading hypotheses of evolution before your minds. (Consult Essay II.)

The chief points in these hypotheses, it will be noticed, are the means of accounting for the origin of variations, and it is upon this general question that philosophical naturalists are at present most divided. It is plain that there can be no evolution without variations or initial differences between individuals; and here is the first and most important direct lesson which the evolution theories bring to the agriculturist,—the importance of individual differences and the means of securing them. You all know that no two plants are alike. Why?

It is not doubted, even by the adherents of Weismann, that environment may cause immediate variation of organisms, but these writers declare that such variations are not transmitted, that is, that they are lost with the death of the individual in which they occur. It is only when any variation is a part of the germ or sex elements, according to Weismann's view, that it becomes hereditary. It is no doubt true that the primary reason for the existence of sex in animals and plants is that offspring may be constantly re-invigorated and diversified by the union of two unlike individuals; for if nothing were to be desired but simple reproduction, the ancestral method of cell-division and bud-propagation would no doubt have been perpetuated, inasmuch as it is a much more economical method than sex-reproduction. But whilst philosophers accept Weismann's assumption that sex has come about for the purpose of imparting variability to the offspring, the contrary proposition,—that all permanent variation is a result of sexual union,—is palpably untrue. It is disproved in many ways, but chiefly by the facts that hosts of fungi are permanently asexual; and that every branch of a tree is really an individual, and is unlike all other branches, the same as any distinct plant is unlike all other plants,—a fact familiar to all careful nurserymen, for they know that the value of a fruit tree depends very much upon what part of the original or cion-bearing tree the cion was borne. (Compare Essay III.)

These three facts, then, I wish to impress upon you: First, that every plant is unlike every other plant; second, that every branch is unlike every other branch in some character of growth, shape, character of flowers or fruit, or the like; and third, that many of these variations may and do originate because of the conditions in which the plants grow. Here, then, is the fundamental source, so far as the horticulturist is concerned, of the evolution of new varieties, and even of the possibility of cultivating plants at all. The expert cultivator must come to look at every plant, and even at every part of it, as capable of producing a new form or variety of promise, if once the conditions under which it grows are made to vary in given or ascertained directions, and if he determines the means by which he can "fix" the variations or make them to become somewhat permanent, or can even augment or "improve" the initial divergence; and he should know, also, that it is impossible to successfully submit a plant taken from the wild to the conditions of cultivation unless the plant adapts itself to the new conditions by means of variation. In a word, the whole structure of the cultivation of plants and, therefore, of agriculture, is impossible without variation and evolution.

Now, let us endeavor to put ourselves in nature's place, if such a conception is possible, and to briefly follow an outline of her methods with plants. We shall find that variation is largely the result, so far as we can see, of excess of food-supply. The seedsman knows that heavy lands make his seed-crops "break" into non-typical forms, and he therefore prefers, for most plants, a soil not very rich in nitrogen or growth-production. Heavy soils make the dwarf peas "viney," and bud-sports of curious leaves and flowers are wont to appear upon over-vigorous shoots. In short, the whole philosophy of the amelioration of plants rests upon excess of food-supply; for what other object have tillage, irrigation, fertilizing of the land, thinning of the plants, pruning, and thinning of the fruit, but to supply more food to the plants or to the parts which remain? Darwin has clearly shown that great numbers of the variations in nature come as the result of this general law,—the plant which gets the better of its fellows generally does so because it has appropriated the food or air or sunlight for which the others were also contending. Man's cultivation is, fundamentally, the same as nature's. He has devised means to augment or emphasize the processes, but the ultimate aims of both are to increase the food; and all this increase beyond the mere point of sustaining the plant in the condition in which man found it goes into the production of variation in one form or another,—for mere increase in bigness is itself a most important departure from the type, and it is usually the primary result of domestication.

I believe that the second important cause of variation amongst domestic plants is the effects of change of climate. It is known that every different or peculiar climate has its own type of plants, showing that, in some way, there has come to be a modification or adaptation to the environment. The same process of adaptation begins with domesticated plants the moment man takes them to climates differing from that in which he found them. These changes are, chiefly, reduction of stature and shortening of form when the transfer is to shorter, colder seasons; increase in intensity of colors of flowers and fruits, and often of saccharine contents, in the north; the diminution of evaporating surface,—of leaves and stems,—in dry climates; the tendency to develop aromatic qualities in arid regions; the shortening or lengthening of habitual periods of growth; the increased or decreased sensitiveness to the progress of the seasons by which plants bloom and expand their leaves relatively earlier in the north and later in the south; the modification of constitution by which plants become hardier or tenderer; the tendency of plants to become annuals or to develop a resting period in regions of severe winters or long dry seasons (see Essay I.); and the development of thickened parts, as tubers and bulbs, in regions of long-enforced rest.

In short, the theories of evolution teach that the keynote of progression, either in untamed nature or in the garden, is adaptation to environment. The selection of varieties to suit one's soil and climate and other conditions, is really a fundamental requisite to success in horticulture; and, if this is true, there must be a constantly-increasing tendency for every locality and every commercial demand to develop a variety of its own. So, instead of coming nearer to the perfect all-round variety in any fruit, we are continually getting farther away from it, for what is perfection for one place may be imperfection, or even failure, for another place. Varieties are not distinct entities, which can be recommended to growers like so many machines or implements, but they are complex combinations of various attributes, so nicely adjusted that every change of conditions is likely to disengage the composition, and often so intangible, in comparison with others, that the nicest description cannot distinguish them.

I must now make an application of these remarks to the testing of varieties by experiment stations, for this is a subject in which every horticulturist is vitally interested. What varieties shall I plant? This and similar questions are always asked of the experimenter, and people seem to think that it is one of the simplest questions to answer. At all events, it is the universal impression that the experiment station officer, of all others, should be able to answer it definitely. He has the facilities and the time for making tests, and it seems, upon the face of it, that he should have exact knowledge of the merits of all novelties. Yet there are so many difficulties and uncertainties pertaining to the so-called testing of varieties that the results often possess nothing of permanent value; and there are certain reasons why the experimenter, if he derives his knowledge wholly from his own tests, is less competent to pronounce upon the merits of novelties than the grower is himself.

What constitutes a test of a variety? Simply this: Obtaining exact knowledge as to whether the variety is distinct from others and whether it is useful for certain places or purposes. It would seem to be simple enough to obtain such knowledge as this; and yet it supposes that the experimenter knows all existing varieties—which no one does or can—and that he is equally expert in judging the merits of any and all plants which may be brought to him, from strawberries to chrysanthemums, and from celery to apples. But there are other difficulties, which inhere in the subject itself. To test a variety for any purpose, it is necessary to actually grow it and use it for that purpose. The chief end of most varieties is for the market, but the experiment station cannot grow varieties for commercial market. One crate or even one shipment does not test the shipping qualities of a variety, for these qualities vary with the season, the weather, the methods of transportation, and with the different pickings of the same variety; and it is, therefore, impossible to give any adequate test to twenty or thirty or even more varieties of any one fruit, let alone the many kinds of fruits and other products with which the experimenter is supposed to deal. It is said that one can judge from the looks and behavior of a variety if it will be a good shipper, but I must remind my reader that this short-cut method of arriving at conclusions is one reason why so many disappointing varieties are introduced. And besides this, the variety may behave differently in different seasons, and in every various soil and treatment. The emphatic impression of this fact upon my mind was the only good result which came of my first test of strawberries. Over forty varieties were grown, and I made the most conscientious attempt not only to make notes upon productiveness and behavior, but to personally eat every kind. I ate across the patch north and south, east and west, backwards and forwards. The results of the whole test were duly published; whereupon a neighbor three miles away said it might all be very well, but the varieties did not behave that way with him!

What the farmer wants to know is the value of the variety upon his place, not upon the experiment station farm, and he is the only person who can find it out. To thoroughly test a variety is to introduce it. When it is once introduced, the general consensus of opinion of men who actually grow it for the purposes for which it is desired, forms the best and the only criterion of its value. Even then there may be farms, as every horticulturist knows, upon which a variety which is generally condemned may succeed; and the variety is then not a failure. Now, the discovering of this consensus of opinion, and publishing it, is just the work which the experiment station can perform when it desires to spread information of varieties. The standard of actual sales in commercial plantations is the only correct one for market fruits, and this is to be had only from farmers themselves. A series of tabulated reports from growers who are capable judges of particular fruits is competent to give reliable information of varieties. If, in connection with such reports, the experimenter can add his own experience, very much will be gained; and he often has the great advantage of receiving varieties before they are put upon the general market. The greater use he makes of the reports of others, the more valuable does his own variety patch become as a means of study and comparison.

But there is another feature of this adaptation of varieties to the conditions in which they are desired to be grown, which I wish to bring to your attention. Thus far, I have spoken of such adaptations as are the necessary means of securing good or profitable crops; but if these changes in the plant, by means of which it becomes fitted to every new condition, are constantly taking place, why is not the modification of the conditions of life the readiest means of securing new varieties? This is one of the sources of new plants or varieties, particularly of those which, like the garden vegetables, are propagated by seeds. One variety gradually passes or varies into another one, and the modification is generally so slow that it is wholly unobserved. Many of our garden vegetables have thus grown away from their original types, although they still retain the original name. The Trophy tomato is probably wholly lost to cultivation, the variety now passing under this name being an "improvement" upon the old type in shape and other features. (Essay XXX.) The fact that varieties are constantly changing in the divers localities in which they are grown, renders exact descriptions of them impossible. Who can describe the Astrachan apple so that it may be always distinguished from its fellows? Observe, if you will, how the same apple varies,—tending to be solid-fleshed and fine-grained, with uniform bright coloring, in northern New England and Canada, coarse-grained and splashy-striped on the Plains, and oblong on the Pacific slope. For all practical purposes, the Baldwin is a distinct variety in each great geographical apple region of the country; and if one is to grow it he should secure trees which are propagated from the type which has developed in his own area.

We are always thinking that the evolution of cultivated plants takes place by fits and starts, but the better part of it proceeds from the gradual unfolding of one variety into another, the present arising from the past under the invariable impulse of a fundamental law of adaptation. Consider, for a moment, that nearly every species of fruit has its one leading variety,—the Baldwin amongst apples, Crawford amongst peaches, Bartlett amongst pears, Concord amongst grapes, Wilson amongst strawberries. These types have sufficient elasticity of constitution to enable them to adapt themselves to many conditions. They are plastic, progressive varieties; and even though many other varieties have superior merits in quality or other attributes, they cannot displace those of cosmopolitan adaptabilities. There are probably other varieties in each of these classes of fruits which possess equal elasticity, but these leading forms have got the start, and are thereby difficult of dislodgment. Taken altogether, the Wilson is evidently still the most popular strawberry in the north. It is strange that, amongst all the new varieties, there are none which are able to supplant it. It is probable, however, that the variety which we now grow as the Wilson is not identical with the original stock. It would be strange if it were so. In hundreds of generations of propagations, many of the variations induced by soil and methods of cultivation are likely to be perpetuated. Careful propagators select young plants from those portions of the plantation which produce what they consider to be the ideal berry, but as no two propagators have the same ideal berry in mind, there must arise a series of divergences in the type. It is certain that there are different strains of Wilson in cultivation, as there are different strains of the Crawford peach; and it is no doubt this very diversity in the variety which adapts it so readily to many soils and uses. I often wonder if the original type of the Wilson, were it to be again introduced, would find so much favor as its modern progeny does. No doubt every decade sees a new type of Wilson strawberry.

Thus all varieties of cultivated plants are moving onward with unbroken front, filling in the unoccupied places here and there, spreading into new territory by virtue of new characters, some dropping out entirely in the eternal shuffle for place and life. And because we have observed the genealogy and have kept one name for the parent and all its descendants, we have never thought to question the identity of all the generations. The Green Gage of to-day is not like the Green Gage of two centuries ago simply because the names are the same. Nature is a congeries of chains, one link giving rise to another under the operation of eternal and inexorable law; and when some of the links die and pass away we notice the breaks, in our retrospect, and conceive that evolution has been capricious. But the closer we study the laws of organic life the more certain we are that all present forms are the gradual outcome of uniform and antecedent causes; and I like to think of cultivation and cultivated plants as agent and objects which are similarly expanding through the passing of time. There cannot be one philosophy for untamed nature and another for tamed nature.

But you want some summary means of producing new varieties. You want varieties quickly, and they must be distinct. You turn at once to hybridization. You must remember, however, that hybrid varieties have not been wrought out with the hammer and the anvil of adaptation, but have been cast forthwith from a mould of conventional pattern. Hybridization is normally rare. Nature rarely does things by jumps. There is no proof that she ever made a species or a potent form in this way. But she mildly crosses one species with itself, and out of the slightly variable offspring selects those which are best adapted to the place in which they live, and uses them for the subjects of another congenial cross; and so the family marches on from generation to generation, each step slow but each one sure. If man makes hybrids, he must generally propagate them by buds, or parts other than seeds, to keep them "true," as in the few hybrid grapes, pears, raspberries and blackberries which we have and in various hybrid ornamental plants; and as a rule these varieties are less adapted to wide ranges of conditions than are those which spring from legitimate sources. Change of seed and crossing between the different stocks are far more important agencies of the evolution of our field crops than hybridization or other forced effects.

Nature, then, gives the variations. Man is ordinarily only a secondary agent in their production. We shall find that in many of those groups of plants in

12 SUR.

which man has done the most to modify and improve, natural forces have been guiding the human ingenuity, and the operator has fallen unconsciously into the very methods which nature had chosen for the same conditions. We pride ourselves upon the increasing number of varieties of fruits of American origin, and we have noticed how they differ from their foreign parents; but we have not thought that it is the American environments which have been at the bottom of the evolution. Man's greatest power, I had almost said his only one, is selection. He may choose the plant which suits him and propagate it. This has been going on half unconsciously for centuries, and this gradual evolution is no doubt the cause of the permanence of many of the types or races of cultivated plants. Intelligent selection, having in mind an ideal form, is man's nearest approach to the Creator in his dealings with the organic world. This has been the greatest force in the wonderful upbuilding of our cultivated flora. "The key," says Darwin, "is man's power of accumulative selection: nature gives successive variations; man adds them up in certain directions useful to him."

There is dispute among scientific men as to the adequacy of natural selection—which is the means so successfully imitated by man—as a method of evolution of the organic world. There are, no doubt, other forces at work, and none of the forces operate equally in all groups of organisms. For plants, I am convinced that natural selection is the chief agent of progression or evolution, once the initial differences given, and for the same reasons I consider human selection to be the one great force in the improvement of cultivated plants. All theories of evolution seem to teach us that the final result of our domestication of plants will come as a result of unobtrusive forces working slowly through the years, not from summary and brilliant creations; and yet this simple truth does not seem to be apprehended by the great body of plantsmen.

This, then, is the main thought which I wish to bring you: that the theories of evolution explain the possibility of the very existence of cultivation itself; that they discourage all sudden and spasmodic attempts at the amelioration of the vegetable kingdom; and that they impress upon us with overwhelming force the importance of those slow and silent processes of adaptation and selection which have been operating throughout all time.

VII.

WHY HAVE OUR ENEMIES INCREASED?[1]

THE burden of complaint among horticulturists now seems to be the destruction and annoyance wrought by insect and fungous enemies. We are all but overwhelmed with the numbers and kinds of our foes, and no sooner do the experimenters learn how to combat one nuisance than another comes upon us. Our fathers tell us of orchards and gardens which were not thus beset upon all sides, and we are led to wonder why it is that these later days are so pregnant of trouble; but we are obliged to give such vigilant attention to fighting these hordes that we afford little thought upon the reasons for their existence. If we can discover the reasons why they appear in ever-increasing variety, we shall be able to prognosticate something for the future; we can learn the natural history of the invasions, so to speak, and we may even be aided in our immediate warfare against them.

At the outset, I may be allowed to say that there can be no doubt of this increase in insect and fungous enemies in any given region. There are men before me who remember the time when they knew no apple-worms, curculios, cabbage-worms, currant-worms, potato-beetles, and a host of lesser worthies; they had

---

[1] Read before the Indiana Horticultural Society, at Indianapolis, December 6, 1892. Printed in Transactions of the Society for that year (thirty-second annual meeting), pp. 62-68.

never heard of apple-scab, black-rot, downy-mildew, leaf-blight, and a score of other plagues which now haunt the orchards by day and the dreams by night. In those blessed days, if the potatoes rotted it was laid to the moon, and that was the end of it. It is strange that so innocent a person as the-man-in-the-moon should have had so many hard things said against him!

Now, this whole problem of the increase of certain kinds of insects and fungi belongs entirely to the interrelations of natural objects,—to insects and plants and animals, and even man himself. If all natural forces and conditions were always equal and unvarying, there would be stability in all forms of life; but just so soon as pressure is removed in any direction do all animals and plants, directly or indirectly and in varying degrees, attempt to fill the breach. It is perfectly apparent, upon a moment's thought, that this pressure exists. The earth is now covered with plants and animals. There is not room for many more. The world is not big enough to hold all the possible immediate offspring of the animals and plants now living upon it. One of the large trees in this city will bear enough seeds in one year to make Indianapolis a forest. So the greater part of the potential offspring of any generation of living objects is destined either not to start into independent growth or to die long before maturity. One can not put ten cats in a bag that will hold but nine, and if there is a hole in the bag every cat will scramble for it. There is something like an equilibrium in any perfectly wild region; the place may be said to be full. But if man cuts off the forest or destroys the animals, other plants and animals endeavor to occupy the vacant places. Weeds and undergrowth come up thickly in the new clearing and bluebirds and sparrows build where the woods' birds once lived. But these disturbances have innumerable secondary and remote influences, which grow fainter as they recede, like the ripples which follow the casting of a stone. The felling of the trees not only destroys the forest, but destroys the food upon which certain animals live, and these animals may have been the food of other animals, which must now decrease, and this will allow the prey of these latter animals to increase, and so the changes run on and on until lost in complexity. Man is now the most disturbing element upon the face of the earth. Wherever he goes, a train of modifications and complications follows. We need not be surprised, therefore, at Wallace's observation that the more old maids the heavier the clover-seed crop, for the maids protect the cats which destroy the mice which rob the nests of the bumble bees which pollinate the flowers.

We are now prepared to admit that this whole question of enemy and friend is a relative one. It does not depend upon right and wrong, but simply upon our own relationship to the given animals and plants. An insect which eats our potatoes is an enemy because we want the potatoes, too; but the insect has as much right to the potatoes as we have. He is pressed by the common necessity of maintaining himself, and there is every evidence that the potato was made as much for the insect as for human kind. Dame Nature is quite as much interested in the insect as in the man. "What a pretty bug!" she exclaims; "send him over to Smith's potato patch." But a bug which eats this insect is beneficial; that is, he is beneficial to man, not to the other insect. Thus everything in nature is a benefit to something and an injury to something: and every time that conditions of life are modified, the relationships readjust themselves.

Cultivation is a powerfully disturbing factor in nature. It affects the relationships of depredaceous insects and parasitic fungi to man chiefly in the following ways:

1. *Cultivation induces change of habit in the insects and fungi.* Animals do not live and plants do not grow where they most desire to live and grow, but where they are allowed to live; and all organisms are susceptible to new enticements or new advantages. A cultivated plant may be a more attractive source of food to an insect than the wild plants upon which it has been forced to live, or it may be a more congenial host to a fungus. In such cases, the organism is likely to abandon its old habits and to spread into cultivated grounds. Or, man may destroy the natural food-plants or host-plants, and the organism is obliged to seek other food, and it is likely to take that which is most nearly like its habitual food, and which is most abundant. We are always liable, therefore, to have insects and diseases transferred to the orchard from our wild crabs and plums. The apple maggot, which lived once upon wild thorn apples, began to attack cultivated apples in New England some thirty years ago, and has now spread westward to the Mississippi Valley. But this same species of insect also occurs in a wild state in this same western region, but it did not so early attack apples here, if, in fact, it has done so to the present day. It is not possible to discover why it

attacked apples in Massachusetts, Connecticut and New York, and not in Illinois; but it may have been due to the lessening number of thorns and the increasing number of apple orchards in the east as compared with the west. In 1841, when Harris made his report upon the injurious insects of Massachusetts, a certain insect known as *Chrysobothris femorata* was briefly described as "resting upon or flying around the trunks of white oak trees and recently cut timber of the same kind of wood;" and he had "repeatedly taken it upon and under the bark of peach trees, also." This insect is now known, however, as the flat-headed apple-tree borer, and Saunders, in his "Insects Injurious to Fruits," in 1883, says nothing about its attacking oaks, but declares it to be "a most formidable enemy to apple culture," and says that "it attacks also the pear, the plum, and sometimes the peach." A certain insect is known in the United States as the buffalo carpet-beetle, because its chief food is carpets and similar fabrics, but in Europe it is not known as a carpet pest, it being found upon a wild plant known as figwort, and in furs and leather articles. The insect changed its habit upon importation into America some twenty years ago. An early naturalist traveling in Colorado found a striped beetle feeding upon wild solanums or nightshades. The insect came to be in demand among collectors, and it is said that handsome prices were paid for specimens for museums. In the course of time the settlers grew potatoes in Colorado, and the insect took a fancy to them and spread rapidly. It is now known as the Colorado potato-beetle. The first attacks were noticed about thirty years ago, but now the insect is a serious pest wherever potatoes are grown in quantity. These are but a few isolated examples out of many which might be cited to show that insects take on new habits when new opportunities arise or when necessity compels. The same thing is true, also, of fungi, but as these do not possess the power of intelligent choice and spontaneous movement, the adaptations are slower than in insects.

2. *Cultivation induces change of habit in the host-plant.* Cultivated plants are eminently variable; and it is apparent, and I believe probable, that varieties may themselves change with age or modification of environment to be congenial to organisms which they once more or less completely repelled. I am inclined to believe that some of the so-called blight-proof and rust-proof varieties now and then advertised are really measurably resistant, but after a time may become amenable to attack.

3. *Cultivation presents large numbers of food- or host-plants in continuous areas.* "It is no doubt true that insects and fungi spread more rapidly than formerly, because of the greater number and continuity of orchards, just as contagious diseases spread faster in cities than in the country. In the small and isolated orchards of former days fungi and insects were confined within closer areas. This phenomenon of rapid distribution, due to greater extent of host-plants, may be termed *communal intensity*."* The more the fuel the hotter the fire. Nothing so stimulates the distribution and development of organic objects as an abundant or excessive food supply. The potato bug could not contain himself when he discovered the great potato fields.

---

*Bailey, Am. Gard. xi. 682. Editorial; (1890.)

Dr. Lintner has written pointedly upon this subject:*
"The excessive ravages of insects in the United States
are largely owing to the cultivation of their food-plants
in extended areas. Two hundred years ago not even
the wild crab, the earliest representative of the apple,
existed in this country, and consequently there were no
apple insects. Later, when a few apple trees became
the adjunct of the simple homes of the early settlers,
those of our insects to which they offered more desirable
food than that on which they had previously subsisted
were obliged to wing their way often for many miles in
search of a tree upon which to deposit their eggs. If
birds were then abundant, how few of the insects could
accomplish such extended flights! But in the apple
orchards of the present day—some of them spreading
in almost unbroken mass of foliage over hundreds of
acres—our numerous apple insects may find the thrifty
root, the vigorous trunk, the succulent twig, the tender
bud, the juicy leaf, the fragrant blossom, and the crisp
fruit spread out before them in broad array, as if it
were a special offering to insect voracity, or a banquet
purposely extending an irresistible invitation. * * *
Careful cultivation has made it the best of its kind;
appetite is stimulated; development is hastened; broods
are increased in number; individuals are multiplied
beyond the conservation of parasitic destruction; facilities of distribution are afforded with hardly a proper
exercise of locomotive organs, and when these almost
useless members have become aborted, as in the wing-
less females of the bark-louse and the canker-worms,
the interlocking branches afford convenient passage

*First Rep. State Entom. N. Y. (1882), 10.

from tree to tree." These remarks will enable us to understand, in part, the wonderful spread of the apple-scab and leaf-blights in recent years. We, as horticulturists, are every year planting new invitations to insect and fungous attacks. If we take this extra risk, we must certainly prepare ourselves to meet it. Our fathers' weapons can not avail against the horde of invaders which we are inviting to our doors. They are coming up out of the woods and the swamps and the bare fields to regale themselves at the banquet which we have spread.

4. *Cultivation affords places of less struggle than organisms are forced to occupy under normal conditions.* Man disturbs the equilibrium or removes the pressure in some direction, and a multitude is waiting to spring into the void. The great potato fields not only provided food, but there were few other insects to dispute the possession of them; the Colorado solanum beetle saw his opportunity, and improved it. He has been a successful bug. This release of the natural tension, which cultivation affords, is to my mind the most potent factor in the increase of our little foes. Dr. Lintner declares that "nowhere else are insect injuries so serious as in the United States," and he attributes the fact to three causes,—the importation of injurious insects, the increased destructiveness of introduced insects, and the large areas devoted to special crops. The last factor we have already discussed. It is not strange that, with all the commerce with foreign countries, various insects and fungi and plants should be introduced, but it does seem strange that the introduced species should become so seriously noxious, for not only do many of our serious insect and fungous

pests come from Europe, but most of our familiar weeds come from that country also. Is it possible that Old World species are inherently more vicious than our own? I think not. The species of the two countries probably possess no constant differences in disposition. They are only what their environments make them to be. Perhaps over half of our plant diseases and noxious insects are of Old World origin, but the indigenous species are equally as assiduous and ambitious. Among native insects we number such species as the potato-beetle, the round-headed and flat-headed apple-tree borers, the grasshoppers and Rocky Mountain locusts, the plant-lice, rose-chafer, the army-worm and the chinch-bug. Among plant diseases there are the black-rot and downy-mildew of the grape, plum-knot, pear-blight and peach-yellows. These are no inconsiderable enemies.

The nativity of an enemy counts for nothing. It is the opportunity which it enjoys for spreading itself rapidly which determines the degree of its noxiousness. This opportunity lies in the environment or external conditions under which it finds itself. The insect or plant cannot spread until it is placed in new conditions; either the plant must be new to the conditions or the conditions must be new to the plant. A given area may be filled to the utmost with the plants and animals of a region, but an entirely different or foreign plant or animal may gain a foothold without dislodging any of the present occupants, because it can fit itself into chinks which they are not fitted to occupy. An area may be full of corn, and yet grow a few cow-peas between. A region may be densely clothed with forest, and yet vines will grow up the tree trunks.

A meadow may be full of timothy, and grow white clover in the bottom. These differences in habits and requirements between different organisms are styled *divergence of character* by Darwin, and the more dissimilar the organisms, within certain bounds, the greater the number which can live together peaceably. Consequently, the foreign or remote species, being different from our own, find places not occupied, and they make the most of them. The same is true to a less degree of any organisms which find themselves in new surroundings. The new enemies come because they see a business opening: there is little competition.

A most interesting result of the struggle for existence, and one which I do not remember to have seen stated, is that it forces plants to grow as single and detached specimens, not as clumps nor in colonies. How true this is for herbs and bushes will be apparent to anyone who recalls how the common plants grow in great solid clumps in gardens, whilst in the adjacent fields and woods they are scattered here and there as small, and usually slender or dwarf specimens. It may be assumed that it is the natural disposition of all plants to occupy the ground continuously and to branch profusely from the base. When they are scattered thinly over any area, it is proof that there are other contestants for the space; and the tendency for trees and other plants to grow to a single trunk is in consequence, also, of the struggle for a place in which to live.

I have now said that our enemies increase because cultivation induces change of habits in wild organisms, because it presents an ever-increasing variety of food- or host-plants, because the food supply is large and in more or less continuous areas, and because the natural equilibrium or tension is disturbed. This may all be summed up by saying that it is a question of readjustment following some disturbance. You will now want to ask how long before this readjustment will have become complete, and equilibrium be again restored, and the enemies in great measure disappear, from lack of food and opportunity. So long as cultivation or disturbance continues, so long perfect readjustment can not occur. Therefore I expect that we shall always find new enemies coming upon us. But, to a considerable degree, readjustment does occur. The potato beetle is less abundant than formerly. It has spread itself over the potato area of the country, and it can not now propagate itself so rapidly as it did in the sixties. It has taken to other plants, but it has met competitors, and is held in check. Enemies have also appeared. Nearly all invaders have their seasons or cycles of great prosperity, and corresponding periods of comparative obscurity. When they are first running over a country they enjoy their greatest license. This is the case in many invasions now progressing in this new country, where the rapid clearing of the land, the great extension of commerce, and the planting and sowing of enormous areas, afford almost unlimited prosperity to a new incursion. (Compare Essay VIII.) The introduction of the phylloxera and downy-mildew into Europe, where they still spread with unabated fury, are examples of new enemies running riot in old and stable countries.

Insects or fungi or weeds are often held in subjection, like a smoldering fire, by the pressure of circumstances, as weather, the presence of enemies, or other conditions. The pressure may be suddenly removed, when they break forth in riot. Thus for over ten years the pear tree psylla was known to exist in the neighborhood of Cornell University before it came to be a serious foe. And now, after a year or two of great activity, the species again appears to have received a check. The gypsy moth is another illustration of the long period of incubation of some invasions. It was not until twenty years after its introduction into Massachusetts that it began to attract attention as an injurious insect. It could not have required all these years for its multiplication into a sufficient horde to arrest attention, for a mathematical calculation will show that this could have occurred in much less time if the species were allowed to propagate to the full extent of its capabilities.

. After a time the check will come. The potato beetle has already passed its zenith. The codlin-moth and the curculio have lost much of their fury in the east. The enemies of insects increase as well as the competitors. Parasites, finding innumerable insects upon which to prey, increase with great rapidity, until they devour their own means of support. They, in turn, succumb, and the defeated host rallies; so the alternate warfare goes on forever. Witness how the tent-caterpillars come and go. The reign of destruction of this insect is apt to be brief, sometimes lasting only a year or two. Other insects hold their own for a longer time. This period of activity is somewhat characteristic of the different species.

We are taught, by these considerations, that we should not become disheartened with the sudden influx of enemies. These invasions are not peculiar to modern times. Egypt has had its plagues. Every country has had similar trials. They are the necessary outcomes of civilization and the clearing of the land. In 1649, there was "a strange multitude of caterpillars in New England."* While we shall always meet these onslaughts, there is reason to believe that they will eventually become less numerous and frequent, for cultivation will become tamer, and we know that after a time every attack loses much of its initial virulence. It is interesting to note that weeds are more numerous in the west than in the east, notwithstanding the fact that they are largely introduced upon the Atlantic sea-board. Here in Indiana the roadside and vacant field are choked with weeds. It is not so bad in New York. The country is newer, the soil is freshly broken, there is little competition from enduring greensward, and there is more waste land for which the weeds compete without difficulty.

We are taught, as well, that new enemies are to come upon us. But we are learning how to contend with them. If insect injuries are more serious in the United States than elsewhere, we have also devised the most perfect means of combating them, and in spite of our difficulties we are growing more and better fruit than any country in the world. Great difficulties inspire great efforts, and the awards of those who succeed are greater than they otherwise could be. The spraying pump has brought a new era into our horticulture, not only because it is a means of dispatching of enemies, but because it has inspired hope and confidence. We can not fear the future when the difficulties of the present have been met in such heroic manner. Both philosophy and recent experience reassure us.

*John Josselyn, New England's Rarities, 110.

VIII.

COXEY'S ARMY AND THE RUSSIAN THISTLE: A SKETCH OF THE PHILOSOPHY OF WEEDINESS.[1]

WITHIN about twenty years, a plant* of the pigweed family,—a tribe noted for its nomadic tendencies,—has established itself over large areas in the Dakotas and adjacent regions; it even threatens to overthrow the agriculture of a present area of some twenty-five thousand square miles, and is rapidly extending itself. The weed has a bad reputation in Russia, whence it came, and where, because of its incursions, "the cultivation of crops has been abandoned over large areas in some of the provinces near the Caspian Sea." People in the infested regions of our western plains have become so much alarmed at this persistent and prolific intruder, that they have appealed to Congress for an appropriation of money to help them to fight it. This demand has been emphasized by representations of hard times amongst the farmers of the west, and the passage of the bill has been urged as a means of utilizing the vast amount of restless labor represented by the Coxey army movement. I suspect that if Congress were to compel these redoubtable warriors to pull Russian this-

---

[1]Read before Section I., American Association for the Advancement of Science, at Brooklyn, August, 1894. The reader may find another presentation of the essential ideas of this Essay in Bulletin 102, Cornell Experiment Station.

*Salsola Kali, var. Tragus. Called also Russian cactus.

tles, it would speedily result in the disbandment of the army; but my purpose is to discuss the weed rather than the soldier.

Two great problems are hereby brought directly before us: We must determine, in the first place, why it is that the weed has spread with such virulent rapidity, and what are the most effective means of checking it; and we must then inquire how far it is the business of the government to interfere.

Weeds, like other plants, grow where they can find room; and the more room any plant can find, other things being the same, the farther and more rapidly will it spread over the earth. But room, used in this connection, does not mean, entirely, space vacant of other plants, but rather conditions of competition into which the given plant can fit itself with prosperity. Ground may be covered with a given plant, and yet a species of wholly different character and habits may thrive along with it. This is well illustrated in the growth of twining or climbing vines in dense thickets of shrubbery, or the practice, common even with the Indians, of growing pumpkins in corn fields. If weeds, then, are to be kept out of grounds, the land must not only be occupied with some crop, but with a crop which will not allow the weed to grow along with it. In practice, it is impossible to select all crops from plants which so completely encumber the ground that no intruder can find a foothold; but this disadvantage is readily and almost wholly overcome by means of the rotation of crops,—one crop in the rotation destroying what weeds may have crept in with the preceding ones. Thorough cropping of the land and judicious rotations of crops, therefore, are conditions against which no weeds can stand; and as these are the vital conditions, also, of successful agriculture, it may be said that weeds are never serious when lands are well farmed.

The converse of the above proposition is that the serious prevalence of weeds is an infallible indication of poor farming, and any one who has thought carefully upon this subject must be compelled to accept the statement. The agricultural conditions in the Dakotas and other parts of our plains region are just such as to encourage a hardy intruder like the Russian thistle. An average of eight or nine bushels of wheat per acre is itself proof of superficial farming; but the chief fault with this western agriculture is the continuous cropping with one crop,—wheat. "The methods of farming in the northwest," says a recent bulletin upon the Russian thistle issued by the Department of Agriculture, "are particularly favorable to the distribution and growth of the Russian thistles. Wheat after wheat, with an occasional barren fallow but no cultivated or hoed crops, gives little opportunity to clear the land of troublesome plants." There is no method of permanently checking the pest except better farming,—by which I mean not only cleaner tillage, but the judicious rotation of crops and management of lands. I am looking to the Russian thistle, therefore, as the apostle of a new agriculture for the northwest. If the statements of its perniciousness are true, it will certainly force the farmers to adopt a different system of agriculture. Wheat must be made a crop of a series, and other crops must be found to supplement it; and with this change of front will come all the benign results of a mixed husbandry, —conservation of fertility and moisture, and a more varied population. I am aware that the lands of these northern plains seem to be better adapted to wheat than to other products, and it is not my purpose to specify other crops for those areas; but it is evident that a region which grows wheat under indifferent cultivation can grow other produce as well, and the Russian thistle will force the inhabitants to discover what these products may be.

What I have thus far stated is only a well-known truth in organic evolution,—that the distribution of an animal or plant upon the earth, and to a great extent the attributes of the organism itself, are the result of a struggle with other organisms. A plant which becomes a weed is only a victor in a battle with farm crops; and if the farmer is in command of the vanquished army, it speaks ill for his generalship when he is routed by a pigweed or a Russian thistle. Let one recall the weedy areas which he has seen, and consider the conditions. The daisy-cursed meadows of the east are those which have been long mown and are badly "run," or else those which were not properly made, and the grass obtained but a poor start. The farmer may say that the daisies have "run out" the grass, but the fact is that the meadow began to fail, and the daisies quickly seized upon the opportunity to gain a foothold; and just so long as the farmer persists in his accustomed methods will the daisies usurp the land. The weedy lawns are those which have a thin turf, and the best treatment is to scratch the ground lightly with an iron-toothed rake, apply fertilizer and sow more seed; in other words, augment the struggle for existence, and the weeds will go down before the June grass, and the grass plants themselves, because of the greater numbers, will be more slender and will make a softer turf. The rank patches of Canada thistles are in neglected fields or along roadsides, where there is least competition with vigorous crops and with the cultivator. The roadsides of the western and prairie states are noticeably more weedy than those of the east, where there are less waste grounds in which the weeds multiply and where the roadside turf is usually stronger. All new countries suffer serious incursions of weeds, because the equilibrium of nature has been broken by removal of forests or breaking up of prairies, and every plant makes an effort, in the resettlement of the land and the reconstruction of competition, to gain a place for itself. The agriculture of a new country is generally one-sided and imperfect, and one crop usually eclipses all others; and in the absence of rotation, the weeds fill in the chinks, spread themselves into waste and half-cultivated lands, and soon threaten the single-handed agriculture like an invading army. But the older and better tilled the region, the less the farmers know about weeds.

I recall an excellent example of the invasion of a weed into an unoccupied area. There is a long stretch of sandy drift near a certain village upon the eastern shore of Lake Michigan. In 1880, I found a strange plant in the loose sand.* It is one of this very family of pigweeds.* It spread rapidly, and in three years had completely occupied a region three or four miles long, and had begun to encroach upon cultivated fields. I considered it a vile weed, and warned the people against it. But presently other wild plants began to dispute possession of the area, and they set up a backfire against it. The weed receded, and it is no longer a prominent plant on that shore. Even the Russian

---

* *Corispermum hyssopifolium.*

thistle finds its match in certain wild plants. The report of the "Russian Cactus Committee" of North Dakota declares that "our native grasses will entirely exterminate the cactus, abundant proof of which can be seen in many once cultivated but now abandoned fields where the cactus has completely disappeared." What was accomplished by these disputatious wild plants can be always accomplished by judicious cropping when new weeds attempt to usurp the land; and if this judicious cropping is already in practice, the weeds will never gain a considerable foothold, and will not attract attention.

All these remarks concerning the relation of weediness to farming are well illustrated by the methods advised by the best authors for the destruction of weeds. The leading "methods of weed destruction" recommended by Professor Shaw's recent book upon weeds are as follows:

"The modification (when necessary) of the scheme of rotation that has been adopted, so that such crops as allow the seeds of the weeds which infest them to ripen may, for a time, be omitted from the rotation."

"The growing of hoed crops upon the farm infested, to the largest extent that is practicable."

"The growing of clover and lucerne, so far as this can be done with profit."

"The growing of soiling crops, to the extent that may be found practicable, both because of the fact that they can be cut almost at any time that is desirable, and also because of their 'smothering' properties."

"The keeping of the land of the farm constantly at work."

VIII.] ATTITUDE OF THE GOVERNMENT. 199

"The stimulation of the soil to a constantly vigorous production by means of thorough working and a large use of manure."

The chief remedies devised for the eradication of the Russian thistle by a report of the Department of Agriculture devoted to the subject, are those which relate to the conditions of the agriculture of the infested region and to the methods of raising crops.

We now come upon the second part of our inquiry: Should the government destroy the Russian thistle? It will first be asked, How can the government destroy it? By going into farming! The government might put a million men to pulling up the weed, but a seed would somewhere be overlooked, and after the lapse of a few years the battle would recur. Sisyphus would forever roll the stone which falls back upon his shoulders the moment his effort is relaxed. The only permanent salvation is the removal of the conditions,—the improvement, diversification of the agriculture and the consequent settlement of the country. But if the government goes to farming, the autonomy of the individual is absorbed, and the result is a long step towards communism.

The Senate amendment to House Bill No. 6937, proposing an appropriation for the relief of the thistle-stricken regions, reads as follows: "For the destruction of the Russian cactus (technically *Salsola Kali Tragus*), one million dollars, or so much thereof as may be necessary, to be apportioned by the Secretary of Agriculture among the several states infested by the Russian cactus, said apportionment to be made in accordance with the necessities of the case, to be ascertained by the Secretary, and to be paid to the governor of each of said states upon his executing an obligation on behalf of his state that the sum so paid shall be faithfully applied in connection with any sum which may be raised for that purpose in his state for the destruction of said cactus."

The expenditure of this money seems to rest with the governors of the various states, but the bill is significantly silent as to the means to be employed in dislodging this inveterate enemy. The first expenditure from this fund, it would seem, should be to clean all state lands of the pest,—which the state should be bound to do, anyhow,—and to enforce the laws concerning the cleaning of roadsides; and if the remainder of the fund could be expended in a vigorous crusade for the betterment of the agriculture of the given regions, in discouraging the breaking up of more land than can be well cultivated, and in the establishment of rotations, the appropriation will have been well made. But beyond this I do not see how the government can go,—certainly not to the point of taking each farm under its surveillance and setting laborers to putting at rights what the owner of the land is himself, in his own welfare, bound to repair, and for the existence of which he may be said, constructively, to have been to blame.

The fact is, this plague is one of those curses which comes upon a new country in consequence of the sudden overturning of established conditions, and the substitution therefor of a very imperfect and one-sided system of land occupancy. It is like the plague of rabbits in Australia, or of cardoons on the pampas. It comes as a vigorous reminder of the weak points in the newly established agricultural system, and demands either that the system be overturned or that the inhabitants move.

I do not doubt that the ultimate result of this bloodless warfare will be of inestimable value to the northwest. Weeds have always been the best friend of the farmer. They taught him how to till the soil, and they never allow him to forget the lesson. Vergil was well aware of it:

> "The father of humankind himself ordains
> The husbandman should tread no path of flowers,
> But waken the sleeping earth with sleepless pains.
> So pricketh he these indolent hearts of ours."

The lesson is painful at the onset, but for that reason it is remembered the longer. Over a half century ago, certain agitators in New York state foresaw untold evil from the incursions of the Canada thistle, and one of them even predicted that it would "establish its fatal empire over the whole of North America," resulting, perhaps, in the depopulation of the country. But good farming and climatic limitations quietly stopped its progress, and it is no longer a terror to the rural communities. So all things find their level, not by legislation but by education. Solomon "went by the field of the slothful, and by the vineyard of the man void of understanding; and lo, it was all grown over with thorns, and nettles had covered the face thereof, and the stone wall thereof was broken down." It is doubtless the privilege of the government to instruct farmers how to improve their farming, but weeds are beyond the reach of the sheriff. Laws cannot correct a vacancy in nature.

IX.

RECENT PROGRESS IN AMERICAN HORTICULTURE.[1]

You have asked me to say something about recent progress in horticulture. I am at a loss to know how you want the subject treated. The subject is a large one, and can be approached in many ways. It is by no means admitted that there is any recent progress. There is a large class of our horticultural public which disparages these modern times as in no way so good as those of several or many years ago. These men are mostly gardeners who were apprenticed in their youth. There is another class which decries the introduction of new varieties of plants, thinking these novelties to be unreliable and deceitful. There are others who are content with the older things, and who have never had occasion to ask if there has been any progress in recent years. Others have looked for progress, but have not found it. A professor of horticulture told me a few days ago that nothing new or interesting seems to be transpiring in the horticultural world. Some people even deny outright that any progress is making at the present time. On the other hand, there are some, perhaps the minority, who contend that they see great advancement. Perhaps these are mostly young

[1] Read before the Agricultural and Experimental Union of Ontario, at the Ontario Agricultural College, Guelph, Dec. 23, 1892. Printed in Science, xxi. 20 (Jan. 13, 1893); and in 18th Annual Report Ontario Agric. College, 1892, p. 300.

men. Then there are the catalogues, with their fascinating impossibilities, pregnant with the glory that is to come. Between all these diversities, where is the young man to stand who loves plants and sunshine, and is yet ambitious? Is there any progress in horticulture? If not, it is dead, uninspiring. We cannot live on the past, good as it is; we must draw our inspiration from the future. This subject is of vital personal interest to me; it must be so to you.

I cannot forego the satisfaction of saying at the outset, that some of this supposed stagnation must be due to blindness on the part of the observer. The apprenticed gardener underwent in his youth the stupendous misfortune of having learned the art and science of horticulture. The apprentice system in itself does not often educate a man; that is, it does not make him a student. It teaches him to base the whole art upon rule, personal experience and "authority;" it is apt to make him a narrow man, and he may not readily assimilate novel methods. Those who have looked for progress and have not found it may have looked in the wrong place. It is possible that they do not understand very clearly just what progress is. Those who are simply indifferent exert little influence upon our inquiry, and may be omitted. Those who see progress upon all sides may be over-sanguine. Perhaps they project something of their own passion into their statements. And the catalogues, being for the most part editorial rather than horticultural productions, may be liberally discounted as evidence. It is apparent, therefore, that we must make an independent inquiry if we are to answer our own question. Several considerations incline me to believe that progress is not only making, but that it is making very rapidly. I may say here that I care little for any facts or illustrations of progress merely as facts. There must be some law, some tendency, some profound movement underlying it all, and this we must discover. I shall not attempt, therefore, to indicate how great the progress has been in any definite time, but endeavor to ascertain if there is progression which gains impetus with the years.

1. *There is a progressive variation in plants.* Horticulture is concerned with the cultivation of plants. The plant is the beginning and the end. For the plant we till the soil, build greenhouses, and transact the business of the garden. All progress, therefore, rests upon the possibility of securing better varieties,—those possessing greater intrinsic merit in themselves, or better adaptations to certain purposes or regions. In other words, all progress rests upon the fact that evolution is still operative, that garden plants, like wild animals and plants, are more or less constantly undergoing modification.

American horticulture may be said to have begun with the opening of the century. It was in 1806 that Bernard M'Mahon wrote his "American Gardener's Calendar." This work contains a catalogue of three thousand seven hundred "species and varieties of the most valuable and curious plants hitherto discovered." Among the cultivated varieties of fruits and vegetables, the present reader will see few familiar names. He will observe among the fruits, however, some American types, showing that even at that date American pomology had begun to diverge from the English and French which gave it birth. This is especially true of the apples, for of the fifty-nine kinds in the catalogue, about 66 per cent are of American origin. Several nurseries were established in the next thirty years, and fresh importations of European varieties were made, so that when Downing, in 1845, described the one hundred and ninety apples known to be growing in this country, American varieties had fallen to 52 per cent. In 1872, however, when almost two thousand varieties were described in Downing's second revision, the American kinds had risen to 65 or more per cent, or to about the proportion which they occupied at the opening of the century. At the present time the percentage of varieties of American origin is much higher, and if we omit from our calculations the obsolete varieties, we find that over 80 per cent of the apples actually cultivated in the older apple regions at the present time are of American origin. The percentage of native varieties, in other words, has risen from nothing to 80 per cent since the apple settlement of the country, and at least once during this time the native productions have recovered from an overwhelming onslaught of foreigners. Except in the cold north and northwest, where the apple industry is now experiencing an immigration not unlike that which befell the older states early in the century, few people would think of importing varieties of apples with the expectation that they shall prove to be a commercial success in America. Other plants have shown most astounding development. In 1889 thirty-nine varieties of chrysanthemums were introduced in North America, in 1890 fifty-seven varieties, and in 1891 one hundred and twenty-one varieties. The chrysanthemum is now the princess of flowers, yet in 1806 M'Mahon barely mentioned it, and there were no named varieties.

All this is evidence of the greatest and most substantial progress, and much of it is recent; and there is every reason to believe that this rapid adaptation of plants to new conditions is still in progress in all cultivated species. In fact, the initial and conspicuous stage of such adaptation is just now taking place in the Russian apples in America, in which the American seedlings are even now gaining a greater prominence than some of their parents. Both the parent stock and the seedling brood are radical and progressive departures of recent date. The same modification to suit American environments is seen in every plant which has been cultivated here for a score or more of years. The mulberries are striking examples, for our fruit-bearing varieties are not only different from those of Europe, whence they came, but many of them belong to a species which in Europe is not esteemed for fruit. The European varieties of almonds are now being superseded in California by native seedlings, which are said to be much better adapted to our Pacific climate than their recent progenitors are. These facts of rapid adaptation are everywhere so patent, upon reflection, that I need not consider them further at this time. They are indisputable evidence that there is permanent contemporaneous progress, and upon them alone I am willing to rest my whole argument.

There is another feature of this contemporaneous variation which must be considered at this point,— the great increase in numbers of varieties. This increase is in part simply an accumulation of the varieties of many years, so that our manuals are apt to contain descriptions of more varieties than are actually cultivated at the time. But much of this increase is an actual multiplication of varieties. That is, there are more varieties of nearly all plants in cultivation now than at any previous time. M'Mahon mentions six beets as grown at his time; in 1889 there were forty-two kinds. Then there were fourteen cabbages, now there are over one hundred. Then there were sixteen lettuces, against about one hundred and twenty now. He mentions fifty-nine apples; now there are about two thousand five hundred described in our books. He mentions forty pears, against one thousand now. There were something over four hundred and fifty species of garden plants native to the United States mentioned by M'Mahon; now there are over two thousand in cultivation. These figures are average examples of the marvelous increase in varieties during the century. I may be met here with the technical objection that M'Mahon did not make a complete catalogue of the plants of his time. This may be true, but it was meant to be practically complete, and it is much the fullest of any early list. Gardening occupied such a limited area a century ago that it could not have been a burdensome task to collect very nearly all the varieties in existence; and any omissions are undoubtedly much overbalanced by the shortcomings of the contemporaneous figures which I have given you. It is certainly true that during the nineteenth century, varieties of all the leading species of cultivated plants have multiplied in this country from 100 per cent to 1,000 per cent. This variation still continues, and the sum of novelties of any year probably exceeds that of the preceding year. Every generation sees, for the most part, a new type of plants.

But I suppose that these statements as to the increase of varieties will be accepted without further proof. The question which you all desire to ask me is whether all this increase represents progress. Many poor varieties have been introduced, beyond a doubt, but I am convinced that the general tendency is decidedly progressive. You may cite me the fact that we have not improved upon the Rhode Island Greening and Fall Pippin apples, the Montmorenci cherry, the Green Gage plum, and other varieties which were in cultivation at the opening of the century, as proof of a contrary conviction; but I shall answer that we now have a score of apples as good as the Greening, although we may have none better. This habit of saying that we have not improved upon certain old plants is really a fallacy, for the reference is always made to quality of fruit alone; and, furthermore, the test of progress is not the supplanting of a good variety, but the origination of varieties which shall meet new demands. The more numerous and diverse the varieties of any plant, the more successful will be its cultivation over a wide area, because the greatest number of different conditions—as soils, climates and uses—will be satisfactorily met. If we had at present only the apples which were grown in M'Mahon's time, apple culture in the prairie states, in our bleak northwest, and even in some of the apple sections of Ontario, would be impossible. We are constantly extending the borders of the cultivation of all fruits by means of these new varieties. The horticultural settlement of our great west and of the cold north is one of the wonders of the time.

We should not ask ourselves of a new variety if it is better in all respects than other varieties, but if it will fill some specific need more satisfactorily. If a variety does better than all other varieties in one locality alone, for one specific purpose, it is not a failure, and it represents progress. Every peculiar or isolated region tends to develop a horticulture of its own, but this is possible only with a corresponding initial variation in plants. No doubt many of our discarded varieties failed to find the place or conditions in which they would have succeeded. We should not look upon adverse reports upon the novelties as necessarily denunciatory; they may only indicate that in some places or for some purposes the variety in question is unsatisfactory.

I must also call your attention to the fact that, while the areas of cultivation have greatly widened in recent years because of the evolution of adaptive varieties, the economic uses of the plants have increased in like ratio. We now have varieties of fruits which are specifically adapted to the making of dried fruit, to canning, to enduring long journeys, and the like; and flowers which meet specific demands in decoration or other uses. The period of maturation of varieties has extended greatly in both directions, so that fruits and flowers are now in season much longer than formerly. The gist of the whole matter is simply this, that our horticultural limits and products have greatly broadened in very recent times by reason of the great increase in number and diversity of varieties; and this leads us to expect that still other wants will be met in like manner, and that the uttermost habitable parts of the country will develop a special horticulture.

2. *There is a constant augmentation in new specific types of plants, both from our native flora and by importation from without.* I suppose that there is no parallel

to the marvelous evolution of native fruits in America. Within a century we have procured the grapes, cranberries, the most popular gooseberries, some of the mulberries, the raspberries and blackberries, the pecans and some of the chestnuts, from our wild species. Perhaps some of the strawberries can be traced to the same source. There are many men still living who remember when there was no commercial cultivation of these fruits. Here is progress enough for one century; yet an overwhelming host of new types is coming upon us. I sometimes think that the improved native plants are coming forward so rapidly that we do not properly appreciate them. Witness the perplexing horde of native plums, the varieties even now reaching nearly two hundred, which are destined to occupy a much larger area of North America than the European plum now occupies. New species of grapes are now coming into cultivation. The dewberries, juneberry, Crandall currant type, buffalo berry, wild apples, and more than a score of lesser worthies, are now spreading into our gardens. Many of these things will be among the staples a hundred years to come. One hundred and eighty-five species of native plants, some for fruit but mostly for ornament, were introduced into commerce last year; and the number of plants native to North America, north of Mexico which have come into cultivation is two thousand four hundred and sixteen. Under the stimulus of new conditions, some of these species will vary into hundreds, perhaps thousands, of new forms, and our horticulture will become the richest in the world. It is a privilege to live when great movements are conceived and new agencies first lend themselves to the dominion of man.

Many species have come to us from various parts of the world throughout the century, but the immigration still continues, and perhaps is greater now than at any previous time. It is well nigh impossible to chronicle the new types of ornamental plants which have come to America during the last two decades. Consider the overwhelming introduction of species of orchids alone. Even the wholly new types of fruits are many. Over twenty-five species of edible plants have come to America comparatively recently from Japan alone, and some of these species are already very important. Two of them, the Japanese persimmons and the Japanese plums, are most signal additions, probably exceeding in value any other introductions of species not heretofore in the country, made during the last quarter-century. During the years 1889, 1890 and 1891, some three hundred and eighty species of plants not in commercial cultivation here were introduced into North America, partly from abroad and partly from our own flora. In 1891 alone, two hundred and nineteen distinct species were introduced.

Valuable as these new types are in themselves, all experience teaches that we are to expect better things from their cultivated and variable progeny. We can scarcely conceive what riches the future will bring.

3. *There is great progress in methods of caring for plants.* The manner of cultivating and caring for plants has changed much during recent years. It is doubtful if all this change represents actual progress in methods, but it indicates inquiry and growth, and it must eventually bring us to the ideal treatment of plants. Some of the change is simply a see-saw from one method to another, according as our knowledge

seems to point more strongly in one direction than another. In one decade we may think lime to be an indispensable fertilizer, and in the next it may be discarded; yet we may eventually find that both positions are tenable. Yet there has been a decided up-uplift in methods of simple tillage and preparation of land and the science of fertilizing the soil; and, moreover, the application of this knowledge is widespread where it was once local or rare. And the application of machinery and mechanical devices to almost every horticultural labor cannot have escaped the attention of the most careless observer.

Among specific horticultural industries, the recent evolution of the glass house has been remarkable. In 1806 the greenhouse was still a place in which to keep plants green, and M'Mahon felt obliged to disapprove of living rooms over it to keep the roof from freezing, because they are "not only an additional and unnecessary expense, but they give the building a heavy appearance." The first American greenhouse of which we have a picture, with a wooden roof and heavy sides, was built in 1764. Glass houses increased in numbers very slowly until the middle of this century, and they can only now be said to be popular. Twenty years ago a glass house was a luxury or an enterprise suited only to large concerns, and the management of it was to most intelligent people an impenetrable mystery. At the present time, even the humblest gardener, if he is thrifty, can afford a greenhouse. In fact, the glass house is rapidly coming to be an indispensable adjunct to nearly all kinds of progressive gardening. The secret of this increasing popularity of the glass house is the simplicity of construction of the modern building. Large glass, low, straight roofs, light frames, simple foundations, small wrought-iron pipes, portable automatic heaters,—these are the innovations which have given the cheap greenhouse a greater popularity and practicability in America, probably, than anywhere else in the world. Yet many of these features would have been heresies when Leuchars wrote his excellent book in 1850.

The simplification and popularization of glass houses has simplified the management of plants in them. Even laymen are now taking to greenhouse plant growing, and many of them achieve most gratifying results. The first days of the commercial forcing of plants are still within the memory of many of this audience; and it is only within the present decade that great attention has been given in this country to the forcing of tomatoes, cucumbers, carnations, and many other plants. The business is yet in its infancy. The greenhouse has also exerted a marked influence upon the plants which are grown in them. There has now appeared a list of varieties of various plants which are especially adapted to the purposes of forcing; and this phenomenon is probably the most important and cogent proof of contemporaneous evolution.

If one were asked off-hand what is the most conspicuous recent advancement in horticulture, he would undoubtedly cite the advent of the sprays for destroying insects and fungi. These are not only eminently effective, but they were perfected at a time when dismay had overtaken very many of our horticulturists, and they have inspired new hope everywhere, and have stimulated the planting of fruit and ornamentals. I fancy that the future historian will find that the advent of the spray in the latter part of this century marked an important epoch in agricultural pursuits. Yet this epoch is not disconnected from the era before it. It is but a natural outcome or consequence of the rapid increase of insect and fungous enemies, which increase, in turn, is induced by the many disturbing influences of cultivation itself. When we devise effective means of checking the incursions of our foes, therefore, we are only keeping pace with the initial progress fostered by the origination of new varieties and the quickening commercial life of our time. Yet the era of spraying is none the less a mark of great achievement, and we have not yet seen the good of which it will ultimately prove to be capable. But a greater achievement than this must be made before we shall have reached the ideal and inevitable method of combating external pests; we must learn to so control natural agencies that one will counteract another. Nature keeps all her forces and agencies in comparative equilibrium by pitting one against another in the remorseless struggle for existence. (See Essay VII.) The introduction of insect parasites and predaceans, entomogenous fungi, colonization of insectivorous birds, and the use of strategy in cultivation and in the selection of immune species and varieties, and the planning of rotations and companionships of plants, will eventually be so skillfully managed that most of our enemies will be kept under measurable control. A short rotation is now known to be the best means of combating wire-worms and several other pests. The first great success in this direction in America is the introduction of the Australian vedalia, or lady-bug, to devour the most pestiferous of the orange-tree scales on the Pacific coast. This experiment is pregnant of greater and more abiding results than all the achievements of the sprays. But in your generation and mine, men must shoulder their squirt-guns as our ancestors shouldered their muskets, and see only the promise of the time when they shall be beaten into pruning-hooks and plowshares and there shall come the peace of a silent warfare!

4. *There is great progress in the methods of handling and preserving horticultural products.* I need not tell the older men in this audience that there has been progress in the methods of handling fruits. When they were boys, apples and even peaches were taken to market loose in a wagon-box. We have all seen the development of the special-package industry, beginning first with rough bushel baskets or rude crates, then a better made and smaller package, which was to be returned to the consignor, and finally the trim and tasty gift packages of the present day. I am sorry to say that some regions have not yet reached this latter stage of development, but their failure to do so only makes the contrast stronger of those who have reached it. Quick transportation and methods of refrigeration have tied the ends of the earth together. Apples in quantity are carried fourteen thousand miles from Tasmania to England, and in 1890 they reached the San Francisco markets to compete with the fruits of the Pacific coast. From a small beginning in 1845, the exportation of American apples to England and Scotland began to assume commercial importance from 1875 to 1880, until nearly a million and a half barrels have been exported

in a single season. It is said that the first bananas were brought to the United States in 1804, and the first full cargo in 1830. Now from eight to ten million bunches arrive annually. The Canary Islands are now shipping tomatoes to London, and the United States will soon be doing the same. Watermelons will follow. California now unloads her green produce in the same market. Even pears are exported from America to Belgium, disputing the old saw that it is unwise to carry coals to Newcastle. The world is our market. But this result may have been achieved with some detriment to home markets and transportation, which have been in some measure overlooked and neglected; but this evil must correct itself in the long run.

Perhaps we owe to a Frenchman the first distinct exposition, some eighty years ago, of a process of preserving perishable articles in hermetically sealed cans; but the process first gained prominence in the United States, and it became known as canning. In 1825, James Monroe signed patents to Thomas Kensett and Ezra Daggett to cover an improvement in the art of preserving, although Kensett appears to have practised his method somewhat extensively as early as 1819. Isaac Winslow, of Maine, is supposed to have been the pioneer in canning sweet-corn, in 1842. About 1847 the canning industry began to attract general attention, and in that year the tomato was first canned. The exodus to California in 1849 stimulated the industry by creating a demand for unperishable eatables in compact compass. North America now leads the world in the extent, variety, and excellence of its canned products, and much of the material is the product of orchards and gardens. In 1891, the sweet-corn pack of the United

States and Canada was 2,799,453 twenty-four-can cases, and the tomato pack was 3,405,365 cases. Over twenty thousand canning factories give employment, it is said, to about one million persons during the canning season. The rise of the evaporated fruit industry is not less remarkable in its way than that of the canning industry.

There are other marvels of progress in methods of caring for horticultural products, but these examples sufficiently illustrate my position. I am aware that all these things are features of commerce and manufacture rather than of horticulture, but they are responsible for much of the phenomenal extension of horticultural interests in recent years. They have also exerted a powerful influence upon the plants which we cultivate, and varieties have appeared which are particularly adapted to long carriage and to canning and evaporating. The vegetable kingdom is everywhere responsive to the needs of man.

5. *There is a corresponding evolution in the horticulturist.* The rapidity with which education and general intelligence have spread in recent years is patent to every one. The rural classes have risen with the rest, but among the agricultural pursuits horticulture has probably shown the greatest advance in this respect. The horticulturist grows a great variety of products, many of which are perishable, and all of which demand expedition, neatness, and care in marketing. These many and various crops bring in a multitude of perplexities which not only demand a ready knowledge for their control, but which are important educators in themselves. The horticulturist lives nearer the markets and the villages than the general farmer does, as a rule, and

he is more in touch with the world. Downing rejoiced in 1852 that there were "at least a dozen societies in different parts of the Union devoted to the improvement of gardening, and to the dissemination of information on the subject." Since that time a dozen national horticultural societies of various kinds have come into prosperous existence, and there are over fifty societies representing states, provinces, or important geographical districts, while the number of minor societies runs into the hundreds. Over fifty states, territories, and provinces have established agricultural schools and experiment stations, all supported by popular sentiment. The derision of "book farming" is well nigh forgotten. Subjects which a few years ago were thought to be "theoretical" and irrelevant are now matters of common conversation. In short, a new type of man is coming onto the farms. This uplift in the common understanding of the science of cultivation, and of the methods of crossing and of skillful selection, is exerting a powerful accelerating influence upon the variation of cultivated plants. But the most important and abiding evolution is that of the man himself; and I expect that the rising intellectual status will ultimately lead people to the farm rather than away from it. We are just now living in a time of conspicuous artificialism; but the farm must be tilled, and it must be inviting. When agriculture cannot pay, something is wrong with the times.

These, then, are the chief lines of progress in horticulture, and they are all still operative and capable of indefinite growth. The achievement of a generation has been phenomenal. The prospect is inspiring to both the cultivator and the student.

X.

ON THE SUPPOSED CORRELATIONS OF QUALITY IN FRUITS.[1]

HIGH quality in fruits is supposed to exist at the expense of some other character; the best fruits are thought to be tender in tree, unproductive, to lack vigor, or to be small or dull in color. This notion is so old that I am unable to find its origin. It is one of the dogmas of horticulture which passes down from generation to generation unchallenged. It finds expression in many of our phrases, as "large and poor," "handsome but poor," and the like, and it is the parent of the assumption that a first-rate market fruit is almost necessarily one that is indifferent or poor in quality. This idea is so prevalent that it demands careful investigation, now that we are entering upon an era of scientific horticulture. It lies at the foundation of all advance in horticulture, for if variation in quality is always correlated with variation in some other character, we should be able to breed directly for quality by choosing parents which have a given combination of characters. We shall take seeds, for instance, from the tenderest tree, the least productive one, the smallest fruit or the one producing fewest seeds.

---

[1] Read before the Biological Section of the American Association for the Advancement of Science, Rochester, August, 1892. Printed in Agricultural Science, vi. 489 (November, 1892).

We must determine if the opinion of Goethe and St. Hilaire is true, that the sum of activity in any plant is fixed with a variation occurring only within the limits; or if we can force the plant beyond its original bounds and increase the sum of its activities. We must determine if the independent variation of members which Wallace has found to exist in nature obtains also in the garden, or if, once inside the garden fence, the plant assumes a law of development in parallelisms. It therefore becomes a philosophical question.

Now, there are about seven characters which are commonly held to be correlated with marked increase in quality, three of which belong to the fruit itself, and the remaining four to the plant as a whole. These are: Decrease in size and seed-production; loss of high color in the fruit; and tenderness, lack of vigor, short life, and unproductiveness in the plant. It is hardly necessary, before this audience, to define what I mean by high quality. I simply refer to that combination of fine texture, tenderness and pronounced agreeable flavor which renders fruits fit for the dessert.

There are two methods of discussing my subject, the statistical and the philosophical. Fortunately, statistics are at hand for our purpose. I have selected as the basis of my investigation the well known Fruit Catalogue of the Michigan Horticultural Society. This is almost wholly the labor of T. T. Lyon, whose discriminating judgment upon the merits of fruits is not excelled in this country. In this catalogue all the varieties are graded upon a decimal scale in three distinct categories—dessert, cooking, and market. Each variety is also rated in size and color. Mr. Lyon's standard of excellence in quality for dessert is high, and only the very choicest varieties reach figures 9 and 10. It therefore offers an opportunity for the selection of extreme types, and the elimination of all such intermediate ones as would be likely to complicate and obscure the results. It does not matter if Mr. Lyon's judgment in certain cases differs from yours or mine; the catalogue is all the more valuable for having been prepared by one man, because it insures uniformity of judgment. The catalogue is also extensive enough to afford a safe basis of estimate: it contains two hundred and nineteen varieties of apples, seventeen of blackberries, fifty-two of cherries, sixteen of currants and gooseberries, forty-seven of grapes, seventy of peaches, sixty-three of pears, thirty-four of plums, thirty of raspberries, and sixty-one of strawberries. And personally I am particularly glad of the opportunity to use this information, because it relieves me at once from any charge of bias in the collection of facts. The following lists contain all the varieties which rank 9 and 10 for dessert:

APPLES.

VARIETY	SIZE	COLOR	SCALE
American Golden Russet	small	yellow russet	9
American Summer	medium	yellow red	10
Belmont	medium	yellow vermilion	9
Chenango	medium to large	whitish carmine	9
Dyer	medium	green yellow red	10
Early Harvest	medium	yellow whitish	9
Early Joe	small	yellow red	10
Esopus Spitzenburgh	large	yellow red	9
Fall Pippin	very large	yellow green brown	9
Fameuse	medium	green yellow red	9
Garden Royal	medium to small	green yellow red	10
Golden Russet (W. N. York)	medium to small	yellow russet	9
Green Newtown (Pippin)	medium	green bright	10
Grimes' Golden	medium	yellow orange	9

APPLES, continued.

VARIETY	SIZE	COLOR	SCALE
Hawley	large	yellow	9
Hubbardston	large	yellow red	10
Jefferis	medium	yellow crimson	9
Jonathan	medium to small	yellow red	9
McLellan	medium	yellow red	9
Melon	medium to large	yellow crimson carmine	10
Mexico	medium	crimson red yellow	10
Newtown (Spitzenburgh)	medium	yellow red	9
Northern Spy	large	green yellow red	10
Pawpaw	medium	yellow red	9
Peck's Pleasant	medium to large	green yellow red	9
Pomme Gris	small	russet red	10
Primate	medium	green whitish crimson	10
Rhode Island Greening	large	green yellow red	0
Scarlet Pearmain	medium	crimson yellow	9
Shiawassee	medium	whitish red	10
Summer Rambo	medium	whitish yellow red	0
Summer Rose	small	yellow red	10
Summer Sweet	large	green yellow	9
Swaar	large	yellow orange brown	10
Wagener	medium	yellow crimson	9
Westfield (Seek-no-Further)	medium to large	green red russet	9
White Spanish Reinette	very large	yellow green orange red	9
Yellow Newtown (Pippin)	medium	yellow red	10

BLACKBERRIES.

VARIETY	SIZE	COLOR	SCALE
Agawam	large	————	9
Kittatinny	large	————	10
New Rochelle (Lawton)	large	————	9
Snyder	medium	————	9
Stone	medium to small	————	9
Taylor	large	————	10
Wallace	large	————	9

CHERRIES.

VARIETY	SIZE	COLOR	SCALE
Bigarreau	very large	yellow carmine red	10
Black Eagle	medium	black	9
Black Hawk	large	purple black	9
Black Heart	large	black	9
Black Tartarian	very large	purple black	9
Burr	large	whitish yellow red	9
Cleveland	large	red yellow	9

CHERRIES, continued.

VARIETY	SIZE	COLOR	SCALE
Coe's Transparent	medium	amber red	10
Delicate	medium to large	amber yellow red	10
Downer's	medium	amber red	9
Downton	large	bright yellow red	9
Early Purple	medium	dark red purple	9
Elton	large	yellow bright red	9
Governor Wood	large	yellow red	9
Rockport	large	red amber	9
Belle de Choisy	medium	yellow amber red	10

CURRANTS AND GOOSEBERRIES.

VARIETY	SIZE	COLOR	SCALE
Red Dutch	medium	———	9
White Dutch	medium	———	10
White Grape	large	———	9
Downing	medium to large	———	10
Smith	large	———	10

GRAPES.

VARIETY	SIZE OF BUNCH	COLOR	SCALE
Brighton	medium	reddish	10
Catawba	medium	reddish	9
Delaware	short	light red	10
Eumelan	long	purple black	9
Ioná	long	reddish	10
Jessica	medium short	yellowish green	9
Lady	medium	yellowish green	10
Rochester	long	reddish	10

PEACHES.

VARIETY	SIZE	COLOR	SCALE
Alexander	medium	green white red	9
Amsden	medium	green white red	9
Atlanta	medium	white purple red	10
Bergen (Yellow)	large	orange dark red	9
Briggs (May)	medium to large	green white red	9
Coolidge	large	white crimson	9
Crawford's Early	large	yellow red	9
Druid Hill	large	green white red	10
Early Newington Free	large	yellow white red	10
George IV.	medium	yellow white dark red	10

PEACHES, continued.

VARIETY	SIZE	COLOR	SCALE
Grosse Mignonne	large	green yellow purple red	10
Hale (Early)	medium	green white red	10
Heath Cling	large	yellow white red black	9
Late Admirable	very large	yellow green red	10
Late Red Rareripe	large	yellow red	10
President	large	green red	9
Rivers	large	yellow pink	9
Steadley	large	white red	9
Tippecanoe	very large	yellow red	9
Van Zandt	medium	white red	10
Variegated	large	white crimson purple	10

PEARS.

VARIETY	SIZE	COLOR	SCALE
Ananas d'Eté	large	yellow brown russet	10
Anjou	large	green russet crimson brown	9
Belle Lucrative	medium	yellow green russet	10
Bloodgood	medium	yellow russet	9
Bosc	large	dark yellow russet red	9
Comice	large	yellow crimson russet	9
Dana's Hovey	small	green yellow russet	9
Emile	large	yellow orange russet	10
Giffard	medium	green yellow red	10
Gray Doyenne	medium	light russet	9
Manning's Elizabeth	small	light yellow red	9
Reeder	small to medium	yellow russet	9
Rostiezer	small	yellow green red brown	9
Seckel	small	yellow brown red russet	10
Stevens (Genesee)	large	yellow	9
Summer Doyenne	small	yellow red	9
Tyson	medium to small	yellow russet crimson	9
Urbaniste	medium to large	yellow russet	9
Washington	medium	yellow red	9
White Doyenne	medium to large	yellow red	10
Winter Nelis	medium	yellow green russet	9

PLUMS.

VARIETY	SIZE	COLOR	SCALE
Bavay's	large	green yellow	9
Green Gage	small	green yellow red	10
Imperial Gage	large	green yellow	9
Jefferson	large	yellow purple red	10
Lawrence's Favorite	large	yellow green	10
McLaughlin	large	yellow red	10

RASPBERRIES.

VARIETY	SIZE	COLOR	SCALE
Caroline	large	orange yellow	9
Herstine	large	bright scarlet	10
Hilborn	very large	black	9
Orange (Brinckié)	large	orange	10
Reder	large	bright red	9
Reliance	medium	bright red	9
Superb	very large	purple red	9
Turner	medium	bright red	9

STRAWBERRIES.

VARIETY	SIZE	COLOR	SCALE
Belmont	very large	bright crimson	10
Bidwell	very large	bright scarlet	9
Black Defiance	very large	dark crimson	9
Boyden	large	bright crimson	9
Cheney	large	bright crimson	9
Cowing	very large	bright crimson	10
Cumberland	very large	bright crimson	9
Duncan	large	dark red	9
Early Canada	medium to small	dark crimson	9
Gandy	very large	bright crimson	9
Gipsy	medium	red	9
Goldsmith	very large	bright scarlet	9
Haverland	large	bright crimson	9
Henderson	large	crimson	10
Jessie	very large	bright crimson	8
Longfellow	very large	crimson	9
Nicanor	medium	bright scarlet	9
Parry	very large	scarlet	10
Pearl	medium	crimson	9
Shirts	very large	bright crimson	9
Triomphe de Gand	large	bright red	10
Warfield	medium	dark red	9
Warren	medium	dark crimson	9

Here we find thirty-eight varieties of apples graded 9 and 10 for dessert, of which only three are rated small, while seven are large, and two are very large. Those rated as medium to small are two, and those medium to large are three. Of these thirty-eight entries, therefore, six, or less than one-sixth, would be called small apples, and thirteen, or over one-third, are large

15 SUB.

apples, the remaining ones being classed as medium or intermediate. In other words, there are over twice as many large apples as small ones of very high quality in this list, and there is every reason to believe that what is true of the two hundred and nineteen varieties here considered is also approximately true of all varieties in cultivation, for the list contains a very large proportion of the total number of varieties of high quality. Of the seven blackberries rated 9 and 10, five are large, one is medium and one is medium to small. Of the sixteen best cherries, eight are large, two very large, one medium to large, and none of them are small. Of the three currants, one is large and the others are medium, and the two gooseberries are large, or medium to large. Among the eight best grapes, there are three large-bunch varieties, and one small-bunch. Of twenty-one best peaches, none are small, twelve, or over half, are large, two are very large, and one is medium to large. Among twenty-one best pears, five, or nearly a quarter, are small, three are medium to small, while six are large and two are medium to large. In this instance the numbers of large and small are equal. In the six best plums, but one is small while five are large. Of eight raspberries, none are small, but four are large and two very large. In the twenty-three best strawberries, none are small, while six are large and eleven, or nearly one-half, are very large.

There can be but one conclusion from the above figures, and that is, that quality is not associated with size of fruit; and a study of any reliable fruit-list of fair proportions will corroborate this conclusion. If the figures were to be interpreted as they stand, it would appear that increase in quality is usually associated with increase in size, but it must be remembered that small fruits are less likely to be propagated extensively than large ones are. It is only when small fruits possess some superlative merits, as in the case of the Early Joe apple and the Seckel and Summer Doyenne pears, that they are worth cultivating in competition with larger fruit. Thus it would be useless to attempt to draw any conclusions from the listed size of poor apples, for poor small apples are not often perpetuated.

We need not resort to figures to show that increase in quality is not a necessary attendant of decrease in size. Every fruit-grower who stops to reason upon the question must recall the fact that seedling apples are usually small and very poor in quality. The fallacy of associating size and flavor, as of other supposed parallelisms, arises from the fact that individual instances have been widened into generalizations. We wonder at the smallness of the Russets, the Early Joes, the Delawares, the Seckels and the Doyennes, but we forget the Fall Pippins, the Hubbardstons, the Spys, the Greenings, the Brightons, the Anjous and the Boscs.

But if it is a fallacy to associate increase of quality and decrease of size, it is perhaps a greater one to associate high quality with low color. A study of the preceding tables shows that red is a very prominent character in all the dessert fruits, and wholly green fruits, even among the apples, are comparatively rare in this country. The question of color is very largely one of climate. The American climate produces high color, while the English climate produces large numbers of green and yellow fruits. Even within our own limits there are great variations in this respect which proceed entirely independently of mere flavor,—a subject further discussed in Essay XVI.

In many varieties the seed-production has decreased, and it has been held by some that there is a correlation between this decrease and quality. The chief exponent of this hypothesis is Dr. E. Lewis Sturtevant, who has made a full discussion of the subject in a recent paper,* in which he asserts that "there seems to exist in fruits a correlation between seedlessness and quality, especially when that quality is expressed by the term tenderness of tissue. In fruits of fine quality, tenderness of the seed coating often seems a marked characteristic, as in grapes, where the seeds of the improved varieties are distinctly softer and more brittle than in those of the wild species; as in peaches and plums, where the tendency of a split stone is often noticeable in fruit of varieties of high quality." I have made no studies concerning the strength or thickness of seed-walls in cultivated fruits, but I do not doubt that there is a general tendency towards fragility. But I cannot look upon this tendency, if it exists, as in any way related to quality. It is undoubtedly due to constant selection for small-seeded fruits. Concerning the relations of seed-production to amelioration, I made some careful studies a few years ago;† and as subsequent study and observation have only confirmed the conclusions at which I then arrived, I may be pardoned for borrowing my present argument from that paper. The paper in question dealt with

---
*Mem. Torr. Bot. Club, i. No. 4 (1890).
†Proc. Amer. Pom. Soc., 1887, 120. Reprinted on p. 251.

the relation of seed-production to amelioration or the effects of cultivation, but as the ultimate aim of amelioration is the production of fruits of high quality, the remarks are germane to this discussion. As a rule, the cultivated varieties of apples contain more seeds than the wild European crabs. Forty specimens of fruit of these crab seedlings I found to contain a total of two hundred and fifty-six seeds, or an average of six and two-fifths seeds to the fruit. Forty Northern Spy apples yielded four hundred and eighty-one seeds, or an average of over twelve to the fruit. Normally, the apple contains five carpels, and each carpel contains two seeds, but some of these Spys had fifteen seeds and one had eighteen. And yet the Northern Spy ranks 10 in Mr. Lyon's dessert scale. I had all the seeds counted in a pound of each of thirty samples of tomatoes, representing twenty-six varieties of very different degrees of amelioration. The lowest comparative seed production was in the Cherry tomato, which is very near the wild type. There was found to be a general, but uncertain, increase in seed production as the variety departs from the Cherry tomato, but this increase bears no relation whatever to the extent of departure. Now and then an orchard fruit appears which is almost or wholly seedless, but it is not necessarily of high quality. So-called "coreless" apples and pears occasionally appear, but none of them have ever had sufficient merit to warrant their extensive propagation, Barron* mentions two No-Core apples, one of which is recommended only for kitchen use and the other is characterized as worthless. Seed-

---

*British Apples, 333 (1889).

production appears to me to be subject to the same laws of variation as other attributes of plants are, and it appears independently of other characters, in the same manner as size and color do.

In comparing the habit and vitality of the trees in the best varieties with the poorer ones, it must be borne in mind that a tender or weak-growing or unproductive tree which bears poor fruit is unfit for cultivation, and such varieties do not often appear in the fruit lists. But on the other hand, such trees are often cultivated when they bear some superior quality of fruit. So it happens that the poorest trees and least productive ones described in our manuals are those which produce fruit of the highest quality, and growers are likely to enlarge this circumstance into a generalization. But the fact that Winter Nelis is a poor grower, that Delaware is slender and particularly liable to mildew, and that the Newtown Pippin is unreliable, is many times overbalanced by the vigorous growth and productiveness of Anjou, Catawba and Northern Spy, and many others. In fact, if figures are compiled for the dessert fruits catalogued in the foregoing tables, it will be found that over 80 per cent of them are hardy, vigorous and productive. It is true that the very hardy Russian apples which have been introduced in late years are very often poor in quality, but this fact is probably due to lack of attention in improving the apple in Russia; pomologists in the extreme north confidently expect to be able to improve the quality of these fruits without losing the hardiness of the tree.

In regard to the notion that the best fruits are short-lived, I have only to say that it is a wholly gratuitous assumption. There are positively no facts in support of it.

If it is true, as the foregoing facts seem to show, that increase in quality is not acquired at the expense of other characters, you may ask me the common question, why it is that most of the market fruits are poor or indifferent in quality. This question is really but a restatement of my original proposition as to whether there is any correlation between quality and other characters; and, furthermore, it is not at all certain that the facts will warrant the question. In considering the question, it must be remembered that many of the best dessert fruits are cultivated solely for the sake of one character,—high quality,—while the best market fruits are cultivated for a variety of features, as size and color of fruit, and vigor, hardiness and productiveness of tree, while quality is usually not considered. Dessert fruits and market fruits are not, therefore, strictly comparable. But if there are any good market fruits which are at the same time good dessert fruits, we shall be obliged to admit that market qualities and table qualities are not incompatible. Of the two hundred and nineteen varieties of apples catalogued by Mr. Lyon, nineteen are rated 9 and 10 for market. Of these, six, or about one-third, also rate 9 and 10 for the dessert, as follows: Golden Russet, Hubbardston, Jonathan, Northern Spy, Peck's Pleasant, and Rhode Island Greening. Of these six, four rate the same for both table and market, and two rank one higher for market than for table. Moreover, there are four other varieties of the nineteen which rank as high as 8 in quality, which is two points higher than the Baldwin. Of the ten best market blackberries, four are included in the select dessert list. Fourteen cherries rate 9 and 10 for market, and just half of them are in the select list. Of the eight best market currants, however, only one is rated high for dessert, but the currant has not been developed in the direction of high quality. Of the four market gooseberries, two are in the other list. Mr. Lyon admits but six market grapes, of which one is a superior table fruit. Of the market peaches, nearly one-fourth are dessert fruits. One-fourth of the market pears rank highest for dessert, while one-third of the remainder rank as high as 8, which is the rating of the Bartlett and Sheldon. One-seventh of the best market plums are best for dessert, and nearly a third rank 8. Of the dozen best market raspberries, one-fourth are best table sorts, while half of them rank 8. Over a third of the market strawberries are dessert varieties. All these facts show conclusively that high quality is not incompatible with that combination of qualities which determines a market fruit, and they show that a very large number of our market fruits actually are dessert fruits. If we take the average quality of all the fruits ranking 9 and 10 for market, we find it to stand uniformly at 7 or above for dessert, or higher than medium quality. Thus the average table rating of all the high market apples is 7.1, or over one point higher than the Baldwin. The average of market blackberries is 8.5. This instance is particularly interesting because the blackberry is probably the fruit oftenest cited as decreasing in quality in proportion as it increases in size. Cherries average 7.3, and grapes 7.8. Peaches average 7.6, which is higher than the rating of Late Crawford, Barnard and other standard sorts. Market pears stand at 7.7, or higher than Angouleme, Flemish Beauty, Superfine and Louise Bonne. Plums average 7. Raspberries give an average of 7.8. Strawberries are 8, which is the rating of Kentucky, Miner, Ohio, Sharpless and Charles Downing. It is impossible to construe these facts to mean anything else than that all desirable characters of fruits may progress simultaneously.

In this connection we should discuss the popular notion that the berry fruits decrease in quality when they are brought into cultivation, because the decrease is supposed to be due to increase of size and vigor. Most people think of the wild strawberries and blackberries of youthful rambles as possessing unusual sweetness and aroma; and I do not doubt that it is true, even allowing for the exaggeration of retrospect, that wild berries are sweeter than those which we commonly obtain from the garden. But I know of no reason for believing that wild fruits are actually sweeter than tame ones. I am convinced that it is mostly a question of ripeness. To be sure, there may be cultivated varieties inferior in quality to some wild berries, but as a rule I do not believe that cultivation has had the effect of decreasing quality. I have given particular attention to this question for two years with blackberries, which are very generally considered to have lost sweetness by transfer to the garden. Among garden varieties I have studied Agawam, Early Cluster, Early Harvest, Ancient Briton, Snyder and Stone, and two of these are rated as low as 8 for dessert by Mr. Lyon, while the poorest of his blackberries go only as low as 7. In the study of wild berries, I visited a region which I had known in boyhood, and which I have always remembered because of its great and luscious blackberries. But the comparison was greatly in favor of the tame berries, if they are allowed to remain upon the bushes until ripe. In the wild patches we practice an unconscious choice and pick only those berries which please us. We pick the ripest and the best. It is noticeable, also, that we pick the largest and base our judgment upon them, while we should find the best quality in the smallest berries, if our assumed logic is sound. Cultivated berries, when marketed, are necessarily picked before they are ripe, and they never reach their full quality. And even when picked for table use, blackness in the blackberry and redness in the strawberry are usually considered as measures of ripeness. But the true measure of ripeness is softness. A well grown, fully ripe blackberry, which falls into the hand when the cluster is shaken, possesses a tenderness, juiciness, and sweetness which I have rarely found in a wild berry. And the same is true, in my experience, of strawberries and raspberries.

But we do not need to rely upon individual tastes, for all chemical examinations which I have been able to find show that sweetness increases with the increase or intensification of cultivation. This would seem to be almost necessarily the case because the ultimate aim of cultivation is to supply more food to the plant, and this food, in fruits, is largely potash, which seems to bear a definite ratio to sugar. Dr. Stone reports* a series of interesting experiments in this direction at the Massachusetts Agricultural College: "A wild

---

*Amer. Gard. vi. 210 (1885).

specimen of *Vitis Labrusca* (our common wild grape) was torn apart at its root; one-half was left in its natural condition, the other transplanted to cultivated ground and treated with nitrate of potash and bone superphosphate. At the end of three years fruit from the cultivated vine contained 12 per cent more potash and 20 per cent more sugar than that from the wild one." Analysis of wild and cultivated strawberries showed a great increase in potash in the cultivated variety: "But the change was not confined to the mineral elements alone, for the same analysis showed that the proportion of sugar to acid in the wild species is as two to one, while in the cultivated varieties it is increased to six to one or more." Dr. Stone further declares that "potash fertilizers have decidedly improved the desirable qualities of fruits. Wherever the percentage of this element has been raised, the change is accompanied by an increase of sugar and decrease of acid." Dr. Stone has made a subsequent examination of the chemical composition of strawberries at the Tennessee Experiment Station* and finds that "in the varieties examined, the average proportion of acid to sugar was 1 to 3.5. For the wild strawberry, the only references available, and these very meagre, show a corresponding proportion of 1 to 2. This indicates that a change for the better has been made, but it is far from probable that the limit has been reached." Fresenius gives the sugar in cultivated strawberries as 7.5 per cent and the free acid as 1.13, and in the wild berries as 3.2 and 1.6 per cent respectively. Cultivated raspberries, according to the

*Bull. 4, vol. ii. Tenn. Exp. Sta.

same authority, contain 4.7 per cent of sugar and 1.3 per cent of free acid, while wild ones contain 3.5 per cent of sugar and 1.9 of acid. Parsons* finds that sugar increases rapidly in oranges as they depart from the wild types, although free acids do not show a corresponding decrease. Thus the wild Bitter-sweet of Florida contains .84 per cent of cane sugar and 5.71 of glucose; and the sour orange .97 cane sugar and 3.36 glucose; the common oranges, 4.38 and 4.60 respectively; russets, 4.51 and 7.29; mandarin, 8.07 and 4.77. The figures and experiences uniformly show that amelioration and sweetness go hand in hand; and every one who has tested seedling or wilding fruits can bear testimony to the same fact.

As a matter of experience, seeds of small or low-colored fruits, or from tender or unproductive varieties, do not give a larger proportion of varieties of high quality than seeds from large, highly colored and vigorous kinds. And it is worthy of remark that while most pomologists hold to the correlation of quality with decrease of other characters, they at the same time recommend that in producing new varieties only seed from the largest, finest and hardiest varieties should be used.

It is evident, from our discussion, that quality and other characters of cultivated fruits appear independently of each other,—that there is no true correlation between these characters. There is a general increase in all characters as amelioration progresses, at least in all characters which are sought by horticulturists; and this fact must ever remain the chief inspiration to man in his efforts to ameliorate plants.

---

*Agric. Science, iii. 29.

XI.

THE NATURAL HISTORY OF SYNONYMS.[1]

Two or three days ago, a man living in the county where we are now assembled, wrote me asking if it is possible for two seedling strawberries to be so much alike that they cannot be told apart. This question is the gist of some sharp controversy in the horticultural world, although it may not be asked in the above form. Is it possible for the same variety to originate twice? Or, is every new seedling a distinct variety?

The confusion attending the discussion of this question arises because there are two opposed views of what constitutes a variety. One view contends that a variety is determined by its origin,—that every plant, amongst fruits at least, coming directly from seed is for that reason distinct from all other varieties. The other view defines a variety by its own tangible attributes: if the plant can be readily distinguished from related forms, it is a new or distinct variety; but if it cannot be distinguished, it is regarded as identical with some older type, wholly irrespective of its origin, and its name—if it has received one—then becomes a synonym. These two positions must be clearly distinguished

---

[1] Read before the American Association of Nurserymen, at Niagara Falls, N. Y., June 6, 1894. Printed in Report of the Nineteenth Meeting, pp. 32 to 35.

if we are to arrive at just conclusions respecting the origin and uses of synonymous names.

In approaching the subject, we must first determine the uses to the vegetable kingdom of reproduction by means of seeds. Inasmuch as all plants have, or may have, the power of reproducing their kind by means of buds or roots or other asexual parts, it must follow that the complex and highly specialized seed or sexual reproduction serves some further purpose than mere multiplication of the plant. It is now considered that this second and most important office of sex is to introduce new features into the offspring, so that, no two of them being alike, all seedlings may tend to subsist in the resulting struggle for existence because each one may be able to live in conditions more or less unsuited to all the others. So it comes that seedlings are more variable or diverse amongst themselves than budded or cutting-made plants are, and this, as you know, is the reason why any variety of fruit—that is, any particular seedling plant—must be propagated by buds rather than by seeds if it is to be kept "true to name." Yet there is some variation or diversity amongst all budded plants. All individuals are unlike: while all Baldwin apple trees, for example, make globular heads and bear a large red winter fruit, there is much minor variation in the shape of top and in size, coloring and season of the fruit. You have all observed that no two trees in your orchard are alike.

Now, therefore, if it is held that every seedling is a new variety simply because it is more or less different from its parents, in like manner it must be held that every budded tree is a new variety, because each one is in some respect unlike its parent. And it is a fact that some of our varieties of fruits and vegetables have originated from what are called bud-variations, or unusual branches or other parts appearing first upon the plant itself; and this proves that this asexual or bud variation may be as pronounced as any variation or difference in seedlings. But those who contend that every seedling is a new variety will now say that marked variation is much more frequent amongst seedlings than amongst bud-propagated plants; and this is true. But it is also true that batches of seedlings are often almost indistinguishable from their parents and are, therefore, no more worthy to be called new varieties than bud-propagated plants are.

We have now found that no two plants are alike, no matter how they have originated; but it is only when the differences are great enough to create some new value in the plants that we regard them as new or distinct varieties. If, therefore, two seedling strawberries are brought together and they are so nearly alike that it is not worth while to distinguish them—as often happens—we are forced to conclude that essentially the same type has arisen twice, or, perhaps, even a half dozen times. In other words, a variety is not determined by the manner of its origin.

Now, synonyms arise in three ways,—by the bringing together of like plants of distinct origin, by the divergence or modification of plants of like origin, and by the simple practice of re-naming. It is commonly held that synonyms are among the misfortunes of horticulture, but the first two classes of synonymous names are not only unavoidable but they may serve distinctly useful purposes. Let us take the Hill's Chili peach as an example of the first class,— the independent origin of like forms. This peach was not described in Downing's original work, nor even in the revision of 1872. It appears only in the appendix, yet even then it is credited with thirteen synonyms. Now it is probable that the major part of these synonyms represent types of distinct origin, for it is well known that this variety has a strong tendency to reproduce itself from seed. Last year a peach grower showed me about a dozen trees, in fruit, of Hill's Chili seedlings, and while each had some minor point of difference, there was only one in the lot which could be called anything else than Hill's Chili. Now, a type of fruit which tends strongly to reproduce itself from seed is one which is virile, because it has the power of renewing itself as often as it may be vitiated by poor treatment or careless propagation; and it is also one which adapts itself readily to a wide range of conditions by means of its recurring variations. Such a type is cosmopolitan. This is one strong point in favor of the Russian apples, which run in families or races, a circumstance which has arisen from long-continued reproduction by seeds with little interposition of graftage.

As a rule, therefore, the more synonyms a plant has, the greater are the assurances that it will thrive over a wide range of country and in many diverse conditions; and, in like manner, varieties which belong to well-marked tribes or families usually have the strongest or most virile characters.

Let us, for illustration, represent the original type of the peach by the hub of a wheel, and each new and distinct variety by the starting-point of a spoke. Now, those spokes lengthen fastest where the greatest number of forms appear. There will be the early white-fleshed half-cling varieties, represented by the Hale, upon one side; on another side the great Crawford family starts off; on another the old Barnard tribe; on another the Hill's Chili type; and on still another the Chinese cling, and so on. Presently, our wheel has lost its symmetry, and instead of presenting a circular outline, it is contorted by numerous swelling prominences, of which the greatest, perhaps, in eastern America, is the Crawford protuberance; and this is the elevation, also, which is most conspicuous in the constitution of our orchards.

I have already said before this association (Essay XVI.) that I believe that the best result of the increasing competition in horticultural pursuits will be the habit of giving much closer attention to the adaptability of varieties to particular conditions and uses. The synonyms, as I have now explained them, will aid us in selecting from particular varieties those strains which may be better suited to given conditions than the pure or original type of the variety itself is. I once attempted to refer the many catalogued varieties of tomatoes to a few well-marked types, and I was sure that I had simplified the matter greatly because I had reduced the varieties more than one-half. But when I asked an experienced gardener for his opinion of the reduction, he remarked: "Excellent! You have put similar kinds together where I can find them, and I have ordered all the kinds which you refer to the Paragon." In other words, his experience had taught him that any variety which represents the Paragon so closely as to be considered to be identical with it, must have exceptional merit. So my effort, instead of lessening the number of varieties, simply emphasized the value or characters of those which I had regarded as synonyms!

I should by no means depreciate the common practice of reducing varieties to synonyms, but I must repeat that varieties which are, by common consent, regarded as synonymous with an older type or name, are not necessarily identical with that type in all respects. While reducing like forms to synonyms, I should still insist upon the distinctions of all those which are peculiar, either by origin or subsequent adaptation, to particular regions or localities. Let us admit, for instance, that, for all purposes of description, Delaware Winter and Lawver are the same; I should still prefer Delaware Winter for planting on the Atlantic seaboard and Lawver for the Mississippi Valley. I am convinced that we need to discover differences rather than similarities, for by that means we come to know varieties intimately. The fact that strains and sub-varieties are quite as important to the discerning horticulturist as the type of the variety itself, has been long recognized by vegetable gardeners, who are under severe competition, and to whom very small differences in varieties are exceedingly important.

The ideal treatment of synonyms is to describe a variable or cosmopolitan variety as a type, and then to treat the synonyms with reference to their history,—placing in one category all those sub-types which have probably sprung independently from seed, in another all those strains which have been developed in certain localities by selection or the effect of environment, and in a third list all those duplicate names which have been given outright to the very same type. These latter only—the re-names—are true synonyms. With such lists as these before me, I should expect the best results in selecting from those types which have the longest list of duplicate or synonymous names. Something of this kind has occurred unconsciously in all generations. The oldest and most prized fruits are generally the ones which have the greatest number of synonyms. Consider, if you will, the multitude of forms of the Green Gage plum which are known in England. This, like most very old and dominant types, tends to repeat itself from seeds, and as the years pass new strains are grouped about the parent stock, each one an independent testimony to the value of the type.

On the other hand, from a nurseryman's point of view, one must look with suspicion upon seedlings of old and variable types, for they are likely to be so nearly like other forms of similar origin that customers will not distinguish them, and the nurseryman may be charged with re-naming old varieties; and the nurseryman may have difficulty, too, in distinguishing the best strains of these variable types. The German Prune is an example. There are several types of this in cultivation, some good and some indifferent, and I should never think of ordering German Prune from a nurseryman unless I knew from what particular strain he has propagated.

In conclusion, therefore, it may be said that a variety, in the horticultural sense, is a plant, and its progeny, which is so distinct from other types that it has some particular value of its own. This variety may be re-originated from seeds. Yet there are few, if any, seedlings which are absolutely identical, and these re-originations may constitute strains or sub-varieties which possess unique value for certain purposes. The types which possess the most synonyms are the strongest and most cosmopolitan, for, if the synonym comes from a new origination, it indicates the power of the type to perpetuate or renew itself; if it comes from the subsequent variation of an old type—as the variation of the Newtown Pippin into the Albemarle Pippin in Virginia and into the Five-Crowned Pippin in Australia—it indicates that the type is sufficiently elastic to adapt itself to wide differences of climate, and that if it remains local in distribution it is because of some external or incidental hindrance, like the apple-scab in the case of the Newtown Pippin above cited; if it comes from a local renaming, the synonym shows that the variety is much prized in the community in which the name was given; or, if the synonym is made by a nurseryman for purposes of trade—a practice which I believe to be much less common than is generally supposed—it is still a testimonial to the merits of the variety.

XII.

REFLECTIVE IMPRESSIONS OF THE NURSERY BUSINESS.[1]

It often happens that one who is not actively engaged in any given business or profession, but who has opportunities to observe the methods and the men concerned in it, may form impressions of certain features of it which may possess quite as much value as those opinions which are held by men who are constantly absorbed in its details. At all events, this is my excuse for coming before this body of nurserymen; and if the impressions which I present to you are wholly irrelevant or even unfounded, you may still be interested to know how certain phases of the nursery business strike an outsider.

In the first place, I look upon the nursery business as the foundation of our fruit growing; and if my remarks seem to have a fruit-grower's bias, it is because I am most fully conscious of the great importance of nursery-culture to the evolution of our agriculture. The old type of farming is gradually crumbling away, and new and special industries are growing upon its ruins. The dominant type in this newer movement in the older states is fruit culture. At the present rate of tree planting, the northern half

---

[1] Read before the American Association of Nurserymen, at Indianapolis, June 13, 1895. Printed in Report of the Twentieth Annual Meeting of the Association, 40-43.

of western New York, for example, will be a continuous orchard by the middle of the coming century. Now, all these trees come from nurseries of one kind or another, and the variety of fruit which the pomologist plants is determined very largely by what the nurserymen can supply. The buyer, of course, makes a choice of varieties, but his range is limited, for the number of varieties which the nurserymen of any locality sell is really very small compared with the number of known meritorious kinds. If so much of the merit or demerit of our fruit growing depends upon the nurseryman, we must first ask what it is that determines the selection of the varieties which he grows.

The nurseryman contends that he grows the varieties which the planters want,—those for which there is a demand. As a matter of fact, he largely forces the demand by magnifying the value of those varieties which are good growers in the nursery. The nurseryman's business ends with the growing of the young tree, and the tree which makes the straightest, most rapid and cleanest growth is the one which finds the readiest sale. Now, it by no means follows that the variety which is the cheapest and best for the nurseryman to grow is the best for the fruit grower to plant. Probably every apple grower is now ready to admit that the Baldwin has been too much planted, whilst Canada Red and various other varieties which are poor growers in the nursery row have been too little planted.

The blame for this condition of things does not rest wholly with the nurseryman, although it is partly his fault. The original difficulty lies in the fact, it seems to me, that our conception, and consequently our definition, of what constitutes a first-class tree is at variance with the truth. We conceive a first-class nursery tree to be one which grows straight and smooth, tall and stocky, whilst we know that very many— perhaps half—the varieties of apples and pears and plums will not grow that way. In order to make our conception true, we grow those varieties which will satisfy the definition, and, as a result, there is a constant tendency to eliminate from our lists some of the best and most profitable varieties.

All this could be remedied if people were to be taught that varieties of fruit trees may be just as different and distinct in habit of growth as they are in kind of fruit, and that a first-class tree is a well-grown specimen *which has the characteristics of the variety*. It seems to me that it is time for nurserymen to begin to enforce this conception upon the public. Why may not a catalogue explain that a tree may be first-class and yet be crooked and gnarly? Why not place the emphasis upon health and vigor, and not upon mere shape and comeliness? And why may not a nurseryman give a list of those varieties which are comely growers, and another list of those which are wayward growers?

I am by no means convinced that the time has come for the extended propagation of many of these excellent but poor-growing varieties which the nurseryman has practically discarded because of their unpleasant habit; but I believe that a beginning should be made in this direction. The question really resolves itself into this: Are nurserymen now growing and pushing the varieties which are most useful to fruit growing? Looking at the question from my own point of view, I cannot escape the conviction that the common staple or commercial varieties are not always the best for the fruit grower. If this is true, then the remedy is education for the grower, that he may select the varieties which are best for his purposes and conditions; but this education, it seems to me, should at least be fostered by the nurseryman, inasmuch as his ultimate success is determined by the success or profitableness of fruit-growing.

It is a common notion that we already have too many varieties of fruits, but I think that it is nearer the truth to say that we have too few, or, at least, that we grow them with too little discrimination as to their uses and the soils and places to which they are adapted. At the World's Fair meeting of this association, I presented a paper upon "Horticultural Geography" (Essay XVI.), in which I tried to point out that the collection of fruits at the Exposition showed that every well-marked geographical region soon comes to have a type of varieties of its own, and I endeavored to prove that the wholesale growing of many ill-sorted varieties by any one nursery, and the indiscriminate dissemination of them over the country, is opposed to the best experience in older countries, and to the best science. Every well-informed fruit grower knows that varieties which are worthless with him may be valuable to one of his neighbors, and the experiment station reports upon new varieties show a remarkable diversity of opinion. These facts mean that varieties have local adaptations, and that the best fruit grower, other things being the same, is the one who most clearly discerns the adaptability of varieties to his own conditions. As countries grow older, these local varieties become more numerous, because more varieties have originated, and because sufficient time has elapsed in which their merits or adaptabilities have been discovered. We may expect, therefore, that the future will see a still greater diversification in varieties, and a greater attention on the part of nurserymen to the selection of varieties for particular regions and special uses,—a condition of things which impresses the American horticulturist when he visits the nurseries and fruit plantations of Europe. If all this is true, the present standard of excellence or merit in nursery stock is fictitious, and must gradually pass away.

Another question which I wish to urge upon you is this: How far is the current nursery practice responsible for the barrenness of orchards? We know that much of the failure of orchards to bear is due to insects and fungi, and some of it to neglect of cultivation and lack of plant food; but there are orchards in which none of these causes seem to be responsible for the fruitlessness. Such orchards seem to be sterile by habit. Now, it is well known that no two trees of the same variety, and standing side by side, will bear equally, any more than they will grow equally. That is, every tree has an individuality, in which it differs from all other trees, and this individuality may consist quite as much in variation in productiveness as in any other character. Furthermore, it is well established that cions or buds tend to perpetuate the features of the plant from which they are taken. Cions from a normally unproductive or non-bearing tree may be expected to yield less productive progeny than those from habitually productive trees. It is also asserted that cions from young unbearing trees, particularly from nursery stock, give later bearing trees than those taken from old bearing trees, and there is much reason for believing this to be often true. At all events, we cannot emphasize too strongly the importance of careful selection of buds and cions for the propagation of nursery stock. Florists know that the selection of a parent plant is a very important consideration in selecting cuttings for the making of floriferous stock, and they are even particular about the part of the plant from which these cuttings shall be taken. Experienced grafters always prefer to take cions from habitually prolific trees, and they even exercise a choice between the branches of the same tree, always avoiding water sprouts and preferring the hard, well-ripened wood from the upper part of the tree. All scientific considerations commend these practices, for we are bound to look upon every branch as in some sense a distinct individual, since it is unlike every other branch, and it is capable of living or of being propagated when severed from the colony or the tree to which it belongs. I will not say that the barrenness of our orchards is ever due to an unwise selection of cions or buds by which they were propagated, but I am so well satisfied in my own mind that such may be true that, in an apple orchard which I am now planting, I am expecting to top-work all the trees from trees which I know to have been productive. It would certainly be a good and safe stroke of business for a nurseryman to select his cions, so far as possible, from trees of known excellence and prolificacy, and to let the fact be known.

XIII.

THE RELATION OF SEED-BEARING TO CULTIVATION.[1]

THERE seems to be much confusion of opinion concerning the supposed relations between seed-production and amelioration. There is a very general notion that production of seeds lessens in direct proportion to the departure, through cultivation, of the plant from the first or wild type. This supposition, it occurs to me, is but partly true, and even when true, is misleading.

For the present purpose, the relation of seed-production to cultivation can be sufficiently studied under three general heads, the first of which discusses selection more particularly. By the term seed-production, I mean to refer to the seed product of the individual fruit, not to that of an entire inflorescence or plant.

1. *Seed-production has increased, as a rule, in those plants which are cultivated for their seeds.* Man would naturally and almost unconsciously select for sowing those seeds which are borne in the most productive fruits. In this way a slow, but continuous, selection has augmented seed-production, and many times, no doubt, almost independently of cultivation. Examples of this increase may be found in certain tropical plants, and in beans and peas. Of course, the converse of this

---
[1] Proceedings of the Twenty-first Session of the American Pomological Society, 120 (1887)

rule will be true in those cases in which man desires a lessening of seed-production in order that some advantage may be gained for the seeds that remain.

2. *Seed-production has decreased, as a rule, in those plants which are propagated exclusively, or nearly so, by separable parts other than seeds.* Under this caption may be cited the banana, sweet potato, potato, horse-radish, sugar cane, some onions, and others. As a rule, all wild plants which propagate readily by tubers, offshoots, or similar means, produce comparatively few seeds, or, in some instances, none whatever. In this connection it is only necessary to cite the instances of quack grass upon certain soils, Canada thistles, and some potamogetons, in support of this proposition. The production of seeds and fruit is an exhaustive process, demanding much of the plant's vitality, and if this vitality is early diverted into growth of other organs, necessarily the fruit and seeds must suffer. This explains why the early varieties of potatoes produce fewer seeds than the late varieties. The tubers form earlier in the life of the plant, and the plant energy is diverted before the blossoms appear. If the tubers are not allowed to form, the plant produces flowers and fruits more abundantly. This has been proved by Thomas Andrew Knight. For the same reason, flowers on young and thrifty fruit trees do not set fruit, although the flowers may produce good pollen and perfect pistils. Luxuriant growth makes the first demand upon the young tree, and seed-production suffers. Cultivation lessens seed-production and fruit-production in some of these cases, simply because it exaggerates the opposing or vegetative methods of propagation through constant breeding

for larger tubers; but the cultivation, of itself, is not opposed to seed-production.

The case of the banana is unique in this section, inasmuch as the rootstock is not the part especially demanded by man. Yet there is reason to believe that in this case selection, rather than cultivation, has had the most to do with the seedless character of this singular fruit. Perhaps a discussion of this case should fall more properly under the next caption.

3. *Seed-production bears no immediate relation to cultivation in those plants which are cultivated for the flesh or pulp of their so-called fruits.* As a rule, the cultivated varieties of apples contain more seeds than the wild apples of Europe do. Forty specimens of the wild crab (*Pyrus Malus*) of Central Europe produced an aggregate of two hundred and fifty-six seeds, or an average of six and two-fifths seeds to each fruit. Forty Northern Spys contained four hundred and eighty-one seeds, or an average of twelve and one-fortieth to the fruit. Normally, the apple should contain ten seeds, two in each carpel, but some of these Spys had fifteen seeds and one had eighteen. Yet some other varieties of apples contain fewer than the normal number, while some are almost entirely seedless. There is generally a slight increase in seed-production as fruits develop away from the first type, especially if the fruits become larger. This is a natural consequence of the increase in size, though it bears no constant ratio to this increase. I am disposed to regard the seedless apples and pears in the light of seminal sports, exactly analogous to red apples, long apples, or other forms of variation; and I should not expect to find this character to possess much stronger

hereditability than form or color does. Relative seed-production can be well studied in the tomatoes, as we have the wild type, or very near it, and numerous monstrous varieties for comparison. I submit a table of seed-production in tomatoes:

Varieties.	No. of fruits in the pound.	No. of seeds in the pound.	Average no. of seeds in a fruit.	Where the variety was obtained.*
Red Cherry	101	7,312	72 2-5	Agricultural College (*Henderson*).
Kirsche Rothe	68	4,830	71 1-3	Prussia.
King Humbert	7	645	92 1-7	Agricultural College (*Rawson*).
King Humbert	7¼	703	97	Prussia.
Criterion	7	1,095	156 3-7	Agricultural College (*Gregory*).
Conqueror	6	1,215	202 1-2	England.
Large Red	7	1,754	250 4-7	England.
Franz Gross Rothe	5	1,480	296	Prussia.
Hubbard's Curled Leaf	7	1,310	187 1-7	Agricultural College (*Nellis*).
Rouge Grosse Hative	8	1,608	201	France.
Tom Thumb	8	1,502	187 3-4	Agricultural College (*Rawson*).
Improved Large Yellow	13	2,250	173	Agricultural College (*Thorburn*).
Persian	5	1,398	279 3-5	Agricultural College (*Nellis*).
The Cook's Favorite	10	1,457	145 7-10	Prussia.
Boston Market	6	1,106	184 1-3	Agricultural College (*Rawson*).
Fulton Market	6	1,441	240 1-6	Agricultural College (*Gregory*).
New York Market	6	925	154 1-6	Agricultural College (*Nellis*).
Trophy	5	886	177 1-5	England.
Trophy	5	702	140 2-5	England.
Trophy	6	1,450	241 2-3	Prussia.
Cardinal	4	941	235 1-4	Thorburn, N. Y.
Livingston's Favorite	6	1,166	194 1-3	England.
New Red Apple	5	1,365	273	Agricultural College (*Gregory*).
Tilden	10	1,696	169 3-5	Agricultural College (*Gregory*).
Paragon	4	763	190 3-4	Agricultural College (*Henderson*).
Paragon	4	1,180	295	Prussia.
Emery	4	781	195 1-4	Agricultural College (*Rawson*).
Acme	5	1,256	251 1-5	Prussia.
Mikado	2	435	217 1-2	Agricultural College (*Henderson*).
French Upright	5	583	116 3-5	Agricultural College (*Thorburn*).

Here the lowest average seed-production is in the Cherry tomato, which is very nearly, if not exactly, the original form of the tomato. There is a general, but uncertain, increase upon this average as the varieties depart from this variety. Yet this increase bears no re-

---

*These tomatoes were grown at the Agricultural College of Michigan. The seeds of some of the samples, as indicated, were from tomatoes grown at the College; but the original source of the stock is given in parenthesis.

lation to the extent of departure. Let us compare the Cherry and the Mikado. The fruit of the Mikado is about fifty times heavier than that of the Cherry, yet the seed-production is only three times as great. If similar comparisons are made between the Cherry and other varieties, we shall find other degrees of dissimilarity between development in number of seeds and size and weight of fruit. In other words, seed-production in all fruits which fall under this third caption is an incidental variation, the same as form, color, size, flavor, texture and other characters are.

XIV.

VARIATION AFTER BIRTH.[1]

AT THE present time, our attention is directed to differences or variations which are born with the individual. We are told that variation which is useful to the species is congenital, or born of the union—or the amalgamation in varying degrees—of parents which are unlike each other. From the variations which thus arise, natural selection chooses those which fit the conditions of life and destroys the remainder. That is, individuals are born unlike and unequal, and adaptation to environment is wholly the result of subsequent selection.

These are some of the practical conclusions of the Neo-Darwinian philosophy. It seems to me that we are in danger of letting our speculations run away with us. Our philosophy should be tested now and then by direct observation and experiment, and thus be kept within the limits of probability. The writings of Darwin impress me in this quality more than in any other, —in the persistency and single-mindedness with which the author always goes to nature for his facts.

In this spirit, let us drop our speculations for a moment, and look at some of the commonest phenomena of plant life as they transpire all about us. We shall find that, for all we can see, most plants start equal, but eventually become unequal. It is undoubt-

[1] American Naturalist, January, 1896, pp. 17 to 24.

edly true that every plant has individuality from the first,—that is, that it differs in some minute degree from all other plants, the same as all animals possess differences of personality; but these initial individual differences are often entirely inadequate to account for the wide divergence which may occur between the members of any brood before they reach their maturity.

The greater number of plants, as I have said, start practically equal, but they may soon become widely unlike. Now, everyone knows that these final unlikenesses are direct adaptations to the circumstances in which the plant lives. It is the effort to adapt itself to circumstances which gives rise to the variation. The whole structure of agriculture is built upon this fact. All the value of tillage, fertilizing and pruning lies in the modification which the plant is made to undergo. Observe, if you will, the wheat fields of any harvest time. Some fields are "uneven," as the farmers say; and you observe that this unevenness is plainly associated with the condition of the land. On dry knolls, the straw is short and the plant early; on moister and looser lands the plant is tall, later, with long, well-filled heads; on very rich spots, the plants have had too much nitrogen and they grow too tall and "sappy," and the wheat "lodges" and does not fill. That is, the plants started equal, but they ended unequal. Another field of wheat may be very uniform throughout; it is said to be "a good stand," which only means, as one can observe for himself, that the soil is uniform in quality and was equally well prepared in all parts. That is, the plants started equal, and they remained equal because the conditions were equal. Every crop that was ever grown in the soil enforces the same lessons. We know that variations in plants are very largely due to diverse conditions which arise after birth.

All these variations in land and other physical conditions are present in varying degrees in wild nature, and we know that the same kind of adaptations to conditions are proceeding everywhere before our eyes. We cannot stroll afield without seeing it. Dandelions in the hollows, on the hillocks, in the roadside gravel, in the garden—they are all different dandelions, and we know that any one would have become the other if it had grown where the other does.

But aside from the differences arising directly from physical conditions of soil and temperature and moisture, and the like, there are differences which are forced upon plants by the struggle for life. We are apt to think that, as plants grow and crowd each other, the weaker ones die outright, because they were endowed with—that is, born with—different capabilities of withstanding the scuffle. As a matter of fact, however, the number of individuals in any area may remain the same, or even increase, whilst, at the same time, every one of them is growing bigger. Early last summer I staked off an area of twenty inches square in a rich and weedy bit of land. When the first observations were made, on the 10th of July, the little plat had a population of eighty-two plants belonging to ten species. Each plant was ambitious to fill the entire space, and yet it must compete with eighty-one other equally ambitious individuals. Yet, a month later, the number of plants had increased to eighty-six, and late in September, when some of the plants had completed their growth and had died, there was still a population of sixty-eight. The censuses at the three dates were as follows:

	July 10	Aug. 13	Sept. 25
Crab grass (*Panicum sanguinale*)	22	20	15
Black Medick (*Medicago lupulina*)	16	17	15
Purslane	14	15	12
White Clover	12	13	8
Red Clover	9	11	8
Red-root (*Amarantus retroflexus*)	4	4	4
Ragweed (*Ambrosia artemisæfolia*)	2	2	2
Pigeon-grass (*Setaria glauca*)	1	2	3
Pigweed (*Chenopodium album*)	1	1	0
Shepherd's Purse	1	1	1
	82	86	68

What a happy family this was! In all this jostle up to the middle of August, during which every plant had increased its bulk from two to twenty times, only the crab grass—apparently the most tenacious of them all—had fallen off; and yet the area seemed to be full in the beginning! How, then, if all had grown bigger, could there have been an increase in numbers, or even a maintenance of the original population? In two ways: First, the plants were of widely different species of unlike habits, so that one plant could grow in a place where its neighbor could not. Whilst the pigweed was growing tall, the medick was creeping beneath it. This is the law of divergence of character, so well formulated by Darwin. It is a principle of wide application in agriculture. The farmer "seeds" his wheat-field to clover when it is so full of wheat that no more wheat can grow there, he grows pumpkins in a cornfield which is full of corn, and he grows docks and stick-tights in the thickest orchards. Plants have no doubt adapted themselves directly, in the battle of life, to each other's company.

The second and chief reason for the maintenance of this dense population was the fact that each plant grew to a different shape and stature, and each one acquired a different longevity; that is, they had varied, because they had to vary in order to live. So that, whilst all seemed to have an equal chance early in July, there were in August two great branching red-roots, one lusty ragweed and eighty-three other plants of various degrees of littleness. The third census, taken September 25th, is very interesting, because it shows that some of the plants of each of the dominant species had died or matured, whilst others were still growing. That is, the plants which were forced to remain small also matured early and thereby, by virtue of their smallness, they had lessened by several days the risk of living, and they had thus gained some advantage over their larger and stronger companions, which were still in danger of being killed by frost or accident. When winter finally set in, the little plat seemed to have been inhabited only by three big red-roots and two small ones and by one ragweed. The remains of these six plants stood stiff and assertive in the winds; but if one looked closer he saw the remains of many lesser plants, each "yielding seed after his kind," each one, no doubt, having impressed something of its stature and form upon its seeds for resurrection of similar qualities in the following year. All this variation must have been the result of struggle for existence, for it is not conceivable that in less than two square feet of soil there could have been other conditions sufficiently diverse to have caused such marked unlikenesses; and I shall allow the plat to remain without defilement, that I may observe the conflict in the years to come, and I shall also sow seeds from some of the unlike plants.* From all these facts, I am bound to think that physical environment and struggle for life are both powerful causes of variation in plants which are born equal.

Still, the reader may say, like Weismann, that these differences were potentially present in the germ, that there was an inherited tendency for the given red-root to grow three feet tall when eighty-five other plants were grown alongside of it in

---

* From two of the red-root (*Amarantus retroflexus*) plants of different stature, seeds were sown in pans in the greenhouse. One of the plants was twelve inches high and had a spread of branches of nine inches. The other was twenty-four inches high and thirty inches broad. The seeds from each were thoroughly ripe and the plants were matured; yet of the seeds from the smaller plant only a few had sufficient vitality to germinate, and all the plants which did appear were very much smaller in stature at maturity than the seedlings of the larger plant. The difference in vigor between the two lots was most remarkable, showing—what every gardener knows to be true—that the acquired habit of a plant generally has a powerful effect upon its offspring.

As this Essay goes to press, June 23, 1896, this little plot presents a most interesting aspect. It is tangled full of luxurious herbage, but the passer-by would see little else than a clump of red clover, and here and there, about the edges, a ragweed. My gardener remarked that the plat contains less plants than last year. Yet here is the census:

Black Medick	3 plants.
White Clover	5 "
Red Clover	11 "
Red-root	78 "
Ragweed	135 "
Pigweed	1 "
Shepherd's Purse	2 "
Mallow (*Malva rotundifolia*)	6 "
Sow-thistle (*Sonchus oleraceus*)	1 "
Alsike Clover	7 "
Spears of grass, about	50 "
	299 "

Notwithstanding all this marvelous population, the greater part of the space

twenty inches square of soil. Then let us try plants which had no germ-plasm, that is, cuttings from maiden wood. A lot of cuttings were taken from one petunia plant, and these cuttings were grown singly in pots in perfectly uniform prepared soil, the pots being completely glazed with shellac and the bottoms closed to prevent drainage. Then each pot was given a weighed amount of different chemical fertilizer and supplied with perfectly like weighed quantities of water. All weak or unhealthy plants were thrown out, and a most painstaking effort was made to select perfectly equal plants. But very soon they were unequal. Those fed liberally on potash were short, those given nitrogen were tall and lusty; and the variations in floriferousness and maturity were remarkable. The data of maturity and productiveness were as follows:

Phosphate of Potash.	Sulphate of Potash.	Phosphate of Soda.	Check.	Phosphate of Ammonia.
68 days	99 days	65 days	67 days	104 days
23½ blooms	18 blooms	27½ blooms	26½ blooms	33 blooms

Here then, is a variation of thirty-nine days, or over a month, in the time of first bloom, and of an average of fifteen flowers per plant in asexual plants from the same stock, all of which started equal and which were grown in perfectly uniform conditions, save the one element of food.

---

was occupied by five burly clumps of red clover. Only two or three of the red-roots were to be seen above the herbage, and they were spindling and unbranched; yet many of the tiny ones under the clover stools were bearing seeds. Of all the ragweeds, none were branched. They were simply etiolated specimens, save about the edges of the area, dying in an attempt to reach the light. Most of them were the merest weaklings, soft and wilted and not more than three or four inches high, and it was plain that many had already died. Of the two shepherd's purses, one was very tall and much branched, whilst the other was a puny thing, with but a single stem; yet both were in full fruit. The grass was mostly but the

But these or similar variations in cuttings are the commonest experiences of gardeners. Whilst some philosophers are contending that all variation comes through sexual union, the gardener has proof day by day that it is not so. In fact, he does not stop to consider the difference between seedlings and budplants in his efforts to improve a type, for he knows by experience that he is able to modify his plants in an equal degree, whatever the origin of the plants may have been. Very many of our best domestic plants are selections from plants which are always grown from cuttings or other asexual parts. A fruit-grower asked me to inspect a new blackberry which he had raised. "What is its parentage?" I asked. "Simply a selection from an extra good plant of Snyder," he answered; that is, selection by means of suckers, not by seedlings. The variety was clearly distinct from Snyder, whereupon I named it for him. The Snyder plants were originally all equal, all divisions, in fact, of one plant, but because of change of soil or some other condition, some of the plants varied, and one of them, at least, is now the parent of a new variety.

But even Mr. Weismann would agree to all this, only he would add that these variations are of no use to the next generation, because he assumes that they

---

merest sprouts on the surface of the ground, and it was evident that most of it could not much longer survive the darkness and dryness of the clover forest. The medick, although sadly reduced in numbers, was making the most of its opportunities. The plants had found a foothold near the borders of the place and had insinuated their wiry branches into the available places in the tangle. The single pigweed had got its head through the forest, and was in good spirits. I suspect that it must have had many fellows, which had been smothered in the scuffle. New adventurers—the sow-thistle and the alsike clover—had been attracted to the spot, and the purslane, needing more sun, had given up the fight. So the merry war goes on; and all the time all the contestants are becoming unlike.

cannot be perpetuated. Now, there are several ways of looking at this Weismannian philosophy. In the first place, so far as plants are concerned in it, it is mere assumption, and, therefore, does not demand refutation. In the second place, there is abundant asexual variation in flowering plants, as we have seen; and most fungi, which have run into numberless forms, are sexless. In the third place, since all agree that plants are intimately adapted to the conditions in which they live, it is violence to suppose that the very adaptations which are directly produced by those conditions are without permanent effect. In the fourth place, we know, as a matter of common knowledge and also of direct experiment, that acquired characters in plants often are perpetuated.

I cannot hope to prove to the Weismannians that acquired characters may be hereditary, for their definition of an acquired character has a habit of retreating into the germ, where neither they nor anyone else can find it. But this proposition is easy enough of proof, viz.: Plants which start to all appearances perfectly equal may be greatly modified by the conditions in which they grow; the seedlings of these plants may show these new features in few or many generations. Most of the new varieties of garden plants, of which about a thousand are introduced in North America each year, come about in just this way. A simple experiment made in our greenhouses also shows the truth of my proposition. Peas were grown under known conditions from seeds, in the same manner as the petunias were which I have mentioned. The plants varied widely. Seeds of these plants were saved and all sown in one soil, and the characters, somewhat diminished, appeared in the offspring. Seeds were again taken, and in the third generation the acquired characters were still discernible. The full details of this and similar experiments are waiting for separate publication.

The whole philosophy of "selecting the best" for seed, by means of which all domestic plants have been so greatly ameliorated, rests upon the hereditability of these characters which arise after birth; and if the gardener did not possess this power of causing like plants to vary and then of perpetuating more or less completely the characters which he secures, he would at once quit the business, because there would no longer be any reward for his efforts. Of course, the Neo-Darwinians can say, upon the one hand, that all the variations which the gardener secures and keeps were potentially present in the germ, but they cannot prove it, neither can they make any gardener believe it; or, on the other hand, they can say that the new characters have somehow impressed themselves upon the germ, a proposition to which the gardener will not object, because he does not care about the form of words so long as he is not disputed in the facts. Weismann admits that "climatic and other external influences" are capable of affecting the germ, or of producing "permanent variations," after they have operated "uniformly for a long period," or for more than one generation. Every annual plant dies at the end of the season, therefore whatever effect the environment may have had upon it is lost, unless the effect is preserved in the seed; and it does not matter how many generations have lived under the given uniform environment, for the plant starts all over again, *de novo*, each year. Therefore, the environment must affect the annual plant in some one generation or not at all. It seems to me to be mere sophistry to say that in plants which start anew from seeds each year, the effect of environment is not felt until after a lapse of several generations, for if that were so the plant would simply take up life at the same place every year. This philosophy is equivalent to saying that characters which are acquired in any one generation are not hereditary until they have been transmitted at least once!

My contention then, is this: plants may start equal, either from seeds or asexual parts, but may end unequal; these inequalities or unlikenesses are largely the direct result of the conditions in which the plants grow; these unlikenesses may be transmitted either by seeds or buds. Or, to take a shorter phrase, congenital variations in plants may have received their initial impulse either in the preceding generation or in the sexual compact from which the plants sprung.

XV.

A POMOLOGICAL ALLIANCE.[1]

SKETCH OF THE RELATIONSHIP BETWEEN AMERICAN AND EASTERN ASIAN FRUITS.

THE fact must have struck every thoughtful horticulturist that Japan is now the most prolific source of profitable new types of fruits and hardy ornamental plants. The recent extension of communication with that country explains the introduction of these plants, but it does not account for the almost uniform success which attends their cultivation in this country. There must be some striking similarity between the climates and other conditions of Japan and America, to enable plants from the very antipodes to thrive at once upon their introduction here. It is well known amongst naturalists that this similarity in climate exists, and that, therefore, there is general accord in the fauna and flora of Japan and eastern America; and that the origin of this resemblance was most strikingly explained by the late Asa Gray, Professor of Botany in Harvard University, as long ago as 1859. But this relationship of Japan and America, with the practical deductions which follow an understanding of it, has never been presented in its horticultural aspects.

Before proceeding to a discussion of Gray's argu-

---
[1] Yearbook of the United States Department of Agriculture, 1894, 437.

mentative paper, it should be explained that a half century ago there was no satisfactory explanation of the means by which plants and animals have become widely disseminated over the earth. This was particularly true respecting the curious phenomena of disconnected distributions, or the fact that some species occur in widely separated and isolated places. Certain plants occur only in eastern America and in Japan, and there may be no other representatives of the genus extant; that is, the genus is monotypic, and has a peculiarly disjointed distribution. There are also certain bitypic genera, of which one species occurs only in eastern America and the other in Japan. There are equally strange distributions of plants and animals in other parts of the world. There were few general hypotheses in vogue at the time Gray wrote, to account for these detached distributions. One was Agassiz's theory, which has been called the autochthonal hypothesis, from the fact that it supposes that each species was borne or brought forth upon the area which it occupies (*autochthon*, one borne of the land itself). It "maintains, substantially," says Gray, "that each species originated where it now occurs, probably in as great a number of individuals occupying as large an area, and generally the same area, or the same discontinuous areas as at the present time."

Much the same view was held by Schouw, of Copenhagen, who advanced the hypothesis of the double or multiple origin of species, but he supposed that the species had the power of greatly distributing itself when it was once created in a given region. It was even then (Schouw wrote in 1837) maintained by various naturalists that species had sprung from one progenitor, but Schouw declared that "when we look at the facts presented by existing geographical distribution, this hypothesis becomes highly improbable; in certain cases altogether inadmissible." All the known agents of the distribution of animals and plants could not account for the fact "that many species of plants are common, on the one hand, to the Alps and the Pyrenees, on the other to the Scandinavian and Scotch mountains, without these species being found in the plains or on the lower mountains lying between; that the flora of Iceland is almost the same as that of the Scandinavian mountains; that Europe and North America have many plants in common, particularly in the northern regions, which have not been transported by man; and still further difficulties, bordering on impossibility, arise for such an explanation, when we know that species occur in the Straits of Magellan and in the Falkland Isles which belong to the flora of the Arctic Pole." In order to account for these anomalous distributions, he supposed that the same species may originate several times, although it would appear that this multiple origination is waning, from the instances which he cites of the less wide and not detached distribution of the mammals and the higher plants, which are, presumably, of comparatively late creation. "Just as we have seen that the leafless and flowerless plants are oftener re-discovered in distant countries than those bearing flowers, we may assume that the more perfect animals are less prone to, perhaps never do, make their appearance in several places independently." Schouw supposed that creation is completed. "I hold it in the highest degree probable," he writes, "if not strictly proved, that no new species originate at present."

The straits to which naturalists were driven to explain the distribution of animals and plants when one progenitor is alone assumed, may be illustrated by the supposition, which Schouw ascribes to an English author, that there must once have been a continental area between Spain and Ireland, inasmuch as certain Spanish plants reappear in the British Isles. Even Alphonse De Candolle, while holding in general to the hypothesis of a single origin, felt obliged to admit that in the case of our modest verbena-like *Phryma Leptostachya*, which grows in eastern North America and again in the Himalayan region, there must have been two independent originations.

Naturalists were ready to believe that species had one origin if only the fact of disconnected distributions could be explained. At this juncture, Asa Gray came forward with his brilliant exposition of the relationships of the eastern American and Japanese floras. The plants collected in Japan in 1853 by Williams and Morrow, in connection with Commodore Perry's visit to that country, and also those procured there by Charles Wright, in connection with Commodore Rodgers' expedition of 1855, went to Gray for study. He was at once struck by the similarity of many of the plants to those of our Alleghany region, a resemblance which he had before noticed. He found that many of the characteristic genera of eastern America and a number of the monotypic and bitypic genera, occur also in the Japanese region. He observed the remarkable fact that the flora of eastern North America is much more like the Japanese flora than those of western America and even of Europe are, and also that our Alleghany flora is more like the Japanese than it is like the European or even like that of our own Pacific coast.

It is well known that the climate of the pliocene epoch, preceding the glacial time, was much milder than now. Over the Dakotas camels, horses, a mastodon, a rhinoceros and an elephant roamed, and the temperate floras extended much further north than they do at the present time. The same conditions prevailed in northern Asia, and the floras of the two continents were coterminous and intermingled. Then came on the glacial epoch,—"an extraordinary refrigeration of the northern hemisphere, in the course of ages carrying glacial ice and arctic climate down nearly to the latitude of the Ohio. The change was evidently so gradual that it did not destroy the temperate flora. * * * These [the plants] and their fellows, or such as survive, must have been pushed on to lower latitudes as the cold advanced, just as they now would be if the temperature were to be again lowered; and between them and the ice there was a band of subarctic and arctic vegetation,—portions of which, retreating up the mountains as the climate ameliorated and the ice receded, still scantily survive upon our highest Alleghanies, and more abundantly upon the colder summits of the mountains of New York and New England;—demonstrating the existence of the present arctic-alpine vegetation during the glacial era; and that the change of climate at its close was so gradual that it was not destructive to vegetable species." So the plants were driven to the southward, both down the Asian and American continents. Gradually the ice melted away, the climate became milder and plants began to return northward. After the glacial epoch had passed away, the arctic regions again became warm. The great fluvial period came in, when arctic lands were lower than at present, when the sea stood five hundred feet above its present level, and when the northern rivers were vastly larger than now. This great expanse of water and low elevation of land caused the warmer climate of the high north. Elephants and rhinoceroses roamed northwards to the very shores of the Arctic Ocean, and lions, elks, horses, buffaloes and mastodons inhabited the high latitudes. In the ice of Siberia the elephants are still found, even with the hair intact, preserved in nature's refrigerator for ages. There is evidence that northwestern America and northeastern Asia were more closely connected by land than now. The Siberian elephant roamed from one continent to the other. "I cannot imagine a state of circumstances," writes Gray, "under which the Siberian elephant could migrate and temperate plants could not." So the floras of America and Asia again became coterminous.

Now came another change. The terrace epoch came slowly on. The arctic lands were elevated, the water receded and the temperature fell. The earth approached its present condition. The plants were again driven southwards down Asia and America. The western coast of America, by reason of ocean currents, was warmer than the eastern region or than the Japanese region, and the temperate floras went down or persisted in similar climates, giving our Alleghany regions and eastern Asian and Himalayan countries similar floras. Subsequently, only minor distributions have taken place. The eastern Asian flora has shown some tendency to extend westward, and some species have reached Europe. Thus we have an explanation of the remarkable fact, long ago noticed by Bentham, that American species have reached Europe through Asia.

"Under the light which these geological considerations throw upon the question, I cannot resist the conclusion," writes Gray, "that the extant vegetable kingdom has a long and eventful history, and that the explanation of apparent anomalies in the geographical distribution of species may be found in the various and prolonged climatic or other physical vicissitudes to which they have been subject in earlier times."

A certain flora "established itself in Greenland," says Sir J. W. Dawson, "and probably all around the arctic circle, in the warm period of the earliest eocene, and, as the climate of the northern hemisphere became gradually reduced from that time till the end of the pliocene, it marched on over both continents to the southward, chased behind by the modern arctic flora, and eventually by the frost and snow of the glacial age." "If, however, our modern flora is thus one that has returned from the south," says Dawson, again, "this would account for its poverty in species as compared with those of the early tertiary. Groups of plants descending from the north have been rich and varied. Returning from the south they are like the shattered remains of a beaten army. * * * It is, indeed, not impossible that in the plans of the Creator the continuous summer sun of the arctic regions may have been made the means for the introduction, or at least for the rapid growth and multiplication, of new and more varied types of plants. * * * * * What we have learned respecting this wonderful history has served strangely to change some of our preconceived ideas. We must now be prepared to admit that an Eden can be planted even in Spitzbergen, that there are possibilities in this old earth of ours which its present condition does not reveal to us; that the present state of the world is by no means the best possible in relation to climate and vegetation; that there have been and might be again conditions which could convert the ice-clad arctic regions into blooming paradises, and which at the same time would moderate the fervent heat of the tropics. We are accustomed to say that nothing is impossible with God; but how little have we known of the gigantic possibilities which lie hidden under some of the most common of his natural laws!"

All these considerations go to establish three general laws: 1. That distribution of plants and animals is determined largely by climatic and other physical causes. 2. That species have a local or single origin. 3. That the origin of our present temperate flora is in the north. These generalizations were written before Darwin's theories appeared, and before Heer had published the fossil histories of the arctic regions, and they at once establish Gray's place amongst philosophical naturalists.

We have now observed that the very facts which led Schouw, De Candolle, and others to accept an hypothesis of the multiple origin of species are the ones which chiefly explain and prove the conclusions of Gray. In the vicissitudes of geologic time, plants retreated up the mountains or persisted along the cold shores of the northern lakes, giving rise to the curious occurrence of arctic and subarctic plants upon Lake Superior, Mt. Marcy, Mt. Washington and Mt. Katahdin. But what is more to our present purpose, we can now understand the similarities of the eastern American and eastern Asian floras, because like plants have persisted in similar climates when they were pushed down from the north upon all sides of the globe. The curiously dismembered diffusion of the *Phyrma Leptostachya* is intelligible; and we can explain Schouw's perplexity concerning the less extended and undetached distribution of the mammals and higher plants, for these may, in many cases, have developed or originated since the epoch of these great dispersions.

The climates of eastern America and eastern Asia are still similar, as shown by the similar floras of the present time. The facies of the Japanese, northern Chinese and Himalayan floras are strikingly those of our own Alleghany flora. The magnolias are peculiar to these two great regions. The tulip-tree, confined to our eastern states, has recently been discovered in China. The story of shortia and schizocodon — independent names for the same type of plant discovered in the two continents — is familiar to botanists. Lately, horticulturists have seen a striking instance of this relationship in the remarkably rapid diffusion in this country of the Japanese plums, fruits which are more closely allied to our native species than the common or European plums are, and which are also unquestionably adapted to a much wider range of our conditions than the European plums are. We all know that the horticulture most resembling that of Europe is upon our Pacific slope,—there the European wine grape, the olive, the citrous fruits, the walnut, the fig, and the prune and raisin industries are already well developed. In like manner, we may expect that in the course of time the horticultural industries of eastern America and eastern Asia will acquire the similarity of facies which the floras of these regions now enjoy. I therefore look with much favor upon the introduction of Japanese plants; and I am convinced, both from the known resemblance of its flora to our own, and from the early introduction of its plants into western Asia and Europe, that the most promising field for horticultural exploration and for the study of the ancestry of our fruits, is now the interior of China and Japan.

It is yet too soon to fully measure the value of the contributions of eastern Asia to our pomology, although the importance of the hardy ornamentals derived in great numbers from that region is everywhere conceded. Yet this antipodean region has already given us quite as important species of fruits as Europe and western Asia have, despite the fact that these latter regions were the source of our colonization and civilization. The following list includes all the fruits of the United States which have come from the Europo-Asian region and from the Chino-Japanese region:

Europo-Asian.	*Eastern Asian.*
Plum,	Japan Plum,
Almond,	Prunus Simonii,
Apple,	Japanese Pear,
Pear,	Peach,
Medlar,	Common Apricot,
Sour Cherry,	Chinese Apricot,
Sweet Cherry,	Wineberry,

Europo-Asian.	Eastern Asian.
Quince,	Kaki, or Japanese Persimmon,
Raspberry,	Orange,
Strawberry,	Mandarin,
(The last two mostly supplanted by the American species.)	Lemon (including lime and citron),
Red Currant,	Kumquat,
Black Currant,	Loquat,
English Gooseberry,	Hovenia,
Wine and Raisin Grape,	Chinese Jujube,
Olive,	Litchi,
Pomegranate,	Elæagnus,
Date,	Myrica,
Fig,	Japanese Walnut,
Filbert,	Japanese Chestnut,
European Chestnut,	Ginkgo.
English Walnut,	—21 species.
Pistachio.	
—22 species.	

The eastern Asian species of fruits now grown in this country are already about equal in number to those from Europe and western Asia—the latter country "the cradle of the human race"—and they comprise some of the most important fruits known to man, as the orange, lemon, peach, apricot and kaki. There is certainly abundant reason for looking towards oriental Asia for further acquisitions, either in other species or in novel varieties.

XVI.

HORTICULTURAL GEOGRAPHY.[1]

"Ultimate results of the World's Fair exhibits of fruits and flowers." This is the subject which your secretary has set before me for discussion. It is one peculiarly difficult to consider, because the ultimate good which comes from such exhibitions as these is subjective rather than objective. In other words, each observer draws certain conclusions for himself which are likely to continue to influence his thought and business for years to come, even after the memory of the exhibits themselves has grown old and dim. For the time being, your mind may rest upon some new variety which you have seen, or upon some new or at least strange method of propagation or management of nursery stock; but after a time the variety becomes old or passes from sight, and the strange methods have lost their first interest to you. These observations are not the ultimate results which are to influence your life, and if you have not seen beyond them, the great exposition can have only a temporary value and interest for you. The visitor may not at first catch any larger truth which seems to fit into his life, but if he has seen the exhibits carefully, he is likely, eventually, to evolve a few general facts which abide with him. So the ultimate value

---

[1] Read before the American Association of Nurserymen at the World's Fair, Chicago, June 7, 1893. Printed in Report of the Eighteenth Annual Meeting, pp. 1 to 5.

of any great exposition comes upon reflection,—and as this value is determined very largely by the temper of the observer himself, it becomes next to impossible for one to forecast what the ultimate results of the display may be. I can only sketch very briefly one or two of the results of this great display which now seem to me to be likely to possess permanent value.

I am greatly impressed with the influence which locality exerts upon the exhibits. It would seem as if the climate of any geographical region determines very largely the character of all the open air plants which grow there, both in modifying whatever varieties have been permanently introduced, and in preventing the establishment of other varieties which may succeed in contiguous areas. Both these influences of climate or locality are admirably shown in the apple exhibits which are now upon the shelves in the Horticultural Building, for while none of these exhibits show the entire apple flora of any state or natural area, they are, nevertheless, fairly representative, and are useful for comparison. I have here transcribed lists of the apples now on exhibition from New York, Illinois, Wisconsin, Washington and New South Wales:

New York.

Aucubæfolia, Baldwin, Belle et Bonne, Ben Davis, Bethlemite, Black, Blue Pearmain, Boiken, Bottle Greening, Broad End, Burtis' Beauty, Burr's Winter Sweet, Cabashea, Camfield, Canada Pippin, Canada Red, Cherry Crab, Cooper's Market, Cranberry, Dyer, Egg Top, Egyptian Russet, English Russet, Esopus Spitzenburgh, Fallawater, Fall Pippin, Fall Seek-No-Further, Flushing Spitzenburgh, Foster, Gilliflower,

Gilpin, Gloria Mundi, Golden Streak, Gold-Flesh Crab, Gold-Flesh Strawberry, Granite Beauty, Gros Faros, Hendrick's Sweet, Hog Island Sweet, Hollow Crown, Honey Sweet, Hubbardston, Jennetting, Jonathan, King, Lady, Leathercoat Russet, Lyon's Sweet, Lyscom, McIntosh Red, Moore's Greening, Newark King, Northern Spy, Norton's Red, Ortley, Oxhead Pearmain, Peck's Pleasant, Pennock, Pewaukee, Pickman Pippin, Pomme Gris, Pound Sweet, Pumpkin Russet, Ragan's Red, Rambo, Randall's Red Winter, Red Romanite, Red Streak, Rhode Island Greening, Roane's White Crab, Rock, Romanite, Roxbury Russet, Rum, Salome, Scott's Winter, Seek-No-Further, Smith's Cider, Spice, Stark, Stone, Swaar, Sweet Pearmain, Sweet Seek-No-Further, Sweet Winter Greening, Talman Sweet, Thomas, Tuft's Baldwin, Twenty Ounce, Vandervere, Vermont Greening, Wagener, Waxen, White Bellflower, White Winter Pearmain, Winter Strawberry, Yellow Bellflower, Yellow Newtown Pippin, Zane's Greening—99.

Illinois.

Baldwin, Ben Davis, Gilpin, Golden Russet, Grimes' Golden, Jonathan, Little Romanite, Northern Spy, Rambo, Rome Beauty, Talman Sweet, Willow Twig, Winesap—13.

Wisconsin.

Bailey Sweet, Ben Davis, Bennett's Seedling, Blaine, Blue Pearmain, Bogdanoff, Crocker, Duchess Seedling, Dutch Mignon, Fall Jennetting, Fameuse, Fatherland, Faulk's Greening, Flushing Spitzenburgh, Golden Russet, Haas, Hibernal, Hinckley Sweet Russet, Jennings' Sweet, Jenny, Jonathan, Little Romanite, Long Keeper, Manning's Russet, Mary, Matthew's Russet, May Seek-No-Further, Myron, Newell, Northwestern Greening, Perry Russet, Pewaukee, Plumb's Cider, President Smith, Randall, Red Romanite, Rich's Greening, Romanite, Scott's Winter, Smith's No. 3, Talman Sweet, Utter, Walbridge, Wall's No. 1, Wall's No. 3, Wall's Sweet Russet, Waterson's No. 2, Waterson's No. 3, Waterson's No. 4, Waterson's No. 5, Waterson's Russet, Wealthy, Wolf River, Wrightman, Yellow Bellflower—55.

Washington.

Ben Davis, Black, Blue Pearmain, Esopus Spitzenburgh, Frazier Seedling, Gloria Mundi, Grindstone, Janet, Lady, Monmouth Pippin, Red Cheek Pippin, Rhode Island Greening, Rome Beauty, Swaar, Vandervere, White Winter Pearmain, Winesap, Wolf River, Yellow Newtown Pippin—19.

New South Wales.

Bailey Sweet, Brown's Perfection, Claygate, Fameuse, Five-Crowned Pippin, Golden Russet, Kentucky Red Streak, New Hawthornden, Northern Spy, Scarlet Pearmain, Seedling Pearmain, Triomphe de Luxembourg, Winter Pearmain—13.

The first thing which strikes one in glancing at these lists are the great differences in lengths or in the numbers of varieties. Of course, the lengths of the lists are not accurate measures of the relative numbers of varieties in the different states, because the collections from the different regions were made with various degrees of thoroughness; yet it is true that the eastern states, because of their age and the great diversity in soils and climates and methods of colonization, possesses a great number of local varieties. New York undoubtedly leads the states in the actual variety of apples cultivated within its borders, and Pennsylvania is probably entitled to second place. Yet no part of our country has developed endemic or peculiar varieties so quickly as Wisconsin and Minnesota have, the fruit lists of those states already containing many varieties of apples and other fruits which are unknown outside that general region. All this indicates that fruits, like other plants, quickly adapt themselves to new conditions through variation into adaptive varieties,—a conclusion to which a closer study of the above lists brings strong additional evidence.

In the above lists there are ninety-nine New York varieties, thirteen in Illinois, fifty-five in Wisconsin, nineteen in Washington and thirteen in New South Wales. Taking the New York list as the basis, we find that 60 per cent of the Illinois varieties occur in it, and less than 20 per cent of the Wisconsin, about 50 per cent of the Washington, and about 20 per cent of the New South Wales varieties. These figures show that Wisconsin and New South Wales have an apple flora very different from that of New York, and moreover, these floras are peculiar,—that is, different, also, from the apple flora of other geographical regions. The Wisconsin-Minnesota apples are more unlike the New York apples in type than the Australian ones are, and they have been developed very largely from an independent stock. If we were to examine the Quebec apples critically we should find them to be nearer the New York apples in type than the Wisconsin apples are, but we should notice a decided influence of European types.

From 50 to 60 per cent of the varieties of Illinois and Washington in the above lists are in the New York list, yet the apples of Illinois and Washington are much unlike; and here we come upon a subject to which nurserymen should give particular attention. While Illinois grows many New York varieties, the leading kinds of the Illinois-Missouri region are different from the leading kinds in the east. The realm of the Baldwin, Rhode Island Greening, King and Hubbardston is practically bounded by Lake Michigan on the west, and we pass southwestward into the area of Ben Davis, Willow Twig, Winesap and Janet, and northwestward into the domain of Duchess, Wealthy and Wolf River. But in the far northwest—Idaho, Oregon, Washington—the leading types are drawn from both the east and the Illinois-Missouri region, with the greater part representing admirable but somewhat local apples in New York state, as Newtown Pippin, Blue Pearmain, White Winter Pearmain, Esopus Spitzenburgh, Swaar, to which must be added, from the prairie region, Rome Beauty, Ben Davis, Winesap and Janet. But the similarity of this remote apple flora to eastern floras ends with the names of the varieties, for the apples themselves are very unlike ours. They have been modified by climate until they are larger, longer and more conical, frequently marked by prominent ridges at the apex, less firm in flesh and often somewhat inferior in quality. To all intents and purposes many of them are distinct varieties from their parents in the east, and they afford as distinct and unequivocal cases of evolutionary modification as the most hypercritical can wish to see. The Newtown Pippin affords one of the best instances of rapid modification of any American fruit. It has always been a local and captious apple in New York state, where it originated, yet in the Piedmont region of Virginia it is the leading apple, known as the Albemarle Pippin; in the far northwest it is again the leading apple over a great territory, and in New South Wales, under the name of Five-Crowned Pippin, it is still again a dominant variety. Yet in each of these four geographical regions the variety attains a specific character which it does not possess in the others. The Albemarle Pippin differs from the true Newtown in a less heavy and somewhat poorer flesh and in poorer keeping qualities; and you can all compare the enormous deep yellow, softer, angular-topped specimens of the Pacific northwest and New South Wales with those of New York. Reviewing these calculations, we find three prominent facts: The whole body of the Wisconsin-Minnesota apple flora is different from that of New York; the prominent types of the Illinois-Missouri region are different from the prominent types of New York, while many secondary varieties are the same in both; the apples of the Pacific northwest, while transplanted from the east, have developed away from their parent stems.

The entire horticultural exhibition seems to force conclusions similar to these upon my mind, and it greatly strengthens the conviction which has been strongly growing upon me in recent years, that the study of the adaptation of varieties to geographical and local conditions is a most imperative demand in horticultural pursuits. I therefore look with much distrust upon the promiscuous distribution of varieties over great areas. If I should not plant a Baldwin orchard in Illinois, I should hesitate in like manner to plant a Ben Davis orchard in New York. I believe that the days of the nursery business which aims to feed the whole country are numbered. We shall develop more nurseries like those in many parts of New York and other eastern states, which attempt to supply the stock which is particularly adapted to their geographical regions, and which are content to leave other lands for other men. Climate and environment must eventually force the nurseries into nearly as narrow limits as the adaptability of the stock which they grow, although this contraction will follow some distance behind the determination or discovery of the limits of adaptability of the varieties themselves. The European nurseries have had this experience to an important extent.

Right here you may wish to cite me to the excellent displays of rhododendrons and azaleas upon these grounds as proof that nursery stock can be successfully grown far away from the geographical area in which it is to mature, for these plants, with unimportant exceptions, are grown in Europe. But I shall contend that the most important reason why these plants do not succeed well in America is because they are European-grown. It is always said that the American climate is not adapted to the rhododendron, but with all due respect to those much older than myself, I must still decline to believe the statement. One of the most important species of cultivated rhododendron is native to our Alleghany region, and evergreen ericaceous plants in variety are indigenous over much of our territory. The trouble is that we have failed to grow with much satisfaction the varieties originated in England and on the continent, and we have then generalized this failure into a maxim that our climate is uncongenial to rhododendron culture; yet the very type from which many of these varieties have come, grows luxuriantly in our woods. There is not the slightest reason to doubt that if American nurserymen were to originate varieties of rhododendrons, we should soon have sufficient adaptive kinds to meet our needs. Even the cultivation of the apple never became an unqualified success in the United States until we produced American varieties. All success in the cultivation of raspberries and strawberries and gooseberries was delayed until we had American species or varieties. It was once thought that we could not grow our own apple stocks, but we now know that the American stocks are as good as the French, and are probably superior to them. All the older men in this audience can remember when it was thought that the American climate would not allow of successful rose-growing out of doors, but now rose gardens are common, and there are more prizes for us among American novelties than among the European. I have the fullest confidence that there is not a more promising field for the faithful and patient American nurseryman than in the evolution of an American race of rhododendrons and azaleas. It would be strange, indeed, if the experience in so many kinds of plants should finally fail in the rhododendrons.

As I now see it, the greatest ultimate good which shall come to the horticulturist from this great exhibition is the lesson that our country is too large and too varied to allow of random and indiscriminate methods and promiscuous distribution of varieties. With the increasing competitions and the refinements of life which are inherent in the coming years, we must confine our efforts to increasingly narrower areas, and must bring larger rewards from more concentrated enterprises.

XVII.

SOME EMPHATIC PROBLEMS OF CLIMATE AND PLANTS.

I.

Speculative Notes Upon Phenology.[1]

1. *The Physiological Constant.* — There are deeper questions involved in the study of the periods of plants than the mere pageant or moods of the seasons. We must determine how it is that climate superintends the periods of plants, or, at least, which one of its many attributes is most intimately and uniformly associated with the periodical phenomena of life. We shall then be able to establish a *physiological constant*, by means of which climate and life-events can be studied and compared. In the first place, it may be well to ask

---

[1] Extract from "Some Suggestions for the Study of Phenology," prepared for the Weather Bureau, United States Department of Agriculture, but yet unpublished. The report has considered a long array of records of phenological phenomena, — such as dates of blooming, leafing, and the like, — and has discussed how these records are influenced by latitude and altitude, and has drawn various conclusions from them. It has also presented the merits of such records as a means of recording meteorological phenomena. It now comes to the consideration of those deeper problems of the inter-relations of plants and climates, and at this point the reader is asked to take up the discussion. He may desire to know that Phenology (contraction of *phenomenology*) is that science which considers the relationship of local climate to the periodicity of the annual phenomena of living things. Its chief records, on the side of organisms, are those of the leafing, blooming and maturation of plants, and the migrations and seasonal habits of animals. The report from which this Essay is extracted gives fuller references to the literature of the subject, together with illustrations.

if we shall assume that all life-events are determined directly by climatal environment. There are some who look for an explanation of these characteristic periods chiefly in the phylogeny or evolution of the species themselves, rather than in the immediate environment. This view has been forcibly presented by Clarke,* who concludes that early blooming of plants is associated with the lower, simpler and more generalized species, whilst the later bloom-periods pertain to species of later or higher developments or to type groups or specialized forms of the lower classes. "In their blooming season, the more perfect succeed the more simple; the aberrant, the normal; the specialized, the generalized." There is certainly a strong argument for this position; but the question now recurs as to why this remarkable correlation exists. Why should the lower or earlier plants have taken to themselves the early season, and the higher or specialized forms to the later season? Mr. Clarke suggests that it is an adaptation to climatic conditions. He assumes that there may have been a constant tendency for plants to bloom earlier, and "the most simple and generalized forms, coming first in the course of floral evolution, have had the longest time in which to adapt themselves to existent climatic conditions; and, reciprocally, climatic conditions have become more and more favorable to the rapid development of the said forms. So a floral type that ages ago would have reached its perfection only after a long continuance of favoring season, now may burst into the fullness of its maturity with the first warmth of spring. * * * * Thus,

---

*Henry L. Clarke, "The Philosophy of the Flower Seasons," Amer. Nat. xxvii. 769 (Sep. 1893).

in the ages to come, the early flowers of to-day will disappear, to be replaced by what are now our later flowers, whose place, in turn, will be filled by forms that are yet to be." All this is offered as a mere suggestion, but there is no hint given us as to the reasons for an assumption that the floral epochs constantly tend to become earlier. I assume that Mr. Clarke means to say that the climatal seasons are becoming shorter, and are thereby crowding back the older forms, but the idea is not expressed. May not the phenomena be better explained upon Darwin's hypothesis of the "divergence of character," by virtue of which a new form occupies places unoccupied by existing forms? We may assume that the primitive plants found the field clear, so to speak, and developed themselves at once upon the arrival of congenial conditions; but later forms, finding the earth occupied early in the season, were obliged to push on and make their greatest development of vegetation later in the season. And specialized types are those which have boldly reached out and have appropriated places of least resistance.

But whatever evolutional explanation may be given of the origin of the periodical epochs of plants, it nevertheless remains that these epochs are evidently adaptations to environments, of which climate is always the chief factor. We may still seek, therefore, for the physiological constant. It is generally conceded that temperature, or relative heat, is more intimately associated with the periods of plants than any other factor of climate, and the physiological constant has been sought in this direction. One of the earliest American expressions upon this point was made in 1859 by

Frederick Brendel, of Illinois,* who, in comparing the late spring of 1857 with the very early spring of 1859, "found in some species a striking coincidence of the sums of the mean temperature, and of the number of days on which the temperature rose above freezing point," when "comparing the periods of flowering with the accumulation of heat in both years, from January to that period." More recently, the same writer has reaffirmed† that the physiological constant is the "sum of daily mean temperature, commencing with January and excluding all temperatures below freezing point," up to the time of the event in question. It is believed by most phenologists that a certain life-event takes place in any species whenever the species has been exposed to a certain sum-total of heat. This sum-total is reckoned from the lowest assumed temperature at which vegetation takes place. This lowest temperature was first put at freezing-point, but in later years it is placed at six degrees Centigrade, or about forty-three degrees Fahrenheit. Below this point all temperatures are disregarded, and the sum-temperature for the life-event is obtained by adding together all the positive daily thermometric readings,—all those above this awakening point. This sum-temperature is itself taken as the physiological constant by Hoffmann, and perhaps most phenologists, but Linsser considers it erroneous, and establishes his constant by ascertaining the *ratio* of this sum-temperature of the event to the sum-temperature for the year. "The sums of temperature above zero which are necessary to the same vegetation-phase in two places are proportional to the sums

---

*Trans. Ill. Agric. Soc. iii. 674.
†Flora Peoriana, 19 (1887).

of all the [yearly] positive temperatures of both places."* In order to construct an actual numerical constant or *aliquote*, Linsser lays down the following rule: "The velocities of development of the events are proportional to the temperatures which influence them, divided by the accustomed yearly sum-temperatures of the mother plants." This law is illustrated as follows: "Every separate seed contains the entire relationship of the life-course of the mother plant to the sum-temperatures of the place of its origin. Two seeds of the same species, one taken from a mother plant having passed its life-course in a yearly sum-temperature of M degrees, the other from a mother plant which has passed its life-course in a yearly sum-temperature of N degrees, possess, therefore, a power of development, or a sensitiveness towards acting equal temperatures, which is inversely proportional to the sums M and N degrees." If, for example, the sum-temperature up to the time of blooming of *Sambucus nigra* is 385 degrees, and the total sum-temperature of the year is 5,200 degrees, then 385 divided by 5,200 equals .07 (approximately), which is the constant or *aliquote*.

It is not my purpose to enter into any discussion as to the true physiological constant of climate and plant epochs, but simply to state the nature of the problem and to emphasize the importance of recording climatological data along with plant data. It should be said, also, that even a physiologically false constant may serve all the purposes of an arbitrary standard

---

*Carl Linsser, Die Periodischen Erscheinungen des Pflanzenlebens in ihrem Verhältniss zu den Wärmeerscheinungen. Mem. Acad. Sci. St. Petersb. ser. vii. vol. xi. No. 7, p. 35 (1867).

of measurement, for it is only necessary that it shall have, approximately, the same comparative value in all cases. Linsser's constants, being quotients, are small numbers, and are therefore handy to use, and they are probably also nearer the true physiological constant than any unit yet proposed. I therefore recommend their use. For myself, I do not believe that it is possible ever to express a life-event in degrees of temperature, from the simple fact that these events are influenced by a multitude of climatal environments. It is quite as easy to express an event of climate by means of a plant-constant, as to attempt to express an event of plants by means of a climate-constant. But these inter-relationships are just the problems which climatological phenology should attempt to solve; and in the collection and tabulation of data to that end, Linsser's *aliquote* may be used to advantage.

2. *The Climatal Modification of Phenological Phenomena.*—Whilst the science of phenology has for its first and prime object the study of climate in terms of plant or animal life, it has an important secondary bearing upon the study of botany and zoölogy. In fact, in most phenological observations the controlling motive has been simply to determine the life-events of plants and animals as a contribution to natural history, and without having coincident records of climate the observations possess small value to the climatologist. Yet, before adequate climatological records of life-events can be made, the observer should acquire a fair understanding of the most apparent ways in which climates modify the epochs of living objects. Some of the general directions in which cli-

mate modifies plants are well known,—such as the dwarfing of plants at the north, the tendency to fastigiate or strict forms of trees at the south, the shortening of the period of growth at the north, the development of high colors of flowers and fruits and high saccharine flavors at the north, the condensing of the plant-body in arid regions, and the like. All these and other changes which inure or adapt a plant to climates at first injurious to it, belong to the general subject of acclimatization.* There are only a very few of these phenomena of acclimatization which directly interest the phenologist,—those which are concerned with the visible modifications in seasons of flowering, leafing, maturation of fruit, defoliation, and the like; and it is these features to which I wish, very briefly, to call attention at this time,—not for the purpose of making any scientific discussion of them, but simply to aid the observer in taking more appreciative records.

It is generally considered that plants become annuals or biennials as a result of adaptation to the environment in which they live. The interposition of a long season of enforced inactivity causes the plant to store up its energy for future use. This storage may be made in the tissue of woody stems, in rhizomes and roots, in bulbs, and sometimes in seeds. When the plant reduces itself to a bulb at the approach of the dry or cold season, it thereby becomes a pseud-annual, but when it reduces itself to a seed it is strictly annual.

---

*For popular discussions of the acclimatization of plants, consult Crozier, "The Modification of Plants by Climate," Ann Arbor, 1885; Bailey, "Acclimatization: Does it Occur?" (Essay XIX.); Pammel, "Climate and Plants," Monthly Review of Iowa Weather and Crop Service, Oct. 1891.

When perennial plants are taken northwards, there is a tendency for them to produce bulbs or seeds relatively earlier in their life history than they do in their normal environments; so, whilst the plant may be killed by frost, it has already provided means for reproducing its kind when congenial conditions again appear. The longer such plants are grown in the northern station, the more completely do they adapt themselves to the short season, not only by confirming the habit of early production of bulbs or seeds, but by an increasing tendency to early maturation of the plant as a whole. Yet the cases are comparatively rare in which a perennial plant becomes a true annual at the north,—that is, one in which the whole plant matures before frost. The tomato is often cited as an example, for it is perennial or at least plur-annual in its original home; but it generally grows in the north until killed by frost, and does not ripen up completely with the normal progression of the season. The egg-plant, red pepper, cotton and castor-bean are similar instances of plants which become potential annuals, or plur-annuals, at the north by adapting themselves to the shorter seasons by means of hastening their life epochs (see page 45).

It is a nice question as to just what elements of climate are responsible for this adaptive change, and what their exact impressions are upon the physiological processes of the plant; but this adaptation to environment in cultivated plants is undoubtedly guided by the same laws which determine the general distribution of plants in the various life-zones. The general limits of floral and faunal zones are probably closely associated with relative temperature, although the minor distributions within these zones are dependent upon a multitude of climatal and physical causes. The method of determining or expressing the physiological unit with which these zonal bounds are associated, has been most satisfactorily presented recently in an admirable paper by Merriam,* who concludes that "animals and plants are restricted in northward distribution by the total quantity of heat during the season of growth and reproduction," and that in their southward distribution they are restricted by "the mean temperature of a brief period covering the hottest part of the year." If it is true that the northward spread of plants is determined by the sum-total of heat units which the plant receives, then it must follow that when a plant is grown northwards beyond its own zone, in a region of lower sum-temperature, it must in some manner conform itself to that lower temperature. If it adapts itself completely to the lower sum-temperature,—as we find it usually does if the change is not too violent,—then it becomes more sensitive to small increments of temperature than it was originally. It should vegetate and bloom relatively earlier in spring at the north than at the south; and I shall now show, by experiment, that this is usually the case.

Cuttings and seeds taken from the south to the north vegetate and germinate later than those grown at the northern station. One of the best experiments in this direction was made by Alphonse

---

*C. Hart Merriam, "Laws of Temperature Control," etc., Nat. Geogr. Mag. vi. 229-238, and charts. 1894.

De Candolle* some twenty years ago. Cuttings of *Populus alba, Carpinus Betulus, Liriodendron Tulipifera* and catalpa were taken at Montpelier and at Geneva, and they were planted at the latter place in glasses of water with sand at the bottom. The Genevan specimens leafed out first. In the case of the poplar, there was a difference of about twenty-three days in favor of the individual of the colder locality, in that of the carpinus about eighteen days, and in that of the tulip-tree a similar result was obtained when the comparison was restricted to buds of the same size and development. The catalpa of the northern locality developed twenty days in advance of the other. The tulip-tree and catalpa are introduced into Europe from America, and yet they had already physiologically adapted themselves to the various stations in which they grew. My own observations along this line have been somewhat extended, and they confirm De Candolle's experiments. Several of my students have studied the matter with reference both to cuttings and seeds from different latitudes. The following test was made by L. C. Corbett, now professor in the Agricultural College of South Dakota, in 1892:

I. Cuttings of Lombardy poplar were procured from southern Maine, and were grown in the greenhouse alongside similar cuttings from our own neighborhood (central New York). The Maine cuttings began to unfold their buds two days earlier than those from New York. The cuttings were pulled up and photographed about two weeks after the buds

*Comptes Rendues, 80, 1369 (June 7, 1875). See also Essay XIX.

started, and it was found that in every case the northernmost cuttings had made the larger growth.

II. Cuttings of Concord grapes were procured from southern Maine, central New York and southern Louisiana, and were all planted at the same time under uniform conditions. The earliest vegetation occurred in the Maine specimens and the latest in the Louisiana specimens. When growth had begun in all the specimens, the ten best ones in each lot were selected for photographing. The least average growth occurred in the southernmost specimens and the greatest in the northernmost. At this time, the average growth per specimen was as follows: Maine, 2.66 inches; New York, 1.6 inches; Louisiana, 1.3 inches.

Similar results have been obtained with potatoes from different latitudes,—those from the north usually giving earliest sprouts, when the stock from the different places is uniform.

Repeated tests have shown that seeds of many plants —and perhaps all plants behave similarly—germinate more quickly when grown in relatively northern latitudes, if the samples which are compared are of equal age and strength. This matter was the subject of experiment by the writer in 1889, when it was found that corn grown in New York germinated much more rapidly than that grown in South Carolina and Alabama. The following comparison of White Dent from Ithaca, N. Y., and Auburn, Ala., indicate the extent of the difference, there having been fifty kernels planted in each case:

	5th day.	6th day.	7th day.	Ultimate total.
New York	14 kernels.	33	2	98 per cent.
Alabama	0 "	34	5	80 "

The difference in rapidity of germination was much

more marked than would appear from the table. The plants from New York seed were by far the largest and most vigorous of any in the test during the month which they remained in the house. This subject was again investigated by two of my students, upon corn, watermelons and kidney beans. The corn gave the most marked results in favor of the northern samples, but there was generally a similar difference in the watermelons and beans, with not one contrary result.

If the cuttings and seeds of northern latitudes start relatively earlier in spring than those of the south, it is reasonable to expect that spring-flowering trees follow the same law. This subject has not been investigated in this country in connection with coincident temperatures, so far as I know, although it is one which promises good results to both the climatologist and the naturalist. "Schübeler states that in the middle latitudes of Europe and North America, flowering is delayed four days for each degree of latitude, but that in higher latitudes, according to Berghaus, the retardation is less,—indicating, apparently, that there a given amount of heat had a greater effect."* Probably the easiest way in which we could accurately express the progression of spring, or compare the differences of any two spring climates, is in terms of a physiological constant of the blooming of spring-flowering trees.

At the present time, the best statement which I can make in illustration of the relative earlier bloom of the north, is to say that most and perhaps all plum trees bloom considerably in advance of the leaves in the southern states, whilst the flowers and leaves are nearly or quite coincident in New York. In other words, with

---

*Crozier, Modification of Plants by Climate, 22.

the first burst of spring in New York, the organs at once put forth simultaneously. I first observed this fact in studying the cultivated forms of the native plums, when I was greatly puzzled by the herbarium specimens from the north and south. Specimens obtained from Maryland had full blown flowers, whilst the leaf-buds were only beginning to swell. In the same variety from New York, the leaves were fully formed and over half grown when the flowers opened. Another remarkable feature of these specimens was the close almost sessile umbels of the Maryland specimens, and the long-pedicelled flowers and prominently stalked umbels of the other,— as if the northern specimens pushed out with such redundant vigor that every organ was forced to its utmost. It would be interesting in this connection to determine if these phenomena are in any way associated with the starch content of the winter twigs in the different regions. These differences are so striking in specimens of the Wild Goose that I could not at first believe that I had the same species of plant from the two states! But subsequent observation has given me many similar instances from various parts of the south and the north (see Cornell Exp. Sta. Bull. 38, pp. 22, 30, 31, 37, and Bull. 51, p. 36). I have now observed this peculiarity in at least six species of plums—*Prunus hortulana*, *P. angustifolia*, *P. Americana*, *P. cerasifera* and its offshoot the Marianna, *P. triflora* and *P. Simonii*,—and I am convinced that most spring-flowering trees and shrubs show more or less difference between the north and the south in the time-epochs of flowering and leafing. These facts may explain some apparent discrepancies in the records of blooming and leafing north and south; and they certainly make it plain that records of either leafing or flowering are not sufficient to measure the comparative oncoming of spring in different latitudes, and that, of the two, the record of flowering is the more important.

This general effect of climate upon the life-events of plants is thoroughly appreciated by phenologists. Linsser declares* that plants originating in the north and transplanted to the south are quicker in their periods than those originating in the south, and southern plants transferred to the north are slower. In like manner, alpine plants taken to the warmer plains are quicker than the resident plants, whilst those from the plains are slower than alpine plants when taken to the mountains.

This crowding effect of the short seasons of higher latitudes and altitudes can often be traced in those northern regions which contain a sprinkling of southern types of plants. The late-blooming and early-blooming plants often modify their periodicities in such cases, so that their epochs overlap or mingle. Professor W. W. Bailey has noticed this phenomenon in New Brunswick:† "In botanizing about the capital city, Fredericton, which is about sixty miles inland, I was impressed with the curious mingling of early summer and autumn flowers. In the same field would be seen, in blossom, *Leucanthemum vulgare*, *Ranunculus acris* in profusion, and several solidagos and asters. The short summer of the region seems to crowd the seasons together; 'spring and autumn here dance hand in hand.'"

---

* Carl Linsser, Die Periodischen Erscheinungen des Pflanzenlebens, etc., Mem. Acad. Sci. St. Petersb. ser. vii. xi. No. 7, 39.

† Bull. Torr. Bot. Club, viii. 129. In this connection, it is interesting to note that Dr. Vroom, of St. Johns, considers, from the probable movements in plant-frontiers, that the New Brunswick climate is ameliorating.

II.

Some Inter-relations of Climatology and Horticulture.[1]

Climatology concerns the agriculturist in two general directions,—in aiding him to anticipate the condition of the weather some hours or days and thereby enabling him to plan his work with confidence, and in explaining the climate of any place in such manner that he can determine its probable influence upon a prospective business. The former office is the one which most readily appeals to the masses, and its direct result is prognostication, which, to most persons, is the only expression of the science. However valuable prognostication may be to the mariner and the general farmer, it serves the horticulturist very little; and its uses are everywhere transient. But local climate exerts a most powerful influence upon the plants which one attempts to grow. In short, it interposes a bar somewhere to the cultivation of all species, and becomes, therefore, the controlling factor in every scheme of rural industry. I speak of local climate, and not of any mere influence of latitude, longitude, or altitude. The climatal limit of any crop, in all directions, is an exceedingly irregular one, presenting a series of sharp curves; that is, the local variations of climate determine the distributions of cultivated plants. Now, it is true that crops are usually valuable in proportion to the difficulty of their successful cultivation, for only the best cultivators can succeed in such regions, and demand is thereby lessened. This is especially true of

---

[1] Extract from Part II. of the Report of the Chicago Meteorological Congress, August, 1893, pp. 431-435.

those products which are very perishable, or for which there exist strong home demands; and these attributes apply particularly to horticultural crops. The horticulturist, therefore, is vitally interested in the climate of his particular neighborhood; and it is the study of this local climate in its relations to plant life which must bring him the greatest good from climatological science.

If the horticulturist is concerned more with climate than with weather, it follows that meteorological records, to be of use to him, should be expressed in terms of plant life rather than in terms of degrees of temperature or other numerical standards. Very good records could be made by an army of careful growers who had neither a barometer nor a thermometer. Let us suppose, for instance, that the peach-growers of a certain geographical area were to make observations for a number of years upon the relative synchronisms of late frosts and blooming time, a subject which is of the most vital importance to every grower of the tender fruits.

The tabulation of these observations would enable us to construct two series of curves, which would indicate at a glance the comparative safety of any station for the cultivation of the given crop. We will suppose that observations have been taken for a number of years by various persons at seventeen closely connected stations, represented by the letters in the margin of the chart, page 305. One curve represents the date of the last killing frost, and the other the date of the opening of the peach flowers. Wherever the frost line lies beyond the bloom line, as in the first five stations, peach growing is impossible. When it lies at the left, peach-growing is possible, and the industry is safe in proportion as the two lines diverge. At the stations J, K and O, peach growing may be considered to be far beyond danger of late frosts. These tabulations would be valuable, of course, in proportion as they include a minute record of every farm in the given territory; but even a somewhat superficial series of observations would possess great value if accurately made, as indicating the probable influence of local climate upon the given industry. If lines tend to converge, or if the frost line passes back of the bloom line, there is indication, at least, that safe peach lands are few in those localities. The information which these records ask could be well ascertained from observations upon a few peach trees here and there long before any general experiment of cultivation had been tried.

There are no doubt many regions of the north which are now almost devoid of peach orchards, which could yield profitable fruit lands if persons could feel sure that there is comparative immunity from late frosts; and, inasmuch as fruit growing is one of the most profitable and pleasant of rural pursuits, it follows that the meteorological bureaus could here perform an inestimable service for the agriculture of the country. Even in the older parts of the country information of this kind would find ready use, for not one of our states is yet developed to even a quarter of its capabilities for fruit growing.

Old lands which have been farmed over and have lost most of their value for grain and stock, may still be invaluable for fruits and other horticultural crops; but fruit growing reaches them very slowly and hesi-

XVII.] LINES OF FROST AND BLOOM-TIME. 305

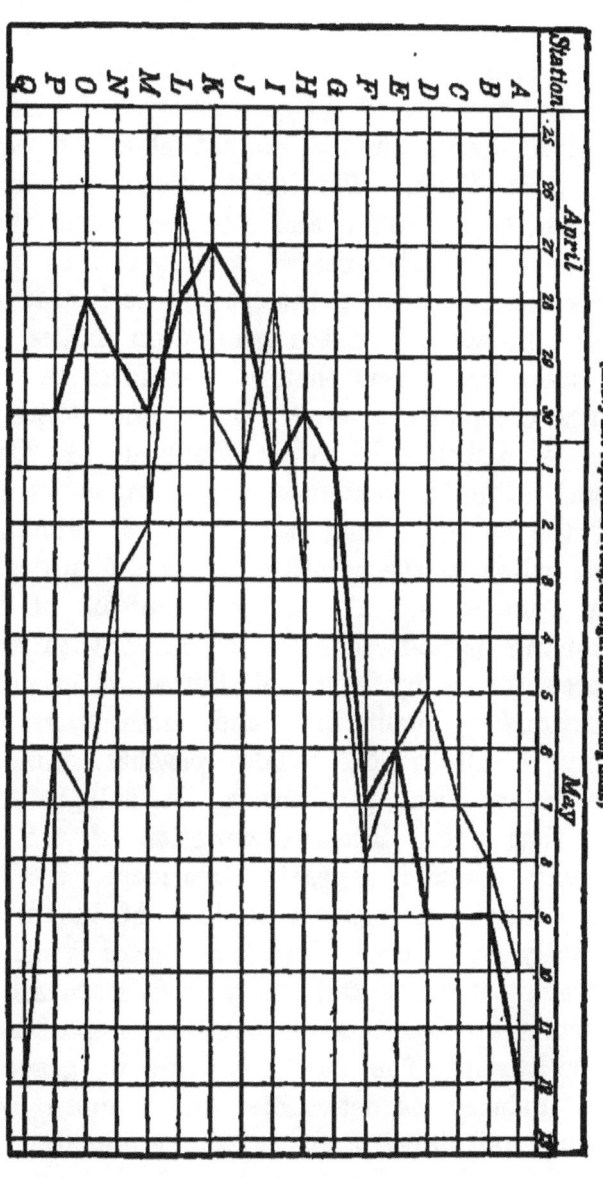

Synchronistic Tabulation of the Least Killing Frost and the Blooming Time of the Peach Tree.

(Heavy line represents Frost, and light line Blooming time.)

tatingly under ordinary circumstances. Even in regions which have once been devoted to fruits there may come a real or apparent change of climate, which overturns the business of the community. An instance of this kind occurs on the eastern shore of Cayuga Lake, in New York. This shore was a well-known peach region a generation and more ago, but the old orchards have now disappeared, and new ones do not take their places because the people feel that some change of climate within the generation makes peach growing more precarious than it was formerly. Orchards are creeping in slowly here and there, but everyone is distrustful. (See Bulletin 74, Cornell Exp. Sta.) Similar instances are common in many parts of the country, and the services of climatology should be called to the solution of the difficulties.

What I have said of the synchronisms of frosts and blooming periods can be repeated with almost equal force for many other attributes of climate in their relations to plant life; and these observations will apply to all fruits, besides peaches, which are liable to injury from late frosts. It will be found, in fact, that even different varieties of the same species may demand separate treatment, for these often vary among themselves in time of bloom quite as constantly as in time of maturation of fruit. The synchronisms of early fall frosts and maturation of certain fruits are subjects of immense importance to the horticulturist. The northern limit of grape culture, for instance, is determined much more by the date of early fall frosts than by winter climates. This is well illustrated by the Catawba, which is our most important native wine grape. It hugs the shores of certain lakes in western New York so closely that the majority of New York grape growers are unfamiliar with its cultivation, and fear that its area can not be greatly extended with safety; yet there are undoubtedly enough isolated Catawba vines in most of the fruit regions of the state to enable observations to be made for a term of years, and which might give rise to a reliable monograph of the climatal limitations of the variety within the state.

Even the cloudiness of winter months is an important consideration for those who force plants under glass, and who must economize every particle of sunlight in order to bring the plants to maturity quickly and cheaply. I am, myself, located in a district so cloudy that forcing of vegetables is scarcely profitable, and if I were to engage in the business commercially, I should seriously consider moving a few miles away into a sunnier area. With the increasing complexities of the future and the niceties which must then be practiced in order to make rural occupations profitable, it will be necessary to construct charts of cloudiness with special reference to horticultural pursuits, for not even the electric light can be expected to stand for normal sunlight.

Winter and summer climates should be studied in terms of plant life quite as much as measured by the customary instruments, for plants record all the influences of climate, while the instruments measure only detached attributes. It follows that the contemporaneous effects of seasonal climates can not be well studied upon the wild plants of a region, for these plants have long since overcome the difficulties of the particular climate, or are acclimatized. Cultivated plants, which have been brought in from other climates must, therefore, be chosen as the registers of the meteorological peculiarities of a given region. We need charts giving the zones or life areas of the cultivation of the different fruits, and these zonal limits should be constructed from the actual behavior of trees in winter, or in summer, rather than from any assumed theoretical temperature at which trees perish. If constructed from the orchard observations, these limits would become much more than mere isotherms, for trees may be injured quite as much by the alternations of temperature, the relative humidity of soil and atmosphere over great areas, the direction and force of prevailing winds, and other features, as by temperature itself.

There are numerous problems of still more local application which are yet of vital importance to the cultivator, and in the solution of which he has the right to expect the aid of the climatologist. The habitual force and frequency of winds during the seasons of maturation of fruits, the prognostication and methods of averting frosts, the influence of windbreaks and orchards upon local climate, the modification of climate in consequence of the removal of forests and the clearing of land, the frequency of droughts, the humidity of atmosphere as affecting the spread of fungous diseases and the ability to prognosticate serious incursions of these diseases from a study of their general relations to climate, the liability to hail storms, the nature of the seasonal variations,— these, in addition to the subjects which I have already indicated, are some of the living problems which await us.

Thus far, I have spoken only of what may be considered the immediately and intensely practical side of horticultural climatology. It will occur at once to the student that these very observations which I have suggested will afford data for the study of all that fertile subject which concerns the inter-relations of climate and plant life in the evolution of the vegetable kingdom, and it opens the whole field of plant variation and distribution in its relation to environment. Every plant is profoundly modified by the climate in which it is placed; and if any species, therefore, is cultivated over a wide range of territory, we must expect to find it widely variable between the extremes of distribution. The same variety of apple, for instance, may lose all its distinguishing qualities and marks through a simple transfer to climates not far removed. A study of the statistics of apple exportations during the next ten years will probably show what states or districts produce fruits of sufficient firmness and long-keeping qualities to withstand the journey profitably. And it is not too much to ask of climatology that it shall tell us why the northern climates develop saccharine elements and high colors, and why the Wisconsin-Minnesota area produces such remarkable waxen and pruinose tints. The influence of climate is nowhere so easily traced, perhaps, as in the business of seed growing. Every seedsman knows that certain climates are not only best adapted to the growth of certain seed crops, but that they exert a profound influence upon the character of the product grown from them. The study of all these inter-relations of climate and plant-life falls into three subjects: Phenology, or the study of the periodic phenomena of plants, a subject which loses half its force and value when considered, as it usually is, without reference to the visible attending features of climate; acclimatization, or a consideration of the means by which plants adapt themselves to climates at first injurious; and secondary variation of plants induced by climatal environment.

The burden of my plea is twofold: First, while not discouraging the instrumental or conventional study of climate, I would encourage its study in terms of plant life. Second, it is essential that the synchronisms of local climate and the phenomena of plants be given the closest attention.

XVIII.

ARE AMERICAN VARIETIES OF FRUITS BEST ADAPTED TO AMERICAN CONDITIONS ?[1]

FRUIT GROWERS assume that the varieties which have originated in this country are better adapted to our soil, climate and market than those imported from other countries. While the presumption favors this idea, the proposition demands investigation, and, if true, it should be capable of proof. It is obvious that domestic varieties are best adapted to the demands of our markets, because those seedlings which most nearly meet these demands have been selected and propagated. The commercial ideals are definite and easily satisfied, and we need not longer consider them here. But the adaptations to all those various conditions and phenomena which we collectively designate as climate are obscure, and they have not been carefully studied; and this relationship of American varieties to American climate, so far as it concerns some of the general adaptations of our fruits, is the particular subject of this paper.

We can draw some useful conclusions from a comparison of our native flora with that of Europe, whence most of our foreign fruits are derived. With the

---

[1] Paper read before the American Horticultural Society, Chicago, September 29, 1892. Printed in Garden and Forest, v. 518 (November 2, 1892).

exception of some arctic and sub-arctic species, the plants of North America are singularly distinct from the European plants, although much like them. There are few species which are common to both continents. Most of the plants which were once thought to be the same in both continents are now separated by botanists, and I am convinced that this separation should proceed to nearly, if not quite all, the remaining supposed identical species of the temperate latitudes. The more closely we study these species the greater the differences of habit and distribution appear to be. All this proves that, while the European and North American floras had a common origin in circumpolar regions, the present floras of the two continents have diverged, until nearly or quite all the specific types in the central and southern areas are dissimilar. This dissimilarity has been brought about by the action of environments — largely of climate — in the two continents. In other words, the habitual dissimilarity of the floras proves that the climatic environments are so different that identical species rarely thrive in both. And this fact lends plausibility to the statement that horticultural varieties, which differ from species only in degree and not in kind, must constantly tend to diverge in the two countries.

The dissimilarity of European and American congeneric species is well illustrated in some of our fruits. Thus our cultivated raspberries, blackberries, gooseberries and grapes are American species, and the profitable cultivation of these kinds of fruits did not begin until we gave up our endeavors to grow the European species. The case of the red raspberries is particularly instructive, because the European and

American species are so much alike that most botanists have never been satisfied that they are distinct; but all berry-growers know that the European varieties will not succeed as market berries in this country. This superiority of the American small fruits and grapes is not due to any greater excellence in quality or appearance in these fruits; on the contrary, they are commonly inferior in these points, for they have not yet had a long enough history to bring them to a high degree of perfection. Their success is due to the perfect adaptation to their surroundings, as an ability to withstand our climate or the attacks of insects and fungi. The capability to withstand or repel attacks is well shown in the grapes, which resist downy mildew and phylloxera better than the European varieties do, and in the American gooseberry, which does not suffer seriously from the mildew. The European plums are also subject to difficulties which the native species, now coming into prominent cultivation, more or less avoid. What is true of a comparison of the European and eastern American floras appears to be true, in varying degrees, of comparisons of other floras with our own, all of which shows that the horticulture of eastern and central North America must constantly tend to differentiate itself from that of all other countries.

If these general conclusions are well founded, we should even now be able to find some corroboration of them in a study of our varieties of fruits, for the literature of our horticulture covers three-fourths of a century, and evolution aided by cultivation is much more rapid than under wholly natural conditions. Among the fruits which have been brought from Europe, the apple has been longest cultivated in this country, and it thrives over the widest range, and we should be able to draw some valuable lessons from its behavior. The first American work on pomology was William Coxe's, published in 1817. In this work is given a list of "one hundred kinds of the most estimable apples cultivated in our country." The list contains one hundred and one kinds, of which only about a half-dozen are now popular, and only one, the Rhode Island Greening, can be classed as a general market fruit. The geographical origins of eighty-nine of these varieties are determinable, of which number thirty-two, or 36 per cent, are of European origin, and fifty-seven, or 64 per cent, are American. The first edition of Downing, 1845, describes one hundred and ninety varieties of apples, one hundred and eighty of which have known origins. Of these one hundred and eighty kinds, eighty-seven, or about 48 per cent, are European, and ninety-three, or 52 per cent, are American. Between 1817 and 1845, therefore, there was apparently a gain in the introduction of European apples over the American; but this need excite no surprise when we consider that those were the pioneer and formative days of American pomology, when great discrimination in varieties was not practiced, and when Europe was the most prolific source of new varieties.

In the second edition of Downing, 1872, we find a decided change. There are descriptions of one thousand eight hundred and fifty-six varieties of apples, and the origins are fairly well determined of one thousand six hundred and eighty-four of them. Of this number, five hundred and eighty-five, or 31 per cent, are European, and one thousand and ninety-nine, or 59 per cent, are American; and these figures undoubtedly give undue advantage to the European apples. Of the one hundred and seventy-two varieties unaccounted for, I should judge that fully three-fourths are American. In the twenty-seven years between the first and second editions of Downing, therefore, there was a remarkable falling off in percentage of apples of European origin and a corresponding increase in American varieties. It would not be safe to say, however, that all of this loss in European varieties is due to lack of adaptation of these varieties to our climate and other environments. Fashion, and the desire to patronize domestic productions, may have influenced this result, yet it is not probable that either of these causes could have defeated a profitable variety. But there is another and more important aspect of the question, and that is the fact that probably over three-fourths of the prominent apples belong to the American part, which comprises 59 per cent of the list; and of the popular market apples a still greater percentage is to be found among the Americans. In this connection we may study with profit the Michigan Fruit Catalogue (1888), prepared by T. T. Lyon, which rates all prominent varieties for Michigan in three categories—dessert, culinary and market—upon a scale of 10. This catalogue contains two hundred and nineteen varieties of apples. Of these, thirty-eight are rated 9 and 10 for dessert, of which two are known to be of European origin and three more are supposed to have come from that country,—that is, somewhat over an eighth of the dessert apples of Michigan are of probable European origin, the remainder being domestic varieties. Mr.

Lyon admits nineteen varieties to the rank of 9 and 10 for market, of which two—Duchess of Oldenburgh and Red Astrachan—are Russian, and another is perhaps of European origin. Less than one-sixth of the Michigan market apples, therefore, are of Old World origin, and one of these—the Duchess—is of recent introduction as a market apple. Of the nine crab-apples admitted by Mr. Lyon, all but the comparatively unimportant Red Siberian are of American origin.

The pear affords an interesting study in this connection, for it is a fruit which has been highly cultivated and developed in Europe, but has received only indifferent attention in this country, so far as the production of varieties is concerned. Coxe, in 1817, described sixty-five pears as grown in this country, of which only four, or less than one-sixteenth, were American in origin. Of the whole list, only the Madeleine is popular now. In 1845 Downing described two hundred and thirty-nine kinds, one hundred and ninety-two of which, or 80 per cent, were European, the remainder being American. In 1872 the Downings admitted nine hundred and ninety-five varieties, of which nine hundred and fifty-four have a known geographical origin. Of these, seven hundred and eight varieties, or 74 per cent, are foreign. There has, therefore, been a gradual increase in the percentages of domestic varieties from the beginning, although the foreign kinds are still predominant. In Mr. Lyon's Fruit Catalogue, twenty-one pears are admitted as 9 and 10 for dessert, of which seven, or just one-third, are American; and exactly the same ratio holds in the twelve varieties standing 9 and 10 for market. All these facts are indications that even in pears the American varieties are prominent and are increasing in number, and they suggest the possibility that European varieties may eventually practically disappear from our horticulture.

What is true of apples and pears appears to be true also of other fruits. Of the seventy peaches which Mr. Lyon catalogues, only five are foreign among those rating 9 and 10 for dessert and market, and of this number only one — the Rivers — is prominent. Next to the pear, the common plum is the most peculiarly European of any fruit of the eastern and central United States, yet of the fourteen varieties admitted by Mr. Lyon as 9 and 10 for dessert, one-half are American, and of the six market sorts, four are American. It is interesting to note, also, that the region of adaptation of the common plum is not large, and that the varieties of the native species are evidently destined to cover a very wide range of our southern and interior territory. (See Essay XXVI.)

If any conclusion can be drawn from all the foregoing figures and remarks, it is to the effect that, as a rule, American varieties are best adapted to American conditions, notwithstanding the fact that there are some foreign varieties which thrive over large areas of this country.

The question of the adaptations of the Russian fruits to this country at once arises, and this brings up a more vital question,— the adaptability of our own eastern fruits to the great interior basin. On a former occasion* I made an examination of the

---

* On the Longevity of Apple Trees, page 335.

reasons for the premature failure of apple orchards in the prairie states, and I satisfied myself that much of this failure is due to the transplanting of New England and New York varieties to those regions. Every fruit grower must have been impressed with the facts that the apples of these prairie states are rapidly assuming a different character from those of the east, and that the leading varieties in the two sections are even now distinct. The dissimilarity between these great regions in climatic conditions is also well illustrated in the floras, for there is a marked tendency for the specific types of the east to stop at the borders of the prairies. In other words, we have floras characteristic of the prairies and plains. Even the wild crab (*Pyrus coronaria*) of the eastern states does not occur freely in the prairie regions, so far as I know, being there represented by its congener, *P. Ioensis*, a well-marked species. More than all this, we know that it is absolutely impossible to grow our common eastern fruits in the cold northwest. Our interior regions must, therefore, be considered apart from the older states, and when we once understand this fact thoroughly much of the prejudice against Russian fruits must disappear. The situation is simply this: The northwest must have an unusually hardy class of fruits, and any type of fruit which will grow there should be encouraged. The Russian is simply one of these types, the Siberian and native crabs being others. But, inasmuch as the Russian type is the most highly developed of them, it follows that quick results are to be expected from it. If the Russian apples and the crabs are more or less adapted to the northwest, I feel sure that American seedlings of them will be still better adapted to those conditions, as a whole, and this must be the opinion of many of the fruit growers of the northwest, else the talk about promising seedlings of Duchess and other families is meaningless. Already the McMahan, Wolf River, Pewaukee, Northwestern Greening and others are great blessings to the northwest. I look for the time when the present imported fruits and crabs will be superseded by their own progeny in the same way that the lists of Coxe and other early writers have been supplanted. Already the tide has set in which shall submerge them. I therefore regard the Russian importations to be of benefit to our horticulture, but I look upon them as a means rather than as an end. The history of our horticulture everywhere emphasizes the probability of a secondary and more important outcome.

The conclusion of the whole matter, as it now lies in my mind, is this: American fruits constantly tend to diverge from the foreign types which were their parents, and they are, as a rule, better adapted to our environments than foreign varieties are. In less than a century we have departed widely from the imported varieties which gave us a start. At the expiration of another century we should stand upon a basis which is nearly, if not wholly, American.

XIX.

ACCLIMATIZATION: DOES IT OCCUR?[1]

THE question is asked in the June *Garden*, if acclimatization does ever really occur. The question is suggested by the definition and explanation of the term as given by myself in the previous issue. In defining the term, I did not intend to defend the question as to whether acclimatization does or does not occur. Being thus drawn into the controversy, however, I submit a few facts in defense of the occurrence of acclimatization.

In order to comprehend clearly the discussion, the reader will need to bear in mind the distinctions between the terms acclimatization, acclimation, naturalization and domestication, as outlined in the May issue. It must be borne in mind that the essential idea of acclimation and acclimatization is the overcoming of a climate which is at first injurious to the plant or the species. It must also be remembered that the difference between acclimation and acclimatization lies in the fact that the former is a process of wild nature, while the latter takes place under the more active guidance or supervision of man. The processes in the two are, of course, the same. Man acclimatizes with the same agencies with which nature acclimates. Hence it happens that in many instances we are unable to deter-

---

[1] American Garden, new series, viii. 295, 325, 357 (September, October, November, 1887). Consult Glossary for definitions.

mine whether a given phenomenon is acclimation or acclimatization. If the phenomenon occurs in plants which are in any manner or degree cultivated, it falls under the head of acclimatization, as the word is used in this discussion. The reader must also remember that plants become acclimatized in various ways without becoming hardier. Increase in hardiness is by no means the only proof of acclimatization, although common opinion seems to consider it so.

The literature of the subject is in most cases valueless, because the idea of overcoming climate is not kept in mind. Nor is it safe to say that because a given sub-tropical plant has been extended over wide temperate areas, it has become acclimatized. The plant may originally have had sufficient flexibility of constitution to allow it to thus extend its range. Again, if acclimatization occur it must necessarily be a very slow process, and the science of plant observation in the garden is not yet old enough to present many definite facts. Add to these difficulties the fact that many writers wholly deny the possibility of acclimatization, and the subject is seen to be exceedingly perplexing.

Those who wholly deny acclimatization are for the most part unreasonable in their demand of what acclimatization should be. They demand that plants be adapted to an opposite extreme of climate before they be called acclimatized. It is not to be expected that the plant can be so radically changed. A slight change, as well as a great one, is acclimatization. I repeat the definition:

ACCLIMATIZATION.—The act or aid of man in inuring or habituating a species or variety to a climate at first injurious to it, or the state or condition of being, thus inured or habituated.

The subject at once divides itself into two heads, and each head divides into two minor captions:*

I. Acclimatization through a change in the individual plant.
   A. Modification of constitution.
   B. Modification of habit.

II. Acclimatization through a variation in offspring.
   A. Variation in constitution.
   B. Variation in habit.

I. A. There is very little record of experience concerning individual adaptation to climate, and nearly all the record which does exist is negative. It is an almost universal opinion that the same plant cannot become modified in constitution so as to endure an injurious climate. Such opinion is not strange if we recollect that the same observer seldom knows the plant in both its original and adopted homes, and is therefore unable to determine if it has acquired any hardiness. Moreover, such change in individual constitution is looked for in plants which have been removed through a great latitude of climate. The fact that plants thus removed usually suffer severely or die outright has given rise to the opinion that such acclimatization does not exist. Yet, although it is difficult to demonstrate individual constitutional adaptation, I am prepared to believe that changes may occur in plants which are removed through small distances, say a degree or so. But the subject is so difficult of determination that we shall not be likely to be speedily enlight-

---

*Some writers contend that acclimatization takes place through the agency of hybridization, but as hybrids are in reality entirely new productions, lying outside the species, they cannot properly be considered under this subject.

ened upon it. There is no physiological reason why such change should not occur, as is witnessed by the practice of "hardening off" cabbages and other plants, whereby a direct and radical change, though not strictly acclimatization, is produced in the individual.

The best direct evidence which I now recall bearing upon the probability of individual constitutional adaptation is that of the vine cited by Darwin.* Vines from Madeira are said to succeed better in the West Indies than those taken from France. Here, obviously, there has been a divergence between the vines of France and Madeira, and, as vines are propagated by cuttings, we can say with truth that the vines in the two countries are but different parts of the same individual. Yet I am not satisfied with this indication of individual acclimatization, as the vines of the two countries may have been separated by seedage or modified in habit.

I. B. Does the individual ever become changed in any external character or habit in a manner to overcome climate? While record of experience upon this caption is meager, as upon the last, it is still valuable. It is well known that the same plant sometimes behaves differently in different years. If this difference is in the direction of enabling the plant to grow in an injurious climate, it is a true means of acclimatization. For instance, if the plant were removed northward it might acquire the habit of blossoming relatively earlier in the spring, so as to take advantage of the shorter season. Peach trees from central Georgia blossom ten or twelve days later in Virginia and Maryland than do those of the same variety from New Jersey or New

---

*Animals and Plants Under Domestication t. 377 Amer. Ed.

York.* As peach trees are propagated by buds, we regard the Georgia and New Jersey trees, being the same variety, as parts of the same individual. The learned and careful Thomas Andrew Knight believed in this method of acclimatization by individual variation, as evidenced by the following remarks concerning offspring of cuttings:† "If two plants of the vine or other tree of similar habits, or even if obtained from cuttings of the same tree, were placed to vegetate during several successive seasons, in very different climates: if the one were planted on the banks of the Rhine and the other on those of the Nile, each would adapt its habits to the climate in which it were placed, and if both were subsequently brought, in early spring, into a climate similar to that of Italy, the plant which had adapted its habits to a cold climate would instantly vegetate, while the other would remain perfectly torpid."

II. Acclimatization through variation in offspring is supported by a multitude of records and by common experience. In this connection a few examples will sufficiently indicate the direction of proof.

A. The offspring of cultivated plants vary much in ability to resist heat, cold, dryness or other peculiarity of climate. Whenever such an individual becomes hardier than the parent species, acclimatization has taken place. Nor is it necessary that in every case the hardiness should exceed that of the species, for there may be cases in which all the domesticated offspring have become more tender than the parent species, and increase of hardiness in any of this

---

* Fitz, Southern Apple and Peach Culturist, 237.
† Horticultural Papers 173.

offspring over its general weakness would be true acclimatization. Variation in constitution is well illustrated by the peach. It is well known that dormant fruit buds and the trees themselves are killed at a much higher temperature in the southern states than in the northern states. Twenty degrees below zero does not often kill mature peach trees in Michigan; but in southern Illinois, as Parker Earle writes me, they are usually killed by a temperature of ten to fifteen degrees below zero.

Mr. Crozier* records testimony to the effect that peach trees in Michigan were injured no more at a temperature of twenty degrees below zero than they were in central Mississippi at a temperature of zero. Peach buds are injured at a much higher temperature at the south than at the north. Mr. P. H. Mell, Jr., director of the Alabama Polytechnic Institute at Auburn, writes me that buds are often killed even at a temperature of thirty-four to thirty-eight degrees above zero. This observation undoubtedly refers to the partially expanded buds, yet it is well known that at the north a considerable frost is required to kill the swelling buds. It is possible that all these instances of the peach should fall under the division of adaptation through modification of individual constitution; but as I cannot be certain, if indeed it is probable, that all these cases represent bud offspring, I place the statements here. If trees of the same variety show this difference in different latitudes, as they undoubtedly often do, then we have indisputable evidence of the acclimatizing of the individual.

It is well known that seedlings grown in the

---

* Modification of Plants by Climate, 21.

north from southern seeds are often much more tender than those grown from northern seeds of the same species. While this fact is generally proof of acclimation rather than of acclimatization, it nevertheless indicates clearly enough that acclimatization could take place after the lapse of sufficient time. Concerning this matter, the veteran Robert Douglas, of Waukegan, Ill., writes me as follows: "*Juniperus Virginiana* grown from seeds from southern Illinois and Tennessee, is not only not so hardy as the same tree from our northern Illinois and Wisconsin seeds, but it is quite tender. My experience in this direction leads me to believe that this is the case with all trees. We planted side by side black walnuts collected from trees here and from trees in southern Illinois. The trees from the latter nuts made nearly double the growth of ours under the same conditions, but the next spring they were found to be killed to the ground, while ours were not injured even in the terminal bud.* *Pseudotsuga Douglasii* from Colorado seeds is hardy here, also in Massachusetts and on the western prairies. The seeds of the same tree from California, Oregon and Washington produce tender trees, which will stand neither our climate nor that of Massachusetts, as has been proved by Professor Sargent and several others." The Philadelphia *Press* for July 6 states that "at the late nurserymen's convention Robert Douglas said that trees from seed of *Pinus ponderosa* brought from the Pacific slope are not hardy, while the same from seed

---

*This experience with the walnut properly falls under the next division of our subject, as the variation in habit of the trees appears to be the cause of differences in hardiness.

gathered from the Rocky Mountains and thereabouts are as hardy as red pine with him." Nurserymen in Scotland find that young *Pinus sylvestris* raised from German seeds become "browned and scorched" in winter, and especially in the frosty breezes of early spring, while plants of the same age grown from seed gathered in the vicinity are not injured.*

But we need not draw all our examples of this sort from plants in wild nature. The four following plants are known in the given localities only in a condition of cultivation or as escapes from cultivation: "*Salix Babylonica* from the Euphrates is tender, while that from the Volga is hardy; *Populus dilatata* from Italy is short-lived and tender, while that from east Europe is perfect; *Spiræa callosa* from France kills back each year, while that from Russia is hardy; *Salisburia* (*Ginkgo*) *adiantifolia* from China is tender, while that of west Asia is hardy."† "As an example of a variety being hardier than the species, we may cite the *Magnolia grandiflora* var. *Exoniensis*, which will retain its leaves uninjured during winters cold enough to destroy young branches of the species in its immediate vicinity."‡ This variety Exoniensis is an English cultural seed variety.

Essentially the same phenomena occur in the case of the apple. Trees from the central plain of Russia are said to be more hardy on our western prairies than are those from the coast of Russia and from other parts of Europe. The same is true of other plants. In this instance we are not able to re-

---

*William Saunders in U. S. Dept. Agr. Rep. 1877, 50. See also Darwin, Animals and Plants under Domestication, ii. 373 Amer. Ed.

†Professor J. L. Budd, in Prairie Farmer.

‡William Saunders l. c.

fer the phenomena directly to acclimatization, as we are unable to determine positively whether or no the common apple is indigenous to Russia. But here are great adaptations to climate, which might have been brought about by disseminations made through the agency of man, as well as those made by nature. According to Buysman,* the cultivated apple grows in Norway at a latitude of sixty-five degrees twenty-eight minutes, while the wild apple grows only as high as sixty-three degrees forty minutes; in Finland the cultivated apple occurs at sixty-three degrees, the wild only at sixty degrees. Schübeler states that while the pear is unknown in a wild state in Norway, it is cultivated as far north as Trondhjem, latitude about sixty-four degrees. The cherry is not certainly known in an original wild condition, yet it is cultivated as far north as the polar circle in the open ground.† These extensions of cultivated plants to the northward are not proof of acclimatization, as in nature the limits of species are often determined by other agencies than climate. Yet the instances cited are indicative of such change. A singular instance of the adaptation of the apple is stated by Mr. T. T. Lyon, who found that apples from the southern states are hardier in Michigan than many kinds of northern origin. This anomaly is perhaps due to the inuring of the trees to the trying southern summers, enabling them to endure our severe northern droughts, so that they enter the winter with unimpaired constitutions.

---

*Am. Jour. Sci., 3rd ser. xxviii. 355.
† Geographische Verbreitung der Obstbäume und Beerentragenden Gesträuche in Norwegen, 22, 29.

In this connection it may be interesting to recall the attempts made late in last century to introduce our wild rice, *Zizania aquatica*, into England. At first the plants did not flourish in those cool, moist summers. Seeds from successive generations sowed themselves, and "in this manner the plants proceeded, springing up every year from the seeds of the preceding one, every year becoming visibly stronger and larger, and rising from deeper parts of the pond, till the last year, 1804, when several of the plants were six feet in height, and the whole pond was in every part covered with them as thick as wheat grows on a well-managed field. Here we have an experiment which proves that an annual plant, scarce able to endure the ungenial summer of England, has become, in fourteen generations, as strong and as vigorous as our indigenous plants are, and as perfect in all its parts as in its native climate."*

II. B. Acclimatization through variation in habit in offspring is common and unequivocal. Variation in habit is usually in the direction of lessening or extending the period of growth. Many herbaceous plants, when taken northward, start relatively earlier in the spring and mature earlier in the fall than they did originally. Others simply shorten their period of growth without obvious change in the direction of early vegetation. Of this latter class Indian corn is a good example. "Thus the season required by maize varies from six months in the elevated plains of Santa Fé, in South America, to four months in the middle United States and two and one-half months in the Rainy

---

*Sir Joseph Banks, Trans. Lond. Hort. Soc. i. 22.

Lake district northwest of Lake Superior."* This wonderful change in the habit of maize has been brought about solely through the agency of man. "Hence it has been found possible, according to Kalm, to cultivate maize further and further northward in America. In Europe, also, as we learn from the evidence given by Alph. De Candolle, the culture of maize has extended, since the end of the last century, thirty leagues north of its former boundary."† The earlier corns, that is, those which require a shorter period of growth, are usually the so-called flint corns, while the later or southern corns are usually dents. Dr. W. J. Beal‡ found that flint corn becomes well marked with dent in three years when taken from Michigan to Kansas. On the contrary, "at Lansing, Mich., dent corn has a tendency to ripen earlier and become round at the tip of the kernel from year to year, unless care is taken by selecting seed which shows prominent dents in the ends of the kernels. In southern Ohio and Indiana there is not that tendency for dent corn to change to flint corn." Those who deny the occurrence of acclimatization cite the fact that Indian corn is no more able to resist frost now than when first known to the white man. This statement is probably true, yet of all plants corn is one of the most ready to adapt itself to climate by way of shortening its period of growth. It habituates itself to a climate at first injurious to it. For instance, the first crop of dent corn grown in Michigan from southern seed will be very poor, most of it being cut by the frost. Successive sowings from the same stock

---

*James S. Lippincott, U. S. Agr. Rep. 1863, 512.
†Darwin, Animals and Plants under Domestication, ii. 370 Amer. Ed.
‡Mich. Agr. Rep. 1880, 283.

give successive gain in yield, other things being equal. This statement will apply to many garden vegetables as well. Red peppers brought from the southern United States give in Michigan a very small yield the first year. The second year's crop is better, and the third or fourth is fair to good. The season of growth becomes so much shortened that the plant can mature. "The races of melons, squashes and gourds, which have long been cultivated in northern Europe, are comparatively more precocious, and need much less heat for maturing their fruit, than the varieties of the same species recently brought from tropical regions."* A single ear of precocious rice has given rise to the only kind that can now be grown north of the great wall of China.† (See also, Bretschneider on the Study and Value of Chinese Plants, 44.)

This shortening of the season of growth is not confined to herbs. Trees mature earlier at the north than at the south. They also start relatively earlier—that is, at a lower temperature. "It occurred to M. De Candolle to test the matter. * * * At some time last winter he had branches sent him from Montpelier of *Populus alba, Carpinus Betulus*, liriodendron and catalpa. These were paired with similar branches taken from trees at Geneva, and after a common sojourn in a cool room long enough to make sure of complete penetration by the same temperature, the pairs were placed in glasses of water with some sand at bottom, and kept in a warm room under exactly the same conditions. * * * The result was that the German trees leafed out first. In the case of the poplar,

---

*Naudin, cited by Darwin, l. c. 376.
†Encyclopedia Brit. 9th Ed. i. 86.

there was a difference of about twenty-three days in favor of the individual of the colder locality, in that of the carpinus about eighteen days, and in that of the tulip tree a similar result was obtained when the comparison was restricted to buds of the same size and development. The catalpa of the northern locality developed twenty days in advance of the other."* In the instances of the tulip tree and catalpa, "of which very few generations can have been raised in Europe," we have clear acclimatization.

Winter and spring wheats afford a striking example of acclimatization. In endeavoring to prove the common origin of these wheats, Monnier has given us a case of distinct adaptation to climate: "He sowed winter wheat in spring, and out of one hundred plants four alone produced ripe seeds; these were sown and re-sown, and in three years plants were reared which ripened all their seed. Conversely, nearly all the plants raised from summer wheat, which was sown in autumn, perished from frost; but a few were saved and produced seed, and in three years this summer variety was converted into a winter variety."†

Plants undoubtedly adapt themselves to dry climates by modifications in form and structure of various organs. Deep-rooted trees endure drought best. Professor Budd writes to the Iowa *State Register* that "it is also interesting to note that the deep-rooted sorts [of apples] that endure drought perfectly are native to sections of the earth where this habit of growth is a necessity. As instances: Gros Pommier is native to the sandy, gravelly knolls of east

---
* Asa Gray, in American Journal of Science, 3d ser. x. 237. Cited also in Essay XVII.
† Darwin, l. c. i. 380.

Poland; Duchess, Romenskoe and many other sorts with green foliage at this time [a time of drought in Iowa when our native apples suffered], are native to the dry, porous, loose bluffs west of the Volga, where the annual rainfall is only from twelve to fifteen inches. We find this general law to hold good with the apple, pear, cherry, plum, forest trees, shrubs, and even with the grasses and weeds."

"It is no exaggeration to say that with almost every plant which has long been cultivated, varieties exist which are endowed with constitutions fitted for very different climates."—*Darwin*.

"We must transport as large number as possible of adult, healthy individuals to some intermediate station and increase them as much as possible for some years. Favorable variations of constitution will soon show themselves, and these should be carefully selected to breed from, the tender and unhealthy individuals being rigidly eliminated.

"As soon as the stock has been kept a sufficient time to pass through all the ordinary extremes of climate, a number of the hardiest may be removed to the more remote station and the same process gone through, giving protection if necessary while the stock is being increased, but as soon as a large number of healthy individuals are produced, subjecting them to all the vicissitudes of climate."—*A. R. Wallace*.

"Domesticated plants can be gradually acclimatized to bear a degree of heat or cold which in their wild state they would not have supported."—*Marsh*.

XX.

ON THE LONGEVITY OF APPLE TREES.[1]

MUCH is said concerning failures in apple orchards, and it is commonly supposed that apple trees are shorter lived than formerly. Many causes are held to account for these conditions, but there have been no definite attempts toward an elucidation of the subject. Any study of the subject, even a mere collocation of opinion from various sources, will be useful in calling attention to facts and in giving direction to argument. In this paper I have endeavored to collate all the opinions of any importance upon the subject of comparative longevity of apple trees, and I have also attempted to analyze them, and to determine their value. In order to obtain as many opinions as possible, I addressed a letter of inquiry to representative men in various parts of the country, with the following requests: "I wish to know if apple trees in your state or region are shorter lived now than formerly. If so, what are your opinions as to the causes? Is the failure due to change in climate, to deterioration of varieties, to methods of cultivation, or to ways of propagation? Do you think that under the better cultivation of later years, apple trees produce more in a short lifetime than formerly in a long

---

[1] Read before the Twenty-fourth Annual Meeting of the Kansas State Horticultural Society, at Topeka, Kansas, December, 1890. Printed in the society's report, vol. xviii. 75 (1889-90).

lifetime? In short, give me your opinions in a definite and clear-cut manner upon the subject of longevity, or lack of longevity, of apple trees at the present day."

In their answers to this appeal, most of the observers state directly that apple trees are shorter lived now than formerly, and even those who oppose the proposition, still admit it indirectly, by making good cultivation and sufficient fertilizing a condition of great longevity. We may assume, therefore, that the average limit of age of apple trees is decreasing.

It is first necessary, in treating the subject, to determine if this falling off in longevity is an inherent tendency in the species or its varieties, or if it is due entirely to external causes, as climate, tillage and neglect. In other words, is the apple tree becoming weakened in constitution through long cultivation, or do we treat it improperly? A few of my correspondents believe in what I may call *cultural degeneracy*, or the doctrine that the more highly we improve the species the weaker in constitution must each succeeding generation of varieties become. No proofs are advanced in support of this proposition, and from our present knowledge, I do not see that it can be sustained. It is an easy matter to find highly improved varieties which are tenderer or weaker in constitution than seedlings; but this proves nothing. It only compares one variety with another, for all varieties were originally seedlings, and they owe their dissemination to the fact that they chanced to be worthy of dissemination. And those that chanced to be unworthy of dissemination—for which we particularly reserve the word seedling—differ as much among themselves in hardiness and vigor, as named varieties differ from seedlings. The seedlings which have survived in waysides and old plantations have been able to do so, no doubt, because they were constitutionally fitted to survive. No one knows how many seedlings have perished because of weakness, and it is certainly not fair to compare those varieties which we chance to cultivate with those wild or half-spontaneous individuals which have chanced to be able to endure all vicissitudes. We are fond of saying that the farther the species departs from its original or wild type, the weaker it becomes, but we have no proof for such statement.

Indeed, the facts cited in support of cultural degeneracy prove conclusively another law, which I may call *varietal difference*, or the proposition that varieties differ widely among themselves in constitution. It is well known, for instance, that some varieties are much hardier than others, and then the question invariably arises if the weaker varieties tend to disappear, or to "run out." This question is too broad for discussion here, but it may be said that in apples, under common methods of propagation, we have little or no reason to believe that varieties are self-limited. (Consult Essay XXIV.)

I am strongly of the opinion, therefore, that the failure in apple trees is due to external rather than to internal causes. The reasons which my correspondents have given for this failure may be named and classified as follows:

   I. *Extra-cultural causes.*
      1. Change in climate.
      2. Greater abundance of insects.
      3. Greater abundance of fungi.

II. *Cultural causes.*
    4. Lack of adaptation of varieties to conditions.
    5. Forceful methods of cultivation.
    6. Lack of fertility, and neglect.
    7. Methods of propagation.
    8. Pruning.

1. *Change in climate.*—It is asserted that climates are becoming more severe, and that varieties which were considered hardy fifty years ago often perish now. Before we can reason definitely upon this point, we must have proof that climate is becoming more severe, yet I do not know that such proofs exist. I had thought of comparing old meteorological records with recent ones in various states, but I find that no adequate studies or records of climate, extending through a series of years, have been made. There are abundant records of temperature, but climate means more than relative heat. It comprises humidity of atmosphere, character, frequency and direction of winds, alternations of variations, progression of seasons, relative cloudiness, and many other conditions. Recollections of climate are peculiarly unreliable and vague, and many of the definite statements concerning changes in climate are founded upon assumptions. The only well-authenticated general fact concerning recent changes in climate appears to be the observation that severe winds are more frequent in deforested areas than in forest regions;—the country is bleaker. But the relations of this bleakness to plant-life have not been carefully studied. There are evidently recurring cycles of climatic differences, and it is probably these more or less marked periodical changes which people have confounded

with the idea of a permanent modification of climate. Over one hundred years ago, Hugh Williamson, M. D., attempted to account for the "very observable change of climate" which had taken place in Pennsylvania within the preceding forty or fifty years. He declared that "our winters are not so intensely cold, nor our summers so disagreeably warm as they have been." Most persons suppose that an opposite change has taken place in recent years.

It is, therefore, useless, in a discussion like the present, to attribute the failure of apple orchards to increased severity of climate. And it is also apparently unnecessary to do so, as other causes appear to adequately explain the falling-off.

2. *Greater abundance of insects.* — There is no question that insects are more numerous, both in individuals and in destructive species, now than formerly. The increase in individuals is due to the greater number of trees grown in later years. The increase of noxious species is due to the changes of habit of various species, and to introductions from foreign countries. But there are comparatively few insects which occasion the death of the tree itself. Insects which weaken the tree are mostly borers, and these species appear to have been common in former times; and although their individual numbers may have increased, their injuries are undoubtedly more than counterbalanced by the greater pains taken in destroying them in later years. Increased insect depredations unmistakably lessen production in recent years, but I cannot believe that they lessen longevity of trees. Some contend that attacks upon the foliage tend to lessen the vitality of the tree, and therefore

to shorten its life. This is an imaginary notion. Plants are not so nicely balanced that comparatively slight injury will disturb their equilibrium and shorten their life. And even if the supposition were true, it may be assumed that the increased attention given to cultivation and fertilizing in later years would counterbalance any weakness induced by increase in incidental insect injury.

3. *Greater abundance of fungi.*—The remarks which have been made in reference to insects apply eqally to fungi. There are few augmentations in fungous injuries which lessen the longevity of the tree.

We have now eliminated the extra-culture hypotheses of failure in apple trees,—all those cases which lie beyond the control of the grower. We have now to consider those assumed causes which are wholly or mostly under direct control of the orchardist.

4. *Lack of adaptation of varieties to conditions.*— In our discussion of *varietal difference*, above, it was observed that varieties of apples, as of other fruits, differ widely among themselves in constitution. It is very evident, therefore, that all varieties are not equally adapted to trying conditions. We have yet scarcely attempted to make any discriminating choice of varieties in respect to their constitutions. It is only within the last few years that search for "ironclads" has been diligent, and much of this has been random.

It is also undoubtedly true that the same variety is not equally adapted to all conditions. This is really but another way of stating the above proposition, but it brings out an important point, viz.:

That the wide dissemination of varieties exposes them to more various conditions than they were obliged to endure in the comparatively small regions near their place of origin. It is to be expected that many of these conditions will be more severe than the original ones, and that the varieties will suffer in consequence. Indeed, this point is so well known that it needs no discussion, yet I do not remember to have seen it stated clearly. Every orchardist of experience can cite examples of varieties which have had greater constitutional vigor in some regions than in others.

These points have great weight in this particular discussion, because in matters of longevity our orchards are usually compared with the seedling orchards of the last generation. These seedling trees were never removed far from their place of origin, and they were not exposed to so many vicissitudes as those sorts which chanced to be scattered far and wide over the country; and it must be remembered, also, that only the hardiest and best of the seedlings were usually selected. Or if an indiscriminate lot of seedlings was planted, some of the trees were very apt to disappear soon, and the orchard became "ragged." This was nature's selection; and yet this fact appears to have been overlooked. The old orchards about which we hear so much were usually ragged or uneven orchards, and only those trees which chanced to stand the longest are used as measures of comparison, while in our orchards we usually count the failure from the trees which succumb first.

My father used to tell me of the old trees upon his father's farm, which had been old from his first recollection; but when, in the expectancy of young manhood, I climbed the Vermont hills to see those trees, I found that they were but a few scattered individuals of an orchard from which the greater part of the trees had long ago perished. In the present generation, the orchard would have been cut out fifty years short of the condition in which I found it. There were few even and regular orchards in the old days. Nature weeded out the poor ones, and the grower was content if three-fourths or even a half of his trees flourished. In these days we count an orchard a failure if such a proportion of its trees weaken and die. Much of the discussion of comparative longevity of apple trees rests not so much upon fact as upon fallacious observation.

Another point needs to be considered in this connection. We are extending apple culture farther and farther into uncongenial regions. Much of the talk of the lessening longevity of orchards originates west of the Great Lakes, or is suggested by western experience, but it must be remembered that this prairie country has a very different influence upon apple trees from that of the eastern states, and that there is no common basis of comparison between the two regions in this respect. It is undoubtedly true that apple trees are shorter lived west of the Great Lakes than east of them, but this is not proof of lessening of longevity in the apple tree. It is simply an experience of the effects of two very unlike soils and climates. Perhaps apple trees will never be so long lived in the northern prairie countries as they are in the east. For myself, I am inclined to think that they will not. But if they ever are, the improvement must certainly come as a result of acclimatization of the species to the region. I do not know why these facts should puzzle us any more than the fact that maize completes its life in Minnesota in half or two-thirds the time that it does in the Gulf States, or that cotton is not adapted to Pennsylvania. It only proves that apple growing in the northwest and prairie countries must be conducted on a different basis than in the east.

5. *Forceful methods of cultivation.*—I am inclined to think that high cultivation and consequent heavy fruit-bearing tend somewhat to shorten life, but I do not see that they can be accepted as general or serious causes of lessening longevity. I should be glad, however, if forceful cultivation should shorten life, for we should then be able to obtain the full returns from orchards sooner than we do now. And in this statement, it seems to me, is to be found the means of determining the relations of high cultivation to longevity. High cultivation, if it really forces the plants, would make varieties more precocious. Do the Northern Spy and the Baldwin bear earlier now than formerly? So far as we know, they do not. It should also be borne in mind that failure of trees oftener follows neglect or poor cultivation than high cultivation, and this brings us to the consideration of our next subject.

6. *Lack of fertility, and neglect.*—Under general conditions of farming, every succeeding crop leaves the ground poorer than it was before, and in this fact, it occurs to me, is to be found the most potent cause of comparative failure of trees. And there appears to be ample proof of this statement in the good results obtained all through the east wherever

apple orchards are well fed. There are numerous instances in this state of well-fed orchards which are longer lived than contiguous ones which are underfed. Soils are not so rich as they were in our grandfathers' days.

Neglect certainly ruins many orchards, but I cannot see that it is any more disastrous now than it was formerly, unless, perhaps, it obtains an accelerated influence because of the lesser fertility of the soil. It was neglect in the old orchards which weeded out the weak trees and emphasized the longevity of the strong ones. It must have the same effect at the present day.

7. *Methods of propagation.*—Much is said concerning the devitalizing influence of the common methods of propagation, but I have yet to find any proof that they have such effect. There are two features of propagation, in particular, which appear to be held accountable for much mischief: Growing stocks from pomace seeds, and grafting.

Domestic apple seeds are obtained indiscriminately from pomace, and imported seeds are procured in essentially the same manner from the crab stocks of Europe. This promiscuous seed-sowing is supposed by some to tend towards the deterioration of the constitution of the species, but there are no facts in support of the assumption. Others contend that by this means we obtain an uneven and variable basis upon which to propagate our orchard trees, and this is certainly true. Seedings vary much among themselves in constitution, and we practice little elimination of the tenderer or least adaptable ones. But I do not see that this unevenness of stock should exercise greater influence upon the vitality of orchards now than it did in past generations. We have observed that the old seedling orchards were usually uneven, from the very fact that the weak individuals could not persist. At the present time, our even and symmetrical orchards are proofs that this unevenness of stock has less marked effects than formerly, probably from the fact that the seedling root is dominated by the grafted top, or that it has disappeared altogether, the cion having rooted from itself. Promiscuous stocks probably influence the character of our orchards, but, as I have stated, the same influences were present in former generations as now, for everywhere and always promiscuous seedlings, whether grafted or not, have formed the basis of orchards.

The last year or two has witnessed a renewed activity of the old assumption that grafting or budding tends to weaken the individual. In the first place, much of the discussion upon this point is misdirected, because graftage is necessary to success, and to discard it means, practically, to discard apple culture itself. There is no other easy and practicable means of perpetuating varieties of apples.

Some contend that graftage is necessarily mischievous, because it is unnatural. This reasoning here, as elsewhere, is puerile. All training of plants is itself unnatural, as is also all cultivation, in this sense, and if we propose to perform all operations just as nature performs them, we must at once abandon all domestication and betake ourselves to barbarism.

No doubt much of the graftage is mischievous,

because not well done; but these instances were no doubt relatively just as common generations ago as they are now. In fact, I should look for worse results from the old, careless methods of top-grafting than from recent methods where the union is protected by the soil, and where every effort is made to heal the wound quickly. In general, I know of no evidence to show that graftage is necessarily a weakening process.*

It is still an open question as to whether or not root-grafting tends to shorten the life of the apple tree. It may be that in certain cases it does, as in particular varieties which do not readily strike root from the cion, or in particular ways of performing the operation. Yet I am inclined to think that root-grafting is not a general cause of lessening of longevity, from the fact that the budded orchards, which are abundant everywhere in the east, appear to fail as soon as grafted ones.

8. *Pruning.*—There are many growers who suppose that pruning weakens the tree and induces shortness of life. I have not yet learned of any reason for this belief, other than the statement that pruning is "unnatural." In our discussion of graftage, we observed that these so-called unnatural processes are not necessarily devitalizing. But pruning is not unnatural. No orchardist prunes so heavily as nature does in destroying the branches of saplings which are to form trees of the forest; and the greater the vigor and persistence required, the more she prunes. And more than this, nature is entirely undogmatic, and

---

*For a more specific discussion of the supposed devitalizing effects of graftage, the reader is referred to the third edition of The Nursery-Book.

prunes at all seasons and in what we should consider the rudest ways.

There are certainly instances in which injudicious pruning has seriously injured orchards, and possibly there are regions where pruning must be cautiously done, but I do not see that it can be held to account for any of the general failure of apple trees.

Conclusions.— Apple orchards appear, as a rule, to fail sooner now than they did formerly, but much of the opinion to this effect is exaggerated because of fallacious observation.

This lessening age is not a degeneracy due to domestication, but it appears to be incidental to methods of cultivation and extensions of apple growing over great areas.

The chief particular causes appear to be lack of **adaptability** of varieties to regions and conditions, climates unfitted to the best development of the species, and lack of fertility of soil.

XXI.

SEX IN FRUITS.[1]

Since the demonstration of the value of sprays for exterminating the insect and fungous enemies of fruits, the most important advance in American pomology is the discovery that some varieties of fruit are unable to fertilize themselves. Much of the failure of apples and pears and native plums to set fruit, even when bloom is abundant, is unquestionably due to too continuous or extensive planting of individual varieties; and it is safe to expect that other fruits are also jeopardized by unmixed planting. This knowledge, as soon as it becomes more extensive and exact, is sure to modify greatly the planting of orchards. But there is also an important philosophical side to the problem which I wish to suggest at this time. Why are varieties infertile with themselves? What relation does such infertility bear to the evolution of varieties? Is it likely to increase or diminish in future varieties?

When sex first appeared, the individual was hermaphrodite; that is, the two sexes were present in the same organism. The two sexes are opposed to each other in their physiological evolution, however, the female sex-elements probably being developed from the constructive or vegetative (anabolic) changes within the

---

[1] Read before the Michigan Horticultural Society, June 14, 1893. Printed in Rept. Mich. Hort. Soc. 1893, 207. For a discussion of the untechnical terminology of sex, see the foot-note, page 66.

organism and the male sex-elements from the destructive or dissociative (katabolic) changes. It is probable, especially in organisms of increasing complexity, that these opposed changes of the organic structure can take place simultaneously, at least in equal degree; and it therefore happens that even in the lowest hermaphrodite or bisexual organisms the sexes develop or operate alternately, the individual being at one time essentially male and at another time essentially female. In this way it first came, no doubt, that self-fertilization was more or less prohibited. Now, as the struggle for existence increased, every organism, whether animal or plant, was obliged to dispense with every superfluous ambition and to concentrate its powers upon those organs and functions which were an absolute necessity to the prolongation of the life of the species. There came a tendency in certain individuals to eliminate one sex and in other individuals to eliminate the other sex; so in time there came to be male and female, or a division of labor. But other advantages besides a mere division of labor resulted from this disjunctive evolution. The male and female individuals became unlike in other features than those of mere sex, and the offspring of their union were more variable than those which might spring from one parent, or which had no father and mother. The more variable the offspring of any species, the greater are the chances that many of them will find congenial or at least tolerable places in nature, and the safer is the species in the contest for life. It is the opinion of some modern philosophers—Weismann and his followers—that the chief use of sex is to originate variation in the offspring.

There must be a general tendency in species toward unisexuality. All the higher animals are male or female, and some of the plants are so, also. The great majority of plants, however, are still hermaphrodite. All our common fruits have what the botanists call perfect flowers, that is, those which contain both male and female elements. Yet nearly all hermaphrodite plants develop their stamens and pistils at different times, so that the flower cannot fertilize itself. This, we suppose, is in consequence of the fundamental law that the constructive and destructive changes upon which the female and male elements respectively rest — or anabolism and katabolism — cannot proceed simultaneously. In many plants, self-fertilization is prohibited or hindered by this simplest of all methods, — the different or alternate maturing of the sex members. But the plant often goes further than this, and the pistil or seed-bearing member refuses to accept the pollen from the same flower, or even from any flower on the same plant; or, to transpose the statement, the pollen is impotent upon its own sisterhood of pistils. It is difficult to account for the physiological origin of this impotency, although we should expect that pollen-bearing members which are prevented from fertilizing associated pistils might in time develop pollen which would be incapable of fertilizing them; but its use to the species is obvious, inasmuch as it insures cross-fertilization, and thereby tends to strengthen or revitalize the species. Darwin was among the first to study this subject, and he published a list of plants which are sterile with their own pollen; but none of the fruits are in his list.

This fact—the impotency of certain plants with themselves—is itself of immense practical importance, but we are anxious to know if such characters are likely to increase among cultivated plants, and if the future holds more perplexity than the present. We have found that as struggle for existence increased and organisms became more complex, animals could not afford to be hermaphrodite or bisexual, for all the surplus energy was needed for the development of a single sex. Among plants, this separation of the sexes has proceeded slowly, perhaps because of their exceedingly constructive or vegetative character, which supplies sufficient nutriment to maintain both sexes in greater or less perfection. But the further we develop fruits, the greater is the energy required in the production of that fruit, and the greater, it would seem, must be the tendency toward the suppression of one sex in given individuals, or toward the evolution of unisexual individuals. Now, it is highly probable that one of the first steps in the separation of the sexes is a differentiation in their mutual relationships, whether a difference in time of maturing of the sex-elements or in the comparative intimacy with which they react upon each other. If these speculations are well founded, it leads us to the conclusion that this impotency among cultivated plants is the beginning of a potential tendency towards unisexuality, and that such impotency is likely to increase, rather than diminish, with the greater amelioration of the species. The reader may think this conclusion counter to the observed facts in the vegetable kingdom, where unisexuality does not appear to be associated with the progressive development of plants; but he will recall that I am speaking of ameliorated or domesticated plants, and not of wild ones. In wild plants, the sex-relation is very largely a specialization in each individual case, but in domestic plants this specialization tends to be overcome by the effects of redundant growth-force.

If it is true that the female sex-elements are the result of constructive or vegetative changes, it would seem to follow that such elements would be most likely to be retained in the great vigorousness of cultivated plants, and that the pollen would first show signs of failing. This is well illustrated in many cultivated species, for deficiency of pollen is by no means uncommon, while good pistils are almost always present. The only important exceptions to this statement are the double and sterile flowers like the roses, carnations, and snowballs; but these plants have been bred directly for their doubleness or sterility, and do not, therefore, influence the present inquiry. The berry-grower knows that all strawberries have pistils or seed-bearing members, while an increasing number have no pollen. Potatoes now fail to set bolls because the anthers are deficient in pollen, and horseradish does not set seed, probably for the same reason. One who undertakes to perform experiments in the crossing of cultivated plants soon finds that it is more difficult, as a rule, to obtain good pollen than good pistils.

An excellent proof that increased amelioration of fruits imposes a severe tax upon the energies of the plant, is afforded by the habitual failure of very many or even the greater part of the flowers upon a fruit tree which blossoms full. Apple flowers are borne in clusters of from five to ten, and yet, except in the crabs, apples are usually borne singly; that is, most of the flowers fail. And trees which bloom full rarely average even one fruit to the cluster. Small wild apples are frequently borne in clusters, and there is every reason to believe that originally all the flowers normally set fruit. With the enormous development in size and other qualities of fruits, the plant is unable to use all its flowers. I am inclined to think, however, that these extra flowers serve a very useful purpose in supplying pollen to those which chance to set, for not only is the supply of pollen in the individual flowers probably becoming less with the improvement of the apple, but it is also probable that more is needed to incite the enormous increase in size over that of the inferior aboriginal apple. What is true of the apple is true in various degrees of all orchard fruits, even of the cherry; and it is most graphically shown in the tomato. It is here worthy of remark, also, that probably the chief reason why the bush fruits, as blackberries, raspberries and currants, do not more rapidly improve in size is because all the flowers upon the clusters still set fruit. All these instances show that cultivation or improvement seriously interferes with the mutual relationships of the sexes, and this disturbance or unbalance is likely to increase rather than diminish.

But it now transpires that not only are some plants impotent or infertile with themselves, but in some cases all the plants of a given variety are infertile among themselves. Thus it has long been known that the Wild Goose plum is usually unproductive when planted in isolated or unmixed blocks, and the same is true in various degrees of most varieties of native plums. Of the pears which have so far been studied in this connection, the self-sterile are Bartlett, Anjou, Clapp Favorite, Clairgeau, Sheldon, Lawrence, Mount Vernon, Gansel Bergamotte, Superfin, Pound, Howell, Boussock, Louise Bonne de Jersey, Souvenir du Congres, Columbia, Winter Nelis, Bosc, Jones Seedling, Easter and Gray Doyenne. Those which appear to be self-fertile are White Doyenne, Le Conte, Kieffer, Duchess, Seckel, Buffum, Manning Elizabeth, Flemish Beauty and Tyson. Among the apples, the following are found to be self-sterile: Talman Sweet, Spitzenburgh, Northern Spy, Chenango Strawberry, Bellflower, King, Astrachan, Gravenstein, Rambo, Roxbury Russet, Norton Melon and Primate; while Codlin (partially), Baldwin and Greening are self-fertile. These are results obtained by M. B. Waite, who has brought this investigation to the fore.

At first thought this fact—that varieties may be self-sterile—looks strange, but it is after all what we should expect, because any variety of tree fruits, being propagated by buds, is really but a multiplication of one original plant, and all the trees which spring from this original are expected to reproduce its characters. If this original tree was self-sterile, therefore, we should expect all trees propagated from it to be equally so, in just the same way that we expect all plants of the Haverland strawberry to be pistillate, like the original parent. To say that any variety of fruit is impotent with itself, therefore, is really the same as saying that the original seedling parent was impotent with itself; and the fact that some varieties are impotent while others are not is proof that fruits vary or differ in this respect when grown from seeds. Perhaps there are as few impotent fruit trees now as there ever were, and that our attention is now called to them simply because they have been propagated or multiplied extensively and because we are now inquiring carefully into all horticultral problems; but I am inclined to think, from reasons already advanced, that there must be a general (though very slow) tendency towards self-sterility in highly cultivated plants. The natural check to this self-sterility is the raising of plants from seeds, by which means a considerable amount of variation is secured in sexual characters. In proof of this, I will cite the case of garden vegetables, in which the various individuals of a variety are fertile with each other, even when a given individual is sterile with itself. Thus blocks of the same variety of tomato or bean fertilize freely. But while this same intra-varietal fertility would undoubtedly result from growing only unbudded or ungrafted fruit trees, the disadvantage, as every one knows, would be so great as to make the practice unprofitable. But the same result can be obtained by planting different named varieties together, for these varieties represent different seed-parents. And this is the conclusion which the best practice enforces, for mixed orchards are, as a rule, the most successful ones.

A broad epitome of the whole problem seems to run something like this: There is a general tendency in nature toward a separation of the sexes, or unisexuality, and this tendency is probably hastened among plants by high cultivation. The first signs of separation—and beyond which most plants may never go—are differences in the time of maturity of the two sex-elements and the failure of pollen to impregnate its associated pistils. Subsequent steps are the failure of many normal flowers to set fruit, and diminution of the pollen supply. The extensive multiplication or division of impotent or self-sterile individuals, and the setting of the resulting plants in large blocks, have given us unfruitful orchards. If increasing amelioration tends toward a sexual unbalance, it must follow that unfruitful orchards are likely to increase unless intelligent mixed planting is brought to the rescue.

XXII.

ARE NOVELTIES WORTH THEIR COST?[1]

IT IS a perennial question, this asking if novelties in fruit pay; and yet it is never settled. The manner of answering the question seems always to be the same: the respondent cites his own experience with the new varieties, with an inclination to dwell most upon those which he considers to be dishonest or unworthy; and so it comes that there are as many opinions of the "novelty question"—as the discussion has come to be called—as there are persons who try to answer it, with a tendency, always, to decry the introduction of new things. It is evident that the fundamental merits of the question can never be determined from individual experiences of a certain number of novelties, for it is rare if any two experiences agree upon even the same variety. If there is not some broader and more scientific basis of judgment, the question may as well be dropped forever.

What we really need to ask is this: Is there a constant tendency for new varieties to surpass the old? Or, in other words, have we yet reached the limit of improvement and evolution in any species of plant? Before attempting a direct answer to these questions, we shall need to consider for a moment if varieties are pre-limited in duration, or if they "run

---

[1] Read before the Western New York Horticultural Society, January 24, 1894. Printed in Proceedings of the Thirty-ninth Annual Meeting, pp. 37 to 41.

out;" for if they do pass away new varieties must take their places, or the cultivated types of the species would cease to exist. Or, to state the proposition differently, if varieties run out, the species can be rescued from oblivion only by new forms; but inasmuch as all valuable cultivated plants tend constantly to increase in extent of cultivation, it follows either that they do not run out, or that new varieties are better than the old and drive them out. And yet there are persons who hold tenaciously to both dogmas,—that varieties run out and that novelties do not pay,—without seeing that the logical result of such opinion is to erase the cultivated flora from the face of the earth. Now, it is true that the varieties of any plant are, as a whole, constantly changing, as one may prove by comparing the catalogues and manuals of a generation ago with those of to-day. These changes are most rapid in plants of shortest duration, or those in which there has been the greatest number of generations, showing that the greater the opportunity for renewal of stock the greater is the variation and number of recorded varieties. Thus the apples of to-day are as much like those of a century ago as the strawberries of to-day are like those of ten years ago; and there is about the same number of generations in the one case as in the other. This means, as I said before, that the rate of change in named varieties is in proportion to the length of life or profitable duration of the species. This at once raises a strong presumption that varieties do not wear out from mere age, but that they pass out by variation in the process of reproduction; and as varieties of standard merit are more numerous in all plants now than they were a century or even a human generation ago, it must follow that new varieties have been appearing all these years which were good enough to obtain the confidence of all careful growers. In two papers which I have presented to this society,* I have shown, I think, that varieties do not wear out; but all plants which are habitually propagated by seeds, as garden vegetables and flowers, tend constantly to change or differ from their parents, and finally to pass so far away from them that they receive new names; and plants which are propagated from cuttings of abnormally developed parts, as the potato, constantly tend to deteriorate unless grown and selected under the very best conditions; but all plants propagated from normal or unvariable parts, as by ordinary cuttings, cions, and layers, remain substantially the same from century to century, as is the actual case with several prominent orchard fruits. If the orchard fruits do not run out, therefore, the only reason why the varieties should change is because better ones appear and drive them out; and inasmuch as it is a matter of common knowledge that change does take place, it follows that profitable novelties have appeared.

Up to this time, therefore, novelties, or at least many of them, have paid. Is there any reason for supposing that they will not pay equally well in the future? Or, to raise my original question: Is profitable variation no longer possible? This question is not new, and there is no special reason for asking

---

* Reprinted in Essay XXIV.

it at the present time. It is certainly as old as commercial horticulture; and, for all I know, Noah, when taking the animals into the ark, may have asked if so many kinds paid. If novelties have furnished all advancement up to the present time, it would seem that they must continue to do so in the future; and the only reason for discussing the question at all must be a prevalent belief that varieties are now so many and so good that the limit of profitable evolution has been reached.

I have said that all advancement in types of cultivated plants has come about through the origination and introduction of new forms. It is necessary, then, that this advancement be defined. A novelty does not necessarily need to surpass every or even any old variety in order that it may have merit. It may possess attributes which fit it for some entirely new condition or use. A currant or gooseberry which is sweet and tender enough to supply the dessert may be a useful novelty, while in all other respects it may be inferior to all existing varieties. And this is a point that we should keep constantly in mind,— that we need new varieties for unfilled gaps, for new regions, various soils, new markets, and new household uses. If, therefore, a variety is successful, or profitable, with one person only, and fails with all others, it is worth introducing. The trouble is not so much that novelties are unworthy, as it is that they are recommended promiscuously, and that their particular and distinctive merits are not discovered. Now, I like to think that the evolution of cultivated varieties follows the same laws as the evolution of new types in nature; and it is pretty well agreed by all naturalists that there are more distinct species or forms upon the earth to-day than there have ever been at any one previous time. We are apt to think that both the animal and vegetable kingdoms have passed the zenith of their development, because the great number of monstrous forms is now extinct. There were giants in those days. But size or bulk is not a measure of the height of development. Evolution is perfected only when every phase and condition of the external world has some type of life particularly adapted to it; and inasmuch as new conditions in the physical features of the globe are constantly appearing, there must be a constantly progressing attempt on the part of animals and plants to adapt themselves to these new conditions. The surface of the earth was probably never so varied in physical characters as at the present time, and it is safe to assume, as I have said—particularly as such facts as are known support the assumption—that there have never been so many diverse forms of life as at present; and this differentiation is proceeding as rapidly to-day, probably, as it has at any time in the past. In other words, the only limit to the expansion and evolution of wild plants is that of the surroundings in which they live; and as cultivated plants modify themselves through the same laws, it must follow that there is no predetermined limit to their amelioration or improvement, so long as man continues to cultivate and modify the earth. Every year may witness better varieties, until the plant becomes so unlike its ancestors that its parentage may be lost or unrecognized, and new specific forms, even, may originate under the hand of man; and this has occurred in many instances. (Compare Essay IV.)

If philosophy teaches us that there is no set or predetermined limit beyond which plants may not progress, reflection must likewise convince every one of us of the essential truth of the same proposition. We know that most important cultivated plants have come from a very inferior ancestry; and some, if not most fruits, have sprung from parents which are scarcely edible to civilized tastes. We have a graphic means of comparing the improved side by side with inferior types in the small-leaved, small and austere-fruited and often weak and tender "crabs" and other seedling apples which, however, are only partially reverted to their aboriginal condition. In America, where vast new regions have been settled with great rapidity, we have seen the extension of fruit growing, by means of new and adaptive varieties, into regions which were thought to be unfitted for such purposes but a few years ago. It is a fact that all plants, especially our fruits, have responded with really remarkable facility to all the new demands which our markets and soils and climatic limitations have placed upon them. This response has been in the way of new varieties, and it has, of course, been most marked in those fruits which were comparatively little developed, and to which almost every condition of cultivation and dissemination was new. You will recall the readiness with which the native plums, within forty years, have given us nearly two hundred varieties adapted to a remarkable range of conditions and uses; and the blackberries and raspberries within a generation have given results which show that they will equal, if, indeed, they do not eclipse, the wonderful evolution of native grapes within a century; and many of you will recall the fact that it is less than a generation ago when it was thought that roses could not be successfully grown out of doors in this country. Evolution undoubtedly becomes slower the more the plant is improved, for it has constantly to compete with its own progress; but if worthy new varieties are less frequent in the old standard fruits, it does not follow that there are none.

I assert, therefore, that the tendency to produce new varieties is the means by which cultivated plants are ever more and more improved and fitted into new conditions and uses; and novelties must pay if horticulture is to forever pay. But not all novelties pay, and the reasons must be apparent. They may not be good enough to pay. Novelties are introduced both hastily and indiscreetly. If the philosophy of the question, as we have considered it, teaches us anything, it is: First, that the older and more improved the type, the less are the chances of securing a worthy novelty; Second, that there is most use for novelties in those plants which are propagated by seeds and by abnormally developed parts, because such plants usually quickly run out by variation; Third, that worthy novelties appear less frequently in old regions than in new ones, because of greater competition of established varieties there; and Fourth, that the merit of a variety lies in its adaptability to some particular use or demand. I therefore look with caution upon novelties in the old standard fruits and in the old horticultural regions, the more especially as these fruits are propagated by buds and the good old varieties remain with us; and I look with suspicion upon all those which are recommended indiscriminately, indefinitely, generally, and for everything, and equally for all regions, because their descriptions cannot be truthful and cannot be founded upon experience. I believe that the time is now at hand when a man can establish a more lucrative nursery or plant business by giving his novelties careful and discriminating tests, and by telling what they are not good for as clearly as he tells what they are good for, as he can by possessing himself of the desire to introduce a certain number of novelties each year, and to paint them in such faultless colors that every thoughtful man knows that the descriptions are false.

XXIII.

WHY DO PROMISING VARIETIES FAIL?[1]

THERE is probably no greater discouragement in horticultural pursuits than the uncertainty which attaches to the purchase and production of new varieties. So great is the fear of new productions that very many people decry the introduction of novelties as hazardous and unfortunate. There must be reason for so widespread feeling. There is one proposition, however, which needs to be presented at the outset in order to arrest your attention upon what seems to be a trite subject. There is probably no variety in existence, whether of fruit, vegetable or ornamental plant, which perfectly meets all the requirements demanded of it; that is, there is none which is ideal. If this perfect variety is not in existence, must it yet appear in the guise of a novelty? It is to the new things, therefore—to the future—that we must look for advancement; the old things are not capable of improvement. I may be asked here if the ideal variety ever can come, if it is among the possibilities. This no man can answer; but we know that there has been a general uplift in the merits and variety of our cultivated productions during the present generation, and if we compare our varieties with those of a century or more ago, we find them to

---

[1] Read before the Illinois State Horticultural Society, at Champaign, December 8, 1892. Printed in Proceedings of the Society, xxvi. 147-154.

be, for the most part, far superior to their predecessors. We are justified, therefore, in expecting better things for the future. But I need not argue this point with you, for the tacit conviction that better varieties are possible is one of the spurs to our labor.

We shall agree, therefore, that there is reason to expect improvement in all plants. But why is it that so many of the promising new things fail? Now, I mean to exclude from this discussion the element of personal dishonesty in the introduction of novelties. There are probably some varieties which are introduced for the sole purpose of money-getting, the introducer knowing that they are inferior, or old sorts renamed. But I am convinced that there is less of this practice than is generally supposed, and that most of the failure that is commonly charged to dishonesty, is to be laid to other causes. I cannot believe that even 10 per cent of the failures in the new varieties is chargeable to any intentional moral fault of the introducer. These inferior varieties are not considered in this paper, for I have confined my inquiry to promising novelties. The reasons why promising varieties fail fall readily into two categories: 1. The false or unfortunate ideals of the purchaser and seller. 2. The uncertain or unfavorable attributes of the varieties themselves.

1. It is a question if we should expect any new variety to exceed the combined merits of existing varieties in all points; that is, it is probably better to look for a variety which shall thoroughly satisfy one or two demands, rather than all demands. The details of horticultural pursuits are now so various

that many of the ideals are contradictory, and therefore unattainable in one variety. We probably need to specialize in varieties as much as in other directions. I therefore look with suspicion upon a new variety which is introduced with the assumption that it shall supplant all other varieties; it should supplant only one other, and that the best of its class. This exaggerated praise is not wholly the fault of the introducer, for there is a demand for it among a very large class of our rural population. (Compare Essay XXII.)

2. But varieties themselves lack merit and persistence; that is, they do not bear out the promises which they seem to make. I may say at the outset that we often mistake the promises and regard the variety as more valuable than it has given us warrant to suppose. This is especially true if the variety is one of our own raising, for our interest in it is so great that we are apt to unconsciously forget or excuse its faults. But varieties often do promise more than they fulfill. Perhaps 80 or 90 per cent of the varieties in our manuals and catalogues never come into cultivation. Some three thousand varieties of apples have been described in American publications, but the important varieties probably do not greatly exceed one hundred, certainly not two hundred. Over eight hundred varieties of apples are offered in the catalogues of 1892. In the year 1889, four hundred and thirty-four varieties of fruits, vegetables and ornamental plants were offered for sale in North America; in 1880, there were five hundred and seventy-five; in 1891, eight hundred and eighty-four. This makes the enormous total for three years of eighteen hundred and ninety-three novelties.

No one can expect that the greater part of these foundlings will find a permanent place in cultivation. In 1869 twenty-eight new strawberries were introduced or prominently mentioned, of which only two—the Charles Downing and Kentucky—are at present known. In that year, also, thirty-six new raspberries were introduced or prominently advertised, of which only the Philadelphia and Turner are now known, and these are rapidly passing from sight. Of the eight newer blackberries of that year, five still persist, however,—the Kittatinny, Missouri Mammoth, Wachuset, Western Triumph and Wilson Early. Of the twelve or fifteen dewberries now named, only three are prominent, and only one has gained a general reputation. All these illustrations show that there are in existence many more varieties than we need, and yet there are few which really satisfy our expectations. This failure has little relation to the mere date of introduction of the varieties, that is, to their novelty, but to the broader and more important facts that very few varieties tend to surpass others which have come into existence earlier, and that variations run largely in similar directions, giving us many essential duplications in leading characters. If these statements are true, it may appear strange that men should introduce so many of these comparatively unimportant varieties. Why have they ever become known and disseminated ? It is largely for the reason, I think, that the varieties mislead us, and in several ways :

1. *New varieties are often not fixed or permanent in their characteristics, or do not show their full attributes at once.* New tomatoes illustrate this fact forcibly. A year ago a chance tomato plant appeared in one

of the benches of our forcing houses. It proved to be the best forcing or winter tomato which I have ever seen, and of a new type. I was proud of it and named it. Seedlings and cuttings were raised from it and set in the field, but none of the offspring seemed to present any decided merits. Many of them were entirely unlike the parent, even in the color of the fruit. Yet this plant stood in an isolated position, where the seeds could not have been crossed. In fact, the cutting-plants varied much more widely from the original than the seedlings did. In 1889 and 1890 I sent out a new tomato under the name of Ignotum. By careful selection we have kept this variety very close to its original characters; yet from seeds of Ignotum, from fifteen seedsmen last year, eight lots failed to produce a single typical Ignotum plant. Varieties of tomatoes are notably unstable, so much so that a variety rarely persists in its original characters for more than ten years unless extra care is exercised to keep it true. This instability is true to a greater or less extent of all varieties which are propagated by means of seeds. But it is sometimes true of fruits as well, which are propagated by buds or divisions of the plant. A young cherry tree stood in an English garden. The fruit was so indifferent that the owner was about to destroy the tree, but his little daughter had become attached to the tree, and pleaded for its life. The tree was left, and the fruit began to improve. The mature tree gave an excellent fruit, which is now known as the Black Eagle. All fruit growers or nurserymen of wide experience know that the first fruit of a plant is not to be accepted as a reliable indication of the permanent character of the plant. Sometimes the first fruit is better than the later fruit and sometimes poorer, but I think that it is oftener better. When the plant first begins to bear, the crop may be unusually profuse or the fruit may be unusually large and fair. If the originator or introducer draws his description from this first crop, he is very likely to be disappointed in after years. On the other hand, some fruits show their full merits only after years of fruiting, like the Josephine de Malines and other winter pears. In these cases, the impatient man might destroy a meritorious variety. This danger of introducing varieties which are not fully fixed or whose habits are not fully known, can be avoided by giving the novelties a longer trial before they are introduced. Of course, the introducer feels that he cannot afford to wait a few or several years before he places a variety upon the market. He is afraid that others may introduce a similar variety, or he is impatient for the gain and notoriety which an introduction may bring. I may say, in answer to this, that the novelty which has the longest record behind it is likely to win the greatest favor, and therefore to bring the greatest gain; and certainly one's reputation gains more from deliberate than from precipitate action.

(2) *New varieties are often not adapted to a wide range of conditions.* However well a variety may thrive in its original place, this is little evidence that it will thrive in other places. Every horticultural convention affords new evidence that few varieties are cosmopolitan. A few days ago I heard a spirited discussion upon the merits of the Cumberland strawberry, and almost every conceivable opinion was expressed concerning it. Some thought it to be

among the most meritorious of strawberries and others had discarded it. Essentially this same discussion could be applied to most varieties of fruits. It does not follow that a variety is necessarily best adapted to the place or conditions in which it originates, but it is true that it stands little chance of being noticed and disseminated unless it is adapted to its birthplace. When we consider the immense area of our country and its great diversity, we cannot wonder that varieties are rarely adapted to a very large portion of it. I am often tempted to construct a detail map of the distribution of some prominent variety of fruit. We should find the distribution to be peculiar, to be dense here and there, sparse in contiguous areas, and to skip entirely an irregular space now and then. Here in Illinois and westward, even the comparatively cosmopolitan Baldwin apple is supplanted by the Ben Davis. It is too much to expect any one variety to thrive equally in all parts of a single state, let alone in all parts of North America. Yet we are likely to regard an adverse report upon any novelty as a necessary condemnation of it, while the report may only define the limits and merits of the variety, and thereby prove to be a decided advantage by tending to restrict the variety to its true place and sphere. I mean, in other words, that the success of a variety is not determined by the number of favorable reports upon it, but rather by its perfect adaptation to certain conditions and requirements. A variety is not a failure if, in one place alone, it is better than all competing varieties.

A very important question now arises: Shall

the originator endeavor to determine the conditions to which his variety is adapted before he introduces it? Now, adaptations often differ very widely between very small contiguous areas. A variety may not be adapted to all the arable soils and all the exposures of a single farm. To discover, therefore, the full range of adaptability of a variety is to introduce it. The originator cannot discover these facts and still hold the stock in his own hands. The experiment stations can help him somewhat, but there are only about fifty of them in all North America. We cannot expect the originator or introducer, therefore, to know all the conditions under which a variety will succeed or fail. But we can expect, however, that he shall tell us all that he does know about it. He should tell us the soil upon which he finds it to succeed, the exposure, and the treatment which it enjoys. It is his duty, also, to give the adverse as well as favorable reports, and the conditions under which they arose.

(3) *Varieties bear a variable and uncertain relationship to disease and insect attacks*. We know that in every species of plant which is ordinarily variable, and which has been cultivated for a century or more, there are some varieties which are more susceptible than others to disease and insect injury, and that in some years these varieties are more injured than in others. If our variety is new, we have not yet learned its relationship to these attacks,—whether it is to be subject to them or immune. When growing in limited quantity in a small space, it may escape attack for several, or even many years, and the originator may think it to be immune; but as the

area of its cultivation enlarges, the enemies find it, and it may turn out to be as liable to injury as any of the older varieties, and, like them, it may fail for this reason. In other words, absence of injury to a new variety may not indicate immunity from disease, but simply escape from it.

I am inclined to believe, also, that a variety may change in its relationship to disease, and possibly to insect attack. May it not be true that many of the so-called blight-proof pears really are measurably immune, and that after a time they become susceptible to attack? It is true, no doubt, that some varieties of pears are freer from attack than others; that is, the species, the pear, varies within itself in this particular. Now, the variety differs from the species in degree only, not in kind; it is variable within itself, and there is no philosophical reason why it may not acquire new habits. More than this, the behavior of many varieties of various plants in reference to disease appears to indicate some such change in character. How many are the old seedling pear trees which, standing near affected ones, rarely or never blight, but whose offspring blight as badly as other kinds! The same variety of plant often behaves differently in different parts of the country in reference to the same disease. The difference in amenability to disease in different varieties of the same species is admirably shown in the tomato. The little-improved sorts, like the Cherry and Plum tomatoes, are not attacked by fruit-rot, but the large modern varieties are seriously affected. In other words, if we had no large tomatoes we should probably fear no such disease as tomato fruit-rot.

Moreover, the rot in any variety appears to depend considerably upon the conditions under which the variety is grown. It is also known that these conditions exert a great influence upon the habit and other characteristics of the variety. The influences of these conditions or environments upon both amenability to disease and upon variation or modification in the variety itself, must, therefore, proceed somewhat in common. It is conceivable, also, if varieties or individual plants become modified with age in reference to productiveness and qualities of fruit without showing other external modifications, as we have already seen, that they can become similarly modified in reference to their attitude toward diseases.

(4) *The standard of merit is constantly rising, and varieties which would have been acceptable at one time may no longer find favor.* Every variety which supplants other varieties, by that much raises the standard of the forthcoming varieties. A grape must now be better than the Concord, if it is worth introduction. Good varieties are not worth introducing; they must be superior if they are to have permanent value. Yet this fact appears to be overlooked by many nurserymen and other introducers, and the simply good or meritorious varieties which they put upon the market fail as soon as they become well known. If the standard of excellence is constantly rising, the question at once arises, if amelioration in plants is keeping pace with this uplift: Are there as many superior variations as there were when the standards were lower? This question is too large for discussion here, but it may be said that there are probably enough superior variations to meet our

present needs. The greatest difficulty, perhaps, is to distinguish them and to bring them properly before the public.

It may here be said, also, that the chance of a new variety to succeed, other things being equal, is in direct ratio to the novelty of its characteristics; that is, the variety which differs most widely from all other varieties finds the field of least competition, or least impediment to its progress. This same principle pertains under wholly natural conditions. That organism spreads most rapidly which differs most widely from all its fellows. This principle has been called by Darwin the divergence of character. Any new character or combination of characters in any organism, gives such organism an immense advantage because it is enabled to occupy places of least struggle. The Lucretia dewberry, for instance, was introduced rapidly because it found no similar plant with which to compete; but every succeeding variety of dewberry will encounter difficulties, and these difficulties will increase with the augmentation of varieties. The new Japanese plums are now spreading rapidly. Varieties of early introduction, because of their wide distribution, are very difficult to dislodge by later and even superior varieties. We all know how hard it was to give up the Isabella grape, the Lawton blackberry, the Houghton gooseberry, the Red Dutch and White Dutch currants and the Wilson strawberry. There are, no doubt, varieties of apples superior to Baldwin and Ben Davis among the three thousand American kinds, and native plums superior in all points to the Wild Goose. Perhaps the merits of these obscure varieties have not been sufficiently advertised ; but the fact remains that it is exceedingly difficult to dislodge an old variety.

If these arguments are well taken, it follows that the blame for the introduction of unsuccessful varieties is not so much moral dishonesty as a misconception of the merits of the varieties and the nature of the demand which they are to meet; and the remedy of the evil is a better understanding of the points at issue, both by the introducer and the purchaser.

XXIV.

REFLECTIONS UPON THE LONGEVITY OF VARIETIES.[1]

I.

Do Varieties Run Out?[2]

FEW questions have occasioned more discussion than this, and few have been so imperfectly answered. At the present time there are the most diverse opinions concerning it, but with a strong trend towards the negative side. And yet the affirmative of the question admits of the most positive demonstration.

It is first of all necessary to define our propositions, and we shall then see immediately that two or three separate questions have been mixed up in this discussion. By "running out" is meant the disappearance of the characteristics of any variety. It does not mean that the line of succession, the series of generations, has actually become extinct, but that the sum of attributes by which we are able to identify the group of individuals has become so modified that we no longer recognize it. Running

---

[1] The reader should also consult Essay V., page 133.
[2] Read before Western New York Horticultural Society, January 29, 1891. Printed in Proceedings of Thirty-sixth Annual Meeting, pp. 86-89; also, in Garden and Forest iv. 58.

out, therefore, is not necessarily deterioration, though the two are commonly confounded; it is simply change, modification.* If we say that the Peachblow potato, for instance, has run out, we simply mean that it has disappeared. It has broken up into many forms, perhaps. We cannot say that it has degenerated, for degeneracy is a relative term, and a variety or an individual which is inferior for one purpose may still be superior for some other; and it is probable that there are many different grades or kinds of variations in the remnants of this variety, some poor, some good.

Again, running out does not mean that the life of the variety is necessarily limited in duration. As a matter of philosophy, we are undoubtedly safe in assuming that the duration of any particular form of life will be limited, for there is evidence that species have become extinct. Yet, as a matter of practice, the limits of the genetic duration of species and varieties in nature concern us little; and, at any rate, there is no reason to suppose that varieties possess necessarily a different limitation from species. The presumption is, however, as Asa Gray long ago pointed out,[†] that the older the variety, that is, the greater the number of its generations, the greater must be its chances of permanence, because it has become pronounced in its character and has proved its capability to persist. But I propose to limit the present discussion to the mere disappearance of varietal characteristics, through which we lose sight

---

*This distinction was clearly made in a recent paper upon tomatoes.—Bull. xxi. Cornell Exp. Sta. 83, 1890.

†N. Y. Tribune, Dec. 8, 1874. Reprinted in Silliman's Journal and Sargent's Scientific Papers of Asa Gray.

of the variety, rather than to extend it to the philosophical question as to whether varieties, like individuals, become old and die, or wear out.

My proposition and the proof of it are simply these: Running out is the disappearance of varietal characteristics through change; all plants vary or change; therefore varieties must tend to run out. While there can be no doubt of this general fact or law, there are still degrees of running out, because no two plants vary in the same way or at the same rate; that is, as there are diverse kinds of variation, so there must be diverse kinds of running out. The causes of running out are, therefore, as numerous as the causes of plant variation, and they include all such considerations as the influences of soils, climates, methods of cultivation, attacks of fungi and insects. It is necessary, however, to distinguish between the disappearance of varieties through natural change and through mere fashion, for the latter often banishes varieties which are useful and well marked.

We can divide variation into two general groups, seed-variation and bud-variation.

Seed-variation may be called a progressive tendency, because the new forms or variations are generally markedly unlike their ancestors, and possess a greater or less tendency to perpetuate themselves. The seed grower is obliged to exercise constant vigilance to keep his stock "true." He knows that, as a rule, stock is more likely to remain true on poor soils than on very rich ones, because on the latter it tends to sport or "break" more. Dwarf peas soon become half-dwarfs upon strong soils, and they possess a tendency to perpetuate the new characteristics. These are instances in which change of soil causes running out. Climate exerts a wonderful effect upon vegetation. Transfer northward dwarfs plants and induces coördinate changes. Dent corn taken far north after a time becomes flint, as has been shown by the experiments of Beal and others. And Beal observes* that in southern Michigan dent "ears grow shorter, kernels become shorter and rounder at the ends." Some plants possess a strong tendency towards variation which appears to be in a measure independent of surroundings. The tomato is a good example; varieties do not long retain their original characters. It is probably impossible to find in the market to-day the Tilden tomato, as it was known when the variety first appeared; and the Trophy has changed considerably from its original character. In short, the very fact that we can improve varieties by good cultivation, and that we are enabled to obtain new varieties at all, are indubitable proofs that varieties run out. Upon these facts depends all possibility of advance in the origination of varieties. And upon this general law, also, hangs the whole framework of evolution.

Bud-variation comprises all change which comes through the agency of grafts, cuttings and tubers. By graftage or cuttage we simply multiply the original plant,—we do not take offspring from it,—and we have every reason to expect, what all observation shows, that propagation by buds should give a less variable result than propagation by seeds. And yet there are instances in which plants do not "come true" from cuttings or grafts. As a philosophical

---

*Rep. Mich. Bd. Agr. 1876, 113. Quoted in Essay XIX.

question, the presumption is that varieties propagated by buds wear out sooner than those propagated by seeds, for the experiments of Darwin and others have shewn that the especial office of seed propagation is to increase the virility of the species through cross-fertilization. It must follow, therefore, that in the absence of cross-fertilization virility must be less.* (See the note on page 382.)

But we do not need to consider this phase of the question, for we are concerned with variation (that is, running out) rather than with ultimate longevity (or wearing out). And it is also probable that any tendency towards weakness through lack of fertilization is fully counterbalanced by the protection which such varieties receive under cultivation.

The question comes simply to this: If buds are taken from parts which possess stable characteristics, they will give stable products under similar conditions. But if the buds are taken from parts which have been developed into abnormal conditions and which tend to vary, they must tend strongly to depart from the parent, especially when the means by which the high development was produced and is maintained are removed. Bud-variation may, therefore, be said to be indeterminate. The best example of running out in plants propagated by buds is the potato. It is a matter of general observation that varieties of potatoes disappear. Beal† has made experiments which show that in eight years varieties which gave good crops ran out so as to produce nothing. These varieties were grown in the same garden

---
* See also Gray, l. c.
† Rep. Mich. Bd. Agr. 1876, 111.

throughout the experiment, but they were constantly shifted over an area of from five to eight acres, so that potatoes were not grown two seasons upon exactly the same ground; and during the time when these potatoes were decreasing in yield, the garden was each year producing better crops of other kinds, and the newer varieties of potatoes did well. In this case it may be argued that the plants showed signs of wearing out rather than of running out by variation, but there is no evidence to show that the plants were in any way weaker or less able to perpetuate themselves after they had run out than before, for it is probable that seed-production increased as tuber-production decreased; at all events, we cannot determine if the varieties wore out so long as we have no record of their seed-production. It seems, rather, that the plants returned to a comparatively tuberless condition. Large potato tubers are abnormal, to begin with, and it is not strange if their characters are transitory. (See page 28.)

At present I see no reason for supposing that fruits propagated by buds run out, to any extent, so long as equal conditions of cultivation and soil fertility exist; but if the buds are taken from parts which are abnormally or unusually developed, as they are in the case of the potato, I should expect that we could not long hold the offspring up to their assumed character.

The conclusion of the whole matter is simply this: Varieties grown from seeds tend to vary or run out, while varieties grown from buds tend to remain permanent or nearly so, unless the parts which are propagated possess abnormal, or what we might call fictitious or unstable characters, in which case further variation or running out may be expected.

NOTE (May 12, 1896).—On page 380 I have said that the presumption is that bud-propagated plants tend to wear out sooner than seed-propagated plants, because the latter are generally cross-bred, and cross-breeding is known to increase the virility of offspring. The reader may derive a very erroneous impression from this statement. I mean to say that inasmuch as bud-propagated plants are less variable than seed-propagated plants, they may be less able to adapt themselves quickly to changing conditions, and may therefore tend to perish; but it is evident, on the other hand, that so long as such varieties do remain they are comparatively true to type, whilst the seed-propagated varieties, from the very fact that they are variable, tend more quickly to vary into new and unrecognizable forms, or to run out. The reader must not hold the common notion that bud-propagation is in-breeding, for it is nothing of the kind. It is simply the division and multiplication of one individual plant (see Essay III.), and all the bud-progeny may be expected to behave very like the parent individual so long as they are subjected to the same conditions.

This erroneous conception of in-breeding might be obtained even from the most admirable paper of Gray, to which I refer. He writes: "When Mr. Darwin announced that the principle of cross-fertilization between the individuals of a species is the plan of nature, and is practically so universal that it fairly sustains his inference that no hermaphrodite species continually self-fertilized would continue to exist, he made it clear to all who apprehend and receive the principle, that a series of plants propagated by buds only must have a weaker hold of life than a series reproduced by seed. The former is the closest kind of breeding." There may be two interpretations of this extract. If it is meant that crosses between plants which were propagated from buds from one plant (as fruit varieties are), are presumably weaker than crosses between plants which have sprung from seeds, then I assent to the statement. But if it is meant, as is obviously intended, that bud-propagation is close-breeding in contradiction to seed-propagation, then I dissent. Bud-propagation is not necessarily breeding at all. The comparison of in-breeding (or close-breeding) with cross-breeding must be made between the offspring of close-fertilization and the offspring of cross-fertilization, and not of such unlike members as seeds and buds.

II.

Are the Varieties of Orchard Fruits Running Out?[1]

Two years ago I presented before this society a

---

[1] Read before the Western New York Horticultural Society, January 26, 1893. Printed in the Proceedings of the Thirty-eighth Annual Meeting, pp. 81 to 85.

discussion [reprinted above] upon the running out of varieties, in which I reached the conclusion that plants grown from seeds constantly tend to vary or run out, as also do those which are grown from buds of highly developed or abnormal parts, but that those grown from buds of normal or natural parts, as the orchard fruits, remain practically permanent. While my general conclusion, that some varieties run out and others may remain more or less permanent, appeared to meet with the approval of those who took part in the discussion, there was some objection to the statement that the varieties of orchard fruits do not run out, and I was cited to the fact that the catalogue of these fruits is constantly changing and that many of the varieties which were popular a generation or more ago have disappeared. It is my purpose at this time to examine more minutely into the permanence of these varieties of orchard or tree fruits. I must say, before proceeding further, that running out does not necessarily mean the deterioration of a variety, but simply a change or modification which obscures its identity; but inasmuch as varieties of orchard fruits — being propagated by buds — do not vary or change to any marked extent, the discussion now in hand really turns upon the question as to whether varieties may not wear out or be limited in duration without having passed by variation into other forms. Is the Esopus Spitzenburgh apple, for instance, approaching the limit of its life?

The most direct means of approaching the subject is through the historical method. What proportion of the varieties cultivated fifty or a hundred years ago are now known? If any of these old varieties are not cultivated at the present day, what are the causes of their disappearance? In 1806, M'Mahon catalogued fifty-nine varieties of apples for cultivation in North America. Of these, twenty-one were offered for sale in 1892. In 1817, William Coxe gave a list of one hundred kinds of the best apples for cultivation in North America, of which forty were still offered for sale in 1892. In 1845, A. J. Downing described one hundred and ninety varieties of apples, of which eighty-four are now offered for sale. The percentages of apples in these lists which have persisted to our time as commercial varieties are 36, 39 and 46 respectively. In other words, from 64 to 54 per cent of them have disappeared within a century. Why?

1. *Have they disappeared because of age?* We do not know if any given type or species of animal or plant is pre-limited in duration. It is true that many of the earlier forms of life have wholly disappeared, but this disappearance may have been due to changed physical conditions to which the organisms were subjected, or to defeat in the struggle for existence, rather than to a wearing out or pre-determined death. But even if species do wear out, the deterioration is so slow that it could not be detected in many centuries, probably; and it is fair to assume that any such tendency would be much overbalanced by the protecting care which man extends to all species or varieties which please him.

But there are now sufficient records to show that mere age of a variety counts for very little. The White Jennetting apple was described as early as

1660 by Evelyn, and it is still grown in England, and Downing describes it fully in 1872. The Ribston Pippin, which is probably the most popular apple in England and which is well known in America, is probably about two hundred years old. Its history is clear for more than a century, at least. The White Doyenne or Virgaleau pear is over two hundred years old, and although this variety has nearly disappeared in America, it has not run out, as we shall presently see. The Bartlett pear originated in 1770. The Green Gage plum was mentioned as early as 1629, and it was probably then an old variety. Similar instances are frequent, especially in European fruits. It is obviously a fallacy to say that certain varieties which were grown a hundred years ago have disappeared because of their age, when certain other varieties of equal age are still in profitable cultivation. About two-thirds of the varieties which M'Mahon catalogued in 1806 appear to have been lost, but the other third, which still persists, contains some of our best apples. These persisting varieties are as follows: Early Harvest, Summer Queen, Margaret, King, Bough (or Bow), Woolman's Harvest, Golden Pippin, Summer Pearmain, Fall Pippin, American Pippin, Orange, Vandevere, Newtown Pippin, Monstrous Pippin, Holland Pippin, Rhode Island Greening, Swaar, Yellow Bellfleur, Harrison, Hughes' Virginia Crab, Cooper's Russeting.

All these facts show either that age does not determine the virility of a variety or that varieties differ widely in this respect. It we can find satisfactory reasons for the disappearance of these lost varieties, we shall be forced to conclude that varieties of orchard fruits do not wear because of age.

2. *Do varieties disappear because they are ill-adapted to new environments?* Most varieties are more or less local in their adaptations; that is, they are not suited to cultivation over wide areas which comprise great differences of soils and climates. It must follow, therefore, that those varieties which are most local, and which must require most skill in cultivation, must constantly tend to disappear, because they cannot compete with the more cosmopolitan sorts which, alone, nurserymen find it profitable to propagate. There is a constant selection among the varieties of fruits, which eliminates the least adaptive kinds. This fact is remarkably well illustrated in the relative behavior in America of the old varieties of European and American origin. In 1817, as I have said, William Coxe made a list of one hundred varieties of apples especially commended for cultivation in North America. Of these, thirty-two are known to be of European origin and fifty-seven of American origin. In 1892, forty of these varieties were sold by American nurserymen, but thirty-three of them belonged to the American group and only seven to the European group. In other words, only 40 per cent of the apples of American origin in Coxe's list have been lost, while 78 per cent of the European group have disappeared. In this instance, therefore, very many of the varieties appear to have passed out of cultivation because they were not well adapted to American conditions. Coxe also listed sixty-five varieties of pears in 1817. Only four of them are now in cultivation, and these are of American origin.

In 1845, there were one hundred and ninety varieties of apples in North America. Eighty-seven of these are known to be of European origin and ninety-three of American origin. At the present time, 77 per cent of the European lot have been lost in America, against only 33 per cent in the American lot. This shows that with the greater number of varieties which had come into use since the time of Coxe, and from which selections had been made, there had appeared more American than European varieties of merit for American conditions. In other words, American varieties are better adapted to American conditions than the European varieties are; and this fact accounts for the disappearance of very many of the apples in the old lists. There has been a constant tendency from the first towards the disappearance of the apples, pears, and all other fruits of European origin, and towards the persistence of American kinds. There is a like tendency, very strongly marked, towards the disappearance of New England apples and other fruits from the prairie states, and a corresponding increase in the percentages of fruits original to those regions. If a certain variety, therefore, as the Baldwin, disappears from large portions of a western state, this fact is an illustration of lack of adaptability to those conditions, rather than of a running out. Many of the varieties which are commonly thought to have run out are now and then found thriving in perfection in some local spot, showing that they still retain their pristine vigor. I may illustrate this point — disappearance due to lack of adaptation — by calling your attention to the fact that very many of the novelties of any year or decade fail to become popular because they are not adapted to a wide range of conditions, and some of them are almost immediately lost from this reason. This is a forcible illustration that disappearance and running out are very different matters. I am becoming more and more convinced that the study of the adaptations of varieties to conditions of soil and climate and other environments, is one of the most important subjects with which the horticulturist has to do, and that the neglect of it in the past has been a serious hindrance and is a source of much confusion now that the least adaptive varieties are being sifted out. (Consult Essays XVIII. and XX.)

3. *Are more meritorious varieties supplanting the old?* Yes; not only because they are better adapted to varying environments, as discussed in the last paragraph, but because varieties of greater intrinsic merit are appearing. This, in fact, is the chief incentive to the origination of new varieties,—this expectation that we shall improve upon present varieties. All the changes in our fruit lists mean nothing if they do not indicate that we are progressing. Poor or indifferent varieties are introduced, to be sure, but they soon find their level and disappear; and thereafter they are classed with those which are said to have run out. If every new country develops varieties specially adapted to itself, then it must follow that changes in the original fruit-lists come most rapidly in such countries and that they will afford the greatest list of discarded varieties in any given length of time. Thus American fruit catalogues appear to contain few very old varieties as compared with European countries, even when allowing

for the great difference in the age of the two countries. That is, varieties disappear more rapidly here; but a certain stability will come with age, as in other countries, and we shall then probably hear less about the running out of the tree fruits.

In 1892, eight hundred and seventy-eight varieties of apples were offered for sale in North America. This great list must contain enough meritorious varieties to supplant all the old ones which have weak points. This leads me to say that nearly all the old varieties which possess superlative merits still exist; and this fact is proof that varieties do not wear out, but drop out. Any nurseryman knows that the Isabella grape has not run out, but that it is crowded out by Catawba and Concord. The Barnard peach, still grown here and there as of old, is driven out in nearly all peach regions by brighter and larger varieties. It would be but a few years before such peaches as Amsden, Alexander and Hale would disappear if a good variety of their season were introduced. You may be inclined to doubt the last statement—that nearly all the superlative old varieties still exist— and cite me to the fact that the Esopus Spitzenburgh apple, White Doyenne pear and some others are little grown now. This leads me to ask:

4. *Are not certain varieties peculiarly liable to disease or insect injury?* It is well known that some varieties are much more subject to fungous and insect attacks than others, and when they are seriously injured year by year the cultivation of these varieties becomes restricted, or may stop entirely. The Kittatinny blackberry, attacked by the red rust, the Iona grape, attacked by phylloxera, and the Fameuse

apple, very subject to scab, are grown only in particular localities, and were it not for the fact that they possess superlative merits, they undoubtedly would have been wholly neglected before this. The White Doyenne pear has been almost entirely driven out by the fruit cracking, and Flemish Beauty, but for the sprays, would follow suit. I am convinced that the chief causes of the failure of the Esopus Spitzenburgh apple are the apple-scab and insufficient fertility of soil, and the experiments in spraying indicate that this good old apple can yet be grown with satisfaction and profit. The decreasing popularity of the Spitzenburgh is regarded as the chief contemporaneous example of the supposed running-out of varieties; but it is chiefly driven out by disease and neglect.

5. *Do fashions and demands change and call for new types?* Yes: and the chief reason why many of the good old dessert fruits are now unknown is because our modern demands are for fruits of greater productiveness, large size, beauty, good carrying qualities, and ease of propagation and growth in the nursery; varieties which least satisfy these demands tend to disappear. There has been no money in Dyer, Jefferis and Mother apples so long as we have had Baldwin and Ben Davis. The persistence of varieties is determined very largely by the profit there is in them, and when fashions and demands change, the varieties change.

I may say here that the merits of many of the old varieties are exaggerated through rosy or unreliable memories. Scarcely a season passes that some one does not regret to me that the old Summer Bell and

Jargonelle pears have passed from cultivation; yet, as compared with even our commonest varieties, these pears are inferior. Memory is at fault.

It is by no means true, I imagine, that only the best varieties are in cultivation. Probably there are as good if not better varieties for particular purposes in the old or obscure fruit-lists as those we now commonly cultivate. They may have been overlooked or neglected, or their merits may not have been properly placed before the public. We have more riches than we know. It is true, also, that it is very difficult to supplant a variety which has once obtained a firm foot-hold. Even a better apple than the Baldwin, for all purposes to which the Baldwin is adapted, would find great difficulty in dislodging it. The lists of tree fruits change more slowly than those of bush fruits and vegetables, because the age of the plant is greater; and for this reason there are fewer epitaphs of dead varieties in the orchard books than in the literature of the smaller fruits. It should be said, too, that there are fewer places to be filled now than there were a century or even a generation ago, when a few varieties had to do duty for all demands. So new varieties come in slowly in orchard fruits; and for this reason they are apt to stay when they do come, and the old varieties may be completely driven out.

The conclusion of the whole matter, as I now see it, is this: Varieties of orchard fruits, which are propagated by buds, very rarely run out, but they may disappear because they are ill-adapted to various conditions, because they are susceptible to disease, and because they are supplanted by better varieties, or those which more completely fill the present demands or fashions. The disappearances are, therefore, so many mile-stones to our progress.

III.

Studies in the Longevity of the Varieties of Tomatoes.

Varieties of tomatoes are, as a rule, short lived. Ten years may be considered the average profitable life of a variety, and many sorts break up and disappear in two or three years. This inconstancy of type is largely due, no doubt, to the haste with which new sorts are put upon the market. A variety should be selected and carefully handled for some time before it is offered to the public.

Almost any of the old sorts afford instances of the running out of varieties. The Tilden tomato, once popular, appears to be extinct. Only two seedsmen in the country advertised the variety last spring, and neither one, as shown by our tests, had the Tilden of fifteen years ago. One of the samples gave us a small round tomato, late in ripening, and much resembling small sorts of the Red Apple kind. The other gave us a somewhat larger angular tomato. In 1887 the writer made an effort to secure the Tilden, but only inferior fruits were obtained. The record of that test is as follows : "This variety, once so popular, appears to have run out. As grown this year, the fruits are very small, irregular and worthless. Last year (1886) the fruits were somewhat larger, though smaller than Hathaway. When first introduced, now many years ago, it was a large tomato."* Mr. W. W. Tracy, of Detroit, an expert in the seed trade, informs me that he has tried in vain for two or three years to secure true stock of the Tilden. The Trophy shows the same tendency to become inferior, and it is difficult to procure a good stock of it. In the test of 1887, this fact was noticed. "The Trophy is evidently not so good as formerly. Our crop this year, from seeds of last year's crop, showed a much greater per cent of poor fruits than the crop of 1886."† Paragon begins to show the same weakness.— *Bulletin X. Cornell Experiment Station, 117 (October, 1889).*

We are still confirmed in our belief that varieties of tomatoes are unstable, and that they soon "run out." The strongest proof of this fact, perhaps, is the difficulty of maintaining any variety true to its type, under good culture and careful selection. The variety, under this treatment, is very likely to "improve" or depart from its original character. An apt illustration of this has come to our experience this year in the Trophy. In our last year's report we observed that this standard variety is running out, and that it is difficult to procure typical stock of it. A careful Long Island gardener opposed the statement, and cited the fact that he had kept the Trophy (though somewhat *improved*) all these years by careful treatment. He furnished us seeds, but we

---

*Bailey, Bull. 31, Mich. Agr. Coll. 22.
† Ibid, 21. See "Origin of the Trophy Tomato," in Essay XXX., for further notes on this variety.

secured few fruits which could be called the Trophy, as that variety was known in the early days. Most of the fruits were smooth and even, medium in size and much flattened, and they were better, in our judgment, than the true Trophy ever was. It is a common but erroneous notion that "running out" necessarily means deterioration.—*Bulletin XXI. Cornell Experiment Station, 83 (October, 1890).*

For some years it has been apparent to the writer that varieties of tomatoes run out or lose their distinguishing characters. The reasons for this loss of varietal character it is not necessary now to discuss. Crossing no doubt hastens it in many cases. But it is well to state that running out does not mean deterioration simply, but disappearance of characters by whatever cause. Studies of this question were made this year by growing the same variety from many seedsmen. This gave us an opportunity to determine if the variety had varied greatly in the course of its history, or if all seedsmen really sold the same thing under a given name. In order to determine how long a variety may persist, we selected Grant and Canada Victor tomatoes, which are old varieties; and to find out how soon a variety may depart from its type, we grew the Ignotum, which was introduced two years ago by ourselves.

The Grant tomato was obtained from seven seedsmen,— all who catalogued it. Of these seven samples, but two were true Grant, as the variety was recognized a few years ago. In these two, the fruits were wrinkled and flattish, somewhat angular, and yellowish about the stem. The remaining five samples gave fruits of various kinds, although somewhat resembling the Grant type. Some of the samples gave two or three distinct types of fruit. One of the samples bore only a few small and shapeless fruits, which were entirely worthless. Some plants bore small and nearly smooth fruits not unlike an overgrown Cherry tomato. One lot gave fruits superior to Grant. They were large and regular, much like Volunteer, but flatter. The plants in this sample were robust. This had undoubtedly been bred away from the Grant by selecting for largest and smoothest fruits. All the other samples were inferior to Grant. It may be said that these variations were due simply to mixing of the seeds during a number of years by careless handling, but there is reason to suppose that such is not the case. The Grant has a peculiar small, slightly curled, light colored foliage and a well marked upright habit of growth of the young shoots. These characters appeared constantly in all the samples. The foliage, being less variable than the fruit and not an object of selection by the horticulturist, had remained constant, while the fruit had lost its characters.

Canada Victor was grown from ten seedsmen. There were none which could be recognized as true Canada Victor, but they were all small, variable, irregular, and practically worthless. Some plants bore small and nearly globular fruits, much like large Cherry tomatoes, and some were thick-walled, suggesting the old Criterion. Yet in all the samples, the peculiar slightly curled foliage of Canada Victor was apparent.

Ignotum was obtained from fifteen dealers. This variety was first offered by seedsmen in 1890. Of the fifteen samples, eight gave small and poor fruits, which were not worth growing, and could not be recognized as Ignotum by any character. The other samples were fairly uniform, and represented a medium type of Ignotum. The Ignotum grown from one of our own savings gave a number of plants which bore inferior fruits, although clearly Ignotum. It is difficult to suppose that in one season a variety could so far have lost its characters that one-half the seedsmen should offer inferior stock of it. The variety is well fixed, for in one of our large plantations it was remarkably uniform, and equally as good if not even better than two years ago. We have been curious to note the reports of Ignotum which have come in from various parts of the country, for, knowing its history, we may be able to discover some facts in the variation of plants. Most of the reports speak well of it, but now and then a grower finds it inferior. A correspondent in New Jersey sends the following account of it:

"It is very smooth and productive, bright in color, ripening up to the stem, and with me that is all that can be said in its favor; it is small as compared with the Matchless; it is not solid, but hollow and full of seeds; worst of all, it has a tendency toward black-heart. I could not find one in ten of my entire crop but was afflicted with this hard black core." It is strange that such a condition should exist so early in the life of a variety, and it would be interesting to know if it is a case of running out or of mixing, or substituting of seeds. [A more recent discussion of this experiment will be found in "Plant-Breeding," page 123.]—*Bulletin 32, Cornell Experiment Station, pp. 171 to 173 (October, 1891).*

Do tomatoes mix in the field ?—For several years we have observed that occasional plants in a tomato field bear fruits not "true" in color, size, and shape. It has been our habit to attribute these "rogues" to mixing of the seed in handling, but these plants appear in seeds of our own saving, where every care has been exercised to keep the seeds separate. The feeling grew upon us that some, at least, of this untrueness to type must be due to crossing. In 1890, therefore, we sought to test the matter. Two or three plants of each of six varieties were set closely together in a row, all the plants of each variety being together. The varieties and the order were as follows :

1. Potato Leaf. 2. German Raisin. 3. Golden Queen. 4. Favorite. 5. Jaune Grosse Lisse. 6. Mansfield Tree.

These represent widely different varieties. The Potato Leaf has very large Mikado-like leaves and purple fruit. The German Raisin is the same as Currant, and belongs to the species *Lycopersicum pimpinellifolium*. Golden Queen and Jaune Grosse Lisse are yellow, Favorite red, and Mansfield purple. Several fruits were saved from each variety, and this year (1891) a few plants were grown from them. The following record shows what took place :

1. Potato Leaf.—Fourteen plants. Thirteen typical Potato Leaf, but one hybridized by German

Raisin. This one crossed plant bore red fruits about three times larger than German Raisin, had much the general habit of that variety, and the foliage was almost exactly intermediate between the two, having very much the form of a hybrid which we had once made by hand. The fruits were borne in long clusters of eight or ten.

2. German Raisin.—Nine plants. Eight typical German Raisin, but one clearly a hybrid with some large tomato, probably either Potato Leaf or Golden Queen. This plant bore red fruits twice larger than normal, and the foliage was a strange intermediate between this species and the common tomatoes. It was small and sparse, but nearer the common tomatoes in form and texture. Thus a spontaneous hybrid was produced with *Lycopersicum pimpinellifolium* as its pistillate parent, but we had not succeeded in making this cross artificially.

3. Golden Queen.—Thirteen plants, of which eleven were true. Two were clearly hybrids with German Raisin. The fruits were deep red, the same as German Raisin, although the seeds came from yellow fruits. The foliage was intermediate, very like that in our artificial hybrids.

4. Favorite.—Fifteen plants, all true.

5. Jaune Grosse Lisse.—Fifteen plants, of which fourteen were true to type, being large and bright yellow. One plant, however, bore large light red tomatoes, indicating a cross with a red variety.

6. Mansfield Tree.—Fifteen plants, fourteen bearing normal purple fruits. One plant, however, bore red fruits, like Favorite.

These records are interesting and valuable, because

they show that mixing occurs spontaneously in the field. It would be an interesting study in probabilities to calculate how many plants untrue to type might have appeared if all the seeds from the plants had been used, instead of from nine to fifteen. In all our crossing studies, it is interesting to note that red varieties have never produced purple or yellow fruits, while both purple and yellow fruits have produced red ones. Spontaneous crossing is no doubt a common means of the running out of varieties of tomatoes. — *Bulletin 32, Cornell Experiment Station, 168 (October, 1891).*

XXV.

WHENCE CAME THE CULTIVATED STRAWBERRY?[1]

The strawberry has been extensively cultivated only during the last century, and the earliest attempt at methodical amelioration extends back little more than two hundred years. The first horticultural variety of which we have any account is the Fressant, which dates from 1660. The wild species of strawberries are few, not numbering more than a dozen under the most liberal estimate, and they are well represented in the great herbaria or botanical centers of the world. Only a part of the wild types have been impressed into cultivation, and exact or very approximate dates can be given for the introduction of these cultivated species.

The strawberry, therefore, is a modern fruit, and its history and evolution would seem to possess no difficulties; and yet, despite all these facts, the botanical origin of the cultivated varieties is unknown, and we have the anomaly of a common fruit, appearing within little more than a century, which the botanist does not refer to any species. Here, then, is a most remarkable instance of the evolution of a new

---

[1] Lecture before the Author's class in Horticulture. Printed in American Naturalist, xxviii. 293. (April, 1894.)

type of plant, taking place under our very eyes: whilst the botanists have written precise histories of its successive progresses, the reasons and methods of its development have escaped them. Perhaps there is no other plant which has more quickly obscured its own origin, or in which the speculative evolutionist can find stronger proof of the instability and elasticity of plants.

I have said that the history of the strawberry is well known. There has been a careful record from the time Casper Bauhin and his contemporaries wrote their voluminous herbals. We cannot expect, at this time, therefore, to add anything to this long and consequential record. We must accept the history essentially as we find it. But it is possible that we shall be able to elucidate the evolution of the strawberry by the application of some of the principles of plant variation, the knowledge of which is now sufficient to warrant a constructive retrospect. At all events, if these laws cannot solve the general problem of the evolution of the strawberry, we must continue to remain in ignorance of its birth and departure. This inquiry will be all the more interesting, also, from the fact that the first monographer of the strawberries, Duchesne, in 1766, made an attempt to explain the origin of known species from the Alpine or Everbearing strawberries of Europe, and this essay, which has apparently not attracted the attention of modern philosophers, is one of the earliest efforts to account for the origin of organisms by means of a course of evolution.

It is necessary at the outset to eliminate the so-called European types of strawberries from our inquiry. These belong to three or four species native to Europe, chiefly to *Fragaria vesca* and *F. moschata* (*F. elatior*), and the botanical characters are sufficiently clear and uniform to allow of little doubt as to their origin. The first strawberries, like the Fressant, are of this type. These European types are mostly small and delicate fruits, which are grown in France and some other parts of continental Europe, but which are little more than curiosities in England and America. It is the class of large American and English strawberries to which I now wish to direct attention, a type which, while grown in all temperate countries, seems to have first come to great prominence in England, and which is the only market strawberry of America.

The first foreign strawberry to reach Europe was the common small species of eastern America, and which is known to botanists as *Fragaria Virginiana*. The first distinct record of it in Europe is in 1624, when it was mentioned by Jean and Vespasien Robin, gardeners to Louis XIII. For more than a century it appears not to have taken on any new or striking forms. It bore a small, bright scarlet berry, with a distinct constriction or neck near the stem and slightly acid flesh. It was in no way very different, probably, from the common wild strawberry which we now pick in the fields. It was never greatly esteemed on the continent, but in England it found greater favor. Duchesne writes of it, in 1766, that "they still cultivate it in England with favor" (*avec honneur*). The original form of the Scarlet or Virginian strawberry was still highly esteemed in England less than three-quarters of a century ago, at which time Barnet* wrote enthusiastically of it. "This" [the Old Scarlet Strawberry], he says, "which has been an inhabitant of our gardens nearly, if not fully, two hundred years, was doubtless an original introduction from North America. It is singular that a kind of so much excellence as to be at present scarcely surpassed by any of its class should have been the first known. It continued in cultivation considerably more than half of the period of its existence as a garden fruit without any variety having been produced of it, either by seed or by importation from America." Yet Barnet knew twenty-six good varieties of the species, and describes them at length; and four of them seem to have come directly from America, probably from wild plants. A considerable progress had been made in the amelioration of the strawberry in England at the opening of the century, therefore, from the Virginian stock or foundation; but the varieties were much alike, and contain little promise of the wonderful development in the strawberry varieties which we now enjoy.

About 1712, a second species of strawberry reached Europe. This is the *Fragaria Chiloensis*, brought from Chile to Marseilles by Capt. Frezier. It reached England in 1727. It is a stout, thick-leaved, shaggy plant, which bore a large globular or somewhat pointed late, dark-colored fruit. In a few places, particularly about Brest, in France, it came to be cultivated for its fruit; but in general it met with small favor, particularly as the flowers were often imperfect and it did not fertilize itself. It did not seem to vary much under cultivation; at least, when

---

*Trans. London Hort. Soc. vi. 152 (1824).

Barnet wrote, about a century later, he knew only three varieties in England which he could refer to it, one of which he considered to be identical with the original plant as introduced by Frezier. The Chilian strawberry grows along the Pacific coast in both North and South America, and it has been introduced into our eastern gardens several times from wild sources; but it always soon disappears. There is little in the record of this species, therefore, of promise to the American horticulturist.

In the middle of the last century, a third strawberry appeared in Europe. Some writers place the date of its introduction with considerable exactness; but the fact is that no one knew just when or how it came. Phillip Miller described and figured it in 1760 as the Pine strawberry, in allusion to the pineapple fragrance of its fruit. There were three opinions as to its origin at that time, some saying it came from Louisiana, others that it came from Virginia, while there was a report, originating in Holland, that it came from Surinam, which is now the coast of Dutch Guiana. None of these reports has been either confirmed or disproved, although Gay, in making extensive studies of the growth of strawberries, may be said to have effectually overturned the Surinam hypothesis in his remark that to find a strawberry growing at sea-level within five degrees of the equator, is like finding a palm in Iceland or Hammerfest.* Duchesne, in his Natural History of Strawberries,† 1766, described a pineapple strawberry as *Fragaria ananassa*, and while he

---
* Ann. Sci. Nat. 4th ser. viii. 203 (1857).
† Histoire Naturelle des Fraisiers. Par M. Duchesne fils, Paris, 1766.

did not know its origin, he argued that it must be a hybrid between the Chilian and Virginian species. The pine-apple strawberries of England and France were found to be different from each other upon comparison, although the differences were such as might arise within the limits of any species or type, and by the end of the century most botanists began to regard the two as variations of one stock. This general type of Pine strawberries, comprising the large-hulled type long represented by the Bath Scarlet and erected into a distinct species by Duchesne as *Fragaria calyculata*, has been collectively known for a century as *Fragaria grandiflora*, a name bestowed by Ehrhart in 1792, although this name, together with the English name Pine, is gradually passing from use. We may say that thus far there are three hypotheses as to the origin of the Pine strawberry,—that it came from North America, from Guiana, and that it is a compound or hybrid of two other species; and we may add a fourth—that apparently accepted by Duhamel and De Candolle, and certainly by Gay—that it is a direct modification of the Chilian strawberry: and also a fifth, advanced by Decaisne,* and accepted by others, that some, at least, of the varieties are products of the large, robust native form of our wild strawberry which is known as *Fragaria Virginiana* var. *Illinoensis*. I shall drop the Guianian origin as wholly untenable, and it will also be unprofitable to discuss directly the question of importation from North America, for we have nothing more than conjecture upon which to found any historical argument. I shall now endeavor

---

*Jardin Fruitier du Museum, ix. under "Frasier d'Asa Gray."

to discover which of the remaining three hypotheses is best supported in the subsequent evolution of the plant itself: Is it a hybrid, a direct development of the Chilian species, or a form of the native variety Illinoensis ?

It is first necessary, however, to determine from what ancestral type our cultivated strawberry flora has sprung. Barnet, writing in 1824, referred all cultivated strawberries to seven groups or classes, three of which comprise the small European varieties, which are outside this discussion. The remaining four classes comprise all the large-fruited types, and they are as follows: (1) The Scarlet or Virginian strawberries, with twenty-six varieties; (2) The Black strawberries or *Fragaria tincta* of Duchesne, with five varieties; (3) The Pines, with fifteen; (4) The True Chile strawberries, with three varieties. The Blacks and Pines are so nearly alike that they can be classed as one. Although the Pine class is the most recent of the lot, it had already varied into twenty forms, and, moreover, it contained the choice of the varieties. In this class is Keen's Seedling, which was then coming into prominence. This variety is the first conspicuous and signal contribution to commercial strawberry culture, and it marks an epoch amongst strawberries similar to that made by the Isabella amongst American grapes. It was grown from seeds of Keen's Imperial, which, in turn was raised from the White Carolina (known also as Large White Chili), which is regarded by Barnet as a Pine strawberry. Thomas Andrew Knight had made various interesting and successful crosses amongst the Scarlet or Virginian strawberries, but Keen's varieties so far excelled them that Knight's productions were soon lost. From Keen's Seedling the present English strawberries have largely descended. The fruit of his remarkable strawberry was first shown in London in 1821. At this time there were apparently no important varieties in this country of American origin. Prince,* writing in 1828, enumerates thirty strawberries of American gardens, of which all, or all but one, are of foreign origin. The two important varieties, and the ones which supplied "the principal bulk of this fruit sold in the New York market," were Red Chili (referred by Barnet and by George Lindley† to the Pines), and Early Hudson, probably a variety of *Fragaria Virginiana*. Keen's berries are in the list, but these, according to Hovey and other later writers, did not thrive in America. As late as 1837, Hovey wrote‡ that "as yet the plants of nearly all the kinds in cultivation have been introduced from the English gardens, and are not suited to the severity of our climate." Mr. Hovey resolved to produce an American strawberry, and with a shrewdness which has rarely been equaled in the breeding of plants, he selected parents representing distinct ideals and the best adaptations to American conditions. Four varieties entered into a certain batch of crosses which he made. These were Keen's Seedling and Mulberry, both Pines, Melon, probably a Pine, and Methven Scarlet, a variety of the Virginian. From these crosses, two varieties were obtained,§ one of which

---

*Short Treatise on Horticulture, 72. New York.
†A Guide to the Orchard and Kitchen Garden, 487. London, 1831.
‡Mag. Hort. iii. 246.
§Mag. Hort. vi. 284 (1840). Fruits of America, i. 25, 27.

fruited in 1836. These were the Hovey and Boston Pine. Owing to the loss of labels, it is not certain which crosses gave these varieties, but Mr. Hovey was always confident that the Hovey sprung from Mulberry crossed by Keen's Seedling. The Hovey strawberry revolutionized strawberry growing in this country. It was to America what Keen's Seedling was to England; and it marks the second epoch in commercial strawberry culture. American varieties now appeared from year to year, and the greater part of them have come directly or indirectly from the Hovey and the Boston Pine. With the passing out of the Boston Pine and its immediate offspring, the term Pine has practically been lost to American strawberry literature, and the word is but a memory in the minds of the older men; but this is not because the class itself has disappeared, but, on the contrary, because it has become the dominant class and has driven out the Scarlet and all other competitors. The Hovey was a true Pine strawberry. Mr. Hovey grew it in his garden till the last, and it was my good fortune to secure a few plants of him shortly before his death. A plant is now before me as I write, and it has all the marks of the old Pine or Grandiflora type,—the thick, rounded, dark leaves, stocky habit, stiff flower cluster, and large, spreading calyx. Practically all our commercial strawberries are Pines, and they compare well in botanical characters with the *Fragaria grandiflora* of the French gardens of a half century ago, and with the famous Bath Scarlet and Pitmaston Black, which were important Pines when Barnet wrote, specimens of all of which I have before me.

Our strawberries, then, are lineal descendants of

the old Pine class, known to botanists as *Fragaria ananassa* and *F. grandiflora*. Now the questions recur, What is the Pine? where did it come from? how did it originate? Three hypotheses, as I have said, have been advanced which an evolutionary review of this subject is capable of considering. Is it (1) a hybrid? (2) a direct development of the Chilian strawberry? or (3) a modified form of our big wild strawberry, *Fragaria Virginiana* var. *Illinoensis*?

1. *Is the Pine a hybrid?* The only reason ever advanced for considering the Pine strawberry to be a hybrid was the supposed impossibility of accounting for its attributes upon any other hypothesis. The ideas of hybridity were indefinite in those times, and intermediateness of characters was often supposed to be enough — as it is, unfortunately, too often at the present day — to establish a hybrid origin. In considering this matter, two questions at once arise: (*a*) Does the Pine bear evidence of being a hybrid? (*b*) Would hybrid characters perpetuate themselves? I am wholly unable to find, either in herbarium specimens of the plants themselves, or in the pictures of the plants, any distinct evidences of hybridity. The Pine strawberries differ from the Chilian chiefly in their greater size, less hairiness and better fruit, and sometimes by somewhat thinner leaves, although this thinness of foliage is usually more apparent than real, being due to the larger size and consequently greater flexibility of the leaf without any real diminution in substance; and I have seen as thin leaves in wild *Fragaria Chiloensis* as in garden berries. But greater size could scarcely be obtained from the smaller or at least more slender Virginian strawberry, and better

sweet fruit would not likely result from the amalgamation of the Chilian with the little acid fruit of the other. On the other hand, there is not a character of the Virginian, so far as I know — save possibly some thinness of leaf — which appears in the Pine. The slender, erect habit, smooth stems, profusion of early runners, comparatively simple and very weak-rayed trusses, the small calyx, the early, light colored, pitted fruit,— none of these marks of the Virginian strawberry appear in the Pine. Again (*b*), it is now known that one of the most characteristic marks of hybrids is their variability when propagated from seeds; and yet Phillip Miller declares that the old Pine strawberry came true to seed! A hybrid left to itself almost invariably departs from its mongrel type and reverts to one or the other parent; and yet here is a supposed hybrid which has held its attributes intact for one hundred and fifty years, and has presented a sufficiently unbroken front to overcome all competitors.* There is not only no evidence in favor of a hybrid origin, but there is very much against it; and I have no hesitation in discarding the hypothesis in favor of a simpler and more philosophical one.

2. *Is the Pine strawberry a direct development of the Chilian strawberry?* Every feature of the Pine strawberry suggests the Chilian species. It differs chiefly in its greater size and sometimes by a slight loss of hairiness, but the relative sizes of the parts remain much the same as in the wild type. It is now well known that variation induced by changed conditions of life, and augmented by subsequent selection,

---

*For a general discussion of the theory of hybridity, consult Bailey, Plant-Breeding, Lecture II.

is the common and potent means of the evolution and amelioration of plants. Hybridization rarely effects a permanent evolution of types. To suppose that the Chilian strawberry should have varied into the type of the common strawberry is in accord with all the methods of nature. But there are two considerations which convince me beyond all question that cultivated strawberries belong to *Fragaria Chiloensis*: (a) Their botanical characters, which I shall discuss more fully in the next paragraph (3), and (b) direct experiment. The experiment which I now record I consider to be of great importance. In 1890, I sent to Oregon for wild plants of *Fragaria Chiloensis*. The strawberries which I secured were short, stocky, thick-leaved, hairy, evergreen plants, at once distinguishable from the garden sorts. They were planted in a spot convenient for observation. I pressed one of the original plants, and have taken specimens from time to time since. A specimen taken in May, 1891, is scarcely distinguishable from the wild plants set the year before, but specimens secured in July of the same year show the longer stalks and larger leaves of garden strawberries; while an average specimen taken in June, 1892, is indistinguishable from common cultivated varieties in botanical features! Here, then, is a change in two years, and not by seeds, either, but in the same original plants or their offshoots. This change, while remarkable, is still not unintelligible, for I have seen many cases of as great modification in plants under cultivation; and the Chilian strawberry is widely variable in its wild state. Barnet has inadvertently recorded a distinct departure from the type of the Chilian plant, for he says that while this strawberry usually loses its leaves in winter, the varieties which have been bred from it keep their leaves. This change in my plants is due primarily, no doubt, to a greater amount of food, arising from the greater space which the plants are allowed to occupy; and it is possible that other environments may have assisted in the transformation. Having this experimental evidence, which so forcibly supplements direct botanical evidence and so well emphasizes the known laws of plant variation, I can no longer doubt that the garden strawberries are *Fragaria Chiloensis*, that the early botanists did not recognize the garden type as a departure from this species, and that this type has finally driven from cultivation the forms of *Fragaria Virginiana*. And I am glad to know that so great an authority as the elder De Candolle accepted the opinion of Seringe (1825) that the Pine, Bath Scarlet and Black strawberries belong to the Chilian species, for the Prodromus makes Duchesne's *Fragaria ananassa*, *F. calyculata* and *F. tincta* all varieties of the Chilian plant. This was evidently the opinion of the Dutch plantsmen of the middle of the last century, also, for even before Duchesne described the Pine strawberry, these merchants sold it under the name of *Fragaria Chiloensis ananæformis*, indicating that it was regarded as a form of the Chilian species. And Duhamel, towards the close of the last century, said that the Pine could be raised from seeds of the Chilian. It is evident, however, that Seringe did not mean to say that all the large garden strawberries are offshoots of the Chilian species, for he has a variety *hybrida* of *Fragaria Virginiana*, which is a supposed compound of this species and the Pine. But if there was any hybridization in the early days, I am confident that it was only incidental and its effect was transitory. Our present strawberries are apparently direct and legitimate progeny of the Chilian species.

3. *Is the Pine strawberry derived from Fragaria Virginiana var. Illinoensis ?* I confess that I have believed until recently that the garden strawberries are offspring of our native berry; certainly I have always hoped that such would prove to be their origin. It is with much reluctance that I give up a pleasant and patriotic hypothesis; but everything is against it. I had long thought that the Pine strawberry of last century was only this robust form of our native species, a feeling to which the early conjectures of an American origin for the Pine lent color. But the Pine and the var. Illinoensis are so unlike in habit that they could not have been confounded. When the var. Illinoensis was really introduced into Europe in 1852 by Asa Gray, who secured it from the "wild and savage" country, in western New York, it was thought to be so distinct from all other strawberries that it was made a new species, *Fragaria Grayana*, although it is scarcely different, except in greater size, from the common *Fragaria Virginiana*. If this plant possessed such eminent and variable qualities as to have made it the parent of our garden varieties, it would certainly have given indications of them somewhere in its wide and varied range. As it is, it has only now and then come into cultivation, when its behavior has been such that it has soon been discarded, as in the well known in-

stance of the recent Crystal City. I have also tried to cultivate it, and its response, like the Crystal City, is mostly in leaves and runners, not in any permanent or striking modification in fruit. It is true that the botanical features of the garden strawberries and the var. Illinoensis are much alike, particularly in herbarium specimens, and for some time I was not able to separate them readily; but there are botanical characters, even aside from habit, which distinguish them. The garden strawberries are lower in habit, producing runners freely only after fruiting, with shorter petioles and more leaves springing from the crown of the plant, and the leaves are spreading,—all of which are striking peculiarities of the Chilian plant,— while in the native plant the leaves stand up on long nearly perpendicular stalks, and the runners are produced at flowering time; the leaflets are thick and firm in texture, broader than in Illinoensis and lacking the long, narrow base of the native, with mostly rounder teeth, and they are particularly distinguished by the dark upper surface and the bluish-white under surface of the mature leaflets, the color of the leaflets in the native plant being light, lively green, with little difference between the two surfaces. In these points of difference, too, the garden berries are characteristically like the Chilian. The truss or inflorescence is different in the two. In the garden berries, the truss stands more or less oblique, or is often prostrate, and it is broken up into two or three strong, often unequal spreading arms, from which the short and stout fruit-stems spring, and this is the distinctive habit of the Chilian species; in the Illinoensis, the truss is erect, and it breaks up more regularly at its top and the inflorescence is less strongly spreading in proportion to the number of fruits it contains, and the fruit-stems are weak and slender and more or less drooping. The calyx is very large in the garden berries, a fact which Duchesne recorded in the name *Fragaria calyculata*, which he applied to the large-hulled forms like the old Bath Scarlet, of which many are in cultivation at the present time. The fruit in Illinoensis is small and soft, and bright scarlet, usually with a distinct neck and deeply embedded seeds ; that of the garden berries still maintains the features of the Chilian berry in its large size, mostly globular-pointed form, dark color, and seeds borne more nearly upon the surface. The garden berries are in every way much farther removed from the native berry than they are from the Chilian. From the latter they differ most widely, as I have said, in the taller growth and less hairiness ;* but even in these features, they do not resemble very closely the Illinoensis. It may be urged that all these differences might have come about under the influence of cultivation if Illinoensis itself had been the parent of the garden forms, to which I reply that direct experiment does not sustain the assumption, and that the excellent engravings of the early forms of the Pine strawberry show the same differences. It was the study of these pictures which first led me seriously to doubt the east-American origin of our straw-

---

* It is often said that the fruit of the Chilian strawberry is erect, and that the garden berries differ in a nodding fruit, but this is an error. While the fruit stems of the true Chilian are stiff, I have never known them to be erect, and in wild plants which I have grown, the fruit has the same drooping habit as in the garden berries. The Chilian species probably varies naturally in its fruiting habit, but I have yet to find an instance in which it holds its fruit upright.

berries. No one can examine the excellent colored pictures of Keen's berries,* and other early varieties, without being struck by the thick, blue-bottomed leaves and wide-spreading, arm-like trusses,—indisputable marks of *Fragaria Chiloensis*.

Yet, despite these important botanical differences, the garden berries and the native Illinoensis are much alike, as I have said; and this similarity is really one of the arguments in support of a different geographical origin of the two. Similar climates or environments produce similar results, and when old berry fields are allowed to run wild, the plants do not revert to the type of the Chilian species, but are modified rather more in the direction of the indigenous plant. In the fall, when the flower trusses are gone and growth has ceased, it is sometimes almost impossible to distinguish between the leaves of spontaneous garden berries and wild Illinoensis; but the flower clusters the following spring will be likely to distinguish the two. As a matter of fact, garden berries probably do not often persist long when run wild. They are unable to contend with the grass and weeds, although Illinoensis may find in similar circumstances an acceptable foothold. It is not strange, therefore, that those individuals from the old cultivated beds which longest persist should be those nearest like the native berries, for such would fit most perfectly into the feral conditions.

There is only one conclusion, therefore, which fully satisfies all the demands of history, philosophy, and botanical evidence, and this is that the garden

---

* See, for instance, the plate of Keen's Seedling in Trans. London Hort. Soc. v. 261.

strawberries are a direct modification of the Chile strawberry. The initial variation occurred when species were thought to be more or less immutable, and, lacking exact historical evidence of introduction from a foreign country, hybridization was the most natural explanation of the appearance of the strange type. This modified type has driven from cultivation the Virginian berries, which were earlier introduced into gardens; and the original type of the Chilian strawberry is little known, as it tends to quickly disappear through variation when impressed into cultivation. The strawberry is an instance of the evolution of a type of plant, in less than fifty years, which is so distinct from all others that three species have been erected upon it, which was uniformly kept distinct from other species by the botanists who had occasion to know it best, and which appears to have been rarely specifically associated with the species from which it sprung.

XXVI.

THE BATTLE OF THE PLUMS.[1]

EVERY naturalist knows that there is a constant struggle amongst animals and plants for a place in which to live. This arises from the two facts that more organisms are born than can find means or place of subsistence, and that the circumstances or the physical environments of life are constantly changing. The struggle for existence operates in the garden and nursery also, but it is frequently so profoundly modified by many counter forces that it generally passes unrecognized. Every person who has made any reflective study of horticulture knows that varieties are coming and going, but the reasons for this change are usually difficult to ascertain. It is oftenest said, perhaps, that such change in varieties is due to the direct and intelligent selection by man, but it will generally be found, upon closer inquiry, that his effort has really been guided by environments and other circumstances which fundamentally affect the species, and of which he may have had little knowledge. In other words, the selection and improvement carried forward by the horticulturist may be determined very largely by the same forces which would have modified the subjects to a less degree,

---

[1] Read before the Peninsula Horticultural Society, at Dover, Delaware, Jan. 10,¹1895. Printed in Transactions of the Society for 1895 (eighth annual meeting), pp. 27-84. See, also, "Evolution of our Native Fruits."

and perhaps in somewhat different directions, had they been left to shift for themselves.

All this is well illustrated in our cultivated plums. Few plants are more generally esteemed or more widely grown in this country than the plums, and yet there are none of our leading fruits which possess so little and so unsatisfactory literature. The natural history of our plums is wholly unwritten. There is not even one good American book devoted entirely or even largely to the cultivation of this fruit, and there is no full account of the interesting botany of the American plum flora. It is, therefore, impossible to determine the various epochs in the evolution of our plums, although it is the purpose of this paper to discuss the general features of this history.

The common garden plum is native to Europe or Asia, and the statement of this fact is sufficient for my purpose. In 1806, M'Mahon mentioned a "select list" of thirty plums, all but one or two of which are undoubtedly of European origin. Coxe, in 1817, selected eighteen kinds, "which comprise a succession for a private garden," of which seventeen are of European origin, and the single American variety (Cooper) was long since lost to cultivation. Our plums, therefore, like other fruits, were almost wholly European varieties seventy-five years ago. But, like these other fruits, varieties originating in America were found to possess, on the whole, rather better features than the imported sorts, and the foreign element began slowly to disappear. By the time that the Downings published the revision of the "Fruits and Fruit Trees of America" (1872), there were two hundred and eighty-three varieties of the

European type of plum described, of which one hundred and twelve, or about two-fifths, were American seedlings. Eighteen varieties cannot be traced, but most of them probably originated in this country. This shows a conspicuous adaptation of the plum to American conditions within a half century. In 1891, this ratio of varieties of American to foreign origin had risen to very nearly one-half for the kinds in actual cultivation, as indicated by the fruit list of the American Pomological Society. This progressive divergence between the two stocks of the common or European species of plum may be expected to proceed until, as in the case of apples (which have received greater attention from our pomologists), we cultivate, almost wholly, varieties of American origin. There is a marked tendency for our pomology to become independent of its European sources. Even when a promising or valuable foreign variety is introduced, it is found, in the course of a generation or two, that it has strong competitors in its American-grown seedlings. The original causes of this divergence are to be sought in the dissimilar environmental conditions of the Old World and the New World, and not in any direct influence exerted by man. These same differences of environment have, no doubt, been the cause of the separation of the indigenous plums of the two hemispheres into the well-marked specific types which are characteristic of each. In other language, the conditions which have been operating in all past time to separate the types or species of plums in the two continents are now operating upon the imported members of the foreign species themselves; and from the new forms which thus arise, the pomologist selects those most peculiarly adapted to his conditions, and thereby hastens or accentuates the differences, while being very little, if at all, responsible for their origin. (See Essay XVIII.)

If the gradual coming in of varieties of American origin is the result of an adaptation of the species to American conditions, there would seem to be the best of reasons for introducing our own indigenous species into cultivation, for they are already adapted to our conditions. These native species may be much inferior to the European type in quality of fruit, but a critical study of the evolution of our fruits will indicate, I think, that it is easier, on the whole, to improve a variable type already adapted to our soil, climate and other conditions, than to permanently succeed with a highly ameliorated type which is not adapted to our circumstances of environment. These native plums of the woods and hedge-rows early attracted the attention of the colonists. William Wood wrote about 1630 concerning New England, saying that "the plumbs of the country be better for plumbs than the cherries be for cherries. They be black and yellow; about the bigness of damsons; of a reasonable good taste." M'Mahon recommends the Chickasaw plum in his list of select fruits in 1806. The first distinct variety of any native plum to be named and propagated appears to have been the one which we now know as the Miner. The seed which produced this plum was planted by William Dodd, an officer under Jackson, in Knox county, Tennessee, in 1814. Dodd appears to have had two batches of seed, one which he gathered the year before upon Tallapoosa creek, and the other given him by an Indian chief. It is not clear from which lot this plum sprung. The plum gained some notice when it came into bearing, and was known as Old Hickory and General Jackson. In 1823 or 1824 Dodd moved to Illinois and settled near Springfield, taking some sprouts of his plum with him. The plums soon attracted attention among Dodd's neighbors, and the variety was called in its new home William Dodd and Chickasaw Chief. The year following William Dodd's removal to Illinois, his brother moved to Galena, Illinois, and took some of the plums. About Galena the plum became known as the Hinckley. Its cultivation spread gradually in the west, because it was found to endure climates which are too severe for the European types of plums. It afterwards found its way eastward, and appears to have been disseminated by a Mr. Miner, of Pennsylvania, whose name it now bears. Here, then, is the beginning of a new race of plums, but the type attracted little attention in the east because the European plums thrive readily east of the Great Lakes and from Pennsylvania northwards.

As late as 1872 only three varieties of native plums are admitted in Downing's great work,—the Miner, Newman and Wild Goose. But in the Mississippi Valley, and southeastward to the Atlantic, this new race found great favor. There is comparatively a small part of the United States which appears to be suited to the European type of plums, the northeastern region and the Pacific coast being the chief. The great interior basin suffers from great heats, droughts, and dry, trying winters, circumstances to which the European plum is at best very imperfectly adapted.

In this great region the native plums are widely distributed, and the inhabitants often had little choice between cultivating them or none. So, whilst the eastern pomologists, who have written our books, were unconscious of the existence of this new race, or were at least indifferent to it, the native plums were gradually spreading over an immense territory in many varieties.

With no historian to record the varieties or even to describe them, these plums, picked up in woods and waste places, became greatly confused; and this perplexity was increased from the fact of the great variability of the forms and the lack of critical knowledge of the botanical status of the types from which they sprung. To the botanist there were two species of native plums producing edible fruit, the common American and the Chickasaw; and to most pomologists there was only one type—the Wild Goose. The Miner had nearly passed from sight and the Wild Goose had taken its place, and was, in fact, the first native plum widely disseminated. When it first began to be propagated extensively it was sold far and wide by agents, and as it turned out to be self-sterile and was introduced into the eastern states where it was not needed, the variety, like many other acquisitions which have been indiscreetly praised and distributed, fell into disrepute. I frequently see isolated plantations of it in New York, and it is uniformly condemned. Nevertheless, it marks the second epoch in the amelioration of our native plums, and it is still the most popular variety in the regions where these plums are needed. The origin of this Wild Goose plum is curious. It was first brought to notice by James Harvey, of Columbia, Tenn. Some time before 1850 a man shot a wild goose near Columbia, and on the spot where the carcass was thrown this plum came up the following spring. It was introduced about 1850 by the late J. S. Downer, of Fairview, Ky. The other native plum mentioned by Downing—the Newman, and which is still popular—originated in Kentucky, so far as we can learn. Here, then, are three leading native plums coming from the same geographical region. If we examine their botanical features we find that they are markedly different from each other; so different, in fact, that the first person who attempted any scientific study of them three years ago, referred two of them to two species and the third to a well marked botanical variety; and one species and the variety were founded for the express purpose of receiving two of the varieties—the Wild Goose and the Miner. But the strange fact is that these two botanical types are not certainly known in a wild state, although the geographical origin of the cultivated forms is well known. There are many varieties with the same botanical features now in cultivation, and nearly all of them have been picked up as wild plants in some portion of the southern Mississippi Valley. The wild species, therefore, cannot be rare. Have the varieties been modified by cultivation so that they are not recognized as identical with the wild plums known to botanists? Or, may they be hybrids? Or, is it possible that the botanists have been less alert than the horticulturists, and are not yet well acquainted with our wild plums? The first two conclusions are the most tenable ones; but the fact nevertheless remains that we are speculating upon the botanical origins of fruits which have sprung from the wild in our own Mississippi Valley within a generation or two. With this lesson before us we may cease wondering at the doubts respecting the origins of those world-wide fruits which were in cultivation when history began.

But the evolution of native plums has not ended here. With the settlement of the northwestern prairie region, a new race of plums came into notice, and these differ widely in fruit and tree from those coming from the mid-country and the south. There is no one variety of this class which stands out clearly as a pioneer. Several well marked forms appeared nearly simultaneously early in the sixties. The chief of these are the De Soto, Forest Garden and Quaker; and about ten years later a very prominent variety, the Weaver, was added to the list. One variety of this class, the Wolf, is probably the oldest native plum, with the exception of Miner, springing from a planted pit. It was raised in Iowa over forty years ago, from a pit taken from a wild tree. Now, this northern type of plums springs from the best known of our native species, *Prunus Americana*, and there would appear to be no difficulty respecting its botanical features. Yet, there is now a discussion as to whether the group from which they have come is one species or two, and some persons are convinced that there are two. And another curious circumstance is yet unexplained—the fact that, while *Prunus Americana* is distributed from Maine to Colorado and south to the Gulf, it is only in the states of the northern Mississippi Valley that cultivable varieties are found, with the single exception of Texas, where another perplexing branch of the group is native.

About two hundred vareties of native plums are now known and named. They are contending with the European type for supremacy in the continental basin, and, whilst still much inferior to the foreigners in quality of fruit, they are destined to win in the ceaseless struggle for existence. They possess great superiority in what we call constitution. But they have other merits which are quite as pronounced. I refer to their comparative immunity from the attacks of the black-knot and leaf-blight fungi, diseases which are very serious upon the common plums. These fungi are both native of this country. The black-knot appears to have traveled chiefly from New England westward, while the leaf-blight is invading the northwestern plum lands from the west and south. At first sight, it seems strange that our native plums should be more immune from our native diseases than the European plums are, but there is excellent reason for it. It is plain that, in the course of the evolution of the species of native plums, those forms which were most susceptible to the attacks of these fungi would be exterminated by them, whilst those forms most immune would stand the best chance of perpetuating their kind. In other words, there has no doubt been a long and fierce battle between the fungi and the plums and both have persisted, but they have developed away from each other. But the European plum, never having had this contest with the two fungi named, is unprepared to meet their attacks. We find this same comparative immunity from indigenous fungous or insect enemies in other native plants. It is best marked in the grapes, which are not seriously injured by phylloxera or downy mildew, both of which are indigenous troubles, whilst the European grape is very quickly decimated by them. The pear blight is a similar instance. It is an American disease which, before the introduction of European fruits, probably lived upon the wild thorn apples, but the pear and quince are less able to resist its attack. The peach yellows is also an American disease which thrives upon an imported host, and I am expecting every year to hear that some one has discovered it upon its original native plant.

But a new factor has now come into this complex battle of the plums. A Japanese type has been introduced within the last quarter century, and, contrary to the expectations of its most sanguine admirers, it has proved to be well adapted to a much wider range of our country than the European type is. And, strangely enough, it is now found that this oriental species is more closely related to our native species than to the European. This fact was first noticed by horticulturists, who discovered that the winter twigs and buds of the Japanese and Wild Goose types are often so much alike that they may be almost indistinguishable when mixed in the same bundle. It was only a year ago this very month that these similarities and some explanations of their origin were first published. The gist of the matter is this: It was long ago shown by the late Asa Gray that the floras of Japan and eastern North America are very similar, due to the persistence of similar types of post-glacial plants in regions of similar geographical position and comparable climate. (Essay XV.) The east-coast floras of the northern hemispheres are more closely related than the more contiguous east and west-coast floras. In fact, the plants of Europe are quite as much like those of California in many particulars as they are like those of our Atlantic slope, a fact which is again well illustrated in the similar horticultural industries of our Pacific slope and central and southern Europe. The only North American region in which many of the characteristic European fruits thrive unequivocally—as the wine grape, olive, walnut, almond and others—is west of the Sierras, although there is a tendency for this belt to extend eastward through Texas and along the Gulf. The Japanese plum is one of the many plants which prove the similarity of east-Asian and east-American conditions, and the dissimilarity of east-American and European conditions. This remarkable correlation extends even to minor or technical botanical characters in the plums. There are two methods in which the plums pack away their leaves in the bud. In some the little leaves are convolute or rolled together, whilst in others they are conduplicate or trough-shaped, one lying inside the other. Now, the two European species which we cultivate, the common plum or *Prunus domestica*, and the myrobalan or *P. cerasifera*, have their leaves convolute or rolled in the bud; and the same thing is true of the one wild plum of the Pacific coast, and also of the *Prunus umbellata* of the extreme south. The Japanese plum, on the other hand, has its leaves conduplicate or folded in the bud, and the same is true of our three native species, the Americana, Wild Goose and Chickasaw types. It is singular, too, that the wild Pacific plum is strikingly like the common European plum in some of its features, whilst the southern *Prunus umbellata* equally resembles in foliage the myrobalan. Another curious circumstance about this Japanese plum is its comparative immunity from leaf-blight and the black-knot, and I have often wondered if we should not yet discover that these diseases are indigenous where it originated, and that it has passed through the conflict with them. But perhaps this immunity is only temporary, because of the comparative rarity of the trees in this country.

If, then, the Japanese plum is so much like our own because it has been evolved in similar conditions, it is not strange that we should find it to be adapted to a wide range of this country. But granting this, why should it be even so well adapted to our circumstances as our native plums are? It has one great advantage over our natives in the fact that it has been cultivated from early times, and is already much improved over its wild condition; but beyond this, I do not see that it can have merits beyond our native. Time will do for our native plums what it has done for the Japanese and European types and for all other plants under the hand of man, and nature has already done the rest. I am looking to the Japanese plums to popularize the natives, because they interpose a type between the widely unlike European and American groups, and divert the attention of conservative pomologists from the familiar old varieties. And, furthermore, I am looking for good results from hybridizing the American and Japanese species, and there is already indication of this amalgamation;

but in all the years that have passed, no undoubted hybrids of recognized value for fruit have arisen between the American and European plums.

I have confused you enough already to spare any allusion to other cultivated types of plums which must some day attract or distract our attention, or to the many botanical perplexities which attach to the subject. It is evident that this complex battle of the plums is only beginning, for the three or four native species and the one Japanese species which are now in commercial cultivation, are of very recent introduction. No less than a thousand varieties of the European plum are known, and each of the other four or five species may be expected to be equally variable. Hybrids will occur. We have an immense country, comprising the widest differences of environment, and nearly all parts of it may be expected, some day, to grow plums of one kind or another. There will be a great mixing and jostling of types, and we cannot foresee the final result; but I believe that a marked feature of that millennial plum flora will be the imprint of our native species.

XXVII.

EVOLUTION OF AMERICAN GRAPES.[1]

The evolution of our cultivated American grapes is interesting, because it may be said to have arisen under pressure. The standards of excellence in grapes are high. They are the European standards,—the outgrowth of centuries of careful cultivation of a fruit which is especially a dessert fruit and a source of wine. In recent years, as grape growers have come to understand that our grapes are wholly different in stamp from those of the Old World, European standards are in large measure forgotten, but in the early days of our grape growing they were almost universally adopted. But even now, what is the meaning of the term "vinous flavor" as applied to our grapes, if it is not a comparison with the European or wine grape? And why do we almost instinctively try to improve the flavor of our grapes by crossing them with foreign blood? Is not the growing American wine industry a direct competition with the product of the European vine? The standard of quality in American grapes is that which flavors the history of Europe. This high standard has had a marked influence upon American varieties,

---

[1] Remarks before a Farmer's Institute at Forestville, Chautauqua county, New York, September 23, 1892. Reported in American Gardening, xiii. 657. (November, 1892), by E. G. Lodeman. A full discussion of the subject will be found in the author's "Evolution of our Native Fruits."

and is one reason for the great improvement of our native grapes.

Attempts to cultivate the European grape in the open air in all the northern and central states have always resulted in failure, although the attempts have been numerous. Only within the last twenty-five years have we discovered that this failure is largely due to the phylloxera and the powdery mildew,— enemies which are native to America, but which do little harm to native grapes. The failure of the foreign grapes drew attention to the wild ones, and the Cape or Alexander grape, which gained prominence about a century ago, was the first of our natives which attracted the attention of vignerons. Not the excellence of the Alexander, but the fact that it would thrive while foreign kinds would not, commended it. It proved a failure for wine, however, and it was not until John Adlum picked up a grape which came from the Catawba river early in this century that American grape culture may be said to have begun. This was the Catawba grape. Subsequently there appeared Isabella and Diana, and our grape culture had received a distinct impetus. In 1853 the Concord appeared, and this incident, more than any other single fact, has greatly extended the cultivation of the grape in this country. So far, our grapes were pure offspring of the fox grape, or *Vitis Labrusca*, of the eastern states; or, in the Catawba, an offspring of the southern type of that species.

At this time definite attempts were being made to introduce foreign qualities into our hardy but harsh natives. John Fisk Allen, of Massachusetts, showed the first hybrid before the Massachusetts Horticultural

Society in 1854. His grape, which is known as Allen's Hybrid, was a cross between Isabella and the foreign Golden Chasselas. About this time, also, E. S. Rogers, of Roxbury, Massachusetts, was making experiments in the same direction, and his thirteen grapes have gained a wide reputation. These grapes are crosses between the wild Labrusca of New England and selected varieties of the European grape. They all combine excellence of flavor with large size and attractive appearance, but none of them has become a popular market grape, because some weakness is present in each one. The introduction of the foreign or *Vitis vinifera* blood, therefore, was not successful in the production of profitable varieties.

But the attempt to add vinifera virtues to American grapes did not end with the phenomenal labors of Rogers. J. H. Ricketts, a resident of Newburgh, New York, soon took up the work, following largely the lines of his predecessor, except that his American parents were taken from among our best named varieties, as Concord, Delaware, Iona and Clinton. Twenty-eight of Ricketts' have been named; of these twenty-seven possess American blood, the Welcome being wholly European. These varieties, as a whole, are of remarkably high quality, and it is not too much to say that they constitute the most marked example of the refinement of American grapes. Every variety, like those of Rogers, affords an instructive lesson in the blending of parentages, but like Rogers', too, they are not market grapes. With the high quality of vinifera we have, also, its weaknesses and disadvantages, and most of Ricketts' remarkable varieties are already lost to cultivation. Adelaide, El Dorado, Highland, Jefferson and Lady Washington have Concord blood, and the last is interesting because one of its parents is the old Allen's Hybrid; but even these have place with amateurs, not with market growers.

It is not improbable that there may exist among our multitude of hybrids some prizes which have been overlooked, for many of them have not been named or introduced, and some of the named varieties have not been thoroughly tested. But it is certainly true that, as a whole, the introduction of the vinifera blood through artificial hybridizations has not been a success. This, after all, is not strange. It is the rule in the vegetable kingdom that violent hybridizations give unsatisfactory results, and any hybridization between the eastern American species and *Vitis vinifera* must be regarded as violent. In fact, primary hybridations between native species have rarely given profitable results. This is well illustrated in Jacob Rommel's seedlings of Labrusca and the common wild *Vitis riparia*, or river-bank grape. His varieties are characterized by great vigor, productiveness and hardiness, but they lack flavor and size of berry. His named sorts are Amber Beauty, Black Delaware, Elvira, Etta, Faith, Montefiore, Pearl, Transparent, and Wilding. If the violence of the cross is responsible for some of the weaknesses in all these hybrids, it would seem to follow that secondary hybridizations would give better results. And in this direction— crossing the best pure native sorts with hybrids of various degrees of attenuation—I look for ultimate success in fusing vinifera characteristics into American grapes. Ricketts' failure in this direction was due to the selection of weak parents, such as the Delaware and Iona. His Golden Gem, which is a union of these two varieties, is of unusually high quality, but very difficult to grow; and this weakness is to be expected from parents which are themselves more or less weak.

Perhaps the most signal successes which have yet come from the introduction of dilute vinifera blood appear in Moore's Diamond, a product of Concord fertilized by Iona, and in the Brighton, also one of Moore's grapes, a cross between Concord and Diana-Hamburg. T. V. Munson, of Texas, whose experiments in American grapes are full of promise, both in extent and importance, is following this method with apparent success. In union with other grapes he has used one of Rogers' hybrids—the Lindley—with most gratifying results. But hybridizing is not to be looked upon as the only, if even as the chief, means of improving our grapes. It is well known that nature discourages hybridization or violent crossing, while she encourages crosses of a mild type, as between different strains or varieties of the same species. These minor crosses impart new vigor and virility to the offspring, and they often afford a sure but very gradual means of directly improving the salient characters of a variety. I should look for good results if a cross were made between Concords from widely separated localities, even if the offspring should itself prove to be true Concord, for such unions usually give plants that outdo the parents in growth and productivenes. Crossing between varieties of one species should give a fair proportion of profitable results. This is well shown in the Niagara, which is a cross between Concord and Cassady, both Labrusca.

Much depends upon immediate parentage. A strong, virile variety, that adapts itself to a great range of conditions, may be expected to give more satisfactory and uniform results than one which has obvious points of weakness and which does not adapt itself to various environments. We turn instinctively to the Concord, for this is preëminently the strongest type of American grape. No other grape has given us such a famous brood. There are nearly or quite fifty named pure seedlings of it, among which are such varieties as Worden, Moore Early, Eaton, Hayes, Cambridge, Rockland, Cottage, Colerain, Esther, Lady, Pocklington and Victoria. These run through deep black-purple to red and white, and all of them possess many strong points, especially in vigor and productiveness. As one parent of hybrids and crosses, Concord has given us Niagara, Moore Diamond, Brighton, Lady Washington, Jefferson, Conqueror and others. It has been said that Concord blood has run out, but in the presence of such a family as this, some members of which are very recent, I am forced to conclude that it is the most desirable single stock upon which to breed, or from which to take pure seedlings.

About three hundred varieties of grapes have been named and prominently disseminated in eastern America. Of these, over one-third are pure Labruscas, nearly one-third are hybrids, about one-fifteenth are æstivalis and one-fifteenth riparia, the remainder being of unknown origin. Of the hybrids, over half contain foreign blood. It is interesting to note, in the lists which I have before me, that four-fifths of our standard market grapes belong to the pure Labrusca class, and that there is not one market hybrid which is known to be a primary hybrid.

It is impossible to draw many definite conclusions from the present state of our viticulture as to the most promising means of improving our grapes, but it appears safe to say that satisfactory results are not to be expected, as a rule, from primary hybridizations, and that a considerable attenuation of the specific blood in one or both parents is essential to the best results; that while most of the former attempts to introduce vinifera blood have been only partially successful, there is every promise of satisfactory results in the future by using hybrids which are already in existence; that crossing between different pure stocks, or varieties of the same native species, gives promise of excellent results; and that the employment of the most profitable and virile stocks, either as parents of pure seedlings or as parties to hybridization, as the Concord, is one of the first requisites of success.

XXVIII.

THE PROGRESS OF THE CARNATION.

I.

Some Types and Tendencies in the Carnation.[1]

THE carnation is wild in the Mediterranean region, where it is a perennial plant of erect, branching habit, long cylindrical calyx, and single flowers with a spreading limb and of a pale lilac color. It has been cultivated for centuries, and it is variable under domestication. No one knows the various forms into which it has run, and doubtless many of these forms have entirely disappeared, leaving no record. The earliest marked varieties appear to have been in color: white, pink, various shades of red, and even yellow, together with many variegations and curious markings, are recorded in the early herbals. The English have always classified the forms largely upon color, distributing them among the Selfs, Flakes, Bizarres, and Picotees. The French and others have classified the forms upon other characters, as habit of plant, shape and texture of flowers, or combinations of various features. Vilmorin recently divides the carnations into seven groups:

---

[1] Read before the Second Annual Meeting of the American Carnation Society, at Pittsburgh, Penna., Feb. 22, 1893. Printed in the Report of the Society for 1893, pp. 21 to 30.

1. GRENADINS—Single, mostly dark self-colored flowers of strong color. These are grown for perfumery, and for coloring and flavoring liquors.

2. FANTASIES—Double, very prolific types, with variously colored or variegated flowers, tending to produce a great proportion of meritorious seedlings.

3. FLAMANDS or FLEMISH—Striped or self-colored pompon-like flowers, with large and nearly entire petals and very attractive habit.

4. PERPETUAL or REMONTANT kinds, or the forcing carnations.

5. DWARFS or VERVIERS, small, sturdy plants, for outdoor cultivation.

6. BICHONS, remarkable for their fresh colors, rather soft substance, and fragrance.

7. SABLES, or Picotee-like forms.

But none of these classifications sufficiently indicate the wonderful and constant variability of the carnation. A classification which was satisfactory a generation ago is of little use at the present time. This fact indicates that new types of carnations are appearing,—not new varieties simply, but wholly new types, adapted to wholly new uses. In our day we have seen the appearance of Malmaison and very recently the Marguerite types,—forms which are as distinct from the carnations in this exhibition hall as some species are from each other. The first of the Malmaison class to gain prominence was the cream-colored Souvenir de la Malmaison, which has now an interesting company of pinks and reds, all agreeing in a strong bushy habit, luxuriant "grass" and enormous fragrant flowers of unique pattern which bloom in late winter or spring if grown inside. It is not a remontant, and yet it forces well.

The Marguerite type is remarkable because it blooms the first year, sometimes in five or six months from seed. It is a half-dwarf Italian class, with fragrant, mostly double fringed flowers, of rather thin substance, and inclined to be tender when young.

Perhaps the most serviceable classification which we can make for the present purpose is to divide carnations into five large and somewhat ill-defined groups :

1. The Grenadins or perfume carnations.
2. The Border Carnations, comprising a great variety of hardy sorts, much used for outdoor cultivation.
3. The Malmaisons.
4. The Marguerites.
5. The Forcing or Bench Carnations.

In each of these groups there are many varieties, and new ones are constantly appearing; yet perhaps the best way that I can impress upon you the fact of the marvelous variation of the carnation plant, is to say that all the four hundred and twenty carnations which are now recorded in America belong to but one of these groups—the forcing varieties. With the exception of a few Marguerites, practically the only class of carnations known in this country is these forcing sorts, so that the very word carnation has come to mean a greenhouse pink. In England, on the other hand, the word, if used without qualification, refers to the border group, and it is only when one speaks of perpetual or tree carnations that these greenhouse kinds are understood.

This peculiarity of vocabulary is very suggestive.

In the first place, it indicates that American carnation cultivation is very one-sided. We have not yet discovered the full merits of the species for decorative purposes. It suggests that this Society should undertake the popularization of the various hardy and dwarf races of carnations, as well as of those particularly adapted to house cultivation. In the second place, it suggests the fact that in England the forcing carnations came into notice after the cultivation of other types of the flower had been long established. It shows, again, that carnation growing had never gained a permanent foothold in this country until these greenhouse kinds came into existence; and they have absorbed our whole attention, and have probably attained a greater popularity than anywhere else in the world. The relative unimportance of the forcing carnations in England is shown by the fact that of the seventeen chapters devoted to special types of carnations in the new English Carnation Manual, only three are devoted to the perpetual kinds. And Williamson, in his recent "Exhibitor's Manual," gives the points of merit in a show carnation to be: (1) Size and form of flower; (2) Distinctness of markings and colors; (3) Substance of petals and regularity of disposition. These are certainly not the only chief points of excellence in the judging of forcing carnations, in which length of stem is quite as important as these features. This schedule indicates that the forcing varieties have made little impression upon the English shows. It is evident, therefore, that if this Society fulfills its complete measure of usefulness, it must speedily enlarge its efforts to comprise the outdoor varieties.

But the most important fact in all this is the very recent origin of the forcing carnations, and to this point I desire to call particular attention. It is scarcely half a century since Dalmais sent out Atim (1844), the first recorded perpetual carnation. Dalmais was gardener to M. Lacene, at Lyons. He crossed a November carnation (St. Martin) with one of the bichons as a starting point, and this crossbreed was crossed again with the Flemish type. Various persons have been concerned in this evolution of the perpetual carnations, especially Schmidtt, Alegatiere and Turner; but to Alegatiere is ascribed, by common consent, the chief merit in this development. Alegatiere's work is little more than half as old as Dalmais'. All this shows how recent has been the beginning of an industry which now enlists a great army of florists. Is it any wonder, then, that the ideals have not yet been reached, and that even the best of the new varieties soon give way to others?

Two new features have come to be essential in this bench type of carnations: (1) The habit of continuous bloom for a period of six or seven months; (2) A tall stature, with long and strong flower stems, fitting them for bouquet work. With these requisites is combined the additional importance attached to a strong, non-bursting calyx. The perpetual character and long stems are rapidly coming to be permanent characters.

It would be interesting to inquire if these perpetual types are really any more productive than the older border varieties, or if only the same amount of bloom is distributed over a longer period. This latter appears to be the truth, for most of our carnation growers are content if a plant produces two flowers a month for six months, making twelve flowers in all, which is by no means a heavy crop for a border carnation in its second year. It would be equally interesting to inquire if the practice of disbudding has had any effect upon the length of the stems in modern varieties. The current theories in evolution dispute any hereditary influence following mere mutilations, and would ascribe all progress in this instance to an intelligent selection of chance long-stemmed seedlings. But it is certainly true that the artificial standard which is set by any custom or fashion is eventually reached by the plants themselves, because the grower constantly selects with reference to it. In this sense, therefore, disbudding is bound to exert a powerful influence upon the character of the forthcoming varieties in the same way that the old practice of "carding" or "dressing," as I showed a year ago (see page 455), has been the means of producing the present flat-bottomed and high-centered flower.

A permanent non-bursting calyx has been the most difficult to secure of all the modern requirements of a perfect carnation. The reason for this is the fact that increased size and fullness of flower are opposed to the resisting powers of the calyx. The increase in number and size of petals is the very attribute which causes the calyx to burst, and it is therefore essential that we modify the ideal of the flower quite as much as the style of the calyx if we desire to secure a uniformly non-bursting flower. I am convinced, as I said a year ago, and as Mr. Lonsdale has also remarked, that the ideal way in which to further increase the size of the carnation flower is by lengthening the outer petals, so as to make the flower broader on the base. So far as I have observed, the worst "bursters" are usually those whose centers are densely packed with petals. There is much to be done, of course, in modifying the style of the calyx itself. There is a common impression that mere shortness in a calyx is all that is desired, but while this may be the chief requisite, it is not the only one. Short calices are frequently the worst bursters, while a long calyx may remain perfectly entire, and these facts are well represented in plants in this hall. Martin R. Smith, an English carnation specialist, writes that "the confirmed burster will always have short, round, blunt-headed buds," but "the non-burster, on the other hand, displays a long bud of about three times its diameter." What is more particularly desired is a calyx relatively short in proportion to its breadth, and one which has a spreading or open mouth and some elasticity. In the single or little improved carnations, the petals unfold or project between the calyx teeth; if it is possible to increase the number of teeth in the calyx as the number of petals have been increased, we may speedily procure the perfect calyx. An elastic cushion or hump on each calyx lobe, which is so conspicuous in the seedlings of Dorner and in some other varieties, is one of the most encouraging signs in recent productions.

But there is reason to expect that all the requisites of a perfect carnation are attainable, and the question then arises if these features will persist. In other words, do carnations run out? This question is full of perplexities, and there are the most opposed opinions concerning it. At the outset, it is important that we understand what is meant by running out. (1) In one sense, it means a wearing out, a predetermined life of a variety at the expiration of which time the type becomes weak and refuses to bear or even to grow. The Buttercup is a variety which is commonly thought to have worn out. (2) In another sense, running out means the disappearance of the variety by variation into other colors or other forms, while the plant still retains its first vigor and productiveness. An excellent example of this is found in the so-called "running" of the striped varieties in England, by which the flakes and bizarres often become self-colored or lose their characteristic markings. (3) In still another sense, running out refers to the crowding out of varieties by better kinds or by changing fashions. These three subjects must be discussed separately.

1. Do varieties wear out? Are they self-limited in duration? There is no evidence yet to show that any variety of plants is pre-limited in period of existence. So long as it receives good care it maintains its pristine virility; if it grows weaker with the years, the fault must be laid to disease or to improper handling or management. The Buttercup is an admirable example of this fact. The most vigorous, most productive and best carnation in our house this year is the Buttercup, and this is evidence that it has not lost its old-time vigor. Some of our Buttercups were weak and would not flower, but careful examination has shown that they were suffering from an

insidious internal disease, the exact nature of which is unknown, but which is readily transferred in cuttings. Here, then, is the probable explanation of the running out of the Buttercup.

I have said that carnations, like other plants, may lose their vigor because of improper handling. It is a common opinion that the nature of the cutting, its age, and its position upon the parent plant, exert a powerful influence upon the resulting plant. On February 26, 1892, a flowering yearling plant of Hinze's White, pot grown, was selected for experiment. Three batches of cuttings were taken from it —(a) from the tips of the strong sterile shoots springing from the root; (b) from the lateral shoots about an inch and a half long which sprung from the flowering stems; and (c) from pieces of the flower stems themselves. These cuttings were placed side by side in the cutting bench; all were set out of doors June 23d, and all were brought into the house October 10th. At this writing (February 18th, 1893) the following notes are taken:

(a) *Cuttings from strong bottom shoots.*—Plants the most vigorous of the lots, with broader grass and stockier shoots than any others. Plants full of buds, but no bloom yet.

(b) *Cuttings from lateral shoots.*—Somewhat less vigorous than lot (a) with narrower grass, but blooming freely now, and as well set with buds as the first lot.

(c) *Cuttings of flower stems.*—Plants weak and poor, with no bloom yet and little promise for the future.

Here, then, is a decided variation between cutting-plants coming from the same parent, as much difference, in fact, as there is between some wholly distinct varieties. If I were to follow up my practice on each of these lots—as I propose to do—I might be able within a few generations to obtain distinct varieties; and there is little doubt that the last lot —made from flower stems — would soon become very weak, and might perish altogether.

I am ready to believe that any noticeably weak plant will produce poor offspring, and by that much hasten the disappearance of the variety. It is well known that stock of a certain kind may be better grown by a given man than when grown by his neighbor, and there is every reason to believe that the treatments which the plants receive are responsible for the difference.

2. Do varieties disappear by variation into other forms? The above experiment shows that cuttings from the same plant vary among themselves in strength when taken from different parts of the parent. It is likewise true that some individual plants change their character from year to year, and cuttings taken from such plants at various epochs in their history produce different offspring. The "running" of carnations in England is an example of the variation of the same plant from season to season. A plant which produces a good bizarre may bear a self the next year. If the individual plant is not stable, the cuttings cannot be expected to be stable. Many other plants often refuse to "come true" from cuttings, as, for instance, some petunias and variegated pelargoniums. I suppose that the reason why the striped varieties do not "run" in

America is because we grow our plants but a single season, and we therefore keep them nearly or perhaps even wholly true to name, so far as this species of variation is concerned; yet it is possible, as these facts show, for even cutting-plants to vary from the original types. So far as known, the running of the colors is confined to the party-colored sorts, although it very rarely affects the picotees. The following interesting remarks upon the vagaries of run flowers are from Martin Rowan, an English grower: "The run flowers, whether taking the form of selfs or fancies, * * * are often very handsome, and one is frequently tempted to layer the stock of them in the hope of fully retaining their new character: but in my experience they are never so good as in the first season of the sport, coming after that always thinner in the flower and less brilliant in color. Occasionally they will go back to their original character, as was the case with Mr. Barlow's fine scarlet bizarre, Robert Houlgrave, which was largely productive of run flowers the first season of its distribution, but the run stock of which for the most part returned to its original character the following season." There is still much discussion as to the cause of running, some attributing it to soil, others to the season and still others to the methods of growing; but it is plain that it is only a spontaneous variation or reversion in varieties which are not well fixed, and it is proof that the cultivated carnation is in a state of great instability.

3. It needs no argument to convince you that changing fashions and the introduction of better varieties are constantly driving out the older car-

nations. This Society will undoubtedly exert a conservative influence upon mere fashion, and by that much contribute to a more permanent merit-list; but it will also stimulate the production of superior varieties and by this means augment the changes in the lists. But change is indication of advancement and should therefore be encouraged.

Varieties also disappear because of mere carelessness in propagating and naming, by which they become mixed.

I have already observed that carnation growing in America is very different from that in Europe, because it concerns itself with but a single branch of a great family. I might go further, and say that even in the bench carnations our varieties are very different from those of other countries. Scarcely any of the forcing varieties which are recommended across the Atlantic are known favorably in America, and less than 5 per cent of our list of four hundred and twenty varieties appears to be of foreign origin, while all the popular varieties here are of American origin. This same tendency to discard European for American varieties is apparent in all classes of plants which have been long or extensively grown in this country. (Essay XVIII.) We shall undoubtedly soon be able to produce meritorious varieties of the Malmaison, Marguerite, border and other types, if they are once seriously introduced into America. This leads me to say that the best results in breeding new varieties of plants are to be attained only when the work is carried on persistently for a long series of years upon the same stock for a basis and by a single individual. The propagator then secures a pure or stable stock, he learns how to handle it to the best advantage, and he is able to constantly augment the merits obtained in preceding years; his work is cumulative. It is effort of this kind which has made so many European horticulturists so eminently successful in their various lines, as Lemoine, Benary, Crozy, Bennett, Paul and others. There is already one example in this country of this persistent effort upon a good foundation applied to the breeding of carnations, as any one knows who is familiar with the work of Fred Dorner.

It seems to me to be important, therefore, that the whole field of carnation culture should be encouraged in America, rather than to confine our attention to a single type of the family. It should be remembered that the perpetual or bench carnations are of recent origin, and are therefore not yet perfect. Varieties do not wear out, but they pass out of sight because of disease, improper methods of propagation and handling, by variation, the appearance of better kinds and the careless mixing of stock. Good results in originating new varieties will come, as a rule, only from persistent effort extended over a series of years and founded upon a strong and uniform stock.

II.

John Thorpe's Ideal Carnation.[1]

Great interest has been awakened in carnation cultivation by John Thorpe's bold prophecy that

---

[1] Read before the First Annual Meeting of the American Carnation Society at Buffalo, New York, February 16, 1892. Printed in First Annual Report of the Society, 58 to 65.

within eight years we shall be able to grow carnation flowers four inches in diameter, and to sell them for one dollar each. The full text of his prophecy, or of the requirements for what he calls his model flower, are as follows :*

"First. The flower is to be not less than four inches in diameter. The petals must be thick and regularly disposed. The color, any color. It must have a decidedly sweet perfume.

"Second. The calyx to be not less than half the diameter of the flower; it must be sufficiently large so as not to burst during the period of the petals emerging from it.

"The stem must be in proportion to the size of the flower, and long enough to be cut not less than eighteen inches long. The lower end of the stem not thinner than an ordinary lead pencil. The stem to be clothed with leaves, as are the best varieties to-day, excepting that the lower leaves are to be eight inches long, one-half inch wide, covered with a glaucous surface, which only carnations have. The leaves to be curved in that lovely way already possessed by the Divine flower.

"Such flowers will sell for one dollar each."

This vivid portrayal piques our curiosity as to the probability of such a consummation, and florists are alert to discover and record every new approach towards this ideal. Blooms nearly three inches in diameter have been recorded within the past few months. Everyone appears to agree that the carnation is rapidly improving in all desirable features. Mr. C. J. Pennock writes as follows in Annals of Horticulture:

---

* Am. Flor. vi. 338 (Jan. 8, 1891).

"A casual observer, if at all interested in floriculture, cannot fail to have noticed that there has been a marked advance in the appearance of carnation blooms as they are now offered for sale, as compared with the blooms as grown even ten years ago; and to those who have watched such improvement critically, it is a prophecy of even greater advancement. Ten years ago the leading varieties were Edwardsii, DeGraw, La Purité, King of Crimson, and Astoria, scarcely any of which are grown now by the commercial florist. Probably greater progress has been made during the last three years in the improvement of the carnation than ever before, and the present year has produced several varieties of striking merit.

"Mr. Thorpe's prediction of the ideal flower, so often referred to among growers — a flower four inches in diameter, with the other highest attributes, and to sell for one dollar each — seemed somewhat chimerical when made two years ago, but now the fulfillment appears to be much nearer at hand. Flowers with particularly attractive qualities are selling readily for one-third to one-half advance over less favored varieties. The production of carnations is rapidly on the increase, while the demand seems to keep pace therewith. As in other industries, the supply of inferior products is often excessive, and the prices received fall below a profitable figure; but first-class flowers will readily sell at wholesale for seventy-five cents to one dollar for one hundred blooms at any time, and during seasons of particular demand two dollars and fifty cents to three dollars per hundred is frequently obtained. It is safe to say that the production of carnation blooms has increased 50 per cent during the past year."

Now, the carnation has been cultivated for several centuries, and the history of it must afford some data to illustrate the laws of its variation and evolution, and to lead us aright in our endeavors for the future. My wish in this discussion, therefore, is not only to discover what hope there may be for the realization of Mr. Thorpe's prophecy, but also to draw from the past some hints which shall be of use for the present.

It is important to notice, at the outset, that Mr. Thorpe's ideal flower differs from those already in existence only in size of bloom, stem and leaves. Our first endeavor must be to determine the extent of variability which the carnation has shown, and then to enquire how near to this new standard varieties have already approached.

At every point in the history of the carnation, we are impressed with the wonderful variability of the species. In 1597, Gerarde declared that there were so many kinds of pinks, most of which appear to have been carnations, "that a great and large volume would not suffice to write of every one at large in particular." In 1702, John Ray catalogued three hundred and sixty distinct kinds. At one of the weekly shows of the Massachusetts Horticultural Society in 1830, "one hundred different varieties of carnation were exhibited."[*] And in recent years, Vilmorin[†] declares that some dealers offer as many as two thousand kinds. Now these varieties differ

---
[*] Hist. Mass. Hort. Soc. 223.
[†] Fleurs de Pleine Terre, 762

among themselves in every direction,— in color, markings, fragrance, habit, vigor, hardiness, time of bloom, shape and size of flowers, so much so, in fact, that several distinct species have been erected upon horticultural varieties. Now, these facts are important to our present discussion, because we are to look for greatest improvement in the most variable species. Some varieties are so unlike the small, slender and single-flowered wild plant, which grows in central and southern Europe, that the two would scarcely be considered to belong to the same species, were they not connected by historical evidence. Almost every character which man has desired has been obtained. This statement is nowhere better illustrated than in the breeding off of the fringes, in securing what the old florists called "whole flowers," or flowers which do not burst the calyx, and in the modification of the shape of the flower itself.

All the old prints and descriptions represent the petals as deeply and sharply fringed. This is well illustrated in Gerarde's figures, printed in 1597. For at least one hundred and fifty years it has been a tenet of gardeners to breed off the fringe, or to strive for "rose leaves," as the old gardeners phrased it. At the present time, the petals are simply erose; and this was the case in some varieties, at least, even a hundred years ago, as illustrated in a cut of a large bizarre of 1788 which is to be found in the Botanical Magazine.

Breeding for flowers which do not burst the calyx is still an important thought with every carnation grower, yet there appears to have been great advance in this direction within the last one hundred and fifty or two hundred years. It was the practice of the early gardeners to split the calyx with a pen-knife or scissors in three or four places, and this appears to have been always necessary in 1752, judging from Phillip Miller's account in the sixth edition of his Gardener's Dictionary. I have not had access to Miller's earlier editions. We find this advice to slit the calyces of carnations in some of the books at the opening of this century. The calyx was sometimes bound with cord. At the present time we expect that a good carnation flower will be a "whole flower" without artificial aid.

The improvement of the form of the carnation flower shows a curious history. A century ago it was the practice to "card" all flowers for exhibition. This operation consisted in securing a circular piece of cardboard to the under side of the flower to act as a support to the lower or guard petals. In the center of this cardboard a hole was cut just the size of the calyx, and a slit was made from this hole to the circumference to allow the cardboard to be adjusted to the flower. The lower petals were flattened out upon this cardboard and the central petals were placed by means of tweezers, as fast as they appeared. All crumpled or imperfect petals were removed. In this manner were the show carnations of a century ago "dressed" for the occasion, the cardboard being allowed to remain permanently upon the flower. The ideal form of a carnation flower one hundred and fifty years ago was essentially the same as that demanded at present. It was "very thick and high in the middle," with flat and spreading borders.

In three directions, therefore, the ideal carnation of last century was like ours: it was fringeless, a "whole flower," and had a rounded center and flat limb. The first of these characters—the fringeless petals—had come to be a varietal character a hundred years ago, but the other features were still, at that time, largely the subjects of artificial dressing. These artificial forms and characters, however, so deeply impressed themselves upon growers that there arose an apparently unconscious effort to breed and select those forms which most nearly approached the artificial standard; so that what was once an arbitrary conception of the mind has now become a characteristic feature of the plant. This is incontrovertible evidence that a conventional standard may serve a useful purpose in the breeding of plants, and it lends new interest to Mr. Thorpe's model flower.

If the carnation has been modified so profoundly in so many directions, is it too much to demand that the size should be increased to four inches? If we examine this question historically, we find that the early ideals said nothing about absolute size of flower or length of flower stem. Characters other than bigness were sought in those days. Miller's points of a good carnation are these (1752):

"1. The stem of the flower should be strong, and able to support the weight of the flower without loping down.

"2. The petals (or leaves) of the flower should be long, broad and stiff, and pretty easy to expand, or (as the florists term 'em) should be free flowers.

"3. The middle pod of the flower should not advance too high above the other part of the flower.

"4. The colors should be bright, and equally marked all over the flower.

"5. The flower should be very full of leaves, so as to render it, when blown, very thick and high in the middle, and the outside perfectly round."

You will notice that nothing is said here about size; and although the ideal plant should have strong stems, nothing is said about long ones, for there was no cut-flower trade in those days. It was some time later than this that definite size began to be mentioned.

In 1807 Martyn added to Miller's model the requirement that "the stem should not only be strong, but straight, and not less than thirty or more than forty-five inches high." But even these figures referred to the total height of the plant and not to the flower stems; and it may be said, also, that these plants were not to be forced, as ours are. But Martyn further adds that "the flower should be at least three inches in diameter." This standard of size was copied by many writers in England and America for a period of thirty or forty years, and there is indication that it was often realized. In fact, Vilmorin says, recently, that "some carnations have flowers three and even four inches in diameter."* Here, then, is the diameter of John Thorpe's flower. But large flowers were known long ago. In 1613 Bessler † figured carnations three and one-half inches in diameter, grown in Switzerland. In 1788, Wm. Curtis ‡ figured a bizarre three and one-fourth inches

---

* "Certains de ces Œillets avaient des fleurs de 8 et meme de 10 centimetres de diametre."—Fleurs de Pleine Terre, 767.
† Hortus Eystettensis.
‡ Bot. Mag. t. 39.

across, and added that it was not the "most perfect flower of the kind, either in form or size." If horticultural literature were searched, we should no doubt be able to find several records of carnations as much as four inches in diameter, but the references I have made will show that such size is possible.

But Mr. Thorpe's flower must possess other virtues than mere diameter of bloom. The most important secondary consideration is the length of flower stem. The carnation grower, familiar with the long stems of recent varieties, will agree that Mr. Thorpe's eighteen-inch stem is among the possibilities: but you will the more readily agree if I show you the character of a good carnation plant of the early days. I have here a photograph of the best plant figured by Bessler in 1613. You will observe that the stems are short and very slender; and the same may be observed in the three and one-half inch carnations from the same author, of which I spoke a few moments ago. The lengthening of the stem is largely a modern character, and the progress in this direction augurs well for the future.

There are evidently two directions in which we are to look for the production of the four-inch flower. We may increase the mass of the flower, or we may increase the length of the outer petals. For myself, I look for better results from the latter method, for by that means we shall probably avoid some of the tendency towards bursting of the calyx, and we shall be likely to obtain a more shapely flower, and one which will not need Mr. Thorpe's pencil-stem for its support. The feature in Mr. Thorpe's flower least likely to be attained, it seems to me, is the two-inch calyx, for the history of the carnation shows that the calyx which we now possess has been secured with great difficulty. And I do not think that it is necessary that a four-inch flower should have a two-inch calyx. A much narrower calyx than this may answer every requirement. It seems to me that better results are to be expected in breeding for a shorter rather than a larger calyx, and this feature is admirably shown in some of Dorner's recent seedlings. And it may be worth while to enlarge the calyx by breeding for a greater number of sepals. I am particularly glad to have my opinion that we should breed for larger petals, reinforced by such an authority as Edwin Lonsdale, who is reported to have said before the second meeting of this Society that it is desirable to develop the length and breadth of the petals rather than their number.*

But you are waiting to ask me why it is that these large carnations of former years have disappeared, and in answering the question I come upon the most interesting feature in the history of the evolution of the garden varieties. The carnation has always been subject to the demands of fashion, and it has alternately risen and fallen in popular estimation. What has been gained in one period of popular favor has been lost in a succeeding period of neglect. The history of the carnation abounds in laments that the plant is less esteemed than it was a few years ago. Even so early as 1752, Miller declares that the large-flowered varieties had mostly disappeared from gardens, and at comparatively short intervals, until the present day, this experience has been repeated. In

---

*Am. Flor. vii. 302. (Nov. 12, 1891.)

1850, carnation cultivation received a new impetus in England from the formation of the Carnation Society. Yet interest appears to have fallen off quickly, for Nicholson writes in 1884[*] that "these charming flowers were, at one time, universal favorites, and the varieties were far more numerous than now. * * For some unaccountable reason, after 1850, they were seriously neglected, and many of the old varieties were entirely lost to cultivation; they are now, however, regaining popular favor." And now the American Carnation Society is bringing the flower into popular notice in this country, and we are already beginning to regain some of the features which have been lost or which have escaped notice. How far we shall regain the large carnations of other days, or how much we shall add to them, depends much upon how assiduously we breed the species, and how long we persist. If in two or three years this Society loses its ardor, we need not look for John Thorpe's flower.

But how shall we obtain the four-inch flower? It is well known that size is largely determined by the food supply, both by means of enriching the soil, and by disbudding by which we lessen the number of flowers to be fed. The inference, then, is plain: Select that variety which most nearly approaches the standard, and by high cultivation and very close pruning force it into great size. This requires extra labor and means less flowers to the square foot. In other words, it means an extra cost, but it is no doubt the only way in which we can hope to secure certain and uniform results, inasmuch as there is little in the history of the carnation to show that such enormous

---

[*] Dict. Gard. i. 269.

size can become a permanent varietal characteristic under common treatment. The four-inch flower can be produced, because it has already been recorded; whether the other characters of Mr. Thorpe's flower will appear will depend much upon the care which we give to forceful cultivation. This means increased cost, and the grower must decide whether it will be worth the while. It is by no means certain that a dollar flower would be profitable.

III.

Border Carnations.[1]

A year ago I urged upon this Society the importance of encouraging the cultivation of the outdoor or border types of carnations, which have been an important feature of European gardens for centuries. I then called attention to the fact that only one of the several leading families of carnations is commonly known in this country,— the winter or forcing types. It is a signal illustration of the fact that plants adapt themselves to our own ideals, that the great development of our greenhouse gardening in recent years has resulted in a wonderful evolution of forcing varieties and in a corresponding poverty of border varieties; so that while the border varieties are the original stock from which all other types of carnations have come and are still the most important family across the Atlantic, in this new country, with

---

[1] Read before the Third Annual Meeting of the American Carnation Society at Indianapolis, Indiana, February 21, 1894. Printed in the Report of the Society for 1894, pp. 47 to 49; also in Florist's Exchange, vi. 218.

distinct ideals, the children have far outnumbered and even obscured the parent.

These two great groups of carnations are opposed to each other in various attributes, but particularly, I think, in three:

The border varieties are low or rather dwarf and tufted; they produce the greater part of their bloom in a comparatively short space of time, and the individual flowers need not be very large.

The forcing type demands a very tall plant, and it loses its habit of standing erect, the production of flowers is distributed over several months, and the individual flowers must be large.

In short, in the one case, the ideal lies in the plant and its effect as a mass; in the other, the only ideal is the individual flower.

I have insisted upon this antithesis in these two types of carnations in order to correct what I believe to be a wrong tendency in the attempt to popularize outdoor or border carnations in this country,—the belief that the forcing varieties can be adapted to this purpose by propagating them in summer and fall, and thus changing their season of bloom. It is true that the forcing kinds will grow and flower well under this treatment, but they are not the type of plant which is adapted to the requirements of outdoor ornamentation. For this purpose we need a plant which requires no staking, which will give a definite and emphatic season of bloom by means of which strong effects can be produced, and the size of individual blooms can safely be sacrificed to productiveness and habit of plant. It is obviously unwise to attempt to impress forcing varieties into service in the open, and it would be a loss of time and effort to endeavor to breed adaptive varieties from them. We should begin, as a foundation, with the best existing border varieties, and endeavor to adapt them, by intelligent cultivation, to American conditions. And it is from these border carnations, too, that we are to expect the best varieties for pot culture.

If we fully accept the above propositions, I am sure that we shall find little difficulty in growing border carnations in America. Gardeners of foreign birth often dismiss the hardy carnations by saying that our climate is too hot and dry for them. While there may be much truth in this position, it is also true that many and perhaps all of the border varieties can be grown here with little trouble. Some persons have grown them with satisfaction for years, and visitors to the World's Fair in early August must have noticed a glowing bed of them upon the Wooded Island. In order to determine if these plants can be successfully grown with only ordinary care, such as any person can give, we secured seeds in the spring of 1892 of the following strains: Early Margaret, Self-colored, Early Dwarf, Mixed Vienna, Red Grenadine, Splendid Rose-leaved, Picotee and some others. These were sown in boxes in the greenhouse on the 8th of March, but they might just as well have been sown out-of-doors when the season opened. The plants were set in the field as the season advanced. A few of them bloomed in the fall. They were allowed to grow through the winter wholly unprotected, although they grew upon a bald hill-top, and the last winter was severe at Ithaca. They all wintered well, and they began to bloom about the middle of June, and gave an uninterrupted display of bright-colored and interesting forms until late in August. Although the lot was a mixed one, having come from seeds, all the varieties were interesting, particularly the single flowers. If any one strain was more pleasing than another, it was probably the Vienna, which bore single and semi-double little flowers of very pure and dainty colors, ranging from ivory white to rose-red. Some of the plants had been taken up in the fall and removed to the house for winter bloom, and here, too, the Vienna was very pleasing. These hardy carnations are perennial, although so good results cannot be expected from the subsequent seasons of bloom, and it is best to raise new plants annually. A collection of the best named border sorts from Europe would undoubtedly afford some excellent varieties for this country. At all events, they could be depended upon to give perfectly adaptive offspring in a course of a very few generations of plants.

XXIX.

EVOLUTION OF THE PETUNIA.[1]

The modern petunia is a strange compound of the two original species which were introduced to cultivation less than three-quarters of a century ago. The first petunia to be discovered was found by Commerson on the shores of the La Plata in South America, and from the dried specimens which he sent home the French botanist, Jussieu, constructed the genus Petunia, and named the plant *Petunia nyctaginiflora*, in allusion to the four-o'clock-like or nyctaginia-like flowers. The plant appears to have been introduced into cultivation in 1823. It was a plant of upright habit, thick, sticky leaves and stems, and very long-tubed white flowers, which exhale a strong perfume at nightfall. This plant, nearly or even wholly pure, is not infrequent in old gardens, and fair strains of it can be had in the market. I remember that it self-sowed year after year in the old garden in my younger days, and even now an occasional plant may be found in some undisturbed corner. This plant is fairly well represented in the drawing (p. 466). The stem leaves of this species are said to be sessile—or without stalks—but the lower leaves in strong specimens like that in the engraving are often conspicuously narrowed into long petioles. Possibly this is a

---

[1] American Gardening, xiv. 278 (May, 1893).

mark of hybridity, but I am rather inclined to think that the pure species has the lower leaves prominently stalked. This old-fashioned petunia is a coarse plant, and is now little known. It was not a difficult matter for the second species to dislodge it.

This second species of petunia first flowered in the

Petunia nyctaginiflora. Half size.

Glasgow Botanical Garden in July, 1831, from seeds sent the fall before from Buenos Ayres by Mr. Tweedie; and in 1831 an excellent colored plate was made of it, under the name of *Salpiglossis integri-*

folia.* This is a neater plant than the other, with a decumbent base, narrower leaves and small violet-purple flowers, which have a very broad or ventricose tube scarcely twice longer than the slender calyx-lobes. This neat little plant has been known under a variety of names, having been referred to Nierembergia by two or three botanists. Lindley was the first to refer it to the genus petunia, and called it *Petunia violacea*, the name which it still bears. It was also early known as *Petunia phœnicea*, but this name is forgotten by the present generation of gardeners. It became popular immediately upon its introduction. In August, 1833, Joseph Harrison wrote that it was "one of the most valuable acquisitions that has been made to our collections of late years."†

Petunia violacea early hybridized with the older white petunia, *P. nyctaginiflora*, and as early as 1837 a number of these hybrids—indistinguishable from the common garden forms of the present day—were illustrated in colors in the Botanical Magazine. Sir W. J. Hooker, who described these hybrids, declared that "it must be confessed that here, as in many other vegetable productions, the art and skill of the horticulturist has improved nature." "Cultivation alone," he wrote, "has, indeed, very much increased the size of the flowers and foliage of this plant [*P. violacea*], so that it can scarcely be recognized as belonging to the same species as the native specimens sent by Mr. Tweedie." This was about the time that *Phlox Drummondii* was becoming popular in England, having been sent there from Texas, in

* Bot. Mag. t. 3113.
† Floricultural Cabinet, i. 144.

1835, by Drummond. These two plants were novelties. "These varieties of petunia and the *Phlox Drummondii*," Hooker continues, "were decidedly

Petunia. Very near the true *P. violacea*. Nearly full size.

among the greatest ornaments of the greenhouse in the Glasgow Botanic Garden during the month of

May (1836), a season too early for them to come to perfection in the open border." These hybrid petunias were even described as a distinct species, *Nierembergia Atkinsiana;* and this fact is still remembered in some books in *Petunia violacea* var. *Atkinsiana.* Harrison gave a colored plate of these hybrid petunias in 1837 in his Floricultural Cabinet, but without description. He says, in an earlier issue of the magazine for that year, that the "impregnation of *P. violacea* and *P. nyctaginiflora* has produced several very charming varieties, such as pale pink with a dark center, sulphur with dark center, white with dark center, and others streaked and veined with dark. The size of the flowers of some of these hybrids has been much increased, some being three inches across." It would be interesting to know if *Petunia intermedia,* which was introduced about the same time as *P. violacea,* and which appears to be lost to cultivation, entered into any of these early hybrids. Here, then, our garden petunias started, as hybrids; but the most singular part of the history is that the true old *Petunia violacea* is lost to cultivation!

The pen drawing (p. 468) shows the closest approach to the true *P. violacea* which I have observed in several years' study of the petunia. Two or three plants came from a packet of mixed seed. But even this shows a flower-tube too long and a limb or border too wide; and perhaps the leaves are too broad. The nearest approach to the true species among the named varieties which I have seen, is the neat little white-tubed, purple-limbed Countess of Ellesmere. Vilmorin makes this variety a subdivision of *Petunia violacea,* and calls it Gloire de Segrez, or

Petunia violacea var. *oculata*. I imagine that even Lindley did not have the pure species when he de-

Cornell Petunia. Hybrid.

scribed *P. violacea* in 1833, for he says that it differs from *P. nyctaginiflora* "in nothing whatever except the inflated tube of its corolla and the size of its embryo." The common form of mixed garden petunia is a diffuse plant, low and slender, like the old *P. violacea*, but the tube is greatly lengthened and reduced in diameter by the influence of *P. nyctaginiflora*, and the colors sport into every combination of the purple and white of the original parents. These little petunias assume a fairly permanent light purple shade when left to themselves for a time, and they then reproduce themselves with tolerable accuracy; and they afford an admirable example of a hybrid which is abundantly fertile and which holds its own year after year.

Various curiously marked types of petunias have appeared and are lost. One of the early forms had a red body color, with grass-green borders. This was figured by Harrison in 1838 under the name of *Petunia marginata prasina*. These green-bordered strains appear now and then, and Mr. Carman, in using them in crossing experiments, obtained "rosettes of green leaves without the rudiments of calyx, corolla, stamens or pistils."* A faintly striped variety, called *Petunia vittata*, was also figured by Harrison at the same time. The stripes originated in the throat of the flower and ran outwards, as they do in most of the striped sorts of the present day; but in 1844 he announced a variety, *Petunia Nixenii*, in which the stripes originate at the border of the flower and proceed inwards.

The most singular development in these hybrid petunias is the appearing of the very broad-mouthed fringed flowers, with short, sessile and more or less

*Proc. Sixth Conv. Soc. Am. Flor. (1890).

trough-like leaves. These highly developed forms may not come true from seed, but among any batch of seedlings flowers of the most remarkable beauty of shape and intensity of color may be found, and in some of them the texture of the flower is almost as firm as that of a rose petal. A seedling from this Burpee's Defiance strain is shown in the pen drawing (page 470). I have called it the Cornell. The flower is of the most intense royal purple, with a velvety texture which reminds one of the richest silk plush. This velvet surface of petunia flowers is very marked in some of the recent forms, and I suppose that the character comes from *Petunia violacea*, which is said by Vilmorin to have had a velvety cast. This Cornell propagates true from cuttings. Some petunias do not. The double fringed petunia is the highest development of the plant; but by most persons the gorgeous single forms of the Defiance and other strains will be preferred.

Of late years the improvement of the petunia has been comparatively neglected, but it is worthy of greater attention from flower lovers. Yet, during 1892 twenty-six new varieties were introduced in this country. To scientists it has particular interest, because the contemporaneous forms have developed widely from the well-known original species within little more than half a century.

XXX.

THE AMELIORATION OF THE GARDEN TOMATO.

I.

The Origin of the Tomato from a Morphological Standpoint.[1]

THERE are two methods by which the cultivator can determine the origin of vegetables which have been long in cultivation. He can follow the history of the plant to its introduction into gardens and may then be able to identify it with a wild species, or he may reason from inference from the morphology and direction of variation of the plant in hand. The latter method may be illustrated by the tomato.

I will suppose, for my purpose, that no record exists as to the introduction of the tomato, or in regard to its characters, at any time before the present.

The fruit of the large tomato is seen at once to be extremely variable. This variability lies mostly in size, form, and number of cells. The number of cells, as seen in a cross-section of the fruit, may be taken as a measure of size and form. Fig. 1 (page 475) represents a cross-section in which ten partial cell divisions project from the walls of the fruit.

---

[1] American Naturalist, June, 1887, 573. This paper is a revision and extension of one which first appeared in the American Garden, viii. 116.

This is a section of a Trophy. If we were to examine a hundred specimens of this variety we should find no two alike in shape and number of cells, and, consequently, in shape and size of fruit. Moreover, we should find the variations to be very great. Now, fruits in wild nature possess a definite number of cells, and of definite shape. The Trophy, then, is a monster; it is unnatural. To find a fruit nearer the original wild type, we must find one more constant in its character. We examine critically every large-fruited sort, and we find each one monstrous in regard to form and number of cells, but some are less so than others. The least monstrous are always those with the fewest cells. The fewest-celled fruits in our garden, then, must be nearest the original type. Fig. 2 represents a sectional view of a normal Criterion. The cells are three, incomplete. The fruit, Fig. 3, is oblong, mostly regular. The smallest, most regular specimens of this variety are incompletely two-celled, Fig. 4. On the other hand, abnormal specimens of this variety are many-celled, as shown by the partially-lobed fruit in Fig. 5. Occasionally the tendency to monstrosity extends to the flowers, and a twin is the result, Fig. 6. The Criterion presents nearly the whole record of development within itself. Its regular, small, normal, two-celled fruits approach the original type. Figs. 5 and 6 attest an excessive influence of cultivation. All the fruits here represented grew upon the same plant. The Criterion must be compared with the pear-shaped and egg-shaped sorts. Fig. 7 represents one of the Pear tomatoes. It is almost uniformly two-celled, or, in its larger form, the King Humbert, it becomes

MORPHOLOGY OF THE TOMATO.

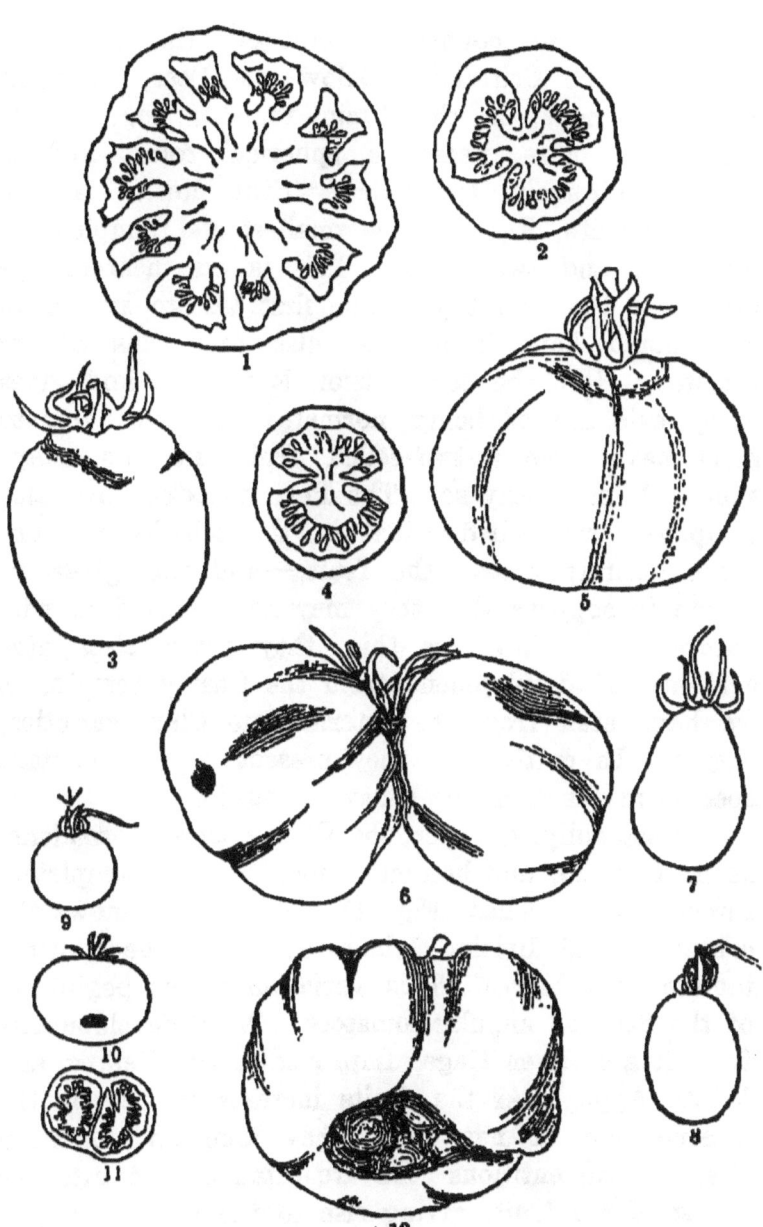

Structure of the fruit of the tomato.

three-celled, and connects completely the Pear tomato and the Criterion. Below the Pear, in point of development, is the Plum tomato, Fig. 8. It approaches more nearly a spherical form, and is almost uniformly two-celled. Still lower is the Cherry tomato, Fig. 9,—the smallest and simplest of them all, and two-celled. This is our nearest approach to the wild type. The first tomato known to man could have been little else than this Cherry tomato. Here the cell-division is perfect, and gives every evidence of being normal. The first tomato must have been a two-celled fruit, and its shape spherical, or nearly so. The Pear tomatoes are also completely two-celled,—that is, the cell-division extends entirely across the fruit,—and this gives us reason to suppose that they may have existed in wild nature also. Granting this, they nevertheless give evidence of development from the Cherry tomato, as we have seen from the intermediate Plum varieties, Fig. 8. In cultivation they present fewer constant specific marks than the Cherry sorts do.

Occasionally, however, the Cherry tomato broadens, as in Fig. 10, and becomes more or less completely three- or four-celled, Fig. 11. This figure shows the complete cell-division which separates the normal tomato into halves. This variation is the beginning of the flat and angular tomatoes. Small developments from it are Green Gage, Improved Large Yellow, and White Apple. As the fruits increase in size by the interposition of new cells, they take on abnormal shapes. Adventitious cells are often pushed into the center of the fruit, giving rise to the familiar structure represented on the top of Fig. 12. Often the rupture caused by these adventitious cells takes the form of an irregular line rather than a ring, as in the illustration. Most of the large varieties of tomatoes give unmistakable evidence of development from the Cherry tomato. So obvious is the direction and manner of variation in the tomato, that among seventy-five varieties grown in our gardens last year, there were none which refused to be classified, in relation to their origins and tendencies, as to whether the earliest variations had been directly from the Cherry tomato or through the Pear tomato. So clear does this manner of variation become, after a few weeks of study, that I am compelled to place more confidence in this method of ascertaining the origin of our cultivated tomatoes than in the records of old herbals.

We cannot so positively determine the color of the original tomato. Five-sixths or more of all our tomatoes are in various shades of red. From this fact we infer that red is the strongest and prevailing, hence the original, color.

The classification of cultivated tomatoes, upon morphological principles, may be represented as follows:

LYCOPERSICUM ESCULENTUM, Miller, Gard. Dict. (1768).

§ A. *Cerasiforme.*—Cherry tomatoes *(L. cerasiforme)* Dunal, Hist. Solan. 113). Fruit spherical, two-celled,—the original type.

§ B. *Pyriforme.*—Pear and Plum tomatoes *(L. pyriforme*, Dunal, l. c. 112). Fruit oblong or pyriform, two-celled, conspicuously pendent.

§§ A. *Vulgare.*—Plant weak, requiring support; leaves ordinary.

Group 1. Angular tomatoes. Fruit medium or below in size, mostly very flat, plane on top, more or less cornered, the lobes most conspicuous on the bottom and sides. (Figs. A and F, pp. 112, 116.) Developments directly from the Cherry tomato, through the type of Improved Large Yellow, etc. Tom Thumb may be taken as the type of the group.

Group 2. Apple-shaped tomatoes. Fruit normally more or less rounded on top, most of the irregularities being due to the interposition of adventitious cells in the centre of the fruit. (Fig. F, p. 116.) Direct developments from the Cherry tomato, through its rounder and more regular forms. The "ringed" or "lined" character of the apex of the fruit is oftenest seen in this group. The Paragon may be taken as a type of the group.

Group 3. Oblong tomatoes. Fruit usually as long or longer than broad, the sides very firm. Developments from the pear-shaped variation. Criterion, in its normal forms, may be considered the type.

§§ B. *Grandifolium.*—Habit the same as in subsection A; leaves very large; leaflets fewer (about two pairs), large (the blade three to four inches long and an inch and a half wide), entire, the lower side strongly decurrent on the petiolule. Leaves of very young plants are entire! Singular plants of recent development, represented by but few varieties, of which Mikado may be taken as the type. (Figs. C and D, p. 114.)

§§ C. *Validum.*—Stem very thick and stout, the plants nearly sustaining themselves, two to three feet high; leaves very dark green, short and dense, the leaflets wrinkled and more or less recurved. Odd plants, with the aspect of potatoes, represented by French Upright and the New Station. (Fig. E, p. 115.)

Another species, *Lycopersicum pimpinellifolium*, Dunal, Solan. Syn. 3, the Currant tomato, is cultivated as a curiosity.

II.

History of the Trophy Tomato.

The Trophy tomato marked one of the most important advances of American horticulture. A generation ago, the tomato was one of the plants of secondary importance in our vegetable gardening. The old traditions respecting its unwholesomeness had not yet disappeared, the masses had not learned to like it, and the great canning industry had not been developed. The fruits were mostly of small size and much corrugated or angled, so that they were prepared for culinary uses with more or less difficulty. About thirty years ago, however, there seemed to have arisen a general interest in the fruit, and many new varieties of peculiar merit appeared. Amongst the first great advances were the Apple and Tilden, both of them precursors and premonitors of the modern race of smooth and plane-leaved tomatoes. The latter was introduced by Henry Tilden, Davenport, Iowa, about 1865.

Into this awakening interest in tomato growing came the Trophy in 1870. It was brought out by Colonel George E. Waring, Jr., of Ogden Farm, Newport, Rhode Island, whose fame as a scientific farmer and an engineer was a guarantee of the excellence of the variety. The reader will be glad to know that this sponsor of the tomato is the same man who has written "Book of the Farm," "Draining for Profit and Draining for Health," "A Farmer's Vacation," "Elements of Agriculture" and various publications upon sanitation, and who is now the energetic Street Commissioner of New York City. It will also astound the reader to know that the Trophy was introduced for five dollars a packet of twenty seeds; and separate seeds were sold for twenty-five cents each. Even this price was not prohibitive, for Mr. Waring declared in 1871 that the seeds were "very widely distributed over the whole country, and the reports received from those who grew them make it evident that henceforth the Trophy will be the only tomato grown in America." Peter Henderson writes of its introduction that "the universal interest taken in this fruit and the confidence placed in Mr. Waring's statements led to the sale of seeds to a large amount to growers in all parts of the country."

The time was ripe for a tomato of a new type,— one which should be large and early and above all with a regular apple-like form, or "smooth." The Trophy came at the right time and it was the right thing. Its success was unbounded. It was almost the making of modern tomato culture. It marks an epoch in tomato growing in this country which has yet scarcely been reached in any other country. It is a great landmark in American vegetable growing; and whilst it is now superseded by several superior varieties, the time has forever gone when another tomato can fill, in history, the place of the Trophy.

The Trophy was judiciously introduced and advertised. In 1871, Colonel Waring offered one hundred dollars "for the heaviest tomato grown from seed purchased directly from me (California, Oregon, and the territories excepted)." In order that unsuccessful competitors might be rewarded for their efforts, he also offered to pay five dollars for every tomato weighing two and one-half pounds; two dollars and fifty cents for every one weighing two and one-fourth pounds; and one dollar for every one weighing two pounds. In 1872, the seeds of these prize tomatoes were offered as follows:

"CLASS 1.—The seed of the tomato to which the one hundred dollar prize was awarded.

"This Tomato was grown by T. J. Hand, Esq., of Sing Sing, New York, (whose entire crop I have secured for seed). It weighed twenty-one and seven-eighths ounces. Many others much larger than this were sent in for competition; but this was the largest *of perfect form*.

"CLASS 2.—The Seed of "Candidates for Premium," *of perfect form* and weighing sixteen ounces or over.

"This fruit was practically hardly at all inferior to the prize-taker.

"CLASS 3.—Early selected fruit of perfect form and ripeness, weighing twelve ounces or over.

"CLASS 4.—Early selected fruit of perfect form and ripeness, weighing eight to twelve ounces.

> "These two classes will be the Standard Seed for the use of amateurs and careful gardeners.

"CLASS 5.—General crop of 1871.

> "This seed was grown from the *very best* of the *selected early fruit* of 1870, and is exceptionable for general use.

"CLASS 6.—Crop of 1870—from selected fruit of that year, weighing eight ounces or over, and of perfect form and ripeness.

> "This seed was sold last season for twenty-five cents per packet, and is undoubtedly as good now as it was then. It has the advantage over the crop of 1871 of having been raised in a more favorable season.

"The prices of these seeds will be as follows:

	Size of Packet.		Price per Packet.	Per Doz.	Per 100.	Per 1,000.
Class 1.	10 seeds.		$1 00			
" 2.	20	"	50	$4 00	$25 00	
" 3.	100	"	(about) 35	3 00	17 50	$125 00
" 4.	100	"	" 25	2 50	12 50	100 00
" 5.	100	"	" 10	1 00	5 00	40 00
" 6.	100	"	" 15	1 50	7 50	50 00

"Not less than six sold at dozen price; fifty at hundred price; and five hundred at thousand price."

The reader now wants to know the origin of this epoch-making tomato. It was the result of a long series of selections. The history of it illustrates the great plasticity of the tomato, and how quickly it responds to good or bad or modified treatment; and this fact is still further illustrated by the passing out of the variety in recent years by variation into other forms. Colonel Waring's original account of the history and merits of the Trophy are here reproduced:

"The Trophy tomato was, until last year, unknown in the seed market. My attention was called to it by a friend, whose father, an amateur horticulturist, commenced, twenty-four years ago, the series of experiments by which he has brought it to its present superb condition. His first step was to cross the old crumpled, large red tomato (which was very heavy, but so rough as to be worthless) with the watery Early Smooth Red. This crossing was continued for several years, until he succeeded in putting the convoluted flesh of the one inside of the smooth skin of the other. In accomplishing this, he adhered as closely to a fixed line of action, and worked as scientifically for the attainment of a predetermined end, as did the originators of the famous Short-horn breed of cattle. The end once accomplished, he has, during nearly twenty years, constantly selected a very few specimens of the best and best-flavored of the earliest fruit for the next year's seed; and now, when properly treated, the seed will, with certainty, reproduce the perfect type—a tomato that has never yet been even remotely approached for excellence. Without wishing to detract from the fame of the popularly favorite tomatoes, all of which I have faithfully cultivated, I have no hesitation in saying that the Trophy is as far superior to the best of them as a herd of Short-horn cattle is superior to the chance stock of an average farm.

"It is *the very earliest*, and it is unquestionably the *largest*, the *smoothest*, the *most fleshy* (and consequently the heaviest), and *much the best flavored of all*; while from its long and careful cultivation (only the best specimens being allowed to breed), it has a *fixity of type* that has heretofore been unknown in its race — that is rarely seen in any vegetable which is reproduced by the seed."

"This tomato is the result of twenty-four years' crossing and careful selection. Every year it has been grown under the most favorable circumstances, and the very best of each year's crop has been saved for seed. By a continuation of the same treatment, it may, no doubt, be still further improved.

"On the other hand, it may be made by simple neglect to revert to the original type in one-half the time that has been required for its development. If planted in poor or cold land, and in exposed situations, it will rapidly deteriorate, and by the selection of the worst specimens of a crop so grown, for planting under similar circumstances the second year, a crop may be produced which will not show one of the good qualities of this really superb fruit.

"Treated tenderly, well warmed, well fed, well watered, and sheltered from cold winds (as all tomatoes should be), the Trophy will, I am confident, be found uniformly much the best ever grown; and if the earliest fine specimens are selected for seed, the best results may be permanently secured. This is all I claim for it, and this I promise; but I do not pretend that, under poor treatment year after year, it will continue to be any better than the common sorts."

The tomato is now one of the great fruits of American gardens and farms. It is a universal favorite, and is canned and otherwise preserved in enormous amounts. The varieties are numerous, but the types which were the ruling forms in 1870 are now practically unknown. The species has taken an enormous reach forward, and the mold into which the modern evolution has been run is that of the Trophy.

The above account of the Trophy tomato was submitted to Colonel Waring, early in 1896, and he makes the following additions to the history:

"The Trophy tomato is a product of crossing and careful cultivation by Dr. Hand, of Baltimore county, Md., who began his work in connection with it about 1850. He crossed the small smooth 'Love Apple,' which was filled with juice and seeds, with the compound, convoluted tomato of that period. This latter was practically four or five separate fruits packed together in one, with the skin running far into the convolutions. He succeeded in putting the solid mass of this compound growth into the smooth skin of the Love Apple, and then, by careful selection, year after year, increased its size and the solidity of its contents until it became a mass of flesh interspersed with small seed cells. The tomato so formed had reached a stable character long before it was brought to my notice by Dr. Hand's son, T. J. Hand, Esq., of New York, who was, at that time, associated with me in the American Jersey Cattle Club.

"Early in the seventies, Mr. Hand placed a small package of selected seeds in my hands. I sold them in packets of twenty seeds each for five dollars per package, and for several years after that for lower, but still very high, prices. I offered a premium each year of one hundred dollars for the largest and best tomato grown from this seed that should be sent me. If I remember rightly, the largest one that I received weighed two pounds and five ounces. It was as smooth as a pippin. I turned over the seed and good will of the enterprise to Peter Henderson & Sons, seed dealers of New York, and they made a specialty of it for several years.

"By this time the seeds have become thoroughly disseminated, and, while the Trophy tomato is, perhaps, no longer widely known under its own name, it was undoubtedly the progenitor of all of the fine fruit now grown." (Compare page 393).

III.

The Probable Course of Evolution of the Tomato.[1]

The Cherry tomato is undoubtedly the original tomato from which have come all the varieties of our garden, with the exception of the Currant, which represents a distinct species. One of the first variations from the primitive type is the augmentation of cells in the fruit, followed by a tendency to irregularity in shape. Later, the flowers become monstrous by the production of an abnormal number of parts. The probable development of the leading sorts is represented in the following diagram:

---

[1] Extract from Bulletin 31, Michigan Agricultural College, pp. 5-6. (1887).

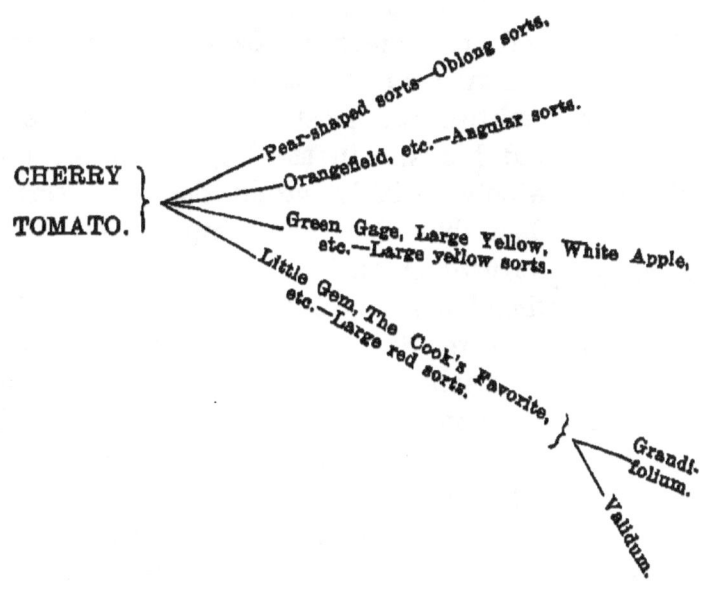

IV.

Direction of Contemporaneous Improvement of the Tomato.[1]

The particular points at present in demand in tomatoes are these: Regularity in shape, solidity, fair size, productiveness of plant.

The ideal tomato would probably conform closely to the following scale of points: Vigor of plant, 5; earliness, 10; color of fruit, 5; solidity of fruit, 20; shape of fruit, 20; size, 10; flavor, 5; cooking qualities, 5; productiveness, 20.

---

[1] Adapted from Bulletin 32, Cornell Experiment Station, 183. (October, 1891.)

Solidity of fruit cannot be accurately measured either by weight or keeping qualities.

Cooking qualities appear to be largely individual rather than varietal characteristics.

Keeping qualities are most marked in the small and unimproved kinds. In the large tomatoes these qualities are widely variably within the same variety, and it is evident that they are comparatively undeveloped as a varietal character.

It is questionable if much farther advance in total productiveness is to be gained by producing larger fruits, for the mammoth varieties may give actually less weight of crop than medium-sized kinds. Increase in the number of fruits of large varieties is usually associated with decrease of size. The greatest increase in productiveness must come probably from increase of vigor and stature of plant, with corresponding increase in fruitfulness. It is noticeable that the angular sorts, which were so largely cultivated a few years ago, are small in stature as compared with our best sorts. The ratio of productiveness to weight of plant was determined for one hundred and seventy-two varieties in 1887. The six best ratios occurred in Island Beauty (resembling Trophy), Hundred Day, King Humbert, Large Red, Yellow Cherry, and Mikado. It will be seen, therefore, that the Cherry tomatoes give as good, or better, ratios of productiveness as the best varieties, and that cultivation has not increased productiveness equally with size of fruit. But if the ratio of productiveness to weight of plant is not increased, increase in size or robustness of plant will give an actual increase of crop per acre, for it is found that the light and spreading plants of Cherry will cover as much ground as the stocky plants of Mikado or Ignotum, which weigh a half more.

With the augmentation in size of the tomato, there has been a loss in earliness. All my observation seems to indicate that if great gain is to be made in earliness, it must be in varieties which are closely allied to the Cherry type. It is probable, however, that it will be found to be more profitable, in the future, to obtain early tomatoes by means of forceful cultivation than by attempting to breed varieties of exceptionally early maturity.

GLOSSARY.

Explanations of certain words used in this book, with which the general reader may be unfamiliar.

ACCLIMATION. The spontaneous or natural process of becoming, or the state or condition of being, inured or accustomed to a climate at first injurious. (Page 321.)

ACCLIMATIZATION. Generally used in a more active sense than acclimation, as denoting the positive means or acts (as of man) in causing an organism to become inured to a climate. The distinctions between the two words are not generally carefully drawn, but acclimatization is preferred for scientific uses. (Page 321.)

ACQUIRED. In contemporary evolution writings, the word *acquired* is used to designate those characters or attributes which arise in the lifetime of the given individual as the result of external or environmental agencies, in distinction to those attributes which are supposed to be the result of antecedent or generation forces.

ADAPTIVE MODIFICATIONS are those which obviously fit or prepare an organism to live in given environments, and which are evidently produced or superinduced by those environments.

ANABOLISM. That kind of metabolism (or chemical change in the compounds of organic bodies) which results in greater or more progressive complexity of organization; ascending, synthetic, or constructive changes. Compare Catabolism. (Page 347.)

ANALOGOUS. Applied to organs or members which have similar function or uses. Compare Homologous.

BATHMISM. A term employed by Cope to designate the force or energy of growth, to which some of the variation of organisms is ascribed. "The vital forces are (nerve-force)

Neurism, (growth-force) Bathmism, and (thought-force) Phrenism."— *Cope*. (Pages 26, 61.)

BUD-VARIATION. Variation or modification from a type through the agency of buds, as distinguished from variation through seeds. (Page 89.)

CATABOLISM. That kind or type of chemical change in organic bodies which results in lesser or retrogressive complexity of organization; descending or destructive changes. Compare Anabolism. (Page 348.)

CATACLYSM. Used in evolution writings to designate the assumption (now mostly given up) that species have been extinguished or created because of sudden physical changes. Literally, the word means a *flood* or *deluge*.

CATAGENESIS. Retrogressive or degenerate evolution; modification by loss of attributes or by simplification of structure. First used by Cope in 1884. "Catagenesis is equivalent to degeneracy and has played an important part in organic evolution."— *Cope*. (Page 17.)

CENTROGENESIS. A term proposed by the present author to designate the rotate or peripheral type of form assumed by members of the plant creation. Compare Dipleurogenesis. (Pages 16, 17, 18.)

COMMUNAL INTENSITY. An expression proposed by the writer to designate the rapid spread of insects and fungi consequent upon the greater number and extent of host-plants. (Page 185.)

CULTURAL DEGENERACY. An expression proposed by the writer to designate the common assumption that plants become weakened in constitution or virility by cultivation. (Page 335.)

DEVELOPMENT. There is a tendency amongst evolution writers to restrict this word to the life-history, or ontogeny, of the individual, in distinction from evolution or the history of the race. See Evolution. "Development is that kind of growth which takes place in a multicellular organism when, by generation, a nucleated cell is set apart, protected, nourished, and by division and differentiation is elaborated into a complex organism, without regard to the growth of the parent—even at its expense, and when fully constructed set free to begin independent life for itself."—*H. S. Williams.*

DIFFERENTIATION. Unlikeness; applied technically to the origination and augmentation of special differences between organs which were once nearly or quite alike.

DIPLEUROGENESIS. A term proposed by the writer to designate the two-sided or dimeric type of form assumed by the members of the animal creation. Compare Centrogenesis. (Pages 16, 17, 18.)

DOMESTICATION. The adaptation or habituating of a plant or an animal to the care and breeding by man.

ECOLOGY. That science which treats of the inter-relationships of organisms. The study of the habits, activities and modes of life of animals and plants. Darwin drew most of his facts from ecology, rather than from embryology, geology, physiology, and the like. Written œcology in the lexicons, but usage now drops the digraph.

ENVIRONMENT. The conditions or circumstances in which a plant or animal lives; as the compound conditions of soil, altitude, climate, struggle for existence, and the like.

EVOLUTION. The doctrine which supposes that one form of life may give rise to another form of life; that each form was not necessarily specially created as we now see it, but that it may have been derived, through modification or variation, from some earlier form. Compare Development.

FACIES. The general aspect or appearance, as of a flora or a collection of plants. How a thing looks, as compared with related things.

FERAL. Wild. Existing in a state of nature, as distinguished from a state of cultivation or domestication.

FORTUITOUS. Accidental. In evolution discussions, used to designate variations or attributes which appear not to be due to any immediate or recognizable agencies, either external or internal. (Page 24.)

GAMETOPHYTE. The sexual generation or stage of the plant. (Pages 18, 67 note.)

GENERALIZED. Used to designate organisms which have attributes that fit them for a wide or common range of conditions. Such organisms are usually simple and fundamental in type. Compare Specialized.

GENESIS. Birth, origin; mode of generation.

GENETIC. Relationship in genealogy; affinity by direct descent from a common type.

GENUS (plural, *genera*). A group or kind comprising a greater or less number of closely related species; as *Quercus*, the oaks; *Rosa*, the roses.

GERM. The earliest generative stage of an organism. The germ-plasm is the assumed original generative substance contained in the body of the parent, from which new individuals arise.

GRAFT-HYBRID. A hybrid produced by the graftage of one species upon another. (Page 93.)

HABIT. In natural history writings, the word denotes the behavior and accustomed appearance of an organism. (Page 55.)

HABITAT. The particular locality or conditions in which an organism grows or lives. (Page 55.)

HOMOLOGOUS. Applied to organs or members which have similar structure, or similar structural relations to a given or fundamental type, or to those members which evidently have similar origins in the organism. Compare Analogous.

KATABOLISM. See Catabolism.

MEMBER. A distinct or integral external part of an animal or plant (as a leg, or a stamen), especially one which is not directly concerned in the maintenance of the vital functions. Compare Organ.

MONISM. The doctrine of oneness; the supposition that all phenomena and all forms of life are derived from the unfolding or evolution of one single principle and substance. (Page 164.)

NATURALIZATION. The establishment of a plant or animal in a country to which it is not native, especially when done through the aid, directly or indirectly, of man.

ŒCOLOGY. See Ecology.

ONTOGENETIC. Pertaining to the life-history or development of an individual organism.

GLOSSARY. 495

ONTOGENY. The life-history and modification of a single, or individual, organism. The history of an individual as distinguished from that of the race. See Phylogeny. Ontogeny is development.

ORGAN. A part of an organized body directly associated with the vital functions, as the heart and lungs of animals. Compare Member. In plants, many parts are at once both organs and members, as the leaves; when one is considering these parts from the standpoint of morphology, or form, it is proper to speak of them as members, but from the standpoint of function or use, they may be spoken of as organs.

ORGANISM. A body exhibiting life. An animal or a plant of any kind or description. Used as a generic term to designate all forms of life.

PANGENESIS. A mechanical theory of the means or vehicle of heredity, proposed by Darwin, which supposes that every part or unit of the corporeal structure is represented in the germ by minute gemmules thrown off from itself. (Page 60.)

PANMIXIA. A term used by Weismann to designate the agency of modification or evolution which results from the cessation of natural selection. "But as soon as an organ becomes useless, the continued selection of individuals in which it is best developed must cease, and a process which I have termed panmixia takes place."—*Weismann.* (Page 29.)

PHYLOGENETIC. Pertaining to the racial history or evolution of any tribe or group of organisms.

PHYLOGENY. The tribal or ancestral history and modification of organisms. The natural history of the race, as distinct from that of the individual. See Ontogeny. Phylogeny is the material of evolution.

PHYLUM (plural, *phyla*). A line of ascent. The stem or main direction of the evolution of any given tribe. A genealogy.

PHYTON, PHYTOMER. That portion of any plant which, when removed and treated as a cutting or a graft, may produce a new plant. It is usually a bud, node, and internode. (Pages 72, 84.)

PLASM, PLASMA. The assumed fundamental, undifferentiated

material or substance of organic beings. It is a general term. Specific applications of it are designated by *protoplasm*, *germ-plasm*, and the like.

PLASMODIAL. Pertaining to the unspecialized plasm of lowly or simple organisms.

PLUR-ANNUAL. A plant which is annual only because it is killed by the closing of the season (as by frost), in distinction to one (the true annual) which dies at the close of the season, or before, because of natural ripeness or maturity. (Pages 45, 295.)

PROTHALLUS. The initial, and often transitory, stage of ferns, and some other flowerless plants, which results from the germination of the spore, and upon or in which the sex-organs are borne.

PROTOPLASM. The fundamental organic material or plasma; the "physical basis of life." It is an exceedingly complex and unstable albuminoid compound, present in all organisms.

PSEUD-ANNUAL (that is, *false annual*). An herbaceous plant which carries itself over winter (or the inactive season) by means of bulbs, tubers, and the like. (Page 294.) First used in this book.

RETROGRESSIVE. Said of organisms or organs which show a loss or decadence of structure.

SOMA. The body, as distinguished from the germ or reproductive portion. (Page 62.)

SPECIALIZED. Adapted, by modification or evolution, to particular environments or functions. Such organisms are unique. Compare Generalized.

SPECIES (plural, *species*). A term used to classify animals and plants, by designating or grouping together all those forms or individuals which are very much alike in taxonomic marks. It is a term used for convenience's sake, and its application, therefore, varies with nearly every author. (Pages 110, 111, 121.)

SPOROPHYTE. The non-sexual or purely vegetative generation or stage of plants. (Pages 18, 67 note.)

SPORT. A marked variety or form which appears suddenly

and apparently without cause, and which is more or less abnormal to the type of the species. (Page 33.)

STIMULUS (plural, *stimuli*). In natural history writings, used to designate the particular active agents which produce definite changes in the organism; for example, abundant moisture may be a stimulus to variation in plants.

TAXONOMIC. Pertaining to taxonomy, or the science of classification. A character which has taxonomic value, is one which may be readily used in classifying the organism of which it is a part. (Page 134 note.)

UNSPECIALIZED. Generalized.

VARIATION. Modification or change in any organism. Departure from the normal type. Red flowers upon a normally white-flowered plant, unusually large leaves, or tall stature, are examples of variation.

VARIETAL DIFFERENCE. A formula proposed by the writer to express the fact that unlike constitutions—or varying abilities to withstand untoward circumstances—may be characteristic of horticultural varieties. (Page 336.)

VARIETY. A form or series of forms which, for purposes of classification, are of less weight or importance than species. The common conception of a variety is a form which it is difficult to distinguish from a species, and which grades or varies into it.

32 SUR.

INDEX.

Acclimatization . 307, 310, 320 et seq.*
Acquired character, heredity as
   an 23
— definitions of . . 56, 76, 77, 78, 79, 264
Adaptation—arguments 51
Africa, bean from 131
Agassiz's theory 268
Age and running out 384
— of type and variability 50
Alabama, corn from 298
Albumen 19
Alchemy 140
Alegatiere, and the carnation . . . 442
Algæ 18
— sex in 104
Aliquote 292, 293
Alleghany flora 270, 275
Allen, John, mentioned 126
— John Fisk, mentioned 432
Alliance, pomological 267
Alkaloids, origin of 52
Almond, nativity of 276
Almonds 206
Alsike clover 261, 263
Alternation of generations . 18, 67, 73
Altitudes and plants 294, 302
Amarantus retroflexus 259, 281
Ambrosia artemisæfolia 259
Amelioration and seed-production 229, 251
America, early fruits in 145
— native fruits in 210
American and Asian fruits 267
"American Gardener's Calendar,"
   quoted 204
American fruits for America,
   .... 311 et seq.
— horticulture, progress in 202

American Pomological Soc., cited . 420
— varieties 178
Ammonia, phosphate of 226
Amœba 21
"Amœnitates Academicæ," quoted . 139
Amphibious animals, number of . 139
Anabolic changes 347
Animals, breeding 160
— number of 139
— vs. plants 82
"Annals of Botany," quoted ... 25
Annuals, nature of 45, 265, 294
Anthemis nobilis 52
Apple, acclimatization 327, 332
— age of 137
— American vs. European . . 205, 314
— Australia 244
— borers 188
— climate and, 99, 174, 244, 282, 283, 337
— cosmopolitan types 370, 374
— Delaware Winter and Lawver . . 242
— dominant types 175
— Downing 205
— Esopus Spitzenburgh . . 383, 389, 390
— exportation of 215
— flower-bearing 351
— fungi 339
— geography of 279
— graftage 344
— Idaho 223
— Illinois .... 280, 282 et seq.
— insects 186, 338
— Knight's work 158
— longevity of 334
— maggot 188
— marketing in early days 215
— Minnesota 262
— Missouri 283

* *Et sequentes*: the pages which immediately follow.

INDEX.

Apple, McMahon 204
— nativity of 276
— New South Wales 281, 282
— New York 279, 282
— number of 366
— nurserymen's varieties 246
— old types 145
— Oregon 283
— Pennsylvania 282
— progress in 207, 208
— propagation 343
— pruning 345
— quality in . . . . 221 et seq.
— Quebec 282
— races in Russian 240
— running out . . . . . 335, 384 et seq.
— Russian in America . . 206, 317, 327
— Russian, quality in 230
— scab 181, 244, 390
— seedling and austere 361
— seed-production in 229, 253
— sports of 90
— sterile and fertile 353
— stocks 286
— synonyms in 244
— Tasmanian 215
— variation in Baldwin 238
— variation in branches 91
— Washington . . . . 281, 282 et seq.
— wild 210
— Wisconsin 280, 282
— World's Fair 279
— worms 180
Apprentice system 203
Apricot, nativity of 276
Araba, evolution amongst 108
"Arbres Fruitiers," considered . . 142
Arctic vegetation . . . . . . 271 et seq.
Army-worm 188
Aromatic qualities 170
Arrows, poison for 52
Artemisia vulgaris 52
Arum 52
Asexual variation 71
Asian plants . . . . 267 et seq.
Asparagus, Cooper on 153
Asters, in New Brunswick 301
Australia, apple in 244

Australia, rabbits in 200
Autochthonal hypothesis 268
Azaleas 285
Bacteria 15
Bailey, L. H., quoted 185, 393
— W. W., quoted 301
Bakewell, Robert, mentioned . . . 160
Banana, seed-production in . . 252, 253
— variation in 71, 99
Bananas, importation of 216
Banks' herbarium 127
— Sir Joseph, cited 155, 329
Bark louse 186
— study of 156
Barlow, mentioned 448
Barnes, Charles R., mentioned . 67
Barnet, cited 403, 406, 407, 408
Barrenness of orchards . . . 249, 252
Barron, quoted 229
Baskets, progress in 215
Bathmism 26, 61, 402
Bauhin, Casper, cited 401
Beal, W. J., quoted 330, 379, 380
Bean 137
— lima, a plur-annual 45
— Soy 132
Beans and latitude 299
— evolution of 129
— seed-production in 251
Beet, progress in 207
Begonia 102
— growth-force in 25
Begonias, rest in 48
Belgium, pears to 216
Benary, mentioned 450
Bengal, bean from 131
Bennett, mentioned 450
Bentham, mentioned 273
Berghaus, quoted 299
Berthollet, mentioned 142
Bessler, cited 458
Biberg, quoted 189
Biennials, nature of 45
Bigness is variation 170
Bilateral development 14
Birds, dispersion of 182
— insectivorous 214
— number of 139

INDEX.

	PAGE		PAGE
Bitypic genera	268, 270	Bulbs, evolution of	171
Bizarres	438 et seq.	— for propagation	101
Blackberries, American	312, 361	— formation of	294
— flower-bearing	352	Bumble bees and clover	182
— hybrid	177	Buysman, quoted	328
— quality in	221, 222, 226, 232, 233	Cabbage, Knight's work	158
		— progress in	207
Blackberry novelties	367	— seed-crops	36, 37
— Lawton	374	— worms	180
— running out	374, 389	Cactus, Russian	193
— progress in	210	California, acclimatization	326
— variation in	263	— almonds of	206
Black-knot	188, 426	— exodus to	216
Black-rot	181, 188	— exporting fruit	216
Blight-proof varieties	185, 372	— growing seeds in	46
Blooming and frost	303	Callas, rest in	48
Bloom-periods	289	Camels in Dakota	271
Book farming	217	Camerarius	67
Book-keeping of nature	139	Canada, apples in	175
"Book of Fruits," mentioned	147	— canned goods in	217
Borago officinalis	52	— thistle	197, 201
Bordeaux mixture, mentioned	144	— thistles, seed-bearing in	252
Border carnation	461	Canary Islands, tomatoes	216
Borer in trees	184, 185	Cane sugar, seed-bearing in	252
"Botanical Gazette," quoted	50	Canker-worm	186
"Botanical Magazine," quoted	467	Canning, history of	216
"Botanisk Tidsskrift," mentioned	121	Carboniferous time	44, 47
Bower, quoted	25	Carding carnations	455
Branches, variation in	86, 168, 249	Cardoons on pampas	200
Brambles, prickles of	51	Carex species	134, 135
Brazil, bean from	131	Caring for plants, progress in	211
Bread-fruit	99	Carman and petunia	471
Breaking	378	Carnation, border	461
— of seed-crops	169	— forcing of	213
Brandel, F., quoted	291	— progress in	438, et seq.
Bretschneider, cited	331	— running out	445
Brinton, mentioned	34	— sports in	92
"British apples," quoted	229	— sterile	351
British Isles, plants	270	— Thorpe's ideal	450
Brucine	52	Carpet-beetle	184
Bryophyllum, growth-force in	25	Carpinus Betulus	297, 331
— propagation	101	Carrière, mentioned	93, 98
Budd, quoted	327, 332	Caspian Sea, thistle at	193
Buds, detachable	100	Castor bean, duration of	295
Bud-variations	72, 82, 89, 169 239, 378	Catagenesis	17
Buffalo beetle	184	Catalogues	203
— berry	210	Catalpa	297, 331
Buffalos, dispersion of	272	Caterpillars in New England	492

	PAGE
Caterpillars, repellants	52
Cats and bumble bees	182
Cayuga Lake, peaches on	306
Centrogenesis	17
Ceratophyllums	100
Chamomile	52
Chaptal, mentioned	142
Chemical test of quality	234
Chenopodium album	259
Cherries, Knight's varieties	158
— quality in	221, 222, 226, 232
Cherry	137
Cherry, acclimatization	328, 333
— flower-bearing	352
— nativity of	276
— progress in	208
— struggle in	88
— unfixity of	368
Chestnut, nativity of	277
— progress in	210
China, exploration in	276
— Soy bean of	132
— tulip-tree in	275
Chrysanthemum	137
— progress in	205
— sports in	92
Chrysobothris femorata	184
Cions, choice of	249
Cion, heredity of	168
Circumlateralism	16
Citron, nativity of	277
Citrous fruits on Pacific coast	276
Citrus	50, 133
Clarke, quoted	289, 290
Climate, acclimatization	320, et seq.
— altitudes	294
— apples	99, 174, 244, 282, 283, 337
— cloudiness	307
— color and	227, 294
— Cooper on	153
— distribution and	274
— essays on	288, 293, 302
— flower seasons	289
— frost	295, 303
— grapes and frost	306
— latitude	295, 297, 298, 379
(See also, Latitude.)	
— onions	46

	PAGE
Climate, peaches and frost	303
— phonology	288 et seq.; 309
— plants, effects on	170, 379
— saccharine qualities	294
— seeds, effects on	46, 309
— shortening period of growth	45
— species and	312
— variability and	32, 44
— varieties and	209
— weather	302
— winter, effects of	47
Cloudiness and plant-growing	307
Clover and bumble bees	182
— alsike	261, 263
— in meadows	189
— red	259, 261 262
— to kill weeds	198
— white	259, 261
Codlin-moth	191
(See also Worm, under Apple.)	
Colorado, acclimatization	326
— potato beetle	184, 185, 187
Color and climate	227
Colors at high altitudes	294
Comfrey	52
Communal intensity	185
Communism and weeds	199
Composites	16, 49, 50
Congress and Russian thistle	193, 199
Conifers	19, 49
Connecticut, apple-maggot in	184
Constant, physiological	288
Continuity of germ-plasm	72, 103, 106
Convolvulus, propagating	70
Cooking fruits	220 et seq.
Cooper, Joseph, quoted	151
Cope, mentioned	14, 26, 31
— quoted	15, 17, 27, 28, 33, 61, 104, 492
Copernicus	108
Corbett, L. C., mentioned	297
Corispermum hyssopifolium	197
Corn	127-129, 137, 153
— acclimatization	329, 379
— and cow-peas	188
— and latitude	298
— and pumpkins	259
— selection in	(see Maize) 154

INDEX. 503

Cornell Exp. Sta., quoted . . 300, 306, 377, 393, 394, 396, 399, 487
Correlation in variation 219
Cotton, duration of 45, 295
Cow, loss of horn 77
Cow-peas and corn 188
Coxe, quoted 152, 314, 316, 319, 384, 386, 387, 419
Coxey's army 193
Crab apples 316, 318, 361
Crab-apples, insects and diseases . 183
— seed-production in 229, 253
Crab-grass 259
Cranberry, progress in 210
Crandall currant 210
Crates, progress in 215
Cretaceous time 44
Cross-breeding and in-breeding . . 382
Crossing 26, 32, 177, 218
— Cooper on 154
— Knight on . . . . 157 et seq.
Crozier, quoted . . . 294, 299, 325, 450
Cucumber, forcing of 213
Cucumber, seed-crops 36, 37
Cucurbits 50
Cultural degeneracy 335
Cultivation and seed-bearing . . . 251
— effect on insects and fungi, ... 183 et seq.
— man's and nature's 170
Curculios 180, 191
Currant, Crandall 210
— Dutch 374
Currants, flower-bearing 352
— nativity of 277
— quality in 221, 223, 226, 232
Currant-worms 180
Curtis, W., cited 457
Cut-leaved, varieties 92
Cuttings, propagation by 16, 69, 85, 94, 262
— experiments with 296
Daggett, Ezra 216
Daisies in meadows 196
Dakotas, camels, etc., in 271
— Russian thistle in 193
Dalmais and the carnation 442
Dana, quoted 44

Dandelions, variation in 258
Daniel, mentioned 86, 93
Darwin, mentioned . . . 26, 27, 28, 49, 56, 57, 62, 64, 76, 82, 86, 87, 92, 94, 108, 110, 140, 141, 148, 151, 158, 164, 166, 169, 189, 259, 274, 290, 349, 374, 382, 493, 495
Darwin, quoted 27, 30, 31, 57, 59, 60, 89, 91, 93, 94, 111, 166, 178, 323, 330, 333
Darwinism 57, 64, 80, 166
Date, nativity of 277
David, quoted 15
Dawson, Sir J. W., quoted 273
Death, origin of 44
Decadence 17
Decaisne 405
De Candolle, cited 270, 274, 297, 330, 331, 405, 412
— — Prodromus 113, 128, 139
Definite variations 23
Degenerate evolution 17
Department of Agriculture and Russian thistle, ... 195, 199
Desmids 15
Dessert fruits . . . . 230, et seq., 231
De Varigny, quoted . . . . 107, et seq.
Dewberry 210, 367, 374
Differences, origin of 19
Dipleurogenesis 17
Diplogenesis 104
Disbudding carnations 460
Diseases and varieties 371, 389
Distribution . . . 268 et seq.; 269, 296
Divergence of character 49, 189, 259, 290, 374
Division of labor . . . . 6_1
Docks in orchards 259
Dodd, Wm. 421
Dorner, F., cited 444, 450
Double flowers 351
Doubling of flowers 26
Douglas, Robt., quoted 326
Downer, J. S., mentioned 424
Downing, mentioned 147, 205
— quoted 218, 240, 314, 315, 316, 384, 385, 419, 422, 424
Downy-mildew . . 181, 188, 190, 313, 426

	PAGE		PAGE
Dressing carnations	455	Fertilizing land, effect of	169, 257
Droughts	308, 324, 332	Fig, nativity of	277
Drummond, and phlox	468	Filbert, nativity of	277
Duchesne	163, 401, 402, 404, 405, 406, 412, 415	First-class tree, what is a	247
Duhamel, cited	405, 412	Fishes, number of	139
Dunal, on tomatoes	112 et seq.; 477	Fixing of varieties	367
Earth-parasites	15	Fitz, quoted	324
Echinoderms	14	Flakes	438 et seq.
Ecology, study in	156	"Floricultural Cabinet," quoted	467, 469
Education, spread of	217	Flower seasons	289
Egg-cell	60	Flowering, latitude and	299
Egg-plant, duration of	45, 295	Flowers and insects	156
Egypt, plagues in	192	Fluvial period	272
Ehrhart, cited	405	Focke, cited	93
Eimer, quoted	26, 71, 83	Food supply and variations	27, 87, 98, 169, 189
Elæagnus, nativity of	277	— — Knight on	159
Elephant, in Dakota, etc.	271, 272	Forcing, and cloudiness	307
Elks, dispersion of	272	— evolution of	156
Endemic plants	282	— houses	213
Enemies, why increased	180	Forest, conflict in	40
England, exportation of apples to	215	— struggle in	189
— rhododendrons in	286	Forests and climate	308
English apples	227	— results of cutting off	181
— plants in America	45	Fortuitous variation	24
Entomogenous fungi	214	Fossil plants	48, 50
Environment, adaptation to	171, 174	Fourcroy, mentioned	142
Eocene-time	50	Fragaria ananassa	404, 409, 412
Equal, plants start	256	— calyculata	405, 415
Equilibrium in nature	181, 187, 190, 197, 214	— Chiloensis	403, 409 et seq.
Equisetums	49	— elatior	402
Ericaceous plants	285	— grandiflora	405, 408, 409
Estimates of animals and plants	139	— Grayana	413
Europe, fruits of	311 et seq.	— moschata	402
Evaporated fruits	217	— tincta	406, 412
Evolution, history of	162	— vesca	402
"Exhibitor's Manual," quoted	441	— Virginiana	402, 405, 409 et seq
Experimental evolution	107	France, vine in	323
Experiment stations, number of	218	French apple stocks	286
— station tests	171	— naturalists	163
Exposition, Columbian	278	Fresenius	235
Extinction of types	48, 49, 377	Fressant strawberry	400
Falkland Islands, plants of	269	Frezier, Capt.	403
Fashions in varieties	390	Frost and plants	295, 303 et seq.
Ferns	18, 47, 49	Fruits, American for America,	311 et seq.
— growth-force in	25	"Fruits and Fruit Trees," mentioned	147
Fertile flowers	351		
Fertilizers and variation	262, 264		

INDEX. 505

	PAGE		PAGE
Fruits, quality in	219	Grafts	16
— sex in	347	Grape	137
Fruit trees, seed-bearing of	252	— acclimatization of	323
Fungi, entomogenous	214	— Catawba	144
— repellants	53	— dominant types	175
— sexless	99, 102	— epoch in	406
— why increased	180 et seq.	— Isabella	374
Gallesio on citrus	163	— nativity of	772
Gametophyte	18, 73	— on Pacific slope	276
"Garden," quoted	320	— progress in	210
Gardener loves his plants	35	— running out	389
Gaudichaud	83, 84	— standard of	373, 431
Gay, quoted	404, 405	— wild, experiment on	235
Gemmules	60	Grapes, American	312, 313
"Genesis," quoted	44	— and frost	306
Geocentric doctrine	108	— hybrid	177
Geography, horticultural	278	— from Maine, etc.	298
"Geological Biology," quoted	21, 48	— quality in	221, 223,
Georgia, peaches in	323		226, 227, 230, 232, 235
Geraniums, rest in	48	— evolution of	431 et seq.
Gerarde and the carnation	453, 454	Grasshoppers	188
Germination affected by latitude	298	Gray, Asa, mentioned	49, 127, 135,
Germ-plasm	62, 65 et seq.;		267, 270, 274, 377, 380, 413, 427
	101, 103, 106, 262, 265	— — quoted	268, 272, 273, 332, 382
Giants	360	Greeks, evolution amongst	108, 163
Gift-package	215	Greenhouse, effect on plants	213
Ginkgo	327	— evolution of	212
— fossil	48, 49	Greenland, flora of	273
— in geologic time	97	Grenadins	439
— leaves	95	Growth-force	25, 30, 32, 53, 61, 351
— nativity of	277	Gypsy moth	191
Glacial epoch	271	Habit	55
Glasgow Botanical Garden	466, 468	Habitat	55
Glass houses, evolution of	212	Haeckel, quoted	111, 121, 165
Glycine hispida	132	"Half-Century of Conflict," quoted	40
— Soja	132	Hairs, origin of	52
Goethe, mentioned	220	Hand, T. J., and Trophy tomato	481, 485
Gooseberries, American	312	Handling, progress in	215
— quality in	221, 223, 226	Hardiness	324
— successful cultivation of	286	Harris, quoted	184
Gooseberry, Houghton	374	Harrison, J., and petunia	467 et seq.
— nativity of	277	Harvey, James	423
— progress in	210	Heer, mentioned	274
Gourds, acclimatization	331	Henderson, P., and Trophy tomato,	
Government and weeds	193 et seq.		480, 486
Graft-hybrids	93	Henslow, quoted	70, 74
Grafting	86, 93	Heredity an acquired force	22
— root, origin of	156	Heredity and evolution	59, 62

33 SUR.

506　　　　　　　INDEX.

	PAGE
Hickories, propagation	85
Himalayan plants	270, 272, 275
Hoffman, cited	78
Hofmeister, cited	67
Holm, cited	96
Homocentric doctrine	108
Hooker, Sir W. J., and petunia	467, 468
Horse-radish	99
— seed-bearing in	252
Horses in Dakota, etc.	271, 272
Horticultural geography	278
Horticulture, progress in	202
Horticulturist, evolution of	217
Host-plants	183 et seq.
Horse-leeks	101
Hovey, cited	147, 407, 408
Hovenia, nativity of	277
Humidity of air	308
Hybridization	177, 322
Hybrid petunias	467 et seq.
Hybrids	94
Ice age	271
Iceland, plants of	269
Idaho apples	283
Illinois, acclimatization	326
— apples in	370
— apple-maggot in	184
— at World's Fair	280, 282 et seq.
Immortality of one-celled organisms	61
Immune varieties	371, 389
Impotent varieties	350
In-breeding and cross-breeding	382
Indiana maize	330
— weeds in	192
Indian corn (see Corn)	127–129, 153
"Insects Injurious to Fruits," quoted	184
Insects and flowers	158
— and varieties	371, 389
— number of	139
— why increased	180 et seq.
Introducing varieties	369
Inventory of nature	139
Ireland, plants of	270
Irrigation, effect of	169
Isotherms	308
Jackson, mentioned	421

	PAGE
Jamaica, Flora of, on beans	131
Japan, corn of	129
— explorations in	270
— fruits of	211, 287 et seq.
— Soy bean of	132
Javanese arrow-poison	52
Jew against Jew	39
Josselyn, John, quoted	192
Juglans regia	52
Jujube, nativity of	277
Juneberry	210
June grass in lawns	196
Juniperus Virginiana	326
Jussieu and petunia	465
Kaki, nativity of	277
Kalm, cited	330
Kansas maize	330
Katabolic changes	348
Kensett, Thomas	216
Kew herbarium, mentioned	120, 121, 126
King, quoted	43
Knight, Thomas A., mentioned	138, 147, 155 et seq.; 164, 252, 406
— — — acclimatization	324
Kœlreuter, mentioned	157
Kumquat, nativity of	277
Lacene, mentioned	442
Lady-bug, Australian	215
Lake-cress	101
Lake Michigan, illustration near	197
Lake Superior, plants of	275
Lamarckism	27, 31, 55
Lamarck, hypothesis of	55, 56, 59, 76. 82, 166
Lamarck, mentioned	140
Lange on tomato	121, 127
Latitude and plants	295 et seq.; 320 et seq.; 379
— beans	299
— corn	298, 379
— grapes	298
— melons	299
— plums	299
— poplars	297
— potatoes	298
Lavoisier, mentioned	142
Lawns, weeds in	196
Laws and weeds	201

INDEX. 507

	PAGE
Leaf-blights	181, 187
Leafing, latitude and	300
Leaves, compounding	26
— germ-plasm in	66, 70
Lemon, nativity of	277
Lemons	133, 137
Lemoine, mentioned	450
Lettuce, effect of thinning	39
— progress in	207
Leucanthemum vulgare	301
Life-events	288
Life-zones	295
Lily propagation	101
Lima bean (see Bean, Lima).	
Lime	133
— nativity of	277
— propagating	70
Lindley and the petunia	467 et seq.
— Geo., cited	407
Linka, missing	176
Linnæus, definition of species	110
— mentioned	33
— on beans	129
Linnæus' work	139
Linsser, quoted	292, 293, 301
Lintner, quoted	186, 187
Lions, dispersion of	272
Liriodendrons, fossil	48
Liriodendron leaves	96
— Tulipifera	297, 331
Lippincott, quoted	330
Litchi, nativity of	277
Locusts	188
Loiseleur-Deslongchamps, quoted,	144, 147, 148
London, tomatoes in	216
Longevity of apple trees	334
— of fruit trees	231
— of species	45
— variations in	45
Lonsdale, cited	443, 459
Loquat, nativity of	277
Louis XIII., strawberries in reign of	402
Lords and ladies	52
Louisiana, grapes from	298
Lucerne, to kill weeds	198
Lycopersicum agrimoniæfolium,	123, 127

	PAGE
Lycopersicum cerasiforme,	113, 126, 477
— esculentum	113, 117, 126, 447
— Humboldtii	122, 127, 128
— Peruvianum	123, 127, 128
— pimpinellifolium,	118, 119, 127, 128, 397, 398, 479
— puberulum	125, 127
— pyriforme	113, 117, 125, 126, 447
— racemiforme	121, 127
— racemigerum	127
Lyon, T. T., cited	220, 315–317, 328
Macfadyen on beans	131
Macfarlane, mentioned	93
Machinery, progress in	212
Madeira, vine in	323
"Magazine of Horticulture," mentioned	147
Magellan, Straits of	269
Magic	140
Magnolias, distribution of	275
Magnolia grandiflora var.	327
Maids and the clover crop	182
Maine forests	40
— grapes from	298
— poplars from	297
Maize (see Corn).	50, 127, 129, 153
Mallow	261
Malmaison carnations	439
Malva rotundifolia	261
Mammals, repellants	52
Mandarin, analyses of	236
— nativity of	277
Manning, Robert, mentioned	146, 147
Map, fruit	370
Marguerite carnations	439
Market fruits	220 et seq.; 231
Marsh, quoted	333
Martens, Von, on beans	129
Martyn, quoted	120, 128, 457
Maryland, peach-trees in	323
— plums from	300
Mass. Agric. College, quoted	234
Massachusetts, apple-maggot, etc., in	184
— gypsy moth in	191
— Hort. Soc., quoted	107, 432, 453
Massee, quoted	51
Mastodon in Dakota, etc.	271, 272
Matlack, Colonel, mentioned	154

INDEX.

	PAGE
Maximowicz, on Soy bean	182
May-apple	101
Meadow, struggle in	189, 196
Medicago lupulina	259
Medick	259, 261
Medlar, nativity of	276
Mell, P. H., Jr., cited	325
Melon	137
Melons, acclimatization	331
— and latitude	299
Melon, selection in	154
Merriam, quoted	296
Mesozoic time	97
Meteorological bureaus	304
Mexico, corn of	128
Mice and clover seed	182
Michigan Hort. Soc., quoted	220
— maize	330
Mildew (see Downy-mildew).	
Miller, Phillip, cited	120, 127, 128, 404, 410, 455, 456, 457, 459
"Miller's Dictionary," quoted	120, 455
Miner, mentioned	422
Minnesota, apples of	282
— fruits in	309
Missing links	176
Mississippi Valley, apple-maggot in,	183
Missouri apples	283
Mixed planting	355
Mixing of tomatoes	396
McMahon, quoted	204, 205, 207, 208, 212, 384, 385, 419, 421
"Modification of Plants by Climate," quoted	294, 299, 325
Mollusks	14
Monism	164
Monnier, cited	332
Monotypic genera	268, 270
Monroe, James, mentioned	216
Moore's grapes	435
Morphology of tomato	473
Mosses	18
— propagation of	72
Mt. Katahdin	275
— Marcy, plants on	275
Mulberries	206, 210
Multifarious variations	23
Munson, T. V., cited	435

	PAGE
Musa, fossil	50
Mutilations	77
Mycetozoa	14
Myrica, nativity of	277
Myxomycetes	14
Nasturtium lacustre	101
Native fruits	210
Nativity of fruits	276
Naturalists, the French	163
Natural selection	30
— — adequacy of	178
— — definition of	57
Naudin, cited	331
Nectarine, Knight's varieties	158
— origin of	90, 91
Nettles	52
Neo-Darwinism	55, 61, 64, 65, 167, 256, 285
Neo-Lamarckism	55, 64, 65, 79, 80
Neurism	492
New Brunswick flora	301
New England, apple-maggot in	183
— apples in	175
— plagues in	192
"New England's Rarities," quoted	192
New Jersey, peach trees in	323
New South Wales at World's Fair,	281, 282 et seq.
New York, apple-maggot in	184
— — Canada thistle in	201
— —: corn from	298
— —: grapes and frost	307
— — — from	298
— — peach trees in	323
— — poplars from	297
— —: weeds in	192
— — western, fruit-growing in	246
— — at World's Fair	279, 282 et seq.
Nicholson, quoted	460
Nierembergia Atkinsiana	469
Nile, example in acclimatization	324
Noah, mentioned	359
North Dakota, Russian thistle in	198
Northwards, taking plants	295
Novelties, numbers of	366
— value of	356, 364
Numbers of animals and plants	139
Nurseries, European	285

INDEX.

	PAGE
Nursery business, impressions of	245
Oaks, borer in	184
Oak, propagating	70, 85
Offshoots, office of	252
Ohio maize	330
Olive	276
— nativity of	277
Oneness	164
Onion, top	99
Onions, effect of climate on	46, 47
— seed-bearing in	252
Orange	137
— nativity of	277
— tribe, development of	164
— tree scale	215
Oranges, analyses of	236
Orchard, insects in	183, 186
Orchards, weeds in	259
— why barren	249
Orchids, increase of	211
Oregon, acclimatization	326
— apples	283
"Origin of Floral Structures," quo.	74
Origin of our flora	274
"Origin of Species," mentioned	111
Ornamentals, hybrid	177
"Our Heredity from God," quoted	22
Ovum	60
Pacific coast, almonds of	206
— — vedalia on	215
— slope, apples on	175
— — pomology of	275
Packages, progress in	215
Pammel, quoted	294
Pampas, cardoons on	200
Pangenesis	60, 64, 67
Panicum sanguinale	259
Panmixia	29
Parallelism in variation	220
Parasites	191, 214
Parkman, Francis, quoted	40
Parsons, quoted	236
Paul, mentioned	450
Pea, Cooper on	153
— Knight's work	158
— seed-crop	37
— variation in	378
Peas, experiments on	264

	PAGE
Peas, seed-production in	251
— viney	169
Peach	137
— borer in	184
— dominant types	175, 176
— growing and climate	303
— Hill's Chili, etc.	240, 241
— nativity of	276
— running out	389
— yellows	188, 427
Peaches, quality in	221, 223, 226, 232
— in early days	215
Peach-trees, acclimatization	323, 325
Pear, acclimatization	328, 333
— American vs. European	316
— Bergamot	145
— blight	188
— borer in	184
— dominant types	175
— Knight's work	158
— nativity of	276
— progress in	207
— psylla	191
— running out	385, 386, 389, 390
— unfixity of	369
— Virgalieu	144
Pears, blight-proof	372
— exporting	216
— hybrid	177
— quality in	221, 224, 226, 227, 230, 232
— sterile and fertile	353
— Van Mons'	146
Pecan, progress in	210
Pelargoniums, from cuttings	447
Pennock, quoted	451
Pennsylvania at World's Fair	282
Pepper, red (see Red Pepper).	
Perennials at the north	295
— nature of	45
Perry, Commodore	270
Persimmon, Japanese	211
— nativity of	277
Petunia, evolution of	465
— experiment with	262
— intermedia	469
— Nixenii	471
— marginata	471
— nyctaginiflora	465 et seq.

	PAGE		PAGE
Petunia, phœnicea	467	Plum, Knight's varieties	158
— violacea	467 et seq.	— knot	186, 426
— vittata	471	— nativity of	276
Petunias, from cuttings	447	— progress in	208
Phaseolus inamœnus	131	— running out	385
— lunatus	131	— synonyms in	243
— multiflorus	130	— Wild Goose	374
— nanus	129	Plums, battle of	418
— vulgaris	129	— native	210, 361
Phenology	288	— and latitude	299
Philistine against Jew	39	— insects and diseases	183, 426
Phillippi, on tomato	127	— quality in	221, 224, 226, 232
Philosophy, the old	162	Plur-annuals	45, 295
Phlox Drummondii	467, 468	Plowshares and pruning-hooks	215
Phosphate of ammonia	262	Poisons, origin of	52
— potash	262	Poiteau, quoted	142
— soda	262	Pollen, office of	334 et seq.
Phrenism	492	Pomegranate, nativity of	277
Phryma Leptostachya	270, 273	Pomological alliance	267
Phylloxera	190, 313, 426	Poplar, Lombardy	297
Phytomer	72	Populus alba	297, 331
Phyton	84, 101	— dilatata	327
Physiological constant	288	Potamogetons	100, 252
— unit	296	Potash, fertilizing with	262
Picotees	438 et seq.	— phosphate of	262
Pigeon-grass	259	— ratio to sugar	234
Pigweed	196, 259, 261	— sulphate of	262
Pineapple	99	Potato beetle	180, 184, 185, 187, 188
Pines by cuttings	85	— Cooper on	153
Pink (see Carnation).		— duration of	45
Pinus ponderosa	326	— Knight's work	158
Pinus sylvestris	327	— latitude and	297
Pistachio, nativity of	277	— mixing in the hill	90
Plains and prairie floras	318	— running out	380
Plane-tree, evolution of	97	— seed-bearing in	252, 351
Plant-breeding, mystery of	161	— variation of	28
"Plant-Breeding," quoted	21, 153, 396	Potatoes, rotting	181
"Plantes Potageres," mentioned	127	Powell, E. P., quoted	22
Plant-lice	183	Prairie and plains floras	318
"Plant World," quoted	51	Predaceans	214
Plum	137	Preserving, progress in	215
— acclimatization	333	"Press, Phila.," quoted	396
— American vs. European	317	Prickles, origin of	25, 52
— borer in	184	Prince, quoted	407
— Cooper	152	Progress in horticulture	202
— Green Gage	145, 176	Promising varieties, why fail	364
— impotent	352	Propagation and longevity	343
— Japanese	211, 275, 314, 427	— of nursery trees	249

INDEX. 511

	PAGE
Prothallus	19
Prune	276
Pruning	87, 88, 169, 257
— and longevity	345
— hooks and plowshares	215
Prunus Americana	300, 425
— angustifolia	300
— cerasifera	300, 428
— domestica	428
— fossil	50
— hortulana	300
— Simonii	276, 300
— spinosa	52
— triflora	300
— umbellata	428
Pseud-annual	294
Pseudotsuga Douglasii	326
Psychological states	23
Paylla	191
Pumpkin	137
Pumpkins and corn	259
Purslane	259
Pyrenees, plants of	269
Pyrus coronaria	318
— fossil	50
— Ioensis	318
— Malus	253
Quack-grass, seed-bearing in	252
Quadrupeds, number of	139
Quality, correlatives of	219
Quebec apples	282
Quiescence of plants	44, 47
Quince, nativity of	277
Rabbits in Australia	200
Races in apples	240
Ragweed	259, 260, 261, 262
Raisin industry	276
Ranunculus acris	301
Raspberries, American	312, 361
— analyses of	235
— flower-bearing	352
— hybrid	177
— quality in	221, 225, 226
— successful cultivation of	286
Raspberry, nativity of	277
— novelties	367
— progress in	210
— propagation	101

	PAGE
Ray, John, cited	33, 110, 453
Red pepper, duration of	45, 295, 331
Red-root	259, 260, 261
Religion and evolution	163
Remnants	98
Rest in plants	48, 170
Retrogressive evolution	17
Reversions	96, 98
Rhine, example in acclimatization	324
Rhinoceros, in Dakota, etc.	271, 272
Rhizomes	294
Rhododendrons	285
Rice, acclimatization	331
Ricketts, J. H., mentioned	433
Riley, quoted	139
Rivers, mentioned	94
Robin, mentioned	492
Rogers, E. S., mentioned	433
Rommel, Jacob	434
Root, evolution of	41
Root-grafting, origin of	156
Roots, Knight on	155
Rose-chafer	188
Rose-growing	286
Roses, Asa Gray on	134–137
— evolution in	133
— fossil	50
— prickles of	51
— sports in	92, 93, 94
— sterile	351
Rotation, to kill weeds, etc.	198, 214
Rowan, Martin, quoted	438
Running out	145, 157, 161, 335, 356, 376
et seq.; 382 et seq.; 392 et seq.; 445
Russia, hardy plants from	327
Russian cactus	193
— fruits	517
— thistle	193 et seq.
Saccharine qualities	294, 309
Sacha, quoted	72
St. Hilaire, mentioned	220
Salisburia (see Ginkgo).	
Salix Babylonica	327
Salpiglossis integrifolia	466
Salsola Kali var. Tragus	193, 199
Salter, quoted	91
San Francisco, Tasmanian apples in	215
Sargent, Professor, cited	326

INDEX.

Sassafrasses, fossil 48
Sassafras leaves 94
Saunders, quoted 184, 327
Scale, orange-tree 215
Scandinavian plants 269
Scotch plants 269
Scotland, exportation of apples to . 215
Schizocodon 275
Schmidt and the carnation 442
Schools, number of 218
Schouw, quoted 268, 269, 274
Schübeler, quoted 299, 328
"Science," quoted 67
Seasons, effects of 170
Sedges . . . . 134 note
Seed-bags, battle in 36
— bearing and cultivation 251
— change of 151, 153, 177
— crops and climate 309
— crops, growing 169
— production and quality . . . 228, 251
— stock 46
Selection, importance of . . . 160, 178
Sequoias, fossil 48
Syringe, quoted 412
Setaria glauca 259
Sex in fruits 347
— significance of 26, 63, 166,
168, 238, 348
— terminology of 67
Sexual mixing 26
— reproduction, meaning of 63
Shaw, quoted 198
Shepherd's Purse 259, 261, 262
Shortia 275
Siberia, elephants in 272
Single specimens, plants as 189
Sisyphus 199
Size and quality 227
Smith, M. R., quoted 444
Snowballs, sterile 351
Societies, number of 218
Soil and variation 378
— effect on plants 169, 171
Soils, influence of 257
"Soil," quoted 43
Soiling crops, to kill weeds . . . 198
Solanum Lycopersicum 128

Solanum racemiflorum 127
Solanums, insect of 184
Soldier, loss of eye 77
Solidagos, in New Brunswick . . . 301
Solomon, quoted 201
Soma-plasm . . . . 62, 65 et seq.
Sonchus oleraceus 261
South Carolina, corn from 298
"Southern Apple and Peach Culturist," quoted 324
Sow-thistle 261, 263
Soy bean 132
Spain, plants of 270
Special creation 19, 163
Species, character of 32
— definitions of . . 33, 110, 111, 121, 129
— dogma 108
— making 134
Spencer, Herbert, quoted 30, 31
Spines, origin of 51
Spiræa callosa 327
Spirifers 49
Spitzbergen 274
Sporophyte 15, 18, 73
Sports 33, 72
Spraying 192, 213
Sprengel, mentioned 157
Spruces by cuttings 85
Squash, Cooper on 153
Squashes, acclimatization 331
Squirt-guns 215
"State Register," quoted 332
Stem, evolution of 43
Sterile flowers 351
Stick-tights in orchards 259
Stock-seed 46
Stone, quoted 234, 235
Storage of food 294
Strawberries, analyses of 285
— quality in . . . 221, 225, 226, 232, 233
— sex in 351, 353
— successful cultivation of . . . 286
— testing 173
Strawberry 100, 101
— dominant types 175
— Duchesne on 163
— Knight's work 158
— nativity of 277

INDEX. 513

	PAGE		PAGE
Strawberry, novelties	367	Tomatoes, forcing	213
— progress in	210	— forms of	112–127
— vagaries of	369	— morphology of	473 et seq.
— whence came	408	— not fixed	367
— Wilson	175, 374	— relation to disease	372
Strasburger	70	— running out	379, 392 et seq.
Struggle amongst branches	87	— scale of points	467
— for existence	88, 131, 189, 214	— seed-crops	36, 37
— induces variation	258	— seed-production in	229, 254
Strychnine	52	— sport	95
Strychnos	52	— Trophy	174, 379, 393, 474, 479
Sturtevant on maize	128	— synonyms in	241
— on seed-production	228	Top-working trees	250
Sugar cane, seed-bearing in	252	Torrey Club Bulletin, quoted	21
Sugar; ratio to potash	234	Tree, a first-class	247
Surinam, Strawberry from	404	— ferns	49
Survival of the fittest	30, 57, 166	Trilobites	49
— of the Unlike	30	Tubers, evolution of	171
Sweet-corn, canning	216	— office of	252
Sweet-potato	137, 252	Tulip, propagating	70
Symphytum officinale	52	— tree	96, 97, 297
Synchronisms of frosts and bloom,	303 et seq.	— tree in China	275
Synonyms, history of	237	Turner and the carnation	442
Tasmania, apples from	215	Tweedie and petunia	466, 467
Taste, origin of	52	Unit, physiological	296
Temperature and plants	291	United States, bananas in	216
Tendrils, study of	156	— — canned goods in	217
Tennessee, acclimatization	326	— — insects in	184, 187, 192
Tenn. Exp. Station, quoted	235	Unlike, Survival of	30
Tent caterpillars	191	Unlikenesses, origin of	19
Terminology of sex	67	Unripe fruits, seedlings from	150
Terrace epoch	272	Urtica species	52
Testing varieties	171, 371	Van Mons	138, 141 et seq.; 155
Thinning, effect of	39, 169	Variation and varieties	27, 35, 159, 168
Thistle, Russian	193 et seq.	— acclimatization and	320 et seq.
Thomson, Sir William	34	— affected by greenhouses	213
Thorn-apples	183	— after birth	256
Thorpe, John, cited	450 et seq.	— age of type	48, 50
Tillage, effect of	169, 257	— American	178
Timothy in meadows	189	— amongst branches	87 et seq., 249
Tomatoes (see, also, Lycopersicum).		— are there too many	248
— Canary Islands	216	— asexual	71, 90 et seq.; 263, 264
— canning	216	— Bigness	170
— currant	118, 120, 121, 126, 127	— blackberry	268
— — duration of	45	— blight-proof	185
— evolution of	473 et seq.	— bud-variation	72, 82, 89, 169, 239, 378
— flower-bearing	352	— carnations	443 et seq.
		— correlation of	219

	PAGE
Variation, Dandelions	258
— definite	23
— and varieties, describing	174, 237
— differences, importance of	242
— due to struggle	258
— fertilizers and	262, 254
— fixing of	367
— food-supply	27, 87, 98, 159, 169
— fortuitous	24
— geography of	282 et seq.
— growth	25
— has it ceased	358, 373
— increase in	206
— insects and diseases in relation to	371
— introducing	369
— merit rising	373
— multifarious	23
— origin of	32, 58
— Parallelism of	219
— pea	254
— petunia	254
— poor growers	246
— production of	138, 177
— progress in	364
— progressive	204, 209
— running out	145, 157, 161, 335, 356, 376 et seq.; 382 et seq.; 397 et seq.; 445 et seq.
— seed-production	251
— soils, influence of	257, 378
— test of a	208
— testing	171 et seq.; 371
— Van Mons on	142
— wheat	257
— why fail	364
Variegation	92
Varietal difference	336, 339
Vedalia	215
Vegetables, number of	139
Vergil, quoted	201
Vermes	14
Vestiges	98
Vilmorin, cited	438, 453, 469, 472
— on tomato	118, 127
Vine, acclimatization of	323
Violets, sports in	92
Virginia, Albemarle Pippin	244

	PAGE
Virginia, peach-trees in	323
Vitality of fruit-trees	230
Vitis Labrusca	235, 432
— vinifera	423 et seq.
Volta, mentioned	142
Von Martens, on beans	129
— Mohl, mentioned	85
Vroom, quoted	301
Waite, M. B., cited	353
Wales, New South, at World's Fair, etc.	281, 282
Wallace, quoted	182, 220, 333
Walnut	52
— acclimatization	326
— nativity of	277
Ward, cited	97
Waring, Geo. E., and the Trophy tomato	480 et seq.
Washington, acclimatization	325
— at World's Fair	281, 282 et seq.
Watermelon, seed-crop	87
— selection in	154
Watermelons to Europe	216
Watson on maize	128
Weather and plants	302
Weediness	193
Weeds in the clearings	182
— from abroad	188
— spread of	192, 193 et seq.
Weed-types	49
Weeping varieties'	92
Weismann, quoted	29, 62, 63, 65, 70, 72, 73, 75, 77, 78, 102, 285, 348, 495
— mentioned	61, 62, 66, 67, 68, 69, 70, 71, 76, 101, 103, 106, 167, 168, 261, 263
Weismannism	64, 79, 81, 103, 167, 264
Wheat	187
— acclimatization	332
— and clover	259
— and Russian thistle	195
— variation in	257
Williams and Morrow, mentioned	270
— H. S., quoted	21, 48, 492
Williamson, cited	441
Willows	100
Willow, weeping	99
Windbreaks	308
Winds and fruit culture	308

Wineberry, nativity of 276	Wright, Charles, mentioned 270
Winslow, Isaac, mentioned . . . 216	Yellows of peach 188, 427
Winter, adaptation to 44, 47	Zea amylacea 128
Wisconsin at World's Fair . 280 et seq.	— amylea-saccharata 128
— fruits in 309	— canina 128
Wood, Wm., quoted 421	— everta 128
World's Fair, carnations at 463	— indentata 128
— — exhibit at 278	— saccharata 128
Worms, number of 139	— tunicata 128
— true 14	Zizania aquatica 829
Wormwood . . . . · 52	Zones of plants 295

The Rural Science Series.

NOW READY.

The Soil. By FRANKLIN H. KING, Professor of Agricultural Physics, University of Wisconsin. 16mo. Cloth. 75 cents.

The Spraying of Plants. By ERNEST G. LODEMAN, Cornell University.

IN PREPARATION.

The Apple in North America. By L. H. BAILEY, Editor of the Series.

The Fertility of the Land. By I. P. ROBERTS, of Cornell University.

Milk and Its Products. By H. H. WING.

Under the editorship of Professor L. H. Bailey, of Cornell University, The Macmillan Co. purpose issuing a series of books upon agricultural subjects, to be known as The Rural Science Series. Professor F. H. King, of the University of Wisconsin, has written upon The Soil, treating the subject from the new attitude, which considers it as a scene of life rather than as a mere mechanical or chemical mixture. The physics of the soil are fully considered, and the physical effects of fertilizers, drainage, and cultivation are discussed, as well as the adaptation of different types of soils to various crops. Professor I. P. Roberts, of Cornell University, will write upon The Fertility of the Land. This volume, while entirely independent of that of Professor King, will carry the subject directly into the practice of the field, giving a full discussion of the philosophy of plowing, cultivating, and the like, and an account of the best methods of maintaining and increasing the productivity of the land. The editor will contribute a monograph upon the cultivation of The Apple in North America, with a discussion of its evolution and the difficulties which now confront the apple-grower. The Spraying of Plants is treated by E. G. Lodeman, of Cornell, in a comprehensive account of the origin and philosophy of the modern means of controlling insect and fungous troubles, and the application of these methods to the leading crops.

Some of the other volumes to be arranged for are:

Psychology of Plants. By J. C. ARTHUR, of Purdue University.
Grasses. By W. H. BREWER, of Yale University.
Bush Fruits. By F. W. CARD, of University of Nebraska.
Plant Diseases. By P. T. GALLOWAY, E. F. SMITH, and A. F. WOODS, of the United States Department of Agriculture.
Seeds and Seed Growing. By G. H. HICKS, of the United States Department of Agriculture.
Leguminous Plants. By E. W. HILGARD, of the University of California.
Feeding of Animals. By W. H. JORDAN, of Maine Experiment Station.
Forestry. Grape Culture. Planting Manual. Landscape Gardening.
Small Fruits. Plant Life. Rural Economics. Etc., Etc.

THE MACMILLAN COMPANY.
66 Fifth Avenue, NEW YORK.

www.ingramcontent.com/pod-product-compliance
Lightning Source LLC
Chambersburg PA
CBHW020858020526
44116CB00029B/364